INTERNATIONAL MONETARY AND FINANCIAL ISSUES FOR THE 1990s

Research papers for the Group of Twenty-Four

VOLUME X

UNITED NATIONS
New York and Geneva, 1999

Note

Symbols of United Nations documents are composed of capital letters combined with figures. Mention of such a symbol indicates a reference to a United Nations document.

*

* *

The views expressed in this compendium are those of the authors and do not necessarily reflect the views of the UNCTAD secretariat. The designations employed and the presentation of the material do not imply the expression of any opinion whatsoever on the part of the Secretariat of the United Nations concerning the legal status of any country, territory, city or area, or of its authorities, or concerning the delimitation of its frontiers or boundaries.

*

* *

Material in this publication may be freely quoted; acknowledgement, however, is requested (including reference to the document number). It would be appreciated if a copy of the publication containing the quotation were sent to the Editorial Assistant, UNCTAD, Division on Globalization and Development Strategies, Palais des Nations, CH-1211 Geneva 10.

UNCTAD/GDS/MDPB/5

Contents

THE WTO AGREEMENT ON FINANCIAL SERVICES: PROBLEMS OF FINANCIAL GLOBALIZATION IN PRACTICE

Andrew Cornford and Jim Brandon 1

STRATEGIC OPTIONS AVAILABLE TO DEVELOPING COUNTRIES WITH REGARD TO A MULTILATERAL AGREEMENT ON INVESTMENT

A.V. Ganesan 19

**KEY ISSUES FOR DEVELOPING COUNTRIES IN A POSSIBLE
MULTILATERAL AGREEMENT ON INVESTMENT**

**CAPITAL-ACCOUNT CONVERTIBILITY AND MULTILATERAL INVESTMENT
AGREEMENTS: WHAT IS IN THE INTEREST OF DEVELOPING COUNTRIES?**

LAX PUBLIC SECTOR, DESTABILIZING PRIVATE SECTOR: ORIGINS OF CAPITAL MARKET CRISES

GLOBALIZATION, ECONOMIC POLICY AND GROWTH PERFORMANCE

Abbreviations

AfDB	African Development Bank
AFTA	ASEAN Free Trade Area
AMF	Asian Monetary Fund
APEC	Asia-Pacific Economic Cooperation
ASEAN	Association of South-East Asian Nations
BIS	Bank for International Settlements
BIT	bilateral investment treaty
BWIs	Bretton Woods institutions
CFA	Communauté financière africaine
CGAP	Consultative Group to Assist the Poorest
CGIAR	Consultative Group on International Agricultural Research
DAC	Development Assistance Committee (of OECD)
EBRD	European Bank for Reconstruction and Development
EC	European Commission
EIB	European Investment Bank
EMU	European Monetary Union
EPU	European Payments Union
ERM	European Exchange Rate Mechanism
ESAF	Enhanced Structural Adjustment Facility (IMF)
EU	European Union
FDI	foreign direct investment
FY	fiscal year
GAB	General Arrangements to Borrow
GATS	General Agreement on Trade in Services
GATT	General Agreement on Tariffs and Trade
GCI	General Capital Increase
GDP	gross domestic product
GNP	gross national product
HIPCs	heavily indebted poor countries
IBRD	International Bank for Reconstruction and Development
ICSID	International Centre for Settlement of Investment Disputes
IDA	International Development Association
IDB	Inter-American Development Bank
IFI	international financial institutions
IMF	International Monetary Fund
IPRs	intellectual property rights
LDCs	least developed countries
LIBOR	London Inter-Bank Offered Rate
LLR	lender of last resort
MAI	Multilateral Agreement on Investment
MDB	multilateral development bank
MEA	Multilateral Environment Agreement
MERCOSUR	Southern Cone Common Market
MFI	Multilateral Framework on Investment

MFN	most favoured nation
MIGA	Multilateral Investment Guarantee Agency
NAB	New Arrangements to Borrow
NAFTA	North American Free Trade Agreement
NGO	non-governmental organization
NIE	newly industrializing economy
NT	national treatment
ODA	official development assistance
ODI	Overseas Development Institute
OECD	Organization for Economic Co-operation and Development
OPEC	Organization of Petroleum Exporting Countries
R&D	research and development
RBPs	restrictive business practices
RDB	regional development bank
SAF	Structural Adjustment Facility
S&L	Saving and Loan
SCA-2	Special Contingency Account II
SDR	Special Drawing Right
SGP	special grants programme
SILICs	severely indebted low-income countries
SPV	special purpose vehicle
SSA	sub-Saharan Africa
TNC	transnational corporation
TRIM	Trade-Related Investment Measure
TRIP	Trade-Related Intellectual Property Right
TRS	total return swaps
UNDP	United Nations Development Programme
WDR	World Development Report
WTO	World Trade Organization

The authors

- **Manuel R. Agosin**, Director, Center for International Economics and Development, and Professor of Economics, Universidad de Chile

- **Jim Brandon**, Consultant to the Division on Globalization and Development Strategies, UNCTAD, Geneva

- **Andrew Cornford**, Economic Adviser to the Division on Globalization and Development Strategies, UNCTAD, Geneva

- **Carlos M. Correa**, Centre for Advanced Studies, University of Buenos Aires, Argentina

- **A.V. Ganesan**, Former Commerce Secretary to the Government of India

- **Devesh Kapur**, Center for International Affairs, Harvard University, Cambridge, Massachusetts

- **Christian Larraín**, GERENS Consulting, Santiago, Chile

- **Percy S. Mistry**, Chairman, Oxford International Associates, Oxford, United Kingdom

- **Paul Mosley**, Department of Economics, University of Reading, United Kingdom

- **Lance Taylor**, Director, Center for Economic Policy Analysis, New School for Social Research, New York

Preface

The Intergovernmental Group of Twenty-Four on International Monetary Affairs (G-24) was established in November 1971 to increase the negotiating strength of the developing countries in discussions that were going on at that time in the International Monetary Fund on reform of the international monetary system. Developing countries felt that they should play a meaningful role in decisions about the system, and that the effectiveness of that role would be enhanced if they were to meet regularly as a group, as the developed countries had been doing for some time in the Group of Ten (G-10).

It soon became apparent that the G-24 was in need of technical support and analysis relating to the issues arising for discussion in the Fund and Bank, including the Interim and Development Committees. In response to representations by the Chairman of the G-24 to the Secretary-General of the United Nations Conference on Trade and Development (UNCTAD), and following discussions between UNCTAD and the United Nations Development Programme (UNDP), the latter agreed in 1975 to establish a project to provide the technical support that the G-24 had requested. This was to take the form, principally, of analytical papers prepared by competent experts on issues currently under consideration in the fields of international money and finance.

Mr. Sidney Dell, a former Director in UNCTAD's Money, Finance and Development Division and subsequently Assistant Administrator of UNDP headed the project from its establishment until 1990. During this period, some 60 research papers were prepared by the Group of Twenty-Four. The high quality of this work was recognized by the Deputies and Ministers of the Group and the reports were given wide currency, some being published in five volumes by North-Holland Press and others by the United Nations.

The project work was resumed in 1990 under the direction of Gerry K. Helleiner, Professor of Economics, University of Toronto, Canada. The UNCTAD secretariat provides both substantive and administrative backstopping to the project. Funding is currently being provided by the G-24 countries themselves, the International Development Research Centre of Canada and the Governments of Denmark and the Netherlands. As a result, it has been possible to continue to provide the Group of Twenty-Four with timely and challenging analyses. These studies are being reissued periodically in compendia. This is the tenth volume to be published.

THE WTO AGREEMENT ON FINANCIAL SERVICES: PROBLEMS OF FINANCIAL GLOBALIZATION IN PRACTICE

Andrew Cornford and Jim Brandon*

Abstract

Negotiations in the WTO on international trade in banking services within the framework of the General Agreement on Trade in Services (GATS) were part of broader negotiations on financial services which also included insurance. The reopened negotiations were designed to achieve a more permanent agreement to replace the interim deal reached in mid-1995. The interests at stake in the negotiations in the WTO varied for different categories of developing countries according to the levels of development of their financial sectors and economies. Under the agreement reached in December 1997 many countries made at most limited changes in their commitments since 1995, but the negotiations did result in substantial additional liberalization in some major cases.

The paper discusses selected issues of special interest to developing and transition economies bearing on the relation of the GATS to financial liberalization. Explicit obligations with respect to the liberalization of capital movements are linked to a country's commitments on market access but governments' autonomy regarding the control of capital movements is not completely clear-cut and might be challenged for various reasons. Governments retain considerable discretion as to lender-of-last-resort operations in support of financial firms affected by banking crises but, in the absence of relevant "case law", the extent of allowable discrimination between domestic and foreign firms is uncertain. Since financial liberalization entails structural changes, its introduction should be gradual if its benefits are to exceed its costs, and this view has helped to shape experience in the OECD area. Liberalization of the banking sector is generally associated with increases in the principal kinds of banking risk and too rapid an influx of foreign financial firms can accentuate these increases. Thus the pace of the opening of banking markets in developing countries should be geared to a conservative timetable determined by the periods required for implementing effective systems of regulation and supervision.

* The authors are grateful for frequently provocative but invariably helpful comments from Chakravarthi Raghavan at all stages of the writing of this paper. They also benefited from accounts of the progress of the negotiations provided by Mina Mashayekhi. However, they are solely responsible for any errors and the views expressed are those of the authors and do not necessarily reflect those of the UNCTAD secretariat.

I. Introduction

This paper begins with a brief description of the General Agreement on Trade in Services (GATS) itself (section II) and of its relationship to the negotiations on financial services recently completed in the WTO (section III). At the time of writing it has not been possible to carry out an analysis of countries' commitments under the agreement reached in these negotiations. Instead the rest of the paper is principally concerned with the major interests at stake (section IV) and with various issues involving the GATS and banking services (sections V-VIII), some of which underlay differences of approach to liberalization and market opening for foreign financial firms among participants in the negotiations. Several of the issues were brought into sharper focus as the Asian financial crisis unfolded. These were less at the forefront of attention during the negotiation of the framework agreement of the GATS which, in comparison with 1997, took place during a relatively calm period in emerging financial markets.

The WTO negotiations on financial services are part of a larger process of putting in place international rules and norms which ultimately will have a significant impact on the autonomy of governments' macroeconomic and financial policies at the national level. The two subjects singled out for treatment under this heading in sections V and VI are the bearing of the GATS on policies towards capital movements and for dealing with the consequences of crises involving both external payments and the banking sector.

At various stages in the negotiations some major OECD countries indicated their objective of achieving rapid market opening from certain developing countries. Figures like five, or even fewer, years for this purpose were proposed. Such demands raise questions about the appropriate time frame for liberalization of financial services. In this context historical experience of OECD countries themselves (which is briefly reviewed in section VII) points to the drawn-out character of many features of their own liberalization process and, in the case of the European Union (EU), to problems which had to be confronted as part of the market opening necessary for the establishment of a single financial market. Questions under the heading of the time frame also include the connections between liberalization of banking services, on the one hand, and instituting or strengthening official regulatory regimes as well as effective internal controls in financial firms them-selves. Consideration of the likely effects of liberalization on various banking risks (the subject of section VIII) suggests that the time frame for liberalization implicit in some of the demands made during the WTO negotiations was too short – indeed, in many cases much too short.

II. The GATS and financial services

The GATS comes in two parts: firstly, a framework of rules, principles and concepts which underlie obligations regarding measures affecting so-called international trade in services; and, secondly, the specific negotiated commitments listed in countries' schedules for service sectors and subsectors. The GATS covers four modes of supply: (a) cross-border supply (that is supply which does not require the cross-border movement of supplier or consumer); (b) supply through the movement of consumers to the location of the supplier; (c) supply through the establishment in a country of the commercial presence of legal entities from another country; and (d) the supply through natural persons of one country in the territory of another. The first part of the GATS, the framework described above whose provisions have many similarities to those of the GATT regarding goods trade, was negotiated as part of the agreement establishing the WTO. The recently completed negotiations on financial services concern the second part, countries schedules of commitments, on which agreement was not reached before the meeting at Marrakesh in April 1994 which inaugurated the WTO.

The key articles in the GATS regarding the scheduling of commitments are Article XVI (on market access) and Article XVII (on national treatment). Market access as such is not defined in the GATS. Rather the approach of the GATS is to list six categories of measure which are prohibited unless specified in a country's schedule (for each of the four modes of delivery). The categories cover the following: (a) limitations on the number of service suppliers; (b) limitations on the value of service transactions or assets; (c) limitations on the number of service operations or on the quantity of service output; (d) limitations on the number of natural persons who may be employed; (e) limitations on the type of legal entity through which a service is supplied (which might refer to branches or subsidiaries, for example, in the case of banking); and (f) limitations on the permissible size of the participation of foreign capital either in terms of a maximum percentage limit on foreign shareholdings or in terms of the total value of individual or aggregate foreign investment. National treatment is defined as treatment no less favourable than that accorded to like domestic services and service suppliers. Under Article XVII measures entailing deviations from national treatment are also to be included in a country's schedule. The classification of some measures under market access rather than national treatment, or vice versa, is somewhat arbitrary: one example is the limitation on the participation of foreign equity capital mentioned above; and another might be restrictions on the licensing of additional branches of a foreign bank which already has a branch in a country, when such restrictions do not also apply to domestic banks. The solution to this problem adopted in Article XX of the GATS is to require inclusion in schedules of commitments under the heading of limitations on market access those measures considered as both restricting market access and resulting in deviations from national treatment. Commitments under the GATS apply only to those service sectors or subsectors actually listed in countries' schedules (i.e. in accordance with the so-called positive list approach).[1]

The reason for the reference earlier to "so-called international trade in services" should now be clearer. A more appropriate term for the coverage of the GATS might be international service transactions, a category which includes, crucially, FDI in entities supplying services in a country.[2] The negotiations over what is included in countries' schedules thus concern those parts of their legal regimes bearing on market access and national treatment for foreign suppliers. The remarks so far cover matters applying to all service sectors and subsectors included in the GATS. But the sequel of this paper will be limited to banking, securities business and asset management[3], although insurance was also part of the negotiations.

III. The restarted negotiations

The reopening of negotiations in the WTO on financial services this summer was designed to achieve by mid-December a new and more permanent agreement to replace the interim deal reached in mid-1995 which expired at the end of 1997. Under this interim deal countries were to leave open their best offers as of mid-1995 but would be free to withdraw them on its expiry. The reopened negotiations were intended to enable countries to make further commitments as to the opening of their financial markets, which, it was hoped, would suffice to persuade the United States to drop its broad Article II Most-Favoured-Nation (MFN) Exemption. Under this Exemption the United States committed itself to maintain market access and national treatment at existing levels for entities already present in its market, but to accord them to future applicants only on the basis of reciprocity considerations involving the openness to United States firms of the markets in their parent countries.

Between mid-1995 and the reopening of the negotiations a number of countries including Brazil, Japan, and the Republic of Korea undertook further liberalization of their financial sectors independently of the WTO process. For many countries from which the United States and the EU were seeking greater openness the focus of the negotiations was as much insurance as banking, securities business, and asset management. But in the event the negotiations were overshadowed by the Asian currency crisis and its links to the banking sector. The effects of the crisis were two-edged: on the one hand, the caution regarding market opening of Asian countries which were major targets of pressure from the United States and the EU was reinforced (despite widespread acknowledgement that infusions of foreign equity capital would inevitably be part of the restructuring of banking sectors made necessary by the crisis); and, on the other hand, reluctance to allow the negotiations to fail was increased by fears of the effects which such failure might have on volatile sentiment in international financial markets.

Agreement was reached on 13 December. The United States withdrew its broad Article II MFN Exemption, replacing it with an Exemption directed exclusively at countries which force United States insurers to divest themselves of equity shares in local firms.[4] This Exemption reflected the dissatisfaction of the United States over Malaysia's unwillingness to accept in its schedule of commitments equity participation of more than 51 per cent in domestic insurers.

Initial impressions indicate that many countries have made at most limited changes in their commitments, but that the negotiations have resulted in substantial additional liberalization in some major cases. The new schedule of commitments of the EU contains a number of movements in the direction of further liberalization by various member countries: restrictions on the entities through which certain operations can be carried out have been relaxed or eliminated; certain restrictions on the portfolio management of investment funds and individuals have been removed; the requirement of an economic needs test for the licensing of the branches and subsidiaries of foreign banks in one country has been dropped; an approval procedure for the acquisition of shares by foreigners giving more than a certain proportion of the voting rights of major banks has also been dropped; and a commitment has been made to reduce delays in processing applications by foreign firms to establish commercial banking or investment subsidiaries. Canada is to allow market access by foreign banks in the form of branches, whereas access had been limited to subsidiaries. Japan has liberalized access by foreign firms to the business of asset management. The Republic of Korea has committed itself to liberalization in several areas: aggregate and individual limits on equity participation in its financial firms have been relaxed; establishment of subsidiaries, joint ventures and branches is permitted in activities where these were previously not allowed; foreigners' access to the country's bond market has been increased; rates of interest on deposits, the issuance of debt instruments by financial firms, and the regulation of foreign-exchange exposure have been liberalized; the categories of securities open to foreign broking have been expanded; and approval requirements have been eliminated for the establishment of representative offices in the securities business and asset management. However, interestingly, some of the measures of liberalization agreed with the IMF as conditions of the Republic of Korea's standby loan (such as those specifying new ceilings on foreign stock holdings and an increase in the limit on foreign bank subsidiaries' equity participation in domestic banks) are not included in its commitments at the WTO.[5] This exemplifies a possibility which may also apply in other cases, that some of the liberalization measures undertaken in Asian countries in conditions of crisis may be intended to be only temporary.

IV. Some interests at stake

One starting-point for discussion of the stakes in the negotiations are estimates of the value of the transactions involved. Data for exports and imports of financial services are available as part of those on the balance of payments on current account for selected countries: a recent study of the WTO, for example, shows that the financial-services exports of nine large suppliers (Austria, Belgium-Luxembourg, France, Germany, Japan, Singapore, Switzerland,

the United Kingdom, and the United States) approximately tripled between 1985 and 1995 (WTO, 1997, p. 13). However, such figures are not generally available. Moreover they are limited to the first mode of delivery discussed above, namely cross-border transactions and thus exclude, for example, revenue or profits due to operations through entities with a commercial presence outside their parent countries.[6]

Other interesting statistics in this context are those on the scale of the presence of foreign banks in different countries. A separate appendix prepared in conjunction with this paper contains data of this kind (of which some are summarised in tables 1-4). The data show the number of banks from developing and transition economies with a commercial presence in a selection of the major OECD economies (table 1), and the number of banks from the latter in the former (table 3). A shortcoming of the figures is that they are largely limited to branches and majority-owned subsidiaries. Thus they do not include banking entities in which foreign firms have equity participation of less than 50 per cent (an important feature of several developing economies where majority ownership by foreign firms is not permitted).

As might be expected, the appendix shows that the largest presence of banks from developing and transition economies in the OECD area is in the United Kingdom and the United States. The region with the smallest presence of OECD banks is Latin America, but this impression may at least partly reflect the incompleteness of the data.

The average number of foreign banking entities per host OECD country shown in tables 2 and 4 is not strikingly different from the number per developing or transition economy.[7] These figures provide at best broad indications as to the character of the likely expansion of foreign commercial presence in response to the agreement reached in the WTO. But they do suggest that the expansion of this presence in the past has not been especially unbalanced as between that in the direction of OECD to developing and transition economies, on the one hand, and that in the direction of developing and transition to OECD economies, on the other. The figures point to the already significant presence of banks from developing and transition economies in the OECD area, thus posing the question of how great is likely to be the pressure for expansion of this presence in the medium term during which the effects of commitments made under the agreement work themselves out.

Table 1

NUMBER OF BANKING ENTITIES FROM DEVELOPING AND TRANSITION ECONOMIES IN SELECTED OECD COUNTRIES, 1996

Host country	Number of foreign banking entities	Number of parent countries represented	Foreign banking entities per parent country
United States	171	34	5.0
Japan	35	11	3.2
France	46	25	1.8
Germany	36	19	1.9
United Kingdom	153	46	3.3
Austria	7	7	1.0
Belgium	9	6	1.5
Greece	3	3	1.0
Italy	5	5	1.0
Luxembourg	16	8	2.0
Netherlands	14	8	1.8
Portugal	1	1	1.0
Spain	7	5	1.4
Switzerland	12	8	1.5
Australia	9	5	1.8

Source: *The Banker*, various issues; *Foreign Banks in Switzerland, 1997* (Geneva: Publications Bancaires, 1997), and industry sources.

Note: The offshore banking centres Bahrain and Bermuda are excluded. Denmark, Finland, Ireland and Sweden have no foreign banking entities from developing or transition economies at all.

Another approach to looking at the interests at stake is to consider the situations of different types of developing economy, using the resulting appreciation as the context for the presentation of information about the scale of, and revenue from, selected financial activities in such economies which may figure significantly in the calculations of foreign banks considering whether to establish a commercial presence. Here it is helpful to frame the discussion in terms of a set of broad categories of country (though some of those participating in the WTO negotiations may not fit precisely into any of them).

Countries in the first category have highly rudimentary banking sectors. Such countries include several with low GDP per capita as well as certain other small economies. In this case policy towards international trade in banking services is often largely governed by the objective of attracting the com-mercial presence of foreign financial firms for the purpose of the contribution they can make to the development of the banking sector. Countries in this category frequently have restrictive regimes for capital transactions (and in many cases also for current ones) which are to a significant extent dictated by limited foreign exchange reserves and access to external financing.

Countries in the second category, typically with somewhat higher levels of GDP per capita, are characterized by more developed financial sectors. These may include some large commercial banks, but organized financial markets (such as stock exchanges) are still small and the range of available financial instruments is limited in comparison with that of most OECD countries (and of a few developing economies). Among these countries there is considerable variation in their policies towards

Table 2

TEN SELECTED DEVELOPING COUNTRIES AND TRANSITION ECONOMIES[a] WITH MOST BANKING ENTITIES IN THE SELECTED OECD[b] COUNTRIES, 1996

Parent Country	Number of foreign banking entities	Number of host countries represented	Foreign banking entities per host country
Republic of Korea	76	9	8.4
Brazil	42	10	4.2
Taiwan Province of China	31	8	3.9
Turkey	25	8	3.1
Singapore	22	4	5.5
Iran	21	6	3.5
India	20	6	3.3
Indonesia	19	6	3.2
Pakistan	17	8	2.1
Hong Kong (China)	17	5	3.4

Source: *The Banker*, various issues, and industry sources.

    a   The offshore banking centres Bahrain and Bermuda are excluded.

    b   United Kingdom, United States, France, Germany, Austria, Belgium, Greece, Italy, Luxembourg, Netherlands, Spain, Australia and Japan.

opening domestic financial markets: acknowledgement of the benefits of increased foreign competition typically has to be balanced against objectives regarding the development of indigenous financial firms (although in some cases the latter consideration is at least partly subordinated to the aim of turning a country into a financial centre). In such countries there are often factors reducing the attractiveness of their financial markets to foreign banks which have nothing to do with the regulatory regime, such as inadequate postal and communications systems and relatively small middle classes. Regimes of exchange control also vary substantially in their restrictiveness. The number of such countries which have assumed the obligations of IMF Article VIII regarding the liberalization of current transactions is steadily increasing, and these obligations facilitate several traditional services provided by commercial banks. But capital transactions are generally still subject to control. Nevertheless, the adoption in such countries of a more open regime for international trade in banking services is sometimes part of a broader liberalization of the financial sector including some relaxation of controls over capital transactions (a relaxation which is particularly likely in the case of countries with ambitions to become financial centres).

The third category of countries includes those with financial sectors which are more diversified but have often been tightly controlled, at any rate until recently. Here, in part owing to higher levels of income and savings, the potential profits to foreign firms from participating in the market through a commercial presence are generally larger than in the first two categories of countries, and are enhanced to the extent that greater opening of the market to foreign financial firms is accompanied by broader liberalization of the financial regime including controls over capital movements.

For example, the profitability of participation for foreign firms in such a country's securities business is increased by access to membership of the stock exchange, which is more likely in a country which has recently undertaken, or is currently undertaking, progressive liberalization of its financial sector.[8] Moreover the attractiveness of such participation is linked to the freedom of inward and outward portfolio investment for non-residents, since foreign firms are often those best placed to provide such investors with brokerage services. Likewise revenues from participation in asset management depend on the regime for capital transactions (as well as on regulations more specifically directed at this

Table 3

NUMBER OF BANKING ENTITIES FROM SELECTED OECD COUNTRIES[a] IN SELECTED DEVELOPING AND TRANSITION ECONOMIES, 1996

Host country	Number of foreign banking entities	Number of parent countries represented	Foreign banking entities per parent country
Albania	4	2	2.0
Bulgaria	7	5	1.4
Croatia	11	3	3.7
Czech Republic	43	11	3.9
Estonia	4	3	1.3
Hungary	1	6	0.2
Latvia	3	2	1.5
Poland	16	6	2.7
Romania	14	8	1.8
Russian Federation	34	14	2.4
Slovakia	10	5	2.0
Slovenia	4	2	2.0
Brunei Darussalam	3	2	1.5
China	31	10	3.1
Hong Kong (China)	108	14	7.7
India	22	8	2.8
Indonesia	7	5	1.4
Republic of Korea	41	7	5.9
Malaysia	9	6	1.5
Philippines	9	6	1.5
Singapore	87	17	5.1
Taiwan Province of China	31	8	3.9
Thailand	26	8	3.3
Viet Nam	7	4	1.8
Argentina	14	9	1.6
Brazil	18	9	2.0
Chile	12	5	2.4
Colombia	4	3	1.3
Ecuador	3	2	1.5
Mexico	9	5	1.8
Panama	9	5	1.8
Peru	9	5	1.8
Uruguay	9	5	1.8
Venezuela	9	5	1.8

Source: *The Banker*, various issues; The Federation of Bankers Associations of Japan, and industry sources.

 a Australia, Austria, Bahrain, Belgium, Canada, Denmark, Finland, France, Germany, Greece, Ireland, Italy, Luxembourg, Japan, Netherlands, Norway, Portugal, Spain, Sweden, Switzerland, United Kingdom, United States.

activity concerning matters such as permitted techniques of selling and the assets which pension funds can hold in their portfolios). Under a regime restricting outward capital transactions foreign asset managers will be limited to selling domestic investment instruments to resident customers, but under a more liberal regime they may also be able to sell them funds which include instruments purchased

Table 4

TEN OECD COUNTRIES WITH MOST BANKING ENTITIES IN SELECTED DEVELOPING AND TRANSITION ECONOMIES, 1996

Parent Country	Number of foreign banking entities	Number of host countries represented	Foreign banking entities per host country
Japan	116	15	7.7
United States	113	28	4.0
France	76	25	3.0
Germany	66	20	3.3
Netherlands	53	27	2.0
United Kingdom	42	17	2.5
Austria	33	11	3.0
Italy	23	9	2.6
Spain	21	14	1.5
Switzerland	13	7	1.9

Source: See table 3.

abroad. Another example in this context is the sale of financial derivatives. Such selling generally requires not only permission from local regulators but also liberalization of certain capital transactions (without which the markets for the instruments involved are likely to be insufficiently liquid). In this context it should be noted that, even in countries with liberal regimes for capital transactions preceding the opening of securities business and other investment banking activities to foreign firms, the scale of inward and outward capital movements is likely to expand after such opening. This expansion is the natural consequence of the generally greater involvement of foreign than domestic firms in cross-border business such as international bank lending and portfolio investment.

These remarks can be made more concrete by some observations concerning the approximate scale of certain categories of business in Latin America and Asia and the identity of foreign firms which are major players in the two regions.

Unsurprisingly estimates are not available of the revenue from retail banking in developing economies where, as explained above, the link between the activities involved and liberalization of capital movements is less important than for investment banking and asset management. Here local habits and preferences as to banking services (as well

as the still limited size of middle classes) slow or impede internationalization. Citibank is generally considered to be the financial firm which has progressed furthest towards global retail banking, though some others such as HSBC Holdings are moving in the same direction.[9] However, several other banks have more limited foreign networks of commercial banking entities with substantial involvement in retail activities, networks whose establishment is often driven by historical business links between banks' parent countries and the host countries where they have a commercial presence.

Foreign involvement in investment banking has recently expanded rapidly in both Asia and Latin America. Factors contributing to this expansion have been the growth in turnover on stock exchanges (which generated commission income in 1996 of almost $6 billion in six Asian economies alone[10]), opportunities for direct investment,[11] revenues from underwriting and advisory work in connection with securities issues and mergers and acquisitions,[12] and revenue from derivatives activities (both over-the-counter (OTC) or customized) sales to customers and participation in the increasing amounts of trading on organized exchanges in some countries in the two regions).[13] Moreover in both regions it is reasonable to anticipate substantial growth of the business of asset management: in Asian countries characterized by high savings and rapid increases in the net worth of the personal sector this business is still fairly underdeveloped,[14] and in Latin America considerable impetus should come from the expansion of privatized pension schemes.[15] Large United States banks (both the country's major investment banks and others whose investment banking activities at home are restricted for regulatory reasons) are involved in investment banking in one or both regions, as are some financial firms from Europe and Japan. Financial firms from the United States and Europe also occupy most of the top slots in international asset management in Asia.[16] A number of financial firms with local origins are responsible for parts of the business of international investment banking in the two regions but their role in international asset management is still limited.[17]

V. Trade in financial services and capital movements

The right of countries to exercise control over international capital movements was a central issue in the negotiations of the Uruguay Round on financial services. At various stages of these negotiations proposals were submitted which, as part of the liberalization of cross-border transactions, would have required the removal of restrictions on capital transactions. However, the eventual text of the GATS acknowledged the need of governments for autonomy in this area. According to Article XI "Nothing in this Agreement shall affect the rights and obligations of members of the International Monetary Fund under the Articles of Agreement of the Fund, including the use of exchange actions which are in conformity with the Articles of Agreement, provided that a [country] shall not impose restrictions on any capital transactions inconsistently with its specific commitments regarding such transactions, except under Article XII [of the GATS] or at the request of the Fund". Under Article XVI of the GATS, if a country undertakes a commitment to market access with respect to cross-border transactions of which cross-border movements of capital are an essential part, then the country is also committed to allow such movements. Here the commitment to the liberalization of capital movements is linked to a country's commitments regarding market access.

Whilst the commitment to liberalization is thus clearly circumscribed, governments' autonomy regarding the control of capital movements under the GATS is not completely clear-cut. Moreover this autonomy may be further limited as a consequence

of the current initiative to extend the IMF's authority to capital movements.[18]

Controls over capital transactions might be challenged in cases where the link between the transactions and a country's commitments was less direct than in the case of the prohibition of their use in the circumstances referred to under Article XVI. An example might be controls (or taxes) imposed to safeguard the balance of payments. Action of this kind which restricts trade in services on which a country has made commitments is allowed under Article XII of the GATS. In determining the incidence of the action countries "may give priority to the supply of services which are more essential to their economic or development programmes" subject to the proviso that the "restrictions shall not be adopted or maintained for the purpose of protecting a particular sector". The reference to "purpose" is important since the incidence of measures to deal with capital movements framed without discriminatory intent may nevertheless be discriminatory in fact between firms supplying different financial services, and thus perhaps have implications for competition between domestic and foreign firms. However, the de facto discriminatory impact of such measures might be queried under Article XVII(3) of the GATS on the grounds that although they were "formally identical" in their treatment of suppliers, they modified "the conditions of competition in favour of services or service suppliers [of the country imposing them] compared to like services or service suppliers [of another country]". Exchange controls have frequently been cited as having a de facto discriminatory impact of this kind. For example, an early study of trade in financial services of the United States Treasury contains the statement that "even-handed application of foreign exchange controls may affect foreign bank operations which are more heavily involved in foreign lending than their domestic counterparts" (United States Department of the Treasury [USDT], 1979). In more recent studies from the same source there is reference to the way in which exchange controls can prevent foreign banks from fully exploiting their competitive strengths and capacity to innovate (see, for example, USDT, 1994). This point is potentially capable of becoming an issue of contention under the GATS since deployment of new financial instruments is increasingly common in association with international investment but their use is often still concentrated among a minority of banks with extensive international operations. Thus measures directed at or having a major effect on such instruments which are adopted as part of restrictions of capital inflows or outflows might be queried by the parent country or countries of such banks as having a de facto discriminatory character which modified the conditions of competition mentioned in Article XVII (3).

This point may prove far from academic. The pace of transactional innovation which has recently characterised the financial sector has already had implications for measures which governments adopt towards the capital account of the balance of payments. For example, in 1995 the Brazilian government restricted participation by non-residents in the country's derivatives markets with the objective of preventing them from using such instruments as a vehicle for the avoidance of the tax payable on fixed-income investments. The restrictions were followed by a contraction of the use of interest-rate derivatives (BIS, 1995, table II.9). Measures such as those taken by Brazil illustrate the way in which financial engineering can now routinely be employed to produce "synthetic" instruments or portfolios whose cash flows through time (inflows and outflows) match or mimic those of other more traditional instruments (in the Brazilian case debt instruments yielding fixed incomes).[19] Thus if a government wants to target such a traditional instrument (for example, for reasons of tax policy, as in the Brazilian case, or for other purposes such as in connection with controls over capital movements), it may also need to extend the scope of its action to "synthetic" instruments or portfolios as well. The potential problem in the context of the GATS is that, owing to differences in capabilities between domestic and foreign firms (which do not appear to have been a consideration in the Brazilian example) the supply of these "synthetic" instruments or portfolios may be carried out exclusively by foreign ones, which may thus take the view that restrictions on these instruments or portfolios are de facto discriminatory and damage their competitiveness in the financial markets of the host country imposing them.

VI. External-payments-cum-banking crises

Recent events in Asia have provided a stark illustration of the processes characterising crises involving both countries' external payments and their banking systems, and of the policy choices with which they confront governments. Such crises bring out the way in which for the financial sector there can be blurring of the distinction often made between

issues involving efficiency and competitiveness, on the one hand, and macroeconomic conditions and policies, on the other. As the Asian crisis has shown, the competitive weaknesses of a countries' banks and other financial firms may be more fully exposed by the strains caused by such features of an external payments crisis as the depreciation of the currency, the rise in interest rates, and consequent collapses in the value of financial and certain real assets (such as property). The train of causation also works in the other direction: in recent instances weaknesses in the banking sector have contributed to the contraction of financial inflows which led to the balance-of-payments difficulties.

The question arises in such cases of the nature of the constraints on governments' policy responses which may result from the rules of the GATS. There is latitude under the GATS for several types of policy action which a country may find necessary in various circumstances: firstly, as already mentioned, to deal with balance-of-payments crises (under Article XII); secondly, to take prudential measures as well other actions which are necessary to preserve the integrity and stability of its financial system (under the Annex on Financial Services); and, thirdly, to protect its financial sector from excessive competition on the part of foreign firms (under Articles XVI and XVII) by inclusion of limitations regarding market access and national treatment in its schedule of commitments (a procedure better adapted to dealing with longer-term problems of "overbanking" than with external-payments-cum-banking crises).

Government action in response to external-payments-cum-banking crises may include lender-of-last resort operations as well as the provision of other types of financing to firms affected (which may comprise finance and mortgage companies and securities firms as well as commercial banks). In such circumstances, under provisions of the Annex on Financial Services of the GATS, governments retain considerable discretion as to the type, scale, and distribution of the support which they provide, but the extent of the allowable discrimination between domestic and foreign firms here is still uncertain. Under the Annex countries "shall not be prevented from taking measures for prudential reasons ... or to ensure the integrity and stability of the financial system". This would appear to permit a broad range of policy responses to crises as they occur. But governments' policy responses also generally include measures to restructure the financial sector and to enhance its competitiveness. Here also issues of the differential treatment of foreign and domestic firms may have to be faced and the proviso of the Annex under which measures not conforming with the GATS "shall not be used as a means of avoiding [a country's] commitments or obligations" might be invoked by the parent countries of the foreign firms against actions perceived as involving such treatment. As mentioned in section II in connection with the impact of the Asian currency crisis on the WTO negotiations, after an external-payments-cum-banking crisis the government may choose to include infusions of equity capital provided by foreign banks as an integral part of the restructuring of the financial sector. But even in cases of this kind governments' objectives regarding such restructuring may be difficult to achieve without measures in contradiction with its commitments under the GATS.

Furthermore in the aftermath of an external-payments-cum-banking crisis decisions may be necessary as to the way in which costs are distributed among affected parties when financial firms with cross-border connections become insolvent. International consensus appears still to be lacking here concerning, for example, the extent to which non-discrimination between residents and non-residents should be applicable to the order in which a failed bank's creditors are paid off.[20] In the absence of "case law" under the GATS it is unclear how far countries' insolvency procedures are covered by the protection for governments' discretion regarding prudential measures provided by the Annex on Financial Services. If they are not so covered, discriminatory features of some countries' insolvency procedures may be in conflict with the principle of national treatment.[21] The possibility of such conflicts means that inclusion by countries in their schedules of the relevant features of their insolvency laws may be well advised – or alternatively that the wording of the provisions of the Annex on Financial Services may need revision.

Article XII should also be mentioned again briefly in this context but only subject to the qualification that this is another area where the lack of "case law" under the GATS makes prognostication particularly difficult. In the discussion in section IV of the scope for government action provided by Article XII reference was made to the prohibition under this heading of the use of measures to safeguard the balance of payments for the purpose of protection. This would appear to imply that any such measures would be carefully scrutinized for the presence of discriminatory effects on the business of foreign suppliers covered by the country's schedule, and

might be a source of contention even in the case of those taken in response to emergencies.

VII. The time frame of financial liberalization: some examples from OECD countries

Financial deregulation and opening-up are species of structural economic change, and mostly require significant periods of time if their benefits are to exceed their costs.

Thus unsurprisingly in OECD countries deregulation itself and the associated longer-term changes in the functioning of financial markets typically have frequently taken place over extended periods of time. This can be illustrated from an OECD study of 1989 on competition in banking, the cut-off date for whose analysis is 1987 (or in a few cases 1988) (Bröker, 1989). The study covered both deregulation and other structural changes of the kind just mentioned, not all of which required legal changes, and several of its findings are summarized in table 5. For example, 11 of a sample of 20 countries actually completed the deregulation of interest rates by 1987 during periods of which some lasted only one to two years (Canada, Ireland and Germany), whilst others lasted seven to 15 years (Sweden, Norway, Denmark, United Kingdom and Finland) or 16 to more than twenty years (Spain, Australia and New Zealand). Nine of the 20 countries had yet to complete the process by the report's cut-off date. Some of the changes shown under the headings of the diversification of commercial banks' activities and of the separation of banks and securities firms belong to the category of those which did not require legal changes. These processes too are typically lengthy and are still continuing in most OECD countries.

The creation of a single market for financial services in the EU also can be studied for the light it sheds on problems facing other initiatives to liberalize international transactions in such services, including those in the WTO. The EU process began with the founding of the EEC in 1957, but the legal framework for the single market eventually took more than 30 years to put in place. There were several reasons why the process was so lengthy: many of the problems entailed could not be properly anticipated in advance and thus had to be faced and solved as they emerged in particular contexts; the banking sector had been traditionally regarded by governments as

Table 5

FINANCIAL MARKETS IN OECD COUNTRIES: DEREGULATION AND STRUCTURAL CHANGE, 1960 - 1987

Country	Interest rate deregulation — Year in which deregulation began[c]	Interest rate deregulation — Year in which deregulation was completed	Creation and development of money markets	Deregulation and diversification of commercial banks[a]	Deregulation and diversification of savings institutions	Deregulaton of separation of banks and securities firms[b]
			Period during which measures or activities were introduced[c]			
Australia	1967	1986	1962 - 1984	n.a.	1963 - 1988	n.a.
Austria	1980	still incomplete	n.a.	n.a.	1979	n.a.
Belgium	1962	still incomplete	n.a.	n.a.	1967 - 1985	n.a.
Canada	1967	1967	1962	n.a.	n.a.	1980 - 1987
Denmark	1973	1982	1970 - 1976	n.a.	1975	n.a.
Finland	1971	1986	1975 - 1987	n.a.	1969	n.a.
France	1966	still incomplete	1981 - 1986	1966 - 1987	1969 - 1984	1984 - 1987
Germany	1965	1967	1986	1961 - 1985	n.a.	n.a.
Ireland	1985	1985	1970	1970 - 1986	n.a.	1987
Italy	1969	still incomplete	1975 - 1983	n.a.	1961 - 1986	n.a.
Japan	1985	still incomplete	1971 - 1985	1981 - 1987	1981 - 1982	1983 - 1986
Netherlands	1961	still incomplete	1986	1962 - 1980	1963 - 1984	n.a.
New Zealand	1962	1984	1962 - 1984	1963 - 1985	1973 - 1988	1975 - 1985[d]
Norway	1977	1985	1985	n.a.	1977 - 1983	n.a.
Portugal	1984	still incomplete	1976 - 1988	1969 - 1988	1979 - 1978	1974 - 1985
Spain	1969	1987	1964 - 1987	1962 - 1987	1962 - 1977	1987
Sweden	1978	1985	1968 - 1983	1960 - 1986	1969	n.a.
Switzerland	n.a.	still incomplete	1979 - 1981	n.a.	n.a.	n.a.
United Kingdom	1971	1984	1966 - 1988	1957 - 1984	1961 - 1988	1982 - 1986
United States	1978	still incomplete	1961 - 1974	1971 - 1983	1966 - 1986	1982 - 1987

Source: G. Bröker, Competition in Banking (Paris: OECD, 1989), Annex III.

a Includes deregulatory changes made possible by changes in law and in regulations and changes within the existing legal framework.

b Includes both deregulation of bank access to the activities of securities firms (including access to stock markets), and vice versa.

c "n.a." indicates that the information is not available in the source or the item is not applicable.

d Dates are approximate.

having several connections to monetary and credit policy which led to reluctance to cede authority in this area to supra-national institutions and rules; key features of disparate national legal traditions had to be reconciled in a single regulatory framework; as was acknowledged in the Treaty of Rome itself,[22] a single market for several categories of financial service required substantial liberalization of capital movements, and such liberalization itself took considerable time; and a crucial but in the event difficult choice had to be made as to the degree of harmonization of the rules under which financial firms would operate throughout the EU.[23]

Divergences between the banking systems of EU countries are smaller than between those of the much larger number of countries which participated in the WTO negotiations. Nonetheless the difficulties posed by the establishment of the EU regime bring out the way in which the opening of financial markets to non-resident firms and to cross-border transactions involves not only issues of microeconomic efficiency but also problems caused by broader qualitative changes in the institutional framework for supplying financial services and in the range of such services available. Concern about the possibility of such qualitative changes appears to have been an important factor in the WTO negotiations, tempering countries' willingness to open their financial markets to increased international competition despite the benefits in terms of microeconomic efficiency which such opening may bring.

VIII. The time frame of liberalization in relation to banking risks

No instance of deregulation or liberalization is quite like any other. But the experiences of OECD countries described above are cautionary as to the feasibility and desirability of very rapid liberalization of financial services and market opening for foreign financial firms by developing countries. For more (though still imprecise) guidance as to a time frame in accord with such caution one approach is to examine in greater detail various banking risks in the context of broader financial liberalization.

Liberalization can be a source of increased profits for financial firms and of benefits for users of financial services. However, as many recent studies have emphasised,[24] it is also the source of new banking risks associated with the greater flexibility of asset prices, the expanded range of sources

of funds and of permissible activities, increased competition amongst financial firms, and the resulting demands on these firms' systems of internal control and on the framework of financial regulation and supervision. Thus these new risks pose challenges to policy.

The greater flexibility of interest rates and asset prices associated with liberalization exposes commercial banks to increased interest-rate and liquidity risks. Interest-rate risk is the result of banks' exposure (through mismatches in their assets and their liabilities) to unexpected changes in interest rates, and liquidity risk of exposure to the inability to meet obligations as they become due (through the sale of assets without incurring losses and acquisition of additional funding at a rate of interest not incorporating an increased risk premium). Liquidity risk is likely to increase as a result of liberalization for two reasons: in the new environment banks are less able to depend on stores of deposits with a low sensitivity to changes in interest rates and thus have to compete in financial markets to meet a larger share of their funding needs; at the same time the greater volatility of asset prices affects their ability to sell assets at par.

Liberalization is also likely to expose banks to increased credit risk. This is partly because of the unfavourable effects of more volatile financial markets on the creditworthiness of many borrowers.[25] But many financial firms will also be pushed by the pressures of greater competition into engaging in more risky lending and other activities. Another result of such pressures is increased technological risk which reflects commercial banks' exposure to their consequences for their costs and revenues of decisions regarding the choice of technology – a risk to which banks are increasingly prone owing to their reliance on electronics, automation and telecommunications.

Financial liberalization may also be accompanied by removal of barriers between commercial and investment banking and by a relaxation of exchange control affording the possibility of more extensive participation in international borrowing and lending. Involvement in the securities business exposes a bank to greater market risk due to fluctuations in the value of its "trading book" or portfolio of tradable assets.[26] Increased participation in international borrowing and lending is a potential source of new kinds of mismatch between banks' assets and liabilities, for example, resulting from their recourse to borrowing in international markets for on-lending to domestic firms.

Liberalization is also a source of risks and opportunities for financial firms other than commercial banks. The position of finance companies is similar to that of commercial banks, although in their case less diversified portfolios of assets and greater dependence on interest-rate-sensitive and foreign-currency-denominated funding may expose them to still greater risks under liberalization. For securities firms and asset management companies the sequel to liberalization is likely include greater market risks due to more volatile asset prices, expansion into new activities, and other effects of increased competition.

The increased banking risks associated with financial liberalization can to varying degrees be reduced or offset through hedging and other techniques of risk management. However, the instruments and banking skills required are less available in the great majority of developing countries.

Susceptibility to systemic banking risk is also generally greater in developing and transition economies.[27] Problems due to banking risks and their interactions are more likely to pose systemic threats in countries where financial firms and regimes are characterised by weaknesses regarding internal controls and financial reporting, and by ineffective regulation and supervision. Systemic crises result not only from processes originating in the banking or securities sectors themselves but also from macroeconomic instability and shocks which are more likely to trigger such crises, the more prevalent are the weaknesses just mentioned.[28] Systemic risk is thus enhanced in developing and transition economies in comparison with major OECD countries to the extent that the generally weaker banking systems of the former are exposed to greater frequency of macroeconomic shocks and instability.[29]

How does increased commercial presence for financial firms fit into this picture ? One effect is likely to be increased competition. Such increased commercial presence may also be associated with macroeconomic developments requiring policy responses by governments.

The potential benefits of greater competition are well rehearsed in the literature. The dangers, on the other hand, are associated primarily with the additional competitive pressures which may result from too great an influx of foreign financial firms. These pressures operate in the same direction as others due to financial liberalization more generally (which were described above), for example, pushing domestic financial firms into new and higher-risk

lending and other activities before the requisite skills and internal controls are in place. The presence of foreign financial firms may also have drastic effects on the balance of supply and demand in the market for people with banking skills, to the detriment of both domestic firms and a country's system of financial regulation and supervision.

On the macroeconomic front the increased presence of foreign financial firms (like the more general financial liberalization which usually accompanies it) is likely to lead to increased capital inflows and outflows, whose beneficial effects have to be reckoned against the problems which they are capable of posing to macroeconomic management. The contribution of foreign financial firms to such capital movements is due to their typically greater involvement than domestic firms in international transactions (a matter mentioned earlier in section III): foreign commercial banks, for example, are more dependent on international borrowing and lending than their domestic counterparts; and the rationale for the commercial presence in a country of foreign securities firms and asset management companies generally includes their greater ability to attract foreign portfolio investment in assets traded in its financial markets and to facilitate or manage investment abroad by its residents.[30]

The above remarks are not arguments against the benefits of either financial liberalization or an expanded presence of foreign financial firms *per se*. But they do point to the disadvantages of excessive haste under either heading. Indeed, they suggest that the pace at which developing countries choosing these policies open up their markets should be geared to a conservative timetable determined by the exigencies of the periods required for the implementation of effective regulation and supervision and the putting in place of effective internal controls by financial firms as well their acquisition of enhanced banking skills.[31]

Notes

1   For more detailed descriptions of the GATS see, for example, Hoekman (1994) and Cornford (1993).

2   According to recent estimates the financial sector accounted for 29 per cent of the stock of OECD countries' FDI at the end of 1995: for the United States the figure was 37 per cent, for the United Kingdom 28 per cent, for Japan 19 per cent, for Germany 24 per cent, for the Netherlands 36 per cent, and for Switzerland 22 per cent (BIS, 1997).

3   Activities under the heading of "banking and other financial services (excluding insurance" are listed in the Annex on Financial Services of the GATS.

4   The Exemption, which is unusual in that it will be triggered by a specific type of future action and does not simply exclude existing laws from MFN treatment under the GATS, in the wording which may still be edited covers "measures [in the insurance sector] according differential treatment in regard to the expansion of existing operations, the establishment of a new commercial presence or the conduct of new activities, in a circumstance in which a Member adopts or applies a measure that compels, or has the effect of compelling a person of the United States, on the basis of its nationality, to reduce its share of ownership in an insurance services provider operating in the Member's territory to a level below that prevailing on 12/12/97".

5   See, for example, the summary of the agreement between the Republic of Korea and the IMF in Morgan (1997b).

6   Financial services in statistics for the balance of payments on current account (other than those related to insurance and pension funds) cover commissions and fees associated with financial intermediation and auxiliary services (IMF, 1993).

7   The substantial overseas network of banking entities from Republic of Korea is of interest in the context of the initial omission from statistics during the recent mobilization of international financial support for the country of a significant part of international banks' exposure to it. Official international banking statistics (such as those published by the Bank for International Settlements) show banks' exposure by the country of residence of the borrower (which in the case of Korean overseas banking entities would be the country in which they are located) rather than that of the parent firm.

8   Concerning restrictions on the access of foreign firms to membership of stock exchanges in selected Asian economies see Cornford (1997).

9   Of Citibank's revenue of approximately $3.8 billion in 1996, 46 per cent was accounted for by global corporate business and 54 per cent by global consumer business, the corresponding percentages in 1988 being 63 per cent and 37 per cent. Under the category of global consumer business 28 per cent was due to its credit- card business, 19 per cent to other retail business, and 7 per cent to private banking (Klee, 1997). HSBC, a London-based holding company, owns entities in Hong Kong (China) (including HongkongBank), the United Kingdom, Canada, Brunei, Malaysia, Singapore, and (since April of this year) Brazil as well as majority or substantial minority participations, *inter alia,* in entities in Argentina, Chile, Egypt, India, Mexico and Peru (Fairlamb, 1997).

10   Cornford, op. cit., p. 11. (The six economies are Hong Kong [China], India, Indonesia, the Republic of Korea, Taiwan Province of China, and Thailand.)

11   Direct investment constitutes a significant part of the involvement of a number of international investment banks in some Asian economies. Such investment typically precedes an initial public offering (IPO) on the stock exchange of the equity of the firm in question, which the bank with the direct investment hopes to manage (and through which it will be able to sell part or all of its investment).

12   The value of major mergers and acquisitions in Latin America amounted to more than $30 billion in 1996 (Engen, 1997).

13   Concerning the order of magnitude of commission income from the trading of financial derivatives on exchanges in Hong Kong (China) and Singapore see Cornford, op. cit., p. 12.

14   For a 1995 estimate of approximately $670 billion for the funds under management by major institutional investors in nine Asian economies (Hong Kong [China], India, Indonesia, the Republic of Korea, Malaysia, Philippines, Singapore, Taiwan Province of China, Thailand) see ibid. pp. 7 and 20.

15   The size of the private pension systems in selected Latin American countries where reforms have led to an expanded role for such systems is as follows: Chile (where the reform dates from 1981), $30.1 billion; Peru (where the reform dates from 1993), $1 billion; Colombia (where the reform dates from 1994), $0.9 billion; and Argentina (where the reform dates from 1994), $6.1 billion (Morgan, 1997a).

16   For example, the major international managers of assets in Asia in 1996 were mostly investment banks and asset managers with parent companies in the United States, the United Kingdom, Germany and Switzerland. They also included the Asian investment arm of the insurance and investment conglomerate, American International Group (AIG) (see Koo, 1997).

17   The first point can be illustrated for the role of adviser on major mergers and acquisitions transactions in Latin America in 1997. Salomon Brothers topped the list as an adviser on 7 deals valued at $5.6 billion, and the identity of other firms and the scale of their involvement in terms of the number and value of deals were as follows: J.P.Morgan, 21 deals/$5.5 billion; Merrill Lynch and Co., 4/$5.4 billion; Chase Manhattan Corporation, 3/$4.6 billion; Banco Bradesco, 2/$3.2 billion; Ernst and Young, 1/$3.1 billion; Banco Patrimônio de Investimentos, 1/$3.1 billion; Robert Fleming Securities, 1/$3.1 billion; Banco Icatu, 1/$3.1 billion; Maxima Corretora, 1/$3.1 billion; Rothschild Group, 1/$3.1 billion; Morgan Stanley, Dean Witter, Discover and Co., 5/$2.9 billion; Credit Suisse First Boston, 7/$2.8 billion; Banco Bozano, Simonsen, 3/$2.1 billion; Dresdener Kleinwort Benson, 4/$2 billion; Banco Santander, 5/$1.5 billion; Banco General de Negocios, 5/$1.2 billion; Violy, Byorum and Partners, 3/$1.2 billion; Bear, Stearns and Co., 2/$1.2 billion; and Lazard Houses, 1/$1.1 billion. See Engen, op. cit., p. 135. (Unfortunately the parent countries of some of these firms are not specified in the article and cannot necessarily be inferred from their names.)

18   In the Interim Committee Statement on the liberalization of Capital Movements Under an Amendment of the IMF's Articles, issued on 21 September in Hong Kong, "the Committee invites the Executive Board to complete its work on a proposed amendment of the IMF's Articles that would make the liberalization of capital movements one of the purposes of the IMF, and extend, as needed, the IMF's jurisdiction through the establishment of carefully defined and consistently applied obligations regarding the liberalization of such movements".

19   In a recent book on financial engineering Fred Arditti, the former chief economist of the Chicago Mercantile Exchange (where he was responsible for the development of the Eurodollar futures contract), provides an elementary illustration of the way in which cash flows resembling those associated with the purchase of six-month United States Treasury bills (T-bills) can be achieved through an alternative portfolio involving the purchase of futures contracts (on T-bills expiring in three months) and of three-month T-bills. The steps described can be generalized to instruments with longer maturities and more complex portfolios (Arditti, 1996, pp. 192-193).

20   Concerning possible deviations from non-discrimination in such cases see Key and Scott (1991, p. 7) and Group of Thirty (1996, p. 6).

21   Potential problems due to such conflicts are not limited to the insolvencies which accompany external-payments-cum-banking crises.

22   According to Article 61(2) of the Treaty establishing the European Economic Community "The liberalization of banking and insurance services connected with movements of capital shall be effected in step with the progressive liberalization of movement of capital".

23   George Zavvos, a former official of the Directorate-General for Financial Institutions and Company Law (DG XV) of the Commission of the European Communities who was involved in the drafting of the EU's Second Banking Directive of 1989, has described the EU's progress on the regulatory harmonization required for a single market in financial services during the first two decades after 1957 as "dismal". In addition to reasons for the slowness such as those cited in the text Zavvos notes the caution of some member countries' central banks (particularly that of the United Kingdom) regarding legally binding harmonized directives owing to their potential lack of flexibility in meeting the needs of the financial sector and to their conflict with non-statutory systems of financial oversight (see Zavvos, 1990).

24   For example, "Few question the long-term benefits of financial liberalisation for developing countries. But such reforms inevitably present banks with new risks which, without the proper precautions, can increase the danger of a banking crisis" (Goldstein and Turner, 1996, p. 17). A study of the World Bank on the effects of greater financial openness (or "financial integration") on cross-border capital flows, states that "Although financial integration may be beneficial for developing countries in the long run, potential risks and losses are greater if the process is poorly managed" (World Bank, 1997, p. 259).

25   Interest-rate and credit risk are frequently connected since unexpected rises in interest rates can threaten borrowers' capacity to meet their interest obligations. Greater volatility of interest rates can also pose special problems in countries whose corporate financing is in many cases characterised by arrangements designed to economize equity capital (which have been a feature of the development models followed by some Asian countries) since borrowers with thin cushions of equity are particularly vulnerable to the resulting fluctuations in their interest obligations. The nature of such arrangements and the contrast with patterns of corporate financing commonly found in major OECD countries are graphically brought in the account by a former banker at Goldman Sachs of his problems in explaining the logic of Mitsui's balance sheet to a management committee considering a proposal in 1969 to act as issuers of commercial paper for the firm in the United States. ("What the hell kind of business is this?" one of the members asked. "It's got almost no equity – more than 90 per cent of its assets are financed with debt..." "The Japanese system of corporate finance is very different from ours ", I began. "As capital is in very short supply, there is a lot of leverage, provided mainly by Japanese banks and suppliers.") (Smith, 1989, pp. 295-299)

26   Market risk is that of loss due to changes in the market value of a position before it can be offset or liquidated.

27   In a 1992 report prepared for the central banks of the Group of Ten, systemic risks are defined as those which have the potential to cause a systemic crisis. Such a crisis is "a disturbance that severely impairs the working of the financial system and, at the extreme. causes a complete breakdown in it ... Systemic crises can originate in a variety of ways but ultimately they will impair at least one of the key functions of the financial system: credit allocation, payments, and the pricing of financial assets. A given financial disturbance may grow into a systemic crisis at one point in time but not another, depending on the financial and economic circumstances when the shock occurs" (BIS, 1992, p. 25).

28   Thus it should not be assumed that progress in the areas of banking management and regulation can eventually eliminate the possibility of banking crises. Much recent experience in OECD countries indicates the contrary. No loan or other asset on a bank's balance sheet, however reasonable the management decision of which it was initially the result, is free of the risk of becoming "bad" or non-performing owing to unfavourable changes macro-economic conditions.

29   Evidence concerning the instability of macroeconomic variables in emerging financial markets is to be found in Goldstein and Turner (1996), pp. 9-14 (who show that for several of them this is also associated with greater volatility of bank deposits and lending). A high proportion of banking crises in developing economies have in fact been closely connected to the instability of macroeconomic variables. See the survey in Caprio and Klingebiel (1996, Annex table 2).

30   It has also been pointed out in this context that the greater international diversification of foreign banks assets and sources of financing means that they may be less threatened (and thus contribute to stability) during crises. See, for example, Goldstein and Turner, op. cit., p. 34.

31   Greater precision concerning the appropriate pace of liberalization is difficult. But a postscript concerning this subject is provided by remarks of a senior financial regulator during a recent talk in UNCTAD that the experience of a major international bank with whose management he was acquainted suggested the need for a period of as much as a decade for the establishment of a reporting system for its entities in different countries which made possible proper supervision of the bank on a consolidated basis, and that a similar period was required for the adequate training of banking supervisors.

References

ARDITTI, F.D. (1996), *Derivatives* (Boston: Harvard Business School Press).

BIS (1992), *Recent Developments in International Interbank Relations*, Report by a Working Group of the Eurocurrency Standing Committee of the Central Banks of the Group of Ten Countries (Basle: Bank for International Settlements).

BIS (1995), *International Banking and Financial Market Developments* (Basle: Bank for International Settlements), November.

BIS (1997), *67th Annual Report* (Basle: Bank for International Settlements).

BRÖKER, G. (1989), *Competition in Banking* (Paris: OECD).

CAPRIO, G., and D. KLINGEBIEL (1996), "Bank insolvencies: Cross-country experience", *Policy Research Working Paper No. 1620* (Washington, D.C.: The World Bank), July.

CORNFORD, A.J. (1993), "Some implications for banking of the draft General Agreement on Trade in Services of December 1991", *UNCTAD Review*, No. 4.

CORNFORD, A.J. (1997), "Selected features of financial sectors in Asia and their implications for services trade", *UNCTAD Discussion Paper*, No. 129, September.

ENGEN, J.R. (1997), "The scramble for Latin America, *Institutional Investor*, September.

FAIRLAMB, D. (1997), "Succeeding Sir Willie", *Institutional Investor*, June.

GOLDSTEIN, M., and P. TURNER (1996), "Banking crises in emerging economies: Origins and policy options", *BIS Economic Papers*, No. 46 (Basle: Bank for International Settlements), October.

GROUP OF THIRTY (in cooperation with INSOL International) (1996), "International insolvencies in the financial sector: discussion draft" (Washington, D.C.: Group of Thirty), August.

HOEKMAN, B. (1994), "The General Agreement on Trade in Services", paper presented at the OECD Workshop on the New World Trading System, Paris, 25-26 April 1994; reprinted in J.H. Jackson, W.J. Davey, and A.O. Sykes (eds.), *Legal Problems of International Economic Relations: Cases, Material and Text on the National and Transnational Regulation of Transnational Economic Relations*, third edition (St. Paul, Minn.: West Publishing, 1995), pp. 921-930.

IMF (1993), *Balance of Payments Manual*, fifth edition (Washington, D.C.: International Monetary Fund).

KEY, S.J., and H.S. SCOTT (1991), *International Trade in Banking Services: a Conceptual Framework*, Occasional Papers 35 (Washington, D.C.: Group of Thirty).

KLEE, K. (1997), "Brand builders", *Institutional Investor*, March.

KOO, C. (1997), "Waiting for the dough", *Institutional Investor*, October.

MORGAN, J.P. (1997a), *Emerging Markets Data Watch*, 28 March.

MORGAN, J.P. (1997b), *Emerging Markets Data Watch*, 5 December.

SMITH, R.C. (1989), *The Global Bankers* (New York: E.P. Dutton).

UNITED STATES DEPARTMENT OF THE TREASURY (1979), *Report to the Congress on Foreign Government Treatment of U.S. Commercial Banking Operations* (Washington, D.C.).

UNITED STATES DEPARTMENT OF THE TREASURY (1994), *National Treatment Study 1994* (Washington, D.C.).

WORLD BANK (1997), *Private Capital Flows to Developing Countries: The Road to Financial Integration* (Oxford: Oxford University Press for The World Bank).

WTO (1997), *Opening Markets in Financial Services and the Role of the GATS* (Geneva: World Trade Organization Publications).

ZAVVOS, G.S. (1990), "Banking integration and 1992: Legal issues and policy implications", *Harvard International Law Journal*, Vol. 31, No. 2 (Spring).

STRATEGIC OPTIONS AVAILABLE TO DEVELOPING COUNTRIES WITH REGARD TO A MULTILATERAL AGREEMENT ON INVESTMENT

A.V. Ganesan

Abstract

In the context of the debate on a comprehensive Multilateral Agreement on Investment (MAI), three important factors need to be kept in view . First, the recent surge in FDI flows has been caused mainly by the autonomous and unilateral liberalization by the developing countries of their FDI policies. Second, nearly 90 per cent of the flows has been received by about 20 developing countries, of which China alone has received over one third. Third, the primary determinant of the flows is the market and investment opportunities that the host countries offer. Therefore, MAI will not be the dominant factor in directing FDI flows to developing countries.

Two basic options are available to developing countries with regard to a MAI. One is to allow the current trends and arrangements to evolve and gather further momentum, and to move towards a possible multilateral framework at an opportune time in the future on the basis of the experience gained. This option is contingent upon developing countries having the collective will and strength to resist pressure by the industrialized countries for entering a MAI at an earlier stage. The other is to prepare for the negotiation of a MAI now, trying to ensure that it reflects the developmental, as well as political and social, needs and concerns of the developing countries, and keeping in mind that the main motive of the industrialized countries behind an MAI is the gaining and consolidation of market access opportunities for their business enterprises around the world. The implications of a MAI will also depend heavily on the forum chosen for its negotiation.

The definition of investment in a MAI can have serious implications not only for the scope and coverage of such an agreement, but also for the obligations relating to the free transfer of funds for foreign investors. The issue of national treatment is also critical. An obligation to grant national treatment for foreign investors in the pre-establishment phase would curb the freedom and flexibility of developing countries to pursue their own policies in consonance with their needs and circumstances. Other key issues requiring the special attention of developing countries are: performance requirements and investment incentives, movement of natural persons, restrictive business practices, transfer of technology and the obligations of the investors. The issues of competition policy and environmental concerns also need careful examination from the perspective of developing countries. Before entering in multilateral negotiations developing countries should aim at a common position on these key issues.

The best forum for developing countries is the WTO. For the majority of developing countries the high standards of the OECD treaty, which are designed for capital exporters and advanced countries, may entail unacceptable costs.

I. Background

The establishment of a comprehensive and legally binding multilateral agreement for the treatment and protection of FDI has now come to occupy a prominent place in the international economic policy agenda. Two recent developments have brought this issue to the fore: first, the negotiations begun in the OECD in September 1995 to establish a Multilateral Agreement on Investment (MAI), which will be a free-standing international treaty open both to all OECD members and the European Communities as well as to accession by non-OECD member countries; and second, the Singapore Ministerial Declaration of December 1996 of the World Trade Organization (WTO). Although the Declaration has established for the present only a working group to examine the relationship between trade and investment, it is widely regarded as having sown the seeds for the negotiation of an MAI under the auspices of the WTO.

There are several reasons why an MAI is now a priority issue for the industrialized countries. First, they are still overwhelmingly the main home and host countries for the flows and stock of FDI as well as for large transnational corporations (TNCs), whose strategies and operations are increasingly becoming globalized. The developed countries still account for over four fifths of global FDI outflows and two thirds of global FDI inflows. Secondly, outward flows of FDI from the developed countries are rising and, more importantly, the share of developing countries in the receipt of these flows is increasing sharply as many developing countries are more and more becoming attractive destinations for FDI. The involvement of developing countries in an MAI – instead of its being confined only to industrialized countries – is therefore a matter of interest to developed countries. These trends in FDI flows are captured in the table below.

However, the fundamental reason behind the demand of the developed countries for a multilateral treaty on FDI is that they see such investment as playing a crucial role in the strategies of their enterprises to gain and consolidate market access opportunities around the world. FDI, trade and technology are growing more intertwined and becoming complementary or alternative ways of accessing foreign markets. FDI in particular is beginning to be more important than trade for delivering goods and services to foreign markets and, in addition, is becoming a powerful vehicle for TNCs

in organizing production internationally and thereby enhancing their competitive edge. With an estimated $7 trillion in global sales in 1995 (the value of goods and services produced by some 280,000 foreign affiliates of TNCs), international production outweighed exports of goods and services (roughly $6 trillion) as the dominant mode for TNCs to service foreign markets.[1] Further-more, while the FDI flow was $350 billion in 1996, the total investment generated by it in foreign affiliates – a true measure of the investment component of international production – was an estimated $1.4 trillion, or four times the volume of the FDI flow alone. In short, industrialized countries are now taking a holistic and integrated view of trade (in goods as well as services), investment and technology, and are therefore pressing hard for binding multilateral disciplines in all these areas with a view to enlarging and ensuring market access opportunities for their enterprises around the world.

This holistic approach has also received an impetus from several other factors. One is the successful conclusion of the Uruguay Round, which has not only extended the multilateral trade regime to new areas of services and intellectual property rights but has also integrated trade in goods, services and technology, and established a strong enforcement mechanism, including the possibility of "cross-retaliation" across sectors to penalize non-compliance. Apart from the GATS and TRIPS Agreements dealing with various investment issues, the Agreement on Trade-Related Investment Measures (TRIMS) has provided an "in-built agenda" to press for multilateral rules for the liberalization of investment regimes. The WTO has thus become a convenient forum for bringing newer issues on the multilateral trade agenda and establishing rules and disciplines for them. A second factor is the ongoing unilateral liberalization of FDI policies by developing countries and the spurt in bilateral treaties for the protection of FDI. A third element is the growing number of regional arrangements on investment, such as the NAFTA, AFTA, APEC Non-binding Investment Principles, MERCUSOR Protocols, etc. These seem to have generated an impression in the industrialized countries that the distance to be travelled to reach an MAI with developing country participation has narrowed and that the time is now ripe to set the ball rolling in the WTO. The Singapore Ministerial Declaration of December 1996 is their first, but decisive, step in this direction.

The current desire of the industrialized countries for a legally binding treaty on FDI must be contrasted

FDI INFLOWS, BY DEVELOPED AND DEVELOPING COUNTRIES, 1985-1996

	World	Developed countries	Share	Developing countries	Share
	($ billion)	*($ billion)*	*(Per cent)*	*($ billion)*	*(Per cent)*
1985-1990 *(Annual average)*	142 *(93 per cent)*	117	82.0	25	18.0
1990-1995 *(Annual average)*	218 *(87 per cent)*	149	68.0	64	29.0
1993	218 *(83 per cent)*	139	64.0	73	33.0
1994	239 *(84 per cent)*	142	59.0	90	38.0
1995	317 *(85 per cent)*	206	65.0	96	30.0
1996	349 *(86 per cent)*	208	60.0	129	37.0

Source: UNCTAD (1996a and 1997).

Note: Figures within brackets in column 2 show the percentage shares of developed countries in outward flows of FDI.

with their attitude towards the multilateral initiatives undertaken in the past within the United Nations system to lay down standards for the conduct, behaviour and obligations of foreign investors, especially the TNCs. The industrialized countries were insistent that the three multilateral instruments negotiated under the auspices of the United Nations system – namely, the "Set of Multilaterally Agreed Equitable Principles and Rules for the Control of Restrictive Business Practices" (negotiated in UNCTAD and adopted by a United Nations resolution in 1980), "Draft United Nations Code of Conduct on Transnational Corporations" (negotiated in the United Nations and not yet adopted) and "Draft International Code of Conduct on the Transfer of Technology" (negotiated in UNCTAD and not yet adopted) – should all be non-binding and voluntary instruments.

Within the OECD itself, although the Code of Liberalization of Capital Movements was adopted as legally binding in 1961, when the OECD itself came into being, it was only in 1984 that the national treatment principle (for the establishment stage) was incorporated into it. The OECD "Declaration on International Investment and Multinational Enterprises", adopted in 1976, which includes *inter alia* a "National Treatment" instrument (establishing national treatment in the operational stage) and "Guidelines for Multinational Enterprises" (establishing voluntary standards for the behaviour of such enterprises), is legally non-binding. The "Recommendation of the Council on Bribery in International Transactions", adopted by the OECD in 1994, is again non-binding.

It is thus clear that as the focus of the industrialized world shifts from the obligations of the owners of capital to the obligations of the host countries, the instruments envisaged, such as an MAI, are sought to be made legally binding. The underlying philosophy behind this approach would seem to be that the obligations of investors/enterprises should be left to be addressed by national laws and regulations (applicable alike to domestic and foreign investors, and consistent with the country's international obligations), while intergovernmental agreements should be confined to the obligations and commitments of the signatory governments. The implications for developing countries of this dual approach are two-fold: first, obligations on investors/ enterprises that may contribute to the developmental objectives of the host countries will be avoided, or at best addressed, only through recommendations for voluntary compliance in a multilateral agreement; and, second, developing countries need to ensure that they have sufficient freedom and flexibility in the agreement to pursue their own policies for achieving their developmental (as well as political and social) objectives.

In contrast, the apprehensions of developing countries over a legally binding MAI stem from the facts that they are net importers of capital and technology and that there is a huge competitive gap between their enterprises, particularly small and medium enterprises, and the TNCs of the industrialized world. There can be little doubt that developing countries recognize the importance and value of FDI and foreign technology to their growth and development; the unilateral liberalization of their FDI and trade regimes and their increasing shift towards a market and outward-oriented approach in economic policy-making bear ample testimony to it. However, their experience shows that the building-up of domestic entrepreneurial, industrial and technological capabilities is essential not only to cope with, but also to realize, the full benefits from FDI and foreign technology. Without sufficient domestic capabilities, FDI and foreign technology seldom permeate the productive system of the national economy to spread their beneficial effects throughout the economy. The selective and judicious intervention of the government is therefore widely considered necessary to support or protect domestic industry and technology creation, sometimes even to ensure a "level playing field" for domestic enterprises. It is also necessary for developing countries to employ an appropriate mix of incentives and performance requirements for FDI to achieve specific developmental objectives. Besides their economic objectives, the regulation of FDI is seen as necessary by developing countries – all the more so since they are overwhelmingly net importers of capital – to also realize certain political and social objectives. Even in the case of the developed countries, it is noteworthy that their attitude towards inward FDI changed only after they became large exporters of capital and

technology (e.g. Canada, Japan). Adequate freedom and flexibility to pursue their own policies toward FDI and foreign technology is therefore regarded as a matter of fundamental importance by developing countries, although it may be argued whether regulation of FDI is the only or the best way for ensuring that FDI contributes to the developmental and social objectives of the host countries.

II. Options open to developing countries

A. *Related issues*

Against this background, what are the strategic options open to developing countries in responding to the demand for a strong, legally binding and effectively enforceable multilateral agreement on investment? This is a complex question considering the socio-political and economic implications of such an agreement but, before the options are analysed, it may be pertinent to take note of some related issues.

The first is the role expected to be played by such a multilateral treaty in the flows of FDI to developing countries. The question is whether a multilateral treaty will enhance significantly such FDI flows in comparison to their own unilateral liberalization measures coupled with the bilateral, regional or plurilateral agreements that they are already entering into on their own volition. The current pattern in FDI flows to developing countries throws some interesting light on this question. Its dominant feature is that the flows are highly skewed in their distribution. Taking the four-year period 1993-1996, total FDI flows to developing countries amounted to $388 billion. Of this, China alone accounted for $139 billion, or about 36 per cent of total flows to all developing countries. The next five largest recipients of FDI flows – namely Brazil, Indonesia, Malaysia, Mexico and Singapore - each of which had a share varying between 4 and 8 per cent, together accounted for about 28 per cent of total FDI flows. The next 14 largest recipients, each of which had a share from 0.8 to 2.5 per cent, together accounted for about 24 per cent of total FDI flows.[2] These included *inter alia* the newly industrialized economies of Hong Kong, the Republic of Korea and Taiwan Province of China. All the remaining developing countries, taken together, accounted for barely 10 per cent of total FDI flows to developing countries. Of these, the 48 least developed countries (LDCs as designated by the United Nations) accounted for a mere 1.3 per cent of the total FDI flows to developing countries (in 1996 the 48 LDCs taken together received $1.6 billion out of a total FDI flow of $129 billion to developing countries).

It is difficult to argue that FDI flows to China or the other top-bracket developing countries would be significantly influenced by their being or not a party to a multilateral treaty on FDI. The driving force behind FDI flows to these countries is the market and investment opportunities that they offer, supported by their macroeconomic conditions, growth prospects and investment climate. They have shown that it is possible to maintain a sound investment climate and guarantee stability of policies and security of investment by their own autonomous measures. Conversely, despite providing a liberal investment climate and incentives for FDI, the poorer countries have been unable to attract FDI, primarily because of their lack of market and investment opportunities. There is no empirical evidence for the view that if there were a multilateral treaty on FDI, the least developed and other developing countries now on the fringe of FDI flows would be able to compete more effectively for such investments and would receive increased flows of FDI.

Two further interlinked questions in this context are:

(i) If developing countries can voluntarily enter into bilateral investment promotion and pro-tection treaties (of which there has been an explosion in the 1990s) as well as regional and plurilateral arrangements, why should they hesitate to move on to the next higher level of a uniform and binding multilateral treaty, and will it not strengthen their investment climate much more than unilateral measures which are not irreversible or regional measures which dis-criminate against non-members?

(ii) If existing arrangements are conducive enough to promoting and securing FDI flows, why should industrialized countries push aggres-sively for a multilateral treaty on FDI?

It is true that there has been a dramatic increase during the 1990s in the number of bilateral investment treaties (BITs) for the promotion and protection of FDI. As of 1 January 1997, there was a total of 1,330 such treaties in the world involving 162 countries compared with less than 400 at the beginning of the 1990s. More than two thirds of these treaties have come into existence in the 1990s, of which around 180 in 1996 alone. Although the number of BITs between developing countries themselves is rising, nearly 62 per cent of the 1,330 such treaties at the end of 1996 involved developed countries. China leads the developing countries in the number of BITs, having concluded 80 treaties, of which 20 with developed countries. The propensity of developed countries to conclude BITs varies widely, with Germany accounting for 111 treaties, the United Kingdom 87, Switzerland 81, France 74, the Netherlands 58, the United States 39, and Japan 4. It must be stated that BITs have not been an important factor in influencing FDI flows to developing countries. In fact, according to a recent survey in the United Kingdom, most TNCs were not even aware of the existence of these treaties.

The main reason why BITs have found favour with developing countries is that they provide for national treatment to foreign investors in the post-establishment phase only, and do not place any restrictions on host countries in following their own FDI policies. This is because the aim of BITs is the protection and equitable treatment of FDI after the investment has taken place in consonance with the host countries' laws and regulations. As regards regional agreements, such as the ASEAN or MERCOSUR arrangements, for one thing they are between developing countries at similar levels of development, and, for another, they do not restrict the autonomy of the participating countries in following their own FDI policies. The APEC Non-Binding Investment Principles (1994), although a voluntary code, also do not impinge on the freedom of host countries in pursuing their own policies. The NAFTA between the United States, Canada and Mexico, however, marks a departure from BITs and other regional agreements in as much as it enshrines the national treatment principle from the pre-establishment phase onwards, though tempered to a significant extent by the exceptions granted to Mexico. Furthermore, the NAFTA does not prescribe any "roll back" obligation, although Mexico on its own volition has undertaken certain rollbacks. In this context, it is worth repeating that the national treatment principle, i.e. the right of establishment, was incorporated in the OECD Code of Liberalization of Capital Movements only in 1984, nearly 23 years after the code was originally adopted. There is also the National Treatment instrument of the OECD "Declaration and Decisions on International Invest-ment and Multinational Enterprises", adopted in 1976, which applies the national treatment principle in the post-establishment phase and is legally a non-binding instrument. It is only the MAI currently under negotiation in the OECD that aims to make the national treatment obligation legally binding both in the pre- and post-establishment stages of an investment.

On the contrary, the main purpose behind the multilateral treaty being contemplated by the industrialized countries is to gain market access for enterprises under conditions of non-discriminatory treatment, as between domestic and foreign investors in regard to the entry, establishment and operation of foreign investment. National treatment from the entry stage itself is crucial to the goal of gaining market access, and therefore, even if some country-specific exceptions are initially permissible under the treaty, they would be subject to standstill and roll-back commitments.

The issue of national treatment (or the right of entry, right of establishment or non-discriminatory treatment at the pre-establishment stage) is thus at the heart of the division between industrial and developing countries in their approach and attitude towards a legally binding multilateral treaty on investment. This issue is also strongly linked to the objective of developing countries that any such treaty on investment should take into account their developmental needs and concerns. While industrialized countries may argue that an investor-friendly agreement is ipso facto also development-friendly, the experience of developing countries is that the development dimension cannot be taken care of merely by statements of principles or exhortations in a treaty, or even by negative lists of exceptions and transition periods. In their view, the pursuit of developmental objectives, in the light of each country's unique needs and circumstances, requires sufficient freedom and flexibility to pursue one's own policies, which in the context of a legally binding treaty on foreign investment means the freedom to regulate the entry of foreign investment and to grant national treatment, subject to such qualifications as may be necessary, only in the post-establishment phase for investments conforming to the host country's policies, laws and regulations.

Lastly, socio-political and economic considerations interact rather strongly in the realm of foreign investment. Foreign investment is much more politically sensitive than foreign trade. Concerns relating to national sovereignty or protection of social and cultural interests tend to figure prominently in the case of foreign investment, arising at least in part from the fact that investment means long-term ownership and control over assets, resources and enterprises. For example, the domestic ownership

requirements in many developing countries stem as much from political sensitivity as from economic considerations. This is also true to a large extent with respect to foreign ownership and control in the so-called "cultural industries" (e.g. media, publishing, films) or State ownership and control in some core industries. These concerns cannot be wished away or countered by purely economic arguments. The notion of non-discriminatory treatment as between national and foreign investors therefore needs to be tempered by political realities as well, particularly against the background of the huge asymmetry in capital ownership between industrialized and developing countries.

B.   The options

In the light of the issues discussed above, there are two basic options open to developing countries in responding to the demand for an MAI. The first option is to allow the current trends and arrangements – namely, autonomous liberalization of their FDI policies by host developing countries together with bilateral and regional arrangements for the promotion and protection of FDI – to evolve and gather further strength and momentum, and to move towards a multilateral framework for FDI on the basis of the experience gained and consensus generated on important issues over time. The second option is to prepare for negotiation of a comprehensive multilateral framework for FDI and try to ensure that the resulting framework takes adequate care of their developmental as well as their political and social needs and concerns. It must be stressed at the outset that the first option does not in any way mean or imply that developing countries should go slow in the liberalization of their FDI regimes or dilute their standards of fair and equitable treatment and effective protection of FDI. In fact, their current unilateral and extensive liberalization of FDI regimes stems from their recognition of the value of FDI in promoting their growth and development and in integrating their economies with the global economy. The fundamental issue in the choice of options is not the need for liberalization of FDI regimes or the standards to be followed for the treatment and protection of FDI, but how the liberalization and high standards of treatment of FDI can be maintained without eroding the capacity of host developing countries to pursue their own developmental, political and social objectives. The choice for developing countries, in other words, is between an evolutionary and a revolutionary approach.

C. First option: the evolution of current arrangements

The developing countries are not the countries seeing the need for or demanding a multilateral treaty on FDI at this juncture. They can therefore consider the option of continually improving their investment climate to attract FDI flows through unilateral measures for liberalization of their FDI policies and regulatory frameworks, supported further by bilateral and regional agreements. As long as they keep their policies stable and transparent, and as long as foreign investors perceive their investment climate to be congenial in terms of fair and equitable treatment and other factors bearing upon the investment decisions of foreign investors, they will continue to receive FDI flows in tune with their market and investment opportunities. There is no a priori reason why a stable, predictable and hospitable investment climate for FDI cannot be maintained at as high a level under a combination of autonomous, unilateral and bilateral/regional measures as under a multi-lateral treaty. At the same time, developing countries will have the freedom and flexibility necessary to ensure that a liberal investment climate is in harmony with their own developmental as well as political and social needs and concerns. They will then be free to decide upon the nature and extent of national treatment to be accorded to foreign investors in the pre- and post-establishment phases of investment in the light of their own specific needs and circum-stances. The upsurge in FDI flows to developing countries in the 1990s shows that investment climates and investment opportunities can be synchronized under the existing arrangements, as the major con-tributory factor behind the FDI upsurge has been the unilateral liberalization of FDI regimes by developing countries.

On the other hand, a legally binding multilateral treaty, in which the chief bone of contention is bound to be the issue of non-discriminatory or national treatment for FDI at the entry and establishment stages, may compel the developing countries to minimize their commitments to as low a level as their negotiating strength will enable them to achieve. This may be attempted through keeping the "negative list" of exceptions as comprehensive as possible or the "positive list" of commitments as short as possible (or a mixture of both), resisting standstill or roll-back obligations, and demanding long transition periods or special safeguards and derogations. Apart from the political and social sensitivities attached to FDI, this kind of a minimalist approach may be considered necessary by developing countries to build the devel-opment dimension into the treaty, which, as noted earlier, cannot be addressed merely by general statements in the preamble or exhortations and best-endeavour clauses in the body of the treaty. In the end, the scope for pursuit of national political, social and developmental objectives will depend upon the host countries having sufficient freedom and flexi-bility to follow their own policies for building up their domestic industrial and technological capa-bilities.

Proponents of this option (of allowing existing arrangements to evolve organically) have therefore pointed out that the momentum for further liber-alization of FDI policies is centred currently at the unilateral, bilateral and regional levels, and that it may be counter-productive if this momentum were disrupted by multilateral negotiations which would bring to the fore the divisive issues, especially that of market access. They have also pointed out that many developing countries have yet to adjust to the impact of the liberalization measures agreed in the Uruguay Round, and it may be too early for them to contemplate another multilateral undertaking for substantial liberalization of FDI, including the important issue of the right of establishment.[3]

Developing countries, therefore, have adequate grounds to consider the option of allowing the existing arrangements to evolve, pursuing unilateral liberalization of their FDI regimes in accordance with their own needs and circumstances, enhancing their investment climate, and entering into bilateral, regional or plurilateral agreements to foster FDI. As these efforts gather more strength and momentum, they can use the experience gained to move further towards a possible multilateral arrangement that is evolutionary in character. Being voluntary in nature, the existing arrangements have acquired a certain strength and durability, which through further evo-lution may provide a good basis for formulating a multilateral arrangement at an opportune time. Developing countries can therefore argue that the time is not yet ripe to begin negotiations on a multilateral treaty for investment.

The option of continuing with the existing arrangements presupposes that developing countries have the collective will and strength to resist the pressure of the industrialized countries to begin negotiations on an MAI now. The Uruguay Round experience and more recently the Singapore Minis-terial Decision, however, do not augur well for this option.

D. Second option: negotiating a multilateral agreement

The proponents of a multilateral framework for investment have advanced several reasons for it. First, foreign investment and trade are inextricably entwined and the present international arrangements governing FDI do not adequately reflect or respond to the contemporary global economic reality. As with the multilateral trade rules ushered in by the Uruguay Round, a multilateral framework of rules is also necessary for investment in order to "catch up with the market" and cope with the dynamics of the ongoing integration of the world economy. In particular, this will enable firms to contest markets, irrespective of the modality used to contest them. The underlying tenets of this argument are that FDI and trade are not substitutes, but are complementary to one another, that FDI has become more important than trade in delivering goods and services to foreign markets, that it is becoming a key instrument in organizing production internationally, and that restrictions on trade or investment are indistinguishable from one another. Barriers to investment need therefore to be reduced under multilateral disciplines, just as barriers to trade have been reduced under GATT/WTO rules.

Secondly, the establishment of a multilateral framework of rules will help create a stable, predictable and transparent environment for investment, enhance business confidence, and thereby promote the growth of FDI flows to developing countries. It is also pointed out that the conditions to help stimulate FDI are precisely the same as those required to stimulate domestic investment. Bilateral investment treaties and unilateral measures, however strong and liberal, do not engender the same degree of business confidence, while regional agreements tend to discriminate against countries not belonging to the regional set-up. Furthermore, the bilateral and regional treaties, besides being limited to the signatory countries, do not adequately address certain vital issues of significance to foreign investors, especially non-discriminatory treatment of foreign investors at the entry and establishment stages of investment. In addition, the same investment issues are addressed in a variety of ways in the bilateral and regional treaties leading to complexity and inconsistency in the treatment of FDI. It is therefore in the interest of everyone that the existing patchwork of bilateral and regional instruments be superseded by a single multilateral instrument laying down uniform rules for the treatment of investment world-

wide. Two subsidiary arguments are also advanced in favour of a multilateral framework: first, small and medium-sized TNCs should be particularly enabled to invest abroad; and second, the least developed countries (LDCs) should be helped in competing for FDI, currently flowing predominantly into developing countries with large, lucrative and growing markets. According to the WTO, if LDCs are signatories to a multilateral treaty on investment, it will substantially improve their investment climate and thereby enable them to attract much needed FDI flows (WTO, 1996, pp. 7 and 75).

However, as noted earlier, the fundamental motive behind the demand of industrialized countries for a strong and comprehensive multilateral framework for FDI is the gaining and consolidation of market access for their business enterprises, particularly in developing countries with large or growing market and investment opportunities. The key to achieving this objective of market access and market consolidation for their enterprises is a legally binding multilateral treaty, firmly enshrining the main elements of liberalization of the FDI regimes of host countries (through, in particular, national treatment at the entry and establishment stages, in addition to the operational stage): fair and equitable standards for treatment of FDI, strong protection of FDI, and effective dispute settlement procedures. From their perspective, as trade, technology and investment are becoming increasingly and inextricably integrated in the strategies and operations of business enterprises, and as multilateral frameworks have already been established for trade and technology (intellectual property rights) under the WTO, it is now time for the third pillar of a multilateral framework for investment to be established.

In considering their response to a multilateral framework for FDI, developing countries may perhaps need to avoid or discount extreme positions on a few issues. While it is valid on their part to argue that the development dimension must be firmly built into any multilateral framework for investment, that there must be a balance between the rights and obligations of investors, and that such a framework must take cognizance of the asymmetry between industrial and developing countries in capital exports and imports, the case against a multilateral framework for investment rest merely on the assertion that there is insufficient evidence as yet on the interlinkages between trade, investment and development. At the other extreme, the assertions of the advocates of a multilateral framework to the effect that it will significantly augment the flows of FDI, reduce the cost of FDI (by reducing the risk perception) or improve the quality of FDI (because of the stability of investment rules) and benefit in particular the least developed countries and small and medium-sized TNCs, need to be discounted to some extent. A multilaterally agreed framework of rules may contribute to the improvement of the investment climate (assuming that its provisions meet substantially, if not wholly, investors' expectations), but it will remain only one of several factors in influencing the investment decisions of TNCs or investment flows into developing countries. Market opportunities and a host of other factors will continue to have a preponderant effect on the destination of FDI flows.

The perceptions of the industrialized and developing countries of the need for and value of an MAI are bound to differ markedly because of the fundamental differences in their situation as capital and technology exporters and importers. However, given the priority attached by the industrialized countries to an MAI and past experience with new issues being brought onto the agenda of the multilateral trade framework, it would be prudent for the developing countries, from a practical standpoint, to be prepared for negotiations. As noted earlier, the industrialized countries, as the demanders, are fairly clear in their negotiating objectives, but the developing countries have yet to develop the same degree of clarity as to what they would wish to see in such a treaty from their own perspective. When the negotiations do take place, the crux of the problem will lie in the scope and content of the treaty, and if developing countries could evolve a common or collective stand on at least some of the key issues, it may still be possible for them to ensure that the treaty has the necessary balance to safeguard their interests.

E. Feasibility of the options

It may be thought that the first option outlined in this paper (that is, allowing existing arrangements to evolve organically – see section C above) has little chance of proving feasible for two reasons. Firstly, developing countries will not have a common stand on an MAI, or the collective will and strength to oppose the establishment of an MAI in the WTO. Secondly, and more importantly, if some developing countries decide to join an MAI, as indeed some will, others will be forced to follow suit as otherwise they will be at a serious disadvantage in competing for FDI. Once an MAI comes into existence, the bilateral treaties will become even more irrelevant, and unilateral liberalization will not be sufficient to compete effectively with the liberalization guaranteed by a multilateral treaty. Regardless of whether an MAI would or would not contribute to enhance FDI flows to developing countries, the only feasible option available to developing countries is the MAI route, once an MAI gets established and some developing countries accede to it.

The validity of this viewpoint needs to be seen from different angles. First, the flows of FDI are predominantly determined by the market and investment opportunities offered by host countries, which in turn depend essentially on the size of their economies and certain other advantages that they may offer. As noted earlier, nearly 90 per cent of the FDI flows are concentrated in about 20 developing countries, with one alone, China, accounting for more than one third of these flows. Therefore, competition between signatory and non-signatory MAI developing countries may at best be limited to this small number of countries. Furthermore, there is no reason to believe that an FDI which otherwise would have been received by a country would be lost by it merely because it is not a party to an MAI. Conversely, if an FDI would not have occurred otherwise, the potential host country would still not receive it even if it were a signatory to an MAI. In other words, if a country maintains a congenial investment climate by its own policies, it can still effectively compete for FDI even if it is not a signatory to an MAI.

Even assuming that an MAI is the better or the only option for developing countries, the cost-benefit equation will depend heavily on the scope and forum of the MAI. In a way, the scope and forum are interrelated. The aim of an MAI in the OECD will naturally be to set the highest possible standards for the liberalization of investment rules and for the widest possible coverage of investment because it is negotiated among countries at more or less the same level of development and with the same outlook. The ultimate elimination of the distinction between a domestic and foreign investor will be the summum bonum of the treaty. This is understandable in the context of the OECD negotiations. For the vast majority of developing countries, however, adherence to such standards would involve substantially more costs than the benefits they may receive. There will be some developing countries who may find it in their interests to join such a treaty, but this by itself is unlikely to weaken the competitive position of other developing countries not joining the treaty.

For pursuing the multilateral route, the WTO offers the best forum for developing countries for reasons explained later in this paper. The negotiations can then take into account the interests of the capital exporters on the one hand and those of the capital importers on the other, and the scope and content of the treaty will hopefully be influenced by this fundamental difference between the two sets of parties. Moreover, if an MAI is in the WTO, it will apply to all members of the WTO, and the question of some developing countries losing their competitive edge for attracting FDI by remaining outside of the MAI will therefore not arise. Negotiations in the WTO will bring to the fore the need for a balanced and evolutionary approach in this matter and will reveal that while developing countries may be able to offer national treatment to FDI in the post-establishment and operational stages, they have still a long way to go before they can take on the obligation of national treatment in the pre-establishment phase. Therefore, even if the first option outlined in this paper is not considered feasible or desirable for any reason, developing countries need to consider seriously the forum for negotiating an MAI, as this will have a vital bearing on the scope, content and further progression of the MAI to which they may be a party.

III. Key issues in a multilateral framework from a developing country perspective

Of the key issues to be considered by the developing countries, the most crucial one is *national treatment in the pre-establishment phase* (i.e. "freedom of entry" or "right of establishment"). As observed earlier, the critical difference between the BITs, so readily being entered into by developing countries, and the proposed multilateral treaty lies in the issue of non-discriminatory treatment of foreign investment at the entry and establishment stages. The other important elements of treatment of foreign investment, such as national treatment in the post-establishment phase (i.e. after the investment has taken place in accordance with the host country's laws and regulations), MFN treatment at all stages, fair and equitable treatment of established investment, freedom for repatriation of capital and remittance of profits and dividends, protection of foreign investment, and dispute settlement through international arbitration, are all more or less guaranteed in the bilateral treaties. Their transposition to

a multilateral treaty, even in a more strengthened fashion, may therefore not pose a serious problem for developing countries. But national or non-discriminatory treatment as between domestic and foreign investors at the entry and establishment stages has consciously and deliberately been excluded from bilateral treaties to enable the developing countries to have the freedom to pursue their own developmental and political objectives. It is this basic freedom that will be eliminated or curtailed substantially by the proposed multilateral treaty.

It may be argued that the concerns of developing countries over national treatment at the entry stage can be taken care of through general exceptions (e.g. for security or cultural reasons) or country-specific reservations. But such an approach would involve keeping the "negative lists" long to take care of current and future requirements, the more so if they are to be further subject to "standstill" and "rollback" commitments. Besides sector or activity-specific reservations (which mean exclusion or restriction of foreign investment in certain sectors, subsectors or activities), the entry-stage national treatment exceptions will need to address also the important issue of the domestic ownership policies of developing countries. At present, such policies in developing countries require, for example, minimum levels of domestic ownership per se, formation of joint ventures with minimum levels of domestic ownership by local partners, minimum volume of foreign investment in any foreign-invested enterprise, maximum level of foreign investment in small and medium enterprises, and the like. Moreover, there has to be a mechanism to ensure that the negative lists are not frozen over time (i.e. at their composition at the time of adhering to the treaty) and that their modification does not require tortuous renegotiations. On the other hand, a "positive list" approach, i.e. of specifying the sectors and activities which alone would be eligible for national treatment in the pre-establishment phase, will run the risk that the initial commitments are kept by countries at as low a level as possible. Thus, both the negative and positive list approaches under a legally binding multilateral treaty will have their own deficiencies, but both of them will tend to make the host country's policies appear more restrictive and less liberal towards FDI than what is actually followed by the country in practice. (An analogy would be the difference between bound tariffs and effective tariffs in the trade regime.)

Some possible ways for tackling the pre-establishment phase national treatment issue, from the standpoint of developing countries, are:

(i) exclusion of the whole issue from the treaty as far as developing countries are concerned and its review, say, after a ten year period;

(ii) having neither a negative nor a positive list, but only a requirement for notification from time to time of the exceptions to national treatment;

(iii) the inclusion of "developmental reasons" in the category of general exceptions in addition to security, public order or cultural reasons;

(iv) freedom for each country to prescribe the quantum of FDI above which only it may grant national treatment; and

(v) freedom from standstill and roll-back obligations.

The "Guidelines on the Treatment of Foreign Direct Investment" (1992) of the World Bank Group provides another model for considering the question of regulation of FDI at the entry stage. It recommends free admission of FDI subject to a "restricted list" of investments, which are either prohibited or which require screening and licensing or which are reserved for nationals on account of the host country's economic development objectives. It maintains the right of host countries to make regulations to govern the admission of FDI. According to the Guidelines, FDI taking place in non-restricted list activities without prior approval would remain subject to the laws and regulations of the host country applicable to investment, which presumably would include domestic ownership requirements also.

There may be other ways, but unless the issue of national treatment at the entry and establishment stages (including domestic ownership requirements, and screening and approval of foreign investment) is carefully examined and mechanisms are found to address the needs and concerns of developing countries on this critical issue, the chasm between industrialized and developing countries on the scope of an MAI will remain unbridged. In this context, it is worth stressing that keeping uniform national treatment rules for developed and developing countries and only allowing a transition period for the latter to comply with the rules will not solve the problems of developing countries.

The second key issue for the consideration of developing countries is the definition of investment for the purposes of a legally binding multilateral treaty that seeks to eliminate the distinction between domestic and foreign investors. The scope and implications of the treaty will rest heavily on the concept and definition of investment. The current (September 1997) draft of the OECD treaty adopts a very broad definition of investment: that "investment means every kind of asset owned or controlled, directly or indirectly, by an investor", including not only equity capital regardless of any threshold percentage, but also portfolio investment, debt capital, intellectual property rights, and every form of tangible and intangible movable and immovable property. The term "investor" has been defined as any natural or legal person of a contracting party, the legal person being any kind of entity constituted or organized under the applicable law of a contracting party, including branch operations. Recognizing the wide coverage of the definition, a proposal is under consideration in the OECD to the effect that the definition of investment consists of an open (i.e. non-exhaustive) list of assets that are considered as investment, and a short closed list of items or operations that, except for purposes of investment protection, are not considered as investment. The latter list would include items such as trade credits, traded goods and foreign-exchange operations. Even with such safeguard provisions, it is clear that the definition of investment in the OECD treaty would go far beyond the traditional notion of FDI.

There has long been confusion and disagreement as to the appropriate definition of FDI, and different practices are in vogue in different countries and international institutions, although basically the definition may aim to exclude portfolio investments. For its annual *World Investment Reports*, UNCTAD follows the definition that FDI is "an investment involving a long-term relationship and reflecting a lasting interest and control of a resident entity in one economy (foreign direct investor or parent enterprise) in an enterprise resident in another economy (FDI enterprise or affiliate enterprise or foreign affiliate). FDI implies that the investor exerts a significant degree of influence on the management of the enterprise resident in the other economy" (UNCTAD, 1997, p. 295). Under this definition, the FDI is comprised of three components: foreign investor's initial equity capital, subsequent reinvested earnings, and intra-company debt transactions between parent and affiliate enterprises. In this context, it needs to be noted that the threshold of the equity stake for determining control by a parent enterprise of an affiliate enterprise differs among industrialized countries, with UNCTAD adopting a threshold equity stake of 10 per cent while some countries like Germany and the United Kingdom use a threshold of 20 per cent or more. For statistical purposes, the International Monetary Fund (IMF) defines foreign investment as direct (FDI) when the investor holds 10 per cent or more of the equity of an enterprise.

The broad definition of investment as envisaged in the OECD draft raises the issue of whether the proposed treaty is really for the treatment of (or a liberal regime for) TNCs and foreign investors, rather than for treatment of FDI per se. To ensure that the obligations undertaken by them are within manageable limits, developing countries need to ensure that the definition of investment is kept within the narrow confines of "direct" investment, as traditionally understood, and that it does not become extended to portfolio investment, debt capital, or financial transactions per se, or to intangible assets. The definition of investment has implications not only for the impact of the national treatment and other obligations of the MAI, but also for the potential need for further exceptions for balance-of-payment reasons under the obligation relating to the free transfer of funds by foreign investors.

In this context, it is also relevant to take note of the struggle for jurisdiction over different kinds of capital movements among international institutions. The question of enlarging the role of the International Monetary Fund (IMF) in the area of capital movements is currently attracting serious attention. According to the Interim Committee communique of 30 April 1997, accepted by developed and developing countries, "the Fund's Articles should be amended to make the promotion of capital movement liberalization a specific purpose of the Fund and to give the Fund appropriate jurisdiction over capital movements". The extension of the jurisdiction of the IMF will naturally involve a discussion of the type of underlying transactions in the capital account that it should cover. Developing countries have cautioned that any extension of IMF jurisdiction beyond payments and transfers on capital account should be confined to transactions that are directly relevant to the IMF's mandate as the overseer of the international monetary system, and should be in harmony with the existing or prospective role of other institutions dealing with capital movements. Most developing countries have also considered it important to exclude "receipts" from such jurisdiction in order to ensure that they maintain their discretion in managing capital inflows. Given the IMF's macroeconomic responsibilities, the extension of IMF jurisdiction in the area of capital movements will most likely exclude *inward* FDI, but it may well encompass *outward* FDI. Developing countries need to take a holistic view of the efforts under way to extend the jurisdiction of international institutions in regard to capital inflows and outflows (specifically in the WTO and IMF) and to ensure coherence in the obligations they undertake in different international fora.

The third major issue for the consideration of developing countries is *performance requirements* and *investment incentives*. The OECD treaty will prohibit several performance requirements totally and a number of other performance requirements when they are not connected to the grant of subsidies and fiscal incentives. Three performance requirements falling under the totally prohibited category are the employment of a given level of nationals, the establishment of a joint venture with nationals, and a minimum level of local equity participation. Exceptions to total prohibition may be carved out for specific purposes, such as, for example, export promotion schemes, development aid, public procurement and environmental concerns. It is important that developing countries try to ensure that the obligations do not go beyond the existing TRIMS Agreement and, if they do, that exceptions are carved out for development reasons as well.

Performance requirements are often linked explicitly or implicitly to investment incentives. Negotiations in the OECD thus far have remained ambivalent in disciplining the use of such incentives. Views vary from having no specific provision at all on investment incentives to constraining their use, including the prohibition of "positive discrimination" (i.e. more favourable treatment of foreign investors as compared to domestic ones) and caps on specific incentives. So far there has been some consensus on only three principles, namely MFN, national treatment, and transparency.

Empirical evidence suggests that incentives are less often used now to attract FDI flows in general, but are used more to achieve specific purposes. However, international competition for FDI with fiscal, financial and other incentives is becoming pervasive, and is even more intense now than it was some ten years ago. Competition with incentives is strong, despite the evidence that incentives play a relatively minor role in the locational decisions of TNCs relative to other locational advantages. There is therefore a strong view that multilateral disciplines must be formulated to restrain investment incentives analogous to the disciplines on trade subsidies in the WTO.[4] Developing countries need to ensure that a multilateral agreement on investment does not evade the issue of investment incentives while disciplining the use of performance requirements and that it allows for "negative discrimination" (i.e. domestic investors being given preference over foreign ones) in the matter of investment incentives.

Beyond these three key issues, there are some other important points which require the special attention of developing countries: *movement of natural persons, curbing of restrictive business practices, transfer of technology, and the obligations of investors.* Briefly stated, the imbalance between the treatment of the movement of capital and that of the movement of investment/trade-related human resources should be minimized under the proposed multilateral treaty. In the area of restrictive business practices, the regulation of the anti-competitive behaviour of TNCs cannot be left to be tackled solely by the domestic laws of host countries. A multilateral instrument seeking to liberalize investment regimes should, beyond prohibiting restrictive business practices that are illegal per se, aim at curbing such practices and thereby strengthen efforts at the national level. As regards transfer of technology, although the problem is complex and there may be no easy solutions, issues such as the dissemination of information on and transfer of freely available technologies, assistance for transfer of environmentally friendly technologies and concrete forms of technical assistance merit consideration, even if it is found difficult to translate them into legally binding obligations. (In the case of proprietary technologies, the argument of industrialized countries has always been that it falls in the domain of enterprises' individual business decisions.) Lastly, the obligations of the investors, legally binding where possible and suggested good corporate practices where this may not be possible, must be spelt out so that there is a balance between the rights and obligations of investors under the multilateral treaty. In respect of the issues of restrictive business practices, transfer of technology and investors' obligations, the three multilateral instruments of the United Nations/UNCTAD referred to in paragraph 5 of this paper provide valuable concepts and formulations for the advocacy of developing countries.

Lastly, there are two further important and complex policy issues that require serious thought in the context of FDI liberalization: *competition policy* and *environmental concerns.* As emphasized in the UNCTAD *World Investment Report, 1997,* the reduction of barriers to FDI and establishment of standards for the treatment of TNCs need to go hand-in-hand with the adoption of measures designed to ensure the proper functioning of markets including, among other matters, measures to control the anti-competitive practices of firms. The Report stresses the imperative need for taking an integrated view of trade, investment and competition policies and for establishing effective competition policy instruments at the international level. It further points out that UNCTAD's "Set of Principles and Rules for the Control of Restrictive Business Practices" (referred to in paragraph 5 of this paper) remains at present the only multilateral instrument on this subject. The Singapore Ministerial Declaration, 1996, of WTO has also resulted in a separate working group in the WTO to study the interrelationships between trade and competition policy. It is important to examine the competition policy issues to identify the rules and disciplines that may be required at the multilateral level, taking into account the developmental needs and problems of developing countries. Their linkage to the proposed multilateral framework for investment would also need particular consideration.

As regards environmental concerns, non-governmental organizations have voiced the apprehension that the increasing thrust towards the liberalization of foreign trade and investment regimes and the unfettered freedom of TNCs to access markets and resources around the world would have an adverse impact on the preservation and protection of the environment. They feel that the top-down approach to liberalization of investment rules contained in the OECD's draft MAI will undermine the ability of national governments to regulate access to and use of their natural and biological resources, and that it will put developing countries and transition economies in a particularly disadvantageous position. They have expressed the view that if the MAI is to be made sustainable, negotiations should not proceed until a comprehensive review of its potential impact on the environment and sustainable development has taken place.[5] In this context, developing countries need to keep in mind that it was with some struggle that they were able to establish the sovereign rights of States over their biological wealth and resources in the Rio Bio-diversity Convention of 1992. As far back as 1962, they had achieved the non-binding United Nations resolution on "Permanent Sovereignty over Natural Resources", which, besides establishing their sovereign rights, provided that "the exploration, development and disposition of such resources, as well as the import of foreign capital required for these purposes should be in conformity with the rules and conditions with regard to the authorization, restriction or prohibition of such activities". It is important that developing countries do not overlook the rights already secured by them in such international instruments, and do not allow those rights to be diluted or whittled down by the national treatment obligations (such as right of entry, right of establishment and freedom of access to resources on a par with nationals) envisaged by the multilateral treaty on investment.

Before they choose the option of the multilateral treaty route, and regardless of whether they join the negotiations for such a treaty with conviction or under compulsion, it is important that developing countries formulate their negotiating objectives on the key issues in order to enhance the prospects of adequate reflection of their political, developmental and social concerns in the multilateral treaty. There can be little doubt that the interests and attitudes of individual developing countries will differ widely, depending on their macroeconomic policies, socio-political cultures, market size, domestic industrial and technological capabilities, skill advantages, and the regional arrangements to which they are, or wish to be, a party. It may therefore be difficult for them to forge a common stand on many of the issues. Even so, there is scope and need for their collective thinking on the key issues enumerated above to ensure that their common or differing interests are addressed within the multilateral framework. Developing countries need to realize that given the complexity and sensitivity of the issues to be tackled, and the divergence in the basic interests of industrialized and developing countries on these issues, the negotiation of a multilateral framework for investment will perhaps prove to be the most difficult negotiations they may be called upon to undertake, with perhaps the most far-reaching long-term implications. Their willingness to join the negotiations for an MAI should therefore be preceded by a strong and collective, as well as individual, application of their minds to their negotiating objectives.

IV. Choice of forum

A. The OECD option

Should the developing countries decide to adopt the multilateral route, they have the choice of the OECD forum or the WTO forum or both for the negotiations. Negotiations in the OECD on a Multilateral Agreement on Investment (MAI) have been in progress since September 1995 and are slated, as of now, to be completed by May 1998. As noted earlier, the MAI will be a free standing international treaty open to all OECD members and the European Communities, and to accession by non-OECD member countries as well. If developing countries choose to accede to the OECD treaty, they should take into account the following basic features of the MAI. Firstly, the objective of the OECD countries is to establish the highest standards for the liberalization of investment regimes and investment pro-

tection, with as broad a definition of investment as possible. This is understandable because the OECD is a group of broadly like-minded countries at similar levels of economic development and in which liberalization is already well advanced. The OECD member countries are also among the largest exporters of capital, technology, goods and services. Secondly, national treatment from the pre-establishment stage onwards (including freedom of entry, right of establishment, etc.), subject only to very general exceptions (e.g. security and possibly cultural exceptions) and certain limited country-specific reservations, is the corner-stone of the treaty. The country-specific reservations are contingent upon each country offering adequate "upfront liberalization" so that there is a satisfactory balance of commitments on the part of all the signatories to the treaty. Thirdly, "standstill" and "roll-back" commitments (the latter according to a pre-determined timetable or through future rounds of negotiations) are fundamental to the treaty, as the goal is to lay down an irreversible initial minimum standard for liberalization and to carry forward the process through future commitments. Fourthly, a wide range of performance requirements will be prohibited excepting some connected to the granting of an advantage. Lastly, it will be comprehensive in scope, covering all sectors and activities.

Thus, the OECD treaty seeks to adopt a top-down approach to the liberalization of investment regimes, as the only reservations permitted will be those listed for each country at the time of adherence to the agreement and which will be further subject to progressive liberalization. The ultimate aim of the treaty is to abolish the distinction between a domestic and a foreign investor.[6]

It is obviously not a mandate of the OECD negotiations to take into account the developmental needs and concerns of developing countries. Moreover, although the treaty will be open to accession by non-OECD member countries, they will only be "consulted" as the negotiations progress; they cannot take part in the negotiations. The OECD is carrying out this consultation process through its "Policy Dialogue Workshops" programme for certain developing countries (Argentina, Brazil, Chile, China, Hong Kong, India, Indonesia, Malaysia, Singapore, Taiwan Province of China and Thailand) and its "out-reach" programme, which also involves a number of other developing countries. The purpose of these consultations is only to keep interested non-member countries informed of the progress of MAI and to obtain their views on the various issues under negotiation.

Developing countries which are invited by the OECD for consultation can certainly take advantage of the opportunity made available to them to keep themselves informed about the progress of the OECD negotiations, to study the documents and statements made available to them and, more importantly, to make known to the OECD their views on matters of concern to them. This does not, however, imply that they should accede to the OECD treaty. Some of the developing countries may take the view that the future thrust and direction of their own FDI policies would be in line with the high standards of liberalization adopted by the OECD treaty and that they may themselves become significant exporters of capital. Their own level of development and their current or possible future participation (or non-participation) in regional arrangements (e.g. NAFTA, FTAA, APEC) may also influence their attitude towards the OECD treaty. They may therefore try to secure possible exceptions or safeguards and decide to join the treaty. For most of the developing countries, however, the consultation process may simply be a valuable educative experience. As the gap between the OECD standards and their own needs will be substantial, they may not find it possible to join the treaty. Participation in OECD's consultative process may also reveal disagreement within the OECD membership on key issues, and such disagreement could be used by developing countries to form alliances, to the extent possible, in the pursuit of their interests in an MAI or within the WTO.

Even if some developing countries accede to the OECD treaty, it will still only be a plurilateral agreement. The vast majority of the developing countries will most likely remain out of its purview. It has been suggested that if some developing countries join the OECD treaty, there may be pressure on other developing countries to follow suit on the apprehension that they will otherwise be at a disadvantage in competing for FDI. Given the factors that influence the locational decisions of the TNCs, such an apprehension is unwarranted and it should not form the basis for a developing country's decision to join the OECD treaty.

Lastly, it is a matter of conjecture at this juncture as to what would be the fate of the OECD negotiations if there were strong and definite indications that there would be a multilateral agreement on investment within the framework of the WTO. Will the OECD negotiations then go forward and culminate in a treaty? On the other hand, if an OECD treaty is established and is followed by a WTO agreement, how will the issues of compatibility

between the two be resolved? Also, how will the provisions of the OECD treaty be harmonized with the existing or future provisions of the GATS, TRIMS and TRIPS Agreements of the WTO? Furthermore, if there is an OECD treaty and it allows the country-specific reservations demanded by a developing country, will it not be better for the developing country to join the OECD treaty than to pursue the WTO route, because the OECD treaty will be a stand-alone treaty and will not involve the risk of cross-retaliation? These are important questions that have not yet been examined or come up for consideration. However, it is fairly certain that a draft OECD treaty or an already adopted OECD treaty, as the case may be, will become the starting point for discussions in the WTO. The industrialized countries will press hard for its adoption in the WTO with as little dilution of the standards as possible. The developing countries must be prepared for this eventuality, which in essence means that they must be ready to put forward alternative concepts and formulations on issues of importance to them.

B. The WTO option

If the multilateral route is to be pursued, the forum of WTO may be the best option for developing countries. First, on the policy plane, the global economic reality is that trade, investment and technology are now becoming increasingly intertwined, although the different facets of the interlinkages and their implications for the developing world undoubtedly need more research. The GATS, TRIMS and TRIPS Agreements of the WTO already address some of the issues related to investment, but the need for a comprehensive framework for investment within the WTO will be felt in the coming years in order to ensure coherence and consistency between trade and investment policies. As noted earlier, the chief message of the *World Investment Report, 1997* of UNCTAD is that there should be coherence between trade, investment and competition policies both at the national and international levels if the problems generated by globalization of the world economy and liberalization of the trade and FDI regimes are to be effectively tackled.

The harmonization of trade and investment rules through the WTO framework can open up some useful options for developing countries. For example, the question of FDI in the services sector could be left to be addressed by the GATS (especially with respect to issues such as MFN, transparency, national treatment and market access), the more so because the GATS envisages successive rounds of negotiations for progressive liberalization of service activities taking into account the interests of developing countries. The question of trade-related performance requirements, especially what is prohibited or permissible, can similarly be left to be handled by the TRIMS Agreement. Some of the performance requirements (e.g. employment of nationals, joint ventures and minimum level of local equity participation) which the OECD treaty seeks to prohibit are not prohibited by the TRIMS Agreement. The issue of national and MFN treatment for IPRs can likewise be left to be covered by the TRIPS Agreement. A multilateral framework for investment under the WTO can thus focus on matters that are not already within the ambit of existing WTO agreements. This will not be the case with a treaty outside of the WTO, which is likely to involve obligations and commitments by developing countries over and above those accepted by them under the WTO agreements.

Secondly, although the principles of "special and differential treatment" for developing countries and "non-reciprocity" in concessions and commitments to be given by them have been dented by the Uruguay Round agreements, the WTO still offers the best forum for developing countries to exercise their collective influence and to bring to bear their developmental concerns on the negotiating agenda. The philosophy that developing countries are at different levels of development as compared to the industrialized countries and that there is therefore a need for differentiated rules and disciplines for them is embedded in the WTO system, notwithstanding the deficiencies in its implementation. The numerical strength of the developing countries and the consensual approach to decision-making in the WTO also make that organization an advantageous forum for them; developing countries as a group have to be carried along in establishing any agreement within the WTO system. To some extent, these advantages may offset the disadvantages arising from their weak bargaining strength and their inability, unwillingness or unpreparedness to adopt a common stand in WTO negotiations.

Thirdly, and most importantly, unlike the negative list and top-down approach of the OECD, it is possible for developing countries to advocate a bottom-up approach in the WTO through a positive listing of the agreed commitments. In this respect, the GATS offers a useful model of a hybrid approach, with a positive listing of sectors opened up and a

negative listing of limitations on market access and national treatment. The MFN and transparency obligations, further rounds of negotiations for progressive liberalization, and special consideration for developing countries will underpin the process of initial commitments and future liberalization under this hybrid approach. Alternatively, as suggested in section III (third paragraph), developing countries could press for the application of only notification requirements for pre-establishment-phase national treatment, with the question of its progressive liberalization to be reviewed after the multilateral agreement has been in force for, say, ten years. These approaches will enable developing countries to have sufficient freedom to pursue the liberalization of their FDI policies on their own volition and to consider legal binding of their commitments at their own pace. Given the number of developing countries participating in the WTO, the prospects of evolving an approach that is compatible with both liberalization of FDI regimes and the developmental needs and concerns of developing countries are greater in the WTO than in any other forum.

A serious disadvantage, it may be argued, in concluding an agreement within the WTO framework is that it will entail the risk of "cross retaliation" across sectors under the WTO dispute settlement mechanism. This may be a genuine concern, but this problem needs to be seen in perspective now that the cross-linkage of sectors has become an integral part of the WTO system. The extreme action of cross-retaliation in the WTO scheme is permissible only after all the previous layers of dispute resolution are exhausted, and thereafter only with the express sanction of the Dispute Settlement Body. Thus far, no plea for cross-retaliation has taken place in the WTO, and only time will tell which types of disputes, and in what circumstances, reach the point of non-resolution so as to invite cross-retaliation across sectors. Also, it is only State-to-State disputes that will fall within the ambit of WTO's dispute settlement mechanism. State-to-investor disputes will continue to be resolved through their own mechanisms, e.g. through international arbitration as in existing bilateral treaties. To avoid the contingency of cross-retaliation, developing countries may try to negotiate for the new multilateral agreement on investment, although falling under WTO's definition of "multilateral trade agreements", to be treated as a distinct agreement (in an Annex other than Annexes 1, 2 and 3 of the Agreement Establishing the WTO) and subjected to the dispute settlement mechanism of WTO barring the provisions applicable to cross-retaliation in that mechanism.

V. Heterogeneity of developing countries

In analysing the implications of any international agreement for developing countries, there is often a tendency towards oversimplification. It is assumed that they are a homogeneous group with similar outlook, problems and constraints. However, the heterogeneity amongst them is a reality, and it comes to the surface nowhere more tellingly than when legally binding agreements in the economic field are being negotiated. This is also true, as it was with the Uruguay Round Agreements, for the proposed multilateral treaty on investment. The newly industrializing economies (NIEs), such as Brazil, Hong Kong, Singapore and Taiwan Province of China, the ASEAN countries like Malaysia and Thailand, and such Latin American countries as Argentina, Chile, Colombia, Peru and Venezuela may consider that the gap to be covered between their own autonomous policies towards foreign investment and the obligations to be met under a multilateral treaty is not so large that it cannot be overcome by them, especially in the light of the regional arrangements to which they are, or are contemplating to be, a party such as the APEC, NAFTA or the Free Trade Area of the Americas. A multilateral treaty with high standards of liberalization could be seen by them as an instrument to attract more foreign investment, provided the treaty takes care of a limited number of their concerns, in particular the safeguards necessary for balance-of-payments reasons.

For developing countries with large and growing domestic markets like China, India and Indonesia, the size of the domestic market is a great advantage, as foreign investors are more likely to access their markets through local presence than direct exports. An autonomous and transparent liberalization of their FDI regimes (e.g. opening up of more sectors to FDI, including the infrastructure and services sectors, liberalization of foreign ownership limits), coupled with national treatment in the post-establishment phase and adequate protection of investment, would still enable them to attract FDI. Their attitude to a multilateral treaty will essentially hinge upon how the issue of national treatment at the pre-establishment stage – which really means freedom and flexibility for them to follow their own policies at the admission stage – is resolved to their satisfaction. This may also be true for a number of other developing countries (e.g. Egypt, Ghana, Morocco, Pakistan, the Philippines, Sri Lanka, Tunisia, Viet Nam and Zimbabwe), which have the potential to attract substantial FDI flows.

The oil-exporting developing countries in West Asia (for example Kuwait, Oman, Saudi Arabia and United Arab Emirates) fall into a distinct category. The availability of capital is not a problem for them. As long as their domestic ownership policies and their system of differential taxation of enterprises based upon the level of domestic/foreign ownership are not altered by legally binding multilateral obligations, other issues, such as liberalized and fair treatment of foreign investment or its effective protection, may not come into conflict with their own autonomous policies. A multilateral treaty on investment may be viewed by them from this limited perspective, as they know that such a treaty per se is not needed to increase FDI flows to them.

At the other end of the spectrum are the large number of low to middle-income countries, including island economies, and in particular the 48 least developed countries (LDCs), which are presently marginal receivers of FDI. Leaving aside those whose basic problem is political and social instability, the others are unable to attract FDI not because their investment policies are restrictive but because their market and investment opportunities are meagre, their infrastructure is weak, and their capacity to utilize FDI is limited. The LDCs in particular are on the horns of a dilemma. They can claim longer transition periods and special exceptions under a multilateral agreement and they will most likely be granted a favoured treatment, as was the case in the Uruguay Round Agreements. But the longer they remain under such exceptions and thereby outside the mainstream of rules and disciplines, the greater is the possibility of the competitive distance between them and other developing countries widening. Although a multilateral investment treaty by itself may not alter dramatically their receipt of FDI flows, they may possibly gain by offering a strong national treatment privilege from the pre-establishment phase onwards, excepting only very small investments and the limited activities that may be within the capacity of their domestic investors. They may therefore wish to join an MAI on the consideration that it will give a boost to their investment climate. Even small incremental flows of FDI may be important to many of the LDCs in view of the small size of their economies.

The preceding broad analysis of the implications of a multilateral investment treaty for different categories of developing countries should not, however, mask the political dimensions of such a treaty for almost all developing countries. The political and social implications explain in substantial measure why so many developing countries are reluctant or unwilling to convert unilateral liberalization of FDI policies into legally binding multilateral commitments. The question of national and non-discriminatory treatment for foreign investors is closely linked to the issue of erosion of political and economic sovereignty much more strongly than in the case of foreign trade. Besides this political sensitivity, the scope for their utilizing FDI to serve their developmental objectives, in particular their need to develop and strengthen their own indigenous industrial and technological capabilities (or in other words their ensuring sufficient "economic space" for their own enterprises to develop), rests crucially upon the freedom and flexibility they have in the admission and regulation of foreign investment. Thus, political and developmental considerations are intermeshed in the issue of national treatment at the entry stage, albeit with varying degrees of intensity, for almost all developing countries, regardless of the category in which they fall.

VI. Summary

The strategic options available to developing countries analysed in this paper may be briefly summarized as follows: developing countries may allow the current trends and arrangements with regard to FDI (namely, pursuing their own autonomous liberalization of their FDI regimes together with bilateral and regional arrangements for the promotion, protection and fair and equitable treatment of FDI) to evolve and gather strength and momentum, and move towards a possible multilateral framework at an opportune future time on the basis of the experience gained and consensus generated on important issues.

The above option is contingent, however, upon developing economies having the collective will and strength to resist the pressure of the industrialized countries to begin negotiations on an MAI in the WTO and/or to join the OECD treaty on investment currently under negotiation among the OECD member countries.

The crux of the difference between existing bilateral treaties/regional arrangements and the multilateral treaty advocated by the industrialized countries is in the issue of national treatment for foreign investors in the pre-establishment phase (i.e. freedom of entry, right of establishment, non-discriminatory treatment between domestic and foreign investors from the admission stage onwards).

This issue has vital implications for the political, social and economic objectives and concerns of developing countries.

Before they choose the option of the multilateral treaty route, whether out of conviction or compulsion, it is essential that developing countries try to evolve a collective or common stand on certain key issues, such as national treatment in the pre-establishment phase, the definition of investment, performance requirements and investment incentives, movement of natural persons, restrictive business practices, transfer of technology and obligations of investors. In addition, the issues of competition policy and environmental concerns require examination from the perspective of developing countries. In the end, the critical question may not be why developing countries joined an MAI, but whether the scope, structure and content of the MAI safeguards adequately their legitimate interests and concerns. This will depend largely on the freedom and flexibility they have under the MAI to pursue their own policies.

Developing countries invited by the OECD may certainly take part in its consultative process, but in deciding whether they should accede to the OECD treaty or not, they need to take into account the basic objectives and features of that treaty, especially its top-down approach to liberalize investment regimes. Those developing countries whose judgment is that the gap between their own autonomous policies and the obligations imposed by the treaty is not substantial and can be managed by them, may wish to join it. But the vast majority of developing countries may not find it possible to subscribe to the high standards set by the OECD treaty. There is, however, no ground for the apprehension that developing countries not joining the OECD treaty will be at a disadvantage in competing for FDI.

If developing countries decide to choose the multilateral route, the best forum for negotiating a multilateral agreement is, for various reasons, the WTO. In particular, this will enable them to negotiate a bottom-up approach, with the GATS providing a useful model for dealing with initial commitments and future liberalization. They should also consider the option that the agreement in the WTO operates as a stand-alone agreement, with a dispute settlement mechanism devoid of cross-retaliation provisions.

Given the heterogeneity of developing countries, the impact and implications of a multilateral treaty will vary widely among them. The vast majority of low-income developing countries and the LDCs are currently on the fringe of FDI flows. Although an MAI may not make a dramatic difference to this situation, they may look upon such an agreement as an additional tool for enhancing their investment climate and thereby increasing the chances of their receiving some incremental FDI flows.

Notes

1 As far as developing countries are concerned, however, exports continue to be the principal mode of delivering goods and services to foreign markets.

2 These 14 developing countries, in the descending order of their individual shares, are: Argentina, Peru, Hong Kong, Colombia, Thailand, Chile, Nigeria, India, Philippines, Republic of Korea, Viet Nam, Taiwan Province of China, Venezuela and Egypt. It may be noted that Turkey and Bermuda have been excluded from these calculations, although the UNCTAD data include them also in FDI flows to developing countries. It should also be noted that Mexico and the Republic of Korea, accounting for nearly 10 per cent of total FDI flows to developing countries, are now members of the OECD negotiating an MAI.

3 For a detailed discussion of this option, see UNCTAD (1996a, pp. 161-166).

4 For a detailed analysis of issues related to investment incentives, see UNCTAD (1996c).

5 For a detailed analysis of this issue, see Werksman (1997).

6 For a comprehensive analysis of the objectives and features of the OECD MAI, see Witherall (1995).

References

BREWER, T.L., and S. YOUNG (1996), "Investment policies in multilateral and regional agreements: A comparative analysis", *Transnational Corporation*, Vol. 5, No. 1 (April).

BRITTAN, Sir Leon (European Commission Vice-President and Trade Commissioner) (1995), "Investment liberalisation: The next great boost to the world economy", *Transnational Corporations*, Vol. 4, No. 1 (April).

ENGERING, Frans (1996), "The multilateral investment agreement", *Transnational Corporations*, Vol. 5, No. 3 (December).

MESSING, J.W. (1997), "Towards a multilateral agreement on investment", *Transnational Corporations*, Vol. 6, No. 1 (April).

MOHAMMED, Aziz Ali (1997), "Issues relating to the treatment of capital movements in the IMF", a position paper for the Intergovernmental Group of 24 on International Monetary Affairs (Washington, D.C.: G-24 Liaison Office), mimeo.

PARRA, A.R. (1995), "The scope of new investment laws and international instruments", *Transnational Corporations*, Vol. 4, No. 3 (December).

RUGGIERO, Renato (Director General, World Trade Organisation) (1996), "Foreign direct investment and the multilateral trading system", *Transnational Corporations*, Vol. 5, No. 1 (April).

SOUTH CENTRE (1977), "Foreign direct investment, development and the new global economic order: A policy brief for the South" (Geneva: South Centre), September.

UNCTAD (1996a), *World Investment Report, 1996* (New York and Geneva: United Nations).

UNCTAD (1996b), *International Investment Instruments: A compendium — Multilateral Instruments*, Vol. I (New York and Geneva: United Nations).

UNCTAD (1996c), *Incentives and Foreign Direct Investment* (New York and Geneva: United Nations).

UNCTAD (1997), *World Investment Report, 1997* (New York and Geneva: United Nations).

WERKSMAN J. (1997), "Is the Multilateral Agreement on Investment sustainable?", *WWF International Discussion Paper* (Gland, Switzerland: World Wide Fund for Nature), October.

WITHERELL, W.H. (1995), "The OECD Multilateral Agreement on Investment", *Transnational Corporations*, Vol. 4, No. 2 (August).

WORLD BANK GROUP (1992), "Guidelines on the Treatment of Foreign Direct Investment", *Legal Framework for the Treatment of Foreign Investment, Vol. II: Guidelines* (Washington, D.C.: World Bank).

WTO (1996), *Annual Report 1996 — Special Topic: Trade and Foreign Direct Investment*, Vol. I (Geneva: World Trade Organization).

KEY ISSUES FOR DEVELOPING COUNTRIES IN A POSSIBLE MULTILATERAL AGREEMENT ON INVESTMENT

Carlos M. Correa*

Abstract

While the national regimes on foreign direct investment (FDI) in developing countries have become more open in the last 10 years, there is no international agreement so far that deals specifically with FDI. This paper analyses current initiatives for a Multilateral Framework on Investment (MFI) in the context of the OECD and the World Trade Organization. According to the proposals, an MFI would include standards of national and most-favoured-nation treatment with regard not only to the operation of investments but also to their entry. Contracting States would not be allowed to select investment projects unless this was specifically permitted by the MFI. An MFI would limit the extent of permissible government intervention with regard to FDI defined as any asset owned or controlled by a foreign investor in any sector of the economy, including agriculture, natural resources, manufacturing and services.

While the negotiation of an MFI would be in line with the trend towards liberalization of FDI, the proposals go beyond the degree of liberalization acceptable to most developing countries, particularly since any liberalizing measures would be "locked in". The basic question is how to guarantee protection of investor interests while ensuring that their investments are consistent with the developmental objectives of the host countries. Specifically, the concerns of developing countries in connection with possible negotiations on an MFI are the following: an MFI should provide for: better control of restrictive business practices by large internationally operating enterprises; the identification and remedy of abuses of transfer pricing; the promotion of technological development in host countries; and specific environmental obligations to be observed by foreign investors. Developing countries should be sheltered against unmanageable short-term capital flows by setting special rules for portfolio investments, and they should retain the possibility to use government procurement as a way to foster the development of local companies by means of preferential treatment in terms of prices or other conditions on supply. Finally, in the context of negotiations on an MFI more symmetrical treatment of the movement of capital, on the one hand, and natural persons, on the other, should be aimed at.

*   The author is grateful for the helpful comments made on an earlier version of this paper by Pedro Roffe (UNCTAD) and Gerry Helleiner (University of Toronto).

I. Introduction

The flows of foreign direct investment (FDI) to developed and developing countries has increased steadily in the 1990s. Most OECD countries, as well as a few developing ones, have joined the largest countries as exporters of capital.

Investment regimes have become more open and welcoming to foreign investors worldwide in the last 10 years. In particular, many developing countries (notably in Latin America) have dramatically changed, or abolished, the regulations on FDI that, under a completely different context, had been implemented in the 1970s. A large number of bilateral investment treaties (BITs) have been signed and are in force, ensuring national treatment and the protection of investments against expropriation and from strife. Similar objectives are sought through a number of plurilateral and multilateral instruments.[1]

The OECD Ministers[2] decided in 1995 to launch negotiations in order to establish an (Multilateral Agreement on Investment) MAI that would ensure high standards of protection and legal security for foreign investors. In the same year the European Commission (1995) also made a proposal to negotiate an MAI within the framework of WTO (see also Brittan, 1995, p. 1-10). A Working Group on the subject was established in the WTO at its first Ministerial Meeting in December 1996, indicating the willingness of its member States to explore the issue, without, however, prejudging the initiation of negotiations in the future.

These initiatives reflect not only the growing flows of cross-border FDI and other investments, but also the increasing interrelationship between trade and investment, which are treated by multinational corporations as "complementary means for carrying out comprehensive global production activities", rather than as alternative strategies for penetrating markets. Simply put, they view trade and investment as "flip sides of the same, market access, coin" (Sauvé, 1997, p. 57).

While there already exists a comprehensive international regime on trade, in the area of investments there is a large number of differing bilateral, regional, plurilateral and multilateral instruments. These instruments do not constitute a coherent international regime for the following reasons (Witherell, 1995, p. 3):

(i)   Despite the large number of common elements contained in the BITs, cross-border investments face an array of different legal frameworks in different countries;

(ii) Barriers to FDI remain in some countries and sectors, including discriminatory treatment against foreign investors, as well as legal uncertainties;

(iii) Although the FDI regimes are more open today, there is no guarantee that they will remain so in the future;

(iv) Existing BITs and other agreements focus on post-establishment conditions and do not generally regulate the conditions for market access as such (in the pre-establishment phase);

(v)   Although the TRIMs and TRIPs Agreements and the GATS contain disciplines relevant in this area, they do not provide a comprehensive framework for FDI.

An Multilateral Framework on Investment (MFI), as proposed by the EC or currently discussed under the auspices of OECD, would mean the creation of a new, legally binding, framework for all types of investments, including a dispute settlement mechanism. An MFI would not amount to the establishment of an absolute standard on investment policy; it would not eliminate differences in national investment regimes, since contracting parties would continue to be able to develop their own investment policies (Charolles, 1997, p. 20).

Nevertheless, if an MFI were approved, contracting parties would be subjected to obligations that would significantly restrain room for manoeuvre to adopt, at the national level, selective policies with regard to admission and to apply instruments to influence the operation of foreign investments.

An MFI, as discussed in the OECD and proposed by the European Commission, would contain a "standstill" requirement, i.e. an obligation not to introduce new restrictions on foreign investments in the future, thus preventing non-conforming changes in policies on foreign investments, even if required by new circumstances and developmental needs.[3] In other words – and particularly if an MFI should be incorporated in WTO agreements – it would imply "the imposition of the status quo ... as an irreversible minimum standard for liberalization" (Graham, 1996, p. 11).

While developed countries – the main sources and destination of FDI – generally seem to support the elaboration and adoption of an MFI, many developing countries fear the implications of a possible MFI on the capacity of host countries to conduct their development process and especially on their ability to foster the development of domestic industries.[4] Such countries have admitted a role for WTO in the discussion of investment issues, but have not agreed to negotiate new disciplines on the matter.

A basic question to be addressed is whether there is a need to establish an MFI at all. Investment issues may continue to be tackled under current arrangements. There is no a priori reason to think that a predictable and stable framework for foreign investments cannot be maintained with the present array of national laws, bilateral agreements and other international instruments (Ganesan, in this volume). If the establishment of an MFI were agreed, a subsequent question would be the extent to which it may adequately address the developmental concerns of developing countries.

Given that the draft MAI[5] under negotiation in OECD is so far the most advanced proposal on such an agreement, this text is taken as a basis for the analysis made here,[6] although there is still (as at November 1997) a long list of pending issues that are unlikely to be resolved in the short term. The negotiating text provides a good model for discussing what the establishment of an MFI[7] may involve.

The aim of this paper is, first, to briefly describe the possible scope and content of an MFI. Section II examines the definition of "investor" and "investment", as well as the basic standards of treatment provided for by the MAI. As discussed below, it is important to note that the draft MAI is not limited to foreign direct investment (FDI), but covers all types of assets owned or controlled by a foreign investor, including intangible property and portfolio investments.

Section III deals with some operational aspects: rules on admission and on ownership and control, performance requirements, transfer of key personnel and incentives. Of special relevance in this section is the eventual application of an MFI to both the pre- and post-establishment phases of an investment.

Sections IV and V address three important regulatory issues: the protection of investment against expropriation and from strife, the system of dispute settlement, and acceptable reservations, safeguards and exceptions to a possible treaty. The first issue is an essential component of any arrangement on investment; the second would "give teeth" to any possible MFI to be negotiated; and the third is an inevitable component in an agreement with such a broad coverage as proposed in the OECD negotiations.

The second aim of this paper is to examine the possible implications of an MFI in pursuing broader developmental objectives. Section VI addresses several concerns, which in fact are not only relevant to developing countries. The issues dealt with include the treatment of restrictive business practices (RBPs), transfer pricing, intellectual property rights, technology transfer, employment, environmental protection, balance-of-payments problems and State contracts. For each of these issues, the current proposals under the draft MAI are briefly described, and their possible treatment in an MFI indicated. Section VII contains the main conclusions of the paper.

II. Scope and standards for treatment

A. *Defining the scope*

A crucial aspect to be considered in order to assess the likely implications of an MFI is its eventual scope of application, which will be determined by the definition of "investor" and "investment".

Most BITs and other instruments (e.g. Energy Charter Treaty) contain a definition of who an "investor" is. In OECD negotiations consensus that the definition of investor should be as broad as possible was quickly achieved (Schekulin, 1997, p. 10). In the MAI, this definition covers all natural persons who are nationals or permanent residents of a contracting party in accordance with its applicable laws, and legal persons or other entities constituted under the applicable law of a contracting party, whether or not for profit, or whether private or government-owned or controlled.

The definition of investor in a possible MFI may raise a number of problems, such as whether it covers any natural or legal person or only "investors" in relation to their current or future investments, the legal status of branches (which generally cannot invest in their own name and on their own account), and the coverage of investments directly made by States (which would be governed by other rules and principles of international law).

The definition of "investment" would be a critical part of an MFI. As contained in many BITs, the Energy Charter Treaty and NAFTA, investment is an all-encompassing concept including all assets of an enterprise, such as movable and immovable property, equity in companies, claims to money and contractual rights, intellectual property rights, concessions, licences and similar rights. The concept used is thus much broader than FDI. If this approach were followed, an MFI would not just be an international instrument on the establishment and operation of FDI, but also a framework applicable to all kinds of assets held by foreign investors. Under such a broad definition, even portfolio investments may be covered (UNCTAD, 1996, p. 174).

It should be noted, in addition, that an MFI may cover all sectors of the economy, including agriculture, natural resources, manufacturing and services. The situation of the financial services sector, subject to special rules in many countries, may deserve special attention.[8] In any case, an important point in the negotiation of an MFI would be to appropriately consider its relationship with other multilateral agreements, such as GATS (Sauvé, 1997, p. 65).

The issue of what "control" of an asset means also requires adequate consideration, if an MFI is intended to apply to both assets owned or controlled by foreign investors. National laws differ on this point. There is no international standard to judge when certain types of rights, or even a de facto situation, may be considered as equivalent to an actual control over certain assets.

An MFI may cover only "direct" or also "indirect" investments. In addition to the difficulties in determining when control exists, a broad concept of indirect ownership or control may lead to the protection of investors that lack a substantial business activity in a contracting party, such as when an investment is made by a firm established in another contracting party, but owned or controlled by a party in a non-contracting party (OECD, 1997, p. 101).

Illustrative of a broad approach to the investments to be covered is the proposed MAI, where a single (i.e. applicable to all obligations in the pre- and post-establishment phases) definition of investment has been negotiated, though not finally agreed upon. It is an asset-based definition ("every kind of asset owned or controlled, directly or indirectly, by an investor"), accompanied by an illustrative list of investments to be covered. Unlike in the NAFTA, in the draft MAI there is so far no negative list (that is,

areas specifically excluded from the scope of the agreement).[9]

The following assets may be covered by an MFI if a broad approach, as proposed by the draft MAI, were followed:

(i) enterprises;

(ii) shares and stocks, bonds, debentures, loans and other form of debt;

(iii) rights under contracts;

(iv) claims to money and to performance;

(v) intellectual property rights;

(vi) legal or contractual concessions, licences, authorizations and permits;

(vii) any kind of movable and immovable property[10] and related rights.

An MFI, as far as it deals with assets, would not apply to trade operations and purely financial transactions as such. However, to the extent that claims to money and any form of debt may be covered assets, an MFI may be applicable – as proposed under the MAI – to the rights arising from trade transactions or from bank operations, including bank deposits.

The adoption of a broad definition on investments may, in particular, have important implications in several areas for the implementation of national policies.[11] Hence, a number of safeguard provisions would be necessary, even inevitable (Schekulin, 1997, p. 12), in order to preserve under the control of contracting States basic instruments necessary to manage their economies both for short- (e.g. financial crisis) and long-term (e.g. conservation of natural resources) objectives.

In particular, if intellectual property rights (IPRs) were deemed to be an investment under an MFI, as currently proposed under the broad definition discussed in OECD, a number of issues would require attention.

First, an MFI may cover all or some of the rights specified in the TRIPs Agreement, and apply only to present or also to future rights. During discussions of the MAI, some delegations proposed excluding copyrights and neighbouring rights, as well as databases (OECD, 1997, p. 117).

Second, the national treatment principle under the TRIPs Agreement and other international agreements on IPRs (such as the Paris, Berne and Rome Conventions) are subject to a number of exceptions. If IPRs were considered an investment under a general national treatment principle of an MFI, such exceptions – carefully negotiated and drafted in such agreements – may be superseded.

Third, possible MFI provisions, such as those negotiated in the draft MAI, relating to general treatment and, in particular, measures that impair the use or enjoyment of an investment, and provisions on performance requirements may be interpreted in a manner that affects the application of exceptions to exclusive rights and compulsory licences, as admitted under the TRIPs Agreement. Illustrative of this possible conflict is the current MAI draft provision on technology-related performance requirements, which would only admit (in one of the alternative texts) compulsory licences granted to remedy anti-competitive practices, while the TRIPs Agreement does not limit the grounds for the granting of such licences (Correa, 1994, p. 331).

Fourth, provisions on monopolies, if included in an MFI, may affect the activities of entities charged with the collective management of IPRs, which may require a specific exception to avoid conflict with the proposed rules.

Finally, the coexistence of two or more mechanisms for the settlement of disputes may add confusion to an already unclear scenario for the interpretation and application of international conventions on IPRs (Geller, 1997). Conflicting decisions and forum shopping may be the likely outcome of such coexistence.

In sum, if current trends were followed in the development of an MFI, it may apply to all types of assets, independently from the sector where they are invested. If the scope of an MFI were defined, for instance, as proposed in the MAI, the concept of investment would be much broader than the notion of FDI, with which the development of an MFI is often associated. An MFI may have far-reaching effects on the ability of host countries to implement a wide range of policies directly or indirectly affecting foreign investments. It may also entail heavier obligations for developing countries in some fields, such as in the area of IPRs.

B. Standards

Existing instruments on foreign investments have been developed on the basis of four principles,

which are likely to be involved in the elaboration of an MFI (as is the case of the MAI):

  (i) national treatment,
 (ii) most favoured nation,
(iii) fair and equitable treatment,
 (iv) transparency.

The national treatment and the most favoured nation (MFN) principles, originally recognized as essential elements of trade agreements, have become a common element of BITs and other international instruments relating to foreign investment. Both standards are contingent, in the sense that they do not oblige a country to provide a certain level or type of treatment but only the same, or a no less favourable treatment, than that accorded to nationals or MFNs, respectively.

One of the major implications of the application of the said principles in an MFI is that the contracting parties would not be able to grant national investors better treatment than that conferred on foreign investors. The latter may, however, receive better treatment than nationals ("positive discrimination"). If a country treated the foreign investors of a contracting party better than its own investors, it would be obliged to extend the same treatment to all foreign investors.

An important point is whether the referred principles would only apply to the operation (post-establishment phase) of an investment or to its entry (pre-establishment phase) as well. Most existing BITs and international instruments on foreign investments only cover the post-establishment phase. In the draft MAI, however, national treatment and MFN provisions would apply to both the pre- and post-establishment phases (see next section).

While, as already noted, an MFI would be based on the national treatment and MFN clauses, which are contingent, relative, standards, it may also contain absolute standards,[12] such as "reasonable" or "fair and equitable" treatment. This kind of standard is found in some BITs and other instruments (generally with regard to the post-establishment phase).

In the draft MAI, for instance, contracting parties are required to grant fair and equitable treatment. Though the wording of this standard is very general, and may allow different interpretations, it sets down a rule against which the policies and regulations of contracting parties would be judged.

In the draft, the provisions relating to fair and equitable treatment are supplemented by an obligation not to impair investments by "unreasonable" and/or "discriminatory" measures.

In the draft MAI foreign investors are to be subject in each contracting party to the regulations and policies generally applicable to the type of activity they undertake. As stated by one commentator of the MAI, it "is not designed to forbid any form of regulation against foreign investors, but only discriminatory policies. This is essential; the MAI does not aim to challenge the legitimacy of a public action connected with investment" (Charolles, 1997, p. 18).

Finally, an important element would be the transparency obligation, under which MFI contracting parties may be bound to disclose any discriminatory measure. In the proposed MAI, this obligation would also include the disclosure of other measures and policies affecting investments, including policies that have not been formalized.

In sum, the development of an MFI is likely to rely on the same contingent and absolute standards that already govern BITs and other international instruments on foreign investments. An important difference from those precedents may arise, however, if under an MFI such standards were also applicable to the pre-investment phase, since this would limit the right of a State to admit or not a foreign investment on the basis of its own national policies and objectives.

III. General operational issues

An MFI is likely to contain a number of provisions relating to the operational aspects of foreign investments. The way in which these issues are addressed will determine the extent to which contracting parties would be able or not to regulate the entry and operation of foreign investments. Such issues include entry restrictions, conditions on ownership and control, performance requirements, the transfer of key personnel, and incentives.

A. *Admission*

Entry restrictions on foreign investments have been applied widely by developing as well as developed countries. They are in most cases, by their nature, discriminatory vis-à-vis foreign persons, and have been based on a wide range of grounds, including willingness to promote the development of local companies, the acquisition of technology, the creation of employment and generation of exports. In some cases, a broad notion of national security has justified such restrictions in areas of critical interest for a country.

Typical pre-establishment measures with respect to FDI applied in many countries (UNCTAD, 1996, p. 176) include restrictions on investment in certain sectors (natural resources, public utilities), conditions on the structure of ownership (minimum participation of local investors), or specific requirements relating to the future operation of the foreign firms (employment of local personnel, utilization of local raw materials and supplies, environment protection, exports of a certain proportion of production, etc.).

A key aspect of an MFI would be whether it would only apply – as most BITs and other international instruments on foreign investments do – to the post-establishment phase, or whether it would also entail obligations with respect to the entry of such investments. If the latter approach were adopted, admission policies applied by many countries with regard to foreign investors, including screening and prior authorization of FDI, may need to be revised or abolished. Though exceptions may be negotiated (see section V), foreign investors would have, under the national treatment principle, the same rights to invest in any asset, localization and industry, as nationals.

As indicated, one distinctive feature of the MAI is that it would apply to both pre- and post-investment operations.[13] Both the national treatment and the MFN provisions would expressly apply to "the establishment, acquisition, expansion, operation, management, maintenance, use, enjoyment, and sale or other disposition of investments".

The approach of the MAI goes beyond that followed in the GATS to liberalize services trade. While the latter applies only to those sectors and activities that a WTO member puts "on offer", the former would be a "catch-all" agreement, in which all sectors and activities would be included, unless specifically excluded.

This means that, subject to any agreed exception or reservation, a contracting party would be unable to prevent foreign persons investing in any asset (as defined above) within its territory, or to condition the investment upon the meeting of certain requirements, if such restrictions and requirements were not applied to nationals as well.

The extension of the national treatment standard to the pre-establishment phase would create a right of market access.[14] In view of the important interests at stake in relation to such a right, national treatment cannot be expected, even in the case of OECD countries, to be granted at once for entry under all circumstances and in all economic sectors (Charolles, 1997, p. 20). Contracting parties may be allowed to make sector-specific reservations. This is likely to be one of the most difficult issues in the negotiation of the MAI. Many countries may be expected to isolate some sectors from national treatment. During the NAFTA negotiations, for instance, neither the United States nor Canada was prepared to roll back any sectoral exception to national treatment (Graham, 1996, p. 44).

Such application of the national treatment standard to the pre-establishment phase in a possible MFI seems even more questionable for developing countries wishing to retain the right to screen and eventually reject an FDI proposal (Ganesan, 1997, p. 4).

To sum up, an MFI initiative including national treatment for the entry and operation of foreign investments would "level the playing field" and ease market access for foreign investors. The adoption of the national treatment principle in a binding international agreement for the pre-investment phase would constitute a significant innovation with respect to existing instruments that many developing countries may find difficult to accept (South Centre, 1997, p. 38).

B. Ownership and control

Many countries apply different types of restrictions regarding the ownership and control of assets by foreign investors. These restrictions, generally established in order to promote the development of local enterprises or based on broad concerns of national interest, discriminate between foreign and national investors. Common limitations on ownership and control include:

(i) restrictions on investment in certain industries,

(ii) requirements for majority local equity participation,

(iii) imitations of foreign equity participation,

(iv) fade-out obligations.

An MFI based on the national treatment clause would prevent contracting parties, in principle, from applying such limitations. For instance, the draft MAI does not permit contracting parties to oblige foreign investors to establish a joint venture or to achieve a minimum level of local equity participation.

Non-discrimination with regard to ownership and control would also apply in the draft MAI with respect to concessions (except when they confer a monopoly). Though this issue is still under considerable debate within OECD, concessions relating to rights to search for, cultivate, extract or exploit natural resources may not be subject to restrictions regarding the participation of foreign capital.

Further, the MAI rules would cover investments relating to the privatization of State enterprises. The point of departure of the proposed rules is that any decision to privatize would remain in the hands of the government. However, once the decision taken, the national treatment principle and the MFN clause would apply[15] to both initial and subsequent sales associated with all kinds of privatization, irrespective of the method employed (whether public offering, direct sale or other methods).

Thus, under the OECD model the general rule would be for the freedom for foreign investors to invest without restrictions on ownership or control. In a number of situations, however, such rules might not apply:

First, contracting parties could reserve certain activities to the State in the form of a State monopoly. The right of governments to designate or maintain a monopoly would therefore not be disputed under the MAI.

Second, contracting parties might seek sector-specific or general exceptions. Most OECD countries, for instance, have means to block takeovers of domestic firms by foreign companies, based on broad, often ill-defined, "national security" grounds that encompass reasons related to the preservation or acquisition of competitive advantages vis-à-vis foreign rivals. For example, under the so-called Exon-Florio authority, the United States Government can block takeovers by foreigners, as it did in the fields of aerospace and capital goods for the production of advanced integrated circuits (Graham, 1996, p. 40).

Third, the prohibition of requirements relating to ownership and control might not be absolute: an MFI could allow a contracting party to apply such requirements as a condition for the receipt or continued receipt of certain advantages (including the provision of incentives),[16] for instance by limiting access to certain advantages to joint ventures or to firms with a minimum level of local equity participation.

In sum, an MFI might oblige contracting parties to avoid, or limit restrictions on, the ownership and control of assets by foreign firms, and would ensure the latter an opportunity to participate in privatization processes as well as in concessions on natural resources.

An obligation of this type – if not qualified and subject to exceptions and reservations – might hence have important implications for national policies aiming at fostering the development of local enterprises.

C.   *Performance requirements*

The admissibility of performance requirements is likely to be one of the key issues in any discussion on an MFI. The current MAI proposal includes a comprehensive list of prohibited performance requirements related to investments in both goods and services.[17] The TRIMs Agreement has already prohibited certain trade-related performance requirements,[18] but an MFI may go far beyond that treaty.

Performance requirements have been regarded by developed countries as having a distortive effect on the entry and/or operation of foreign investments (Brewer and Young, 1997, p. 184). In the perspective of the developing countries, however, a "TRIMs-plus" agreement prohibiting an expanded list of performance requirements may negatively affect the options available for pursuing development policies. Such requirements may be necessary to secure benefits for society from foreign investments.

Various analyses suggest that the countries benefiting the most from FDI were those (China, Republic of Korea, etc.) which had established frameworks that selectively attracted "quality" FDI, that is, FDI that did not displace local investments but complemented it and supported capacity-building in their economies (Kumar, 1996a, p. 7; South Centre, 1997, p. 38; UNCTAD, 1997, p. 9). It has also been

pointed out that developed countries have used investment incentives with much the same effect as developing countries using TRIMs (Brewer and Young, 1997, p. 184).

The draft MAI specifies the performance requirements that contracting parties may not apply, either as a condition for entry or for the operation of a foreign investment. In the draft, performance requirements would not be allowed with regard to the "establishment, acquisition, expansion, management, operation or conduct" of an investment, that is neither as a pre- or post- establishment condition.

The draft MAI contains a dozen specific performance requirements that would be prohibited, inter alia: to export a certain level or percentage of goods of services; to achieve a certain level of domestic content; to relate the volume of imports or sales to exports; to transfer technology; to locate headquarters; to supply exclusively from a territory to a specific region or the world market; to achieve a certain level of production, investment, sales, employment or research and development (R&D); to establish a joint venture, and to achieve a minimum level of local equity participation. The prohibition of these requirements would be subject to some exceptions based on such grounds as environmental concerns, export promotion and foreign aid programmes, government procurement and privatization (OECD, 1997, pp. 18-24).

In addition, a distinctive feature of the draft MAI provisions on performance requirements is that they distinguish between requirements that would depend on the granting of an advantage from those that do not. This means that contracting parties might impose some requirements (such as those related to the location of production, provision of particular services, training or employment of workers/employees, construction or expansion of particular facilities or to carrying out R&D) to the extent that they are linked to the enjoyment of, for instance, investment incentives (Ahnlid, 1997, p. 28).[19]

In sum, a critical aspect of an MFI would be whether it would restrict, beyond the TRIMs Agreement, the policy options available today to maximize the benefits and minimize the costs for host countries of foreign investments by means of performance requirements, whether related or not to the concession of certain advantages. This is likely to be a major and controversial issue in any possible discussion on an MFI, to the extent that developing countries wish to retain the possibility of determining conditions for the entry and operation of foreign investments in line with their own developmental policies.

D. *Transfer of key personnel*

The possibility of transferring personnel to perform managerial and other key functions in the host country is often viewed by foreign investors as a necessary condition for the successful operation of an investment.

The GATS already contains some provisions on the movement of personnel.[20] An MFI may contain more general rules on the matter, applicable to all foreign investments. Thus, the MAI, as drafted,[21] would subject the entry, stay and work of "key personnel" (including executives, managers and specialists) and of the investors themselves to national immigration and labour regulations. However, the MAI would not permit denial of entry, stay or authorization to work for reasons related to labour markets or other economic needs tests or numerical restrictions in national laws, regulations and procedures.

While the interest of national investors in transferring their own personnel is understandable, a restriction, as proposed in the MAI, might conflict with the immigration policies of certain countries. Some national laws, for instance, provide for "needs tests": if the country requires certain specialists or professionals from outside, they may be allowed work permits. Permits are denied if foreigners are likely to compete with available local people able to perform the same tasks. In some countries such tests are regarded as an important public policy issue (Khanna, 1996, p. 2).

If an MFI were negotiated an important issue would therefore be how to reconcile the interests of foreign firms and of governments on this matter.

E. *Incentives*

A vast array of incentives is granted in developed and developing countries in the framework of industrial, technological and other policies.[22] The discussion of this issue in the context of a possible MFI involves at least two important dimensions: application of the national treatment principle for access to incentives by foreign investors, and disciplines on the concession of investment incentives.

The application of national treatment – as currently provided for in most BITs and other instruments on investments – requires, in principle, the granting of incentives without discrimination between national and foreign investors.

However, since scarce public funds are committed (via tax exemptions, financial or other mechanisms) to promote R&D, employment, local value added, or to pursue other aims, governments often wish to limit the granting of incentives to national firms or to a certain category thereof. In some cases, discrimination in favour of local companies is based on national economic interests, such as obtaining or maintaining a competitive edge. The desire of governments to reserve incentives to nationals has been particularly strong in relation to R&D incentives, as illustrated by tensions observed among some industrialized countries.[23]

In OECD negotiations the type of incentives to be covered and the exceptions to be admitted to the national treatment principle are still undefined. Tax incentives, in particular, may be excluded altogether.[24] On the other hand, even if incentives were subject to this principle, nothing would prevent their limitation to certain categories of firms (such as small and medium enterprises), which would normally be only or predominantly locally owned. However, if no exception were provided for, strict application of national treatment might prevent member countries from tying certain incentives to the nationality of the capital owners, as in the case of special measures for "indigenous" firms applied in Malaysia and in some African countries so as to overcome the dominance of ethnic minorities.

A second dimension of the incentives issue specifically relates to disciplines on investment incentives. Despite the limited impact of incentives on investment decisions (Wheeler and Mody, 1992, pp. 57-76; World Bank, 1985, p. 130; UNCTAD, 1996, p. 181), costly competition has often arisen among countries seeking foreign investments, based on the offering of different kinds of *investment incentives* in general, or with respect to particular investment projects. Competition via incentives involves not only national governments, but very often also municipalities and States.[25]

The extent to which an MFI may address, and in particular, limit the use of investment incentives is unclear. In the OECD negotiations, no final consensus has so far been reached on the extent to which the MAI should include disciplines (including prohibitions) on investment incentives,[26] or on the relationship of future MAI rules with the relevant provisions of the WTO Agreement on Subsidies and Countervailing Measures.

IV. Investment protection and dispute settlement

One of the main components of an MFI, as illustrated in the draft MAI, would relate to investment protection, including:

(i) disciplines on expropriation,

(ii) obligations regarding compensation,

(iii) protection from strife,

(iv) free transfer of payments related to an investment,[27]

(v) subrogation.

Disciplines on expropriation constitute one of the typical and important provisions found in BITs and other international instruments on investments. In some of those instruments, the application of such disciplines is conditional upon the meeting of certain conditions[28]. In other cases, rules on expropriation and other forms of appropriation of property are non-contingent and not subject to any conditions. NAFTA and the Energy Charter Treaty, in particular, include strict criteria on the legality of expropriations and elaborate provisions on the payment of compensation.

The prevailing standard on expropriation requires "prompt, adequate and effective compensation" in case of expropriation on other protected investment,[29] and the right of the investor to substantiate its case before a judicial court or any other independent authority in the host country. In OECD negotiations, for instance, there has been agreement on the following elements (Karl, 1997, p. 14):

(i) "prompt" means without delay;

(ii) "adequate" means that the compensation must be equivalent to the fair market value immediately before the expropriation took place, without any deduction owing to the fact that the pending expropriation became publicly known in advance;

(iii) "effective" means that compensation shall be fully realizable and freely transferable; and

(iv) "due process of law" includes the right of an investor to have its case reviewed by a judicial authority or any other independent body in the host country.

The expropriation clauses are generally associated with a subrogation clause, under which a host country is bound to recognize the assignment of the rights and claims of an investor to its home country when the latter has made a payment under a guarantee, indemnity or contract of insurance in respect of an investment. In this case, the home country may exercise by virtue of subrogation the rights and claims of the foreign investor.

Under protection from strife clauses, as provided in BITs and other instruments, a host country would be obliged, in principle, to confer foreign investors with national and MFN treatment. In the draft MIA it is proposed to supplement this contingent standard with an absolute obligation. The host country would be obliged to pay compensation for losses arising from war, any other armed conflict, state of emergency or similar cases, if the losses were caused by requisition or destruction by the host country's forces or authorities. Moreover, if a contracting party decided to pay, even when not obliged, it would be subject to national treatment and MFN principles.

If an MFI were negotiated, another important issue would be the extent to which it would contain specific rules and mechanisms on dispute settlement, and whether they would apply to State-to-State and/or investor-to-State relationships. Those rules and mechanisms would "give teeth" to an MFI and overcome what is regarded by some countries as a major shortcoming of existing instruments, even within the OECD (European Commission, 1995).

In the case of the draft MAI, one of the proposals is a dispute settlement mechanism characterized by the following elements:

(a) State-to-State arbitration

Following the WTO system of dispute settlement, the first step under the MAI would be consultations attempting an amicable solution to the dispute. If not reached, an arbitration panel (consisting of three or five members) would be appointed, based on a proposal by the Secretary-General of the International Centre for Settlement of Investment Disputes (ICSID). The treaty would establish the basic rules and procedures for arbitration, although the parties to a dispute would always be allowed to apply agreed modifications to the rules.

The substantive law to be applied would be the provisions of the MAI, while other international rules might be applied for the interpretation and application of the treaty. Domestic laws would be taken into account only if relevant to and consistent with the MAI. The awards issued by a panel would be final and binding upon the parties to the dispute.

(b) Investor-to-State arbitration

The system would operate as follows (Baldi, 1997, p. 39):

(i) The investor would be free to choose whether:

- to submit the dispute for resolution to any competent court or administrative tribunal of the contracting party to the dispute;
- to solve the dispute in accordance with any dispute settlement procedure agreed upon before the dispute arose; or
- to follow the procedures provided for by the MAI itself.

(ii) MAI contracting parties, through the adoption of the treaty, would give unconditional consent to the submission of a covered dispute to arbitration under:

- the rules of arbitration of ICSID, or under the rules of the ICSID Additional Facility;
- the UNCITRAL rules; or
- the Court of Arbitration of the International Chamber of Commerce.

Prior consent by the contracting parties, as indicated in (b) above, would mean, in practice, that it would be exclusively up to the investor to decide whether or not to refer the dispute to arbitration (Baldi, 1997, p. 40). Unconditional prior consent, without any possible exception, could in some countries raise problems of a constitutional nature (OECD, 1997, p. 130).[30]

A number of important issues still remain to be defined in OECD negotiations on this matter, including the consequences if a contracting party failed to comply with a final award. They may include the suspension of voting rights in the Parties Group (the body that would monitor and interpret the treaty in order to facilitate its operation) and the withdrawal of concessions under the MAI (with the exception of rules relating to the general treatment and expropriation of investments). Other countermeasures, including trade retaliations, are under discussion.

The debates taking place in OECD illustrate the type of issues that would have to be tackled in a possible MFI. If an MFI is not integrated into the WTO system, accession to it would not mean a waiver of rights and obligations under WTO agreements, particularly under the Dispute Settlement Understanding. Hence, there would be a possibility of conflicting decisions in different fora and of a duplication of mechanisms of sanctions.

Another delicate problem is whether a dispute settlement mechanism could be applied with regard to the pre-establishment phase. How would it be possible for a potential – and not an actual – investor to initiate proceedings against a contracting party that is not yet established?

To sum up, any MFI would contain provisions for the legal protection of investments that follow more or less closely existing precedents in BITs and other instruments on investments. Though this might not represent a major innovation vis-à-vis the existing situation, the establishment of an independent system of dispute settlement would. Given the possible overlapping of jurisdiction with WTO in many areas, a critical point to be considered is the desirability of a new system that could facilitate "forum shopping" and eventually lead to complex conflicts.

V. Exceptions, derogations and reservations

Given the likely implications of a possible MFI for the design and application of a wide range of domestic policies on foreign investments, an issue of critical importance is the flexibility left to the eventual contracting parties to derogate from the obligations under the treaty.

The draft MAI has adopted a "top-down approach" according to which, as a general principle, only the sectors explicitly excluded from its disciplines would not be subject to national treatment and other obligations.[31] In addition, the MAI would include "standstill" and "rollback" provisions which, taken together, would produce a "ratchet effect", i.e. any new liberalizing measure adopted by a contracting party would be "locked in" so it could not be nullified over time (Sikkel, 1997, p. 23).

As negotiated in the framework of the MAI, there would be five types of provisions allowing derogations from the general obligations of the treaty:

(i) *General exceptions*: Contracting parties would be allowed to take measures to protect their essential security interests and the fulfilment of their obligations under the United Nations Charter concerning the maintenance of international peace and security. Discussions have also taken place with regard to a general exception for public order, for cultural industries and for regional economic integration organizations.

(ii) *Taxation*: Though it is a vital aspect for foreign investment decisions, taxation would be carved out from the MAI, except for certain specific provisions such as expropriation and transparency.

(iii) *Temporary derogations*: Under exceptional circumstances affecting balance of payments, a contracting party would be able to introduce exchange restrictions and capital controls during a temporary period of time. Such measures would be subject to a number of conditions, including the MFN treatment, a review by the Parties Group and approval by the International Monetary Fund.

(iv) *Prudential measures*: A contracting party could apply measures that do not conform with the national treatment, MFN and other provisions of the treaty in the financial services only, in order to protect investors, depositors, etc., or to ensure the "integrity and stability" of the financial system. Thus, a provision is being considered to "carve out" transactions carried out by a central bank or monetary authority in the pursuit of monetary or exchange rate policies.

(v) *National reservations*: States would be obliged, in order to become parties to the MAI, to disclose all non-conforming measures when the MAI is signed or when they join. As mentioned above, "standstill" and "rollback" provisions would imply the prohibition of new or more restrictive exceptions to the treaty's minimum standards and the elimination over time of non-conforming measures.[32]

VI. Developmental issues

The foregoing discussion indicates that if an MFI were negotiated many complex issues would require careful attention and a variety of options would be available. In view of the possible broad implications of an MFI, it is not surprising that views

on its merits differ among countries with different levels of development, and even among institutions and groups within the same country (see, for instance, Woellert, 1997).

For countries that are sources of FDI and other forms of investment, an MFI may facilitate the establishment and operation overseas of their enterprises, particularly if such an agreement provides not only substantive rules but also mechanisms to ensure enforcement in cases of non-compliance. Investment supplier countries may, thus, substantially benefit from such a framework. Developing countries, which are mainly recipients of foreign investments have already liberalized to a great extent their FDI regimes. In this sense, an MFI would not be in contradiction with present trends in such countries. Most of them recognize that FDI may play a positive role in their economies. However, the possible negotiation of an MFI has raised their concerns, since host States may loose the right to regulate FDI in a manner that ensures that a positive role is effectively fulfilled by FDI, with minimum negative effects for the host country (Kumar, 1996a; Khor, 1996, p. 29; South Centre, 1997, p. 38).

In principle, an MFI would not challenge the right of countries to develop their own investment policy, including common investment policies that may be developed in regional economic integration organizations (Charolles, 1997, p. 20). Nevertheless, the above analysis indicates that the adoption of an MFI may limit certain aspects of investment policies with respect to the promotion of capacity building, for instance:

(i) Contracting parties would not be able to select project investments based on the complementarity of investment with local firms, the level of local content, or the development of networks with local suppliers;

(ii) Incentives would have to be granted on a non-discriminatory basis,[33] thus preventing preferences for local firms. Foreign investors may, in certain circumstances, be better positioned than local firms to respond to the available incentives;

(iii) "National buying" policies would be prohibited, except regarding acquisitions for purely public, non-commercial, purposes.

Given the different views that developed and developing countries may have on the impact of a possible MFI, an important issue is whether it would allow for differential treatment with regard to developing countries, as generally permitted under GATT/WTO agreements.

As already said, the MAI, if adopted, would be open to accession by any non-OECD country. The proponents of the MAI assume that a multilateral regime would equally benefit developed and developing countries at very different stages of development (Shelton, 1997, p. 6). There is nothing in the draft MAI in terms of differential treatment for developing countries. Though a number of national exceptions could be negotiated, the "bottom-up" approach, the "rollback" provision and the likely continuing pressures by other contracting parties to reduce or eliminate non-conforming measures, would make it very difficult to preserve a certain margin of manoeuvre to implement policies consistent with different levels of economic development.

The accession to an MFI is not likely to increase per se the attractiveness for foreign investors from a given country. It is well proven that the legal regimes on FDI are not generally the crucial factor in determining FDI flows, which are rather dependent on other conditions, such as the size and growth of the market, infrastructure, political, legal and economic stability, and the availability of human resources (UNCTAD, 1997, p. 7).

As the experience of many African countries shows, providing high standards of protection to foreign investors has not been enough to foster FDI flows, while other countries with more restrictive frameworks (e.g. China) have shown a dramatic growth in FDI (Kumar, 1996a, p. 6). Moreover, once a majority of countries adopt similar standards for the treatment of FDI, the relative importance of the legal framework as a factor of attraction of FDI will be completely overshadowed by the other above-mentioned factors.

If an MFI were established, its impact may significantly vary according to the level of development of the countries concerned. If the proposals by the European Commission and OECD were taken as a model, some developing countries would have to make substantial concessions in different policy areas. Such concessions may be more difficult to make in countries already receiving important FDI flows than in those (like most least developed countries) where FDI inflows are scarce.

It would be speculative, at this stage, to judge whether the concessions to be made in order to adhere to a possible MFI might be compensated by any

potential benefits to be derived from the new set of rules. If, as stated, an MFI is not likely to substantially change current trends in FDI flows, developing countries may be expected, if negotiations on an MFI were initiated, to press for differential treatment in order to retain their ability to implement different kinds of developmental policies, as, for example, in the case of the prior screening of FDI projects, ownership needs and use of performance requirements.

Differential treatment may be granted in terms of the scope of the MFI obligations applicable to developing countries, for instance by limiting them to capital movements in the form of FDI, as proposed by the European Commission (1995). A special provision for least developed countries may also be considered, as provided for in WTO agreements.[34] Another possibility would be for an MFI to contain provisions that specifically address developmental concerns, such as those generally dealt with by FDI regimes adopted in developing countries and in other international instruments. These issues include the treatment of RBPs, transfer pricing, technology transfer, employment, environmental protection, balance-of-payments problems and State contracts.[35] There is no comprehensive international set of rules dealing with such issues in relation to foreign investments. Some of them where unsuccessfully addressed in the negotiation of a Code of Conduct on Transnational Corporations, and have been dealt with by the OECD Guidelines for Multinational Enterprises (hereinafter the Guidelines), which are of a voluntary nature.

The draft MAI does not contain rules addressing these developmental concerns, although the agreement would be open to signature by non-OECD countries. It would only make a reference to the Guidelines, without incorporating them in the Agreement or altering their non-binding nature. As a result, developmental concerns would be mainly subject to the general legislation concerning contracting parties, as limited by their international obligations under the MAI or other instruments.

A. Restrictive business practices

The control of RBPs has not been addressed in BITs and investment agreements. It basically remains an area subject to national and regional rules.[36]

The UNCTAD Principles and Rules on Restrictive Business Practices constitute the most important international instrument on the matter, but of a non-binding nature. Part I, section 8, of the TRIPs Agreement, which is binding, only applies with regard to restrictive practices in licensing agreements. The Ministerial Meeting held in Singapore in December 1996 agreed to establish a working group to study the interaction between trade and competition policy, but without prejudging whether negotiations will be initiated in the future.

The relationship between a possible MFI and the control of RBPs exercised by foreign investors is not evident. For instance, the MAI, as drafted, does not include provisions on RBPs, while the Guidelines only contain a clause (article 4 on competition), indicating the need to comply with competition rules as applied in the OECD area.

If an MFI were not to address the issue of RBPs, national laws would be free to determine the regulations on the matter, subject only to the provisions of the TRIPs Agreement relating to voluntary licence agreements. Under an MFI, the only restriction would be not to discriminate in the application of RBPs laws against foreign investors.

National regulations, however, may not suffice to effectively prevent or remedy abuses by large enterprises that operate internationally (Kumar, 1996a, p. 6). The Guidelines themselves recognize that the RBPs of multinational enterprises may impact on trade and competition and on the process of national and international concentration more significantly than those of national enterprises, because of the more international character of their operations (p. 27).

Hence, if an MFI were negotiated, an important question would be what kind of obligations should be assumed by contracting parties in order to ensure an effective control of anti-competitive practices by foreign investors.

B.   Transfer pricing

Transfer pricing may be used by multinational corporations to seek undue tax benefits, to evade exchange controls, to reduce the profit to be shared in joint ventures with local owners, and to influence local wage bargaining, among other reasons.

One of the most common reasons for the abuse of transfer pricing is tax evasion (that is, an artificial increase in the price of inputs acquired by a subsidiary from the parent company to reduce the subsidiary's income subject to taxation), thus depriving host countries of tax revenues. National laws as well as bilateral and double taxation agreements often contain provisions with respect to transfer pricing, but there are not yet international rules on the matter. The Guidelines only refer to the publication of "the policies followed in respect of intra-group pricing". In accordance with current proposals under discussion in OECD, the MAI would not apply to tax issues at all, thereby leaving the matter to domestic tax laws only.

Since the abuse of transfer pricing is difficult to detect, international cooperation may be an important element in identifying it and adopting the necessary remedies. A possible MFI might contain specific disciplines on such practices in order to assist developing countries in preventing and condemning such abuse.

C.   Technology transfer

Access to foreign technology is a critical issue for developing countries, given their relatively low R&D capabilities. In addition to access via licences and other contractual arrangements, many developing countries have been interested in attracting FDI in R&D activities, but with little success so far (Kumar, 1996b).

Since the failure of the initiative in the 1980s to establish a (voluntary) International Code of Conduct on the Transfer of Technology, there have been no attempts to develop specific international rules on the matter. The TRIPs Agreement contains, as mentioned above, provisions that are relevant to access to and utilization of technology protected by IPRs, particularly with regard to RBPs in licensing agreements.

So far, the proposed MAI draft focuses on and strengthens protection of the proprietary rights of producers of technology. The treaty would prohibit performance requirements related to a given level or value of R&D, except if linked to the granting of an advantage. Moreover, the treaty would prevent a contracting party from requiring the transfer of technology as a condition for access to or operation of a foreign investment. On the other hand, the OECD Guidelines only contain very general statements relating to the creation, transfer and diffusion of technologies.

An important issue in terms of the developmental impact, therefore, is whether an MFI would consider the essential interests of developing countries in the area of technology transfer and building up of local R&D capabilities. An MFI, if negotiated, might address such interests by including rules on the terms and conditions of technology transfer, as well as elements for promoting the transfer of technology linked to investment activities, particularly in least developed countries.

D. Employment

Investors have certain responsibilities with regard to wages, work conditions, safety and health, training and other individual and collective rights of workers. Such responsibilities might be dealt with in a possible MFI. These issues are addressed in the Guidelines and in the ILO Tripartite Declaration of Principles Concerning Multinational Enterprises and Social Policy. However, the MAI as proposed by the OECD focuses on the rights of investors and would leave these issues without a binding regulation.[37]

On the other hand, an MFI may contribute to developing a less asymmetric treatment between the movement of capital and of natural persons – one of the problems of concern for certain developing countries (Ganesan, 1997, p. 5). This issue is not addressed in the MAI draft, which deals exclusively with the movement of key personnel associated with FDI.

Finally, an important issue is whether contracting parties under a possible MFI would be allowed to establish performance requirements relating to a certain level of employment or an obligation to hire a given level of local personnel/nationals. Such requirements, including training of workers/employees, could be only imposed, according to the draft MAI, if linked with certain advantages.[38]

E. Environmental issues

The protection of the environment, and the ability of States to implement sustainable development policies, including with respect to the operation of foreign investors, are important concerns of developing countries. Several issues are relevant to this topic (see also World Wildlife Fund, 1997):

(i) The inclusion of concessions and other authorizations or permits under the national treatment principle – as proposed under the draft MAI – may create conflicts with a number of national regulations, such as those relating to the conservation and management of living resources (including those in the sea), and property rights over and exploitation of hydrocarbons. Contracting parties eventually joining an MFI may call for precise exceptions. The parties to NAFTA, for instance, exempted their fisheries and other environmentally related sectors from national treatment obligations.

(ii) Would an MFI recognize the State's right to adopt legitimate environmental measures, even if they disadvantaged foreign investors? Such measures may include, for instance, requiring foreign investors to carry additional liability insurance, to maintain a minimum level of assets within the host country, or to post a bond or deposit to guarantee regulatory compliance (World Wildlife Fund, 1997, p. 5). On the other, an MFI should ensure that its provisions do not impair the capacity of contracting parties to implement their obligations under Multilateral Environment Agreements (MEAs). Exemptions to an MFI rule may be necessary, as provided for, for instance, under NAFTA.

(iii) Would an MFI enhance the accountability of foreign investors for environmental damage? As drafted, the MAI does not set forth specific obligations relating to the environment. Its basic approach would seem to be that governments would retain their freedom to implement environmental policies, as long as the standards for foreign investors are not more stringent than those for domestic ones. The latter, however, would not be subject to specific obligations.

(iv) Even if no obligations were imposed on investors by a possible MFI, environmental reasons could be the basis for exempting host countries from certain conducts or policies. For instance, performance requirements to achieve a certain percentage of domestic content, and to purchase or use goods produced or services provided in a contracting party's territory, might be acceptable under the draft MAI[39] if necessary to protect human, animal or plant life or health, or for the conservation of living or non-living exhaustible natural resources.

(v) Finally, an important issue in a possible MFI may be the obligation by contracting parties not to lower environmental standards/measures as an encouragement to FDI. The MAI, for instance, would prevent this kind of action.

In sum, if an MFI were internationally negotiated, attention should be given to environmental issues in a way that ensures a high degree of compliance with national environmental laws and MEAs.

F. *Balance of payments*

The way in which balance-of-payments-related issues are dealt with by a possible MFI is likely to be of critical importance for developing countries. An MFI may have significant implications for the management of the balance of payments by contracting parties. Given that a possible instrument would apply to both the pre- and post-establishment phases, its application could substantially limit the ability of a country to face balance-of-payment difficulties.

A possible MFI could affect the balance of payments in a variety of ways. If "portfolio" investments were included[40] as a component of covered investments, as proposed under the draft MAI, cases of unmanageable short-term capital flows may arise. The volatility and pro-cyclical behaviour of portfolio investment might, in particular, create financial instability via overvaluation of the host country's currency and subsequent pressures for devaluation (South Centre, 1997, pp. 29-30). A broad derogation clause may be needed to handle such situations.[41]

A more liberal framework for and increased flows of FDI – if this were the outcome of the adoption of an MFI – may also have a structural impact on the balance of payments, depending on a large number of factors, including the steadiness or volatility of FDI inflows, the profits and royalties remitted abroad, the rate of capital repatriation, and the import-saving or export-earning characteristics of investments (South Centre, 1997, pp. 29-30).

The freedom to transfer funds is an issue of critical importance for foreign investors, and a typical element in investment treaties. An important point is the extent to which an MFI would allow general exceptions or temporary safeguards for cases of balance-of-payments problems.

The freedom-to-transfer provision, as envisaged by OECD, would only allow temporary limitations. The issue of general exceptions for reasons of public order, preservation of monetary union, and balance-of-payments problems, is still to be considered by the Negotiating Group.[42]

In the draft MAI, foreign investors have the right to transfer capital, returns and other payments, including the remuneration of foreign personnel, in a freely convertible currency and at the market exchange rate. An exception is under discussion for cases in which the rights of creditors and other rights-holders may be impaired. The MAI would only accept a "temporary safeguard" to limit the transfer of funds "in exceptional circumstances", where movements of capital could cause serious difficulties for the operation of economic/monetary or exchange rate policies, or in the event of balance-of-payments and external financial difficulties or the threat thereof.

Finally, another issue is the potential for jurisdictional confusion or conflict over the issue of capital flows, in view of a possible expanded role for the International Monetary Fund in order to ensure the liberalization of capital flows. If the relevant articles of the Agreement were amended, the Fund would extend its jurisdiction through the establishment of obligations regarding the liberalization of capital movements, at least those of a financial character (Mohammed, 1997). There would be a need, hence, to examine the possible relationship between the provisions of a revised Fund Agreement and of an MFI.

In sum, only limited and temporary exceptions seem to be admissible under the OECD proposal to tackle balance-of-payments problems. A possible MFI – particularly were it to include portfolio investments – might affect the developing countries' ability to manage balance-of-payments problems, and should therefore contain the safeguards and exceptions required to preserve the government's capacity to act promptly and effectively in such circumstances.

G. *State contracts*

Government procurement has been extensively used in both developed and developing countries to promote the development of local industries by means of preferential treatment in terms of prices or other conditions of supply.

The MAI, as proposed by OECD, would not affect the right of a State to establish or maintain State (or private) monopolies, but would discipline their behaviour in order to prevent discrimination against foreign investors. It has been agreed so far in OECD negotiations that monopolies should provide non-discriminatory treatment to foreign firms with regard to the sale of goods and services made by a monopoly, as well as to its purchase of goods and services from third parties. The non-discrimination obligation concerning the purchase of goods and services by the monopoly would not extend to government procurement, so long as the purchase is not made with a view to commercial resale or for use in the production of goods and services for commercial sale. Hence, under the MAI, contracting parties would be allowed to continue the application of schemes that provide preferential treatment to domestic investors in State buying, but only where the State does not operate as reseller or producer of goods of services for commercial purposes. This limitation would exclude the application of national buying regimes whenever the purchasing agency undertakes a commercial activity. However, from a developmental perspective, a possible MFI should be flexible enough to permit the use of public purchasing power as an instrument to promote the development of local firms.

VII. Conclusions

The climate for foreign investments has changed dramatically in developing countries since the 1980s. Most countries now see the importance of foreign investment and are trying their best to attract it.

As proposed by the European Commission and currently negotiated in the OECD, an MFI would consist of a number of basic obligations, notably the national treatment and MFN principles, the (absolute or conditional) prohibition of performance requirements, and the protection of investments. A possible MFI would encourage the resolution of disputes through negotiation or consultation among the parties concerned. If not settled amicably, the disputes would be submitted to a binding investor-to-State and State-to-State dispute settlement process.

A basic innovation of the proposed MFI with respect to most existing BITs and other instruments on investments is that it would include national and MFN treatment with regard to the pre-establishment phase. Contracting States would not be allowed, therefore, to screen and select investment projects unless, and as long as, admitted by specific exceptions, to be eventually incorporated into the MFI.

An MFI would limit the extent of permissible government intervention with regard to foreign investments defined in a broad sense, but, as currently proposed, it would leave little room, if any, to lay down international standards on the conduct of foreign investors.

From the point of view of countries that are capital exporters and hold assets (including intangible property) abroad, an MFI would ensure that investment regimes, which have already become much more open and welcoming in the recent past, remain so in the future. In particular, an MFI would increase the flexibility for investors to select the nature and location of investments, and to manage them in accordance to their own business strategies.

The negotiation of an MFI would be in line with the trend towards liberalization of FDI regimes observed in most developing countries. However, as proposed, the underlying concept of an MFI goes beyond the degree of liberalization accepted by most developing countries which have retained the right and powers to regulate the entry of FDI. In addition, an MFI would not only apply to FDI, but to all types of foreign-owned assets, including intellectual property rights and monetary claims, and would "lock in" any liberalizing measure by preventing its eventual removal.

The current proposals for an MFI do not take into account the possible developmental concerns of developing countries that have not participated in the elaboration of such proposals. The MFI would limit national room for manoeuvre in various policy areas, while it would not include international rules to support actions in certain fields of interest for developing economies, such as RBPs, technology transfer, control of transfer pricing and environmental protection.

Undoubtedly most developing countries actively seek foreign investments. The point is how to guarantee the protection of investors' legitimate interests while, at the same time, ensuring that such investments are consistent with the developmental objectives defined by the host countries and actually do have the expected positive effects on their economies.

Notes

1   For a review of the international arrangements on FDI, see UNCTAD (1996).

2   OECD countries account for nearly 85 per cent of global outflows of FDI and nearly 65 per cent of global inflows (UNCTAD, 1996).

3   The OECD MAI (as well the EC MIA) would also include a "rollback" commitment to gradually eliminate measures that run counter to the new rules. This means that, even if certain measures were exempted, this would be accepted only on a temporary basis.

4   See Kumar (1996a), South Centre (1997), Khor (1996), and the NGO Joint Statement on the Foreign Investments Issue in WTO, Penang, November 1995.

5   The analysis made in this paper is based on OECD (1997).

6   The analysis explicitly recognizes, and is limited by, the provisional nature of the draft text, still under discussion and open to changes and additions in many important areas. The choice and analysis of particular aspects of the OECD text should not be deemed as prejudging the eventual outcome of the ongoing negotiations. There is no intention either to suggest that the OECD draft treaty should be the basis for eventual negotiations on the matter involving non-OECD countries.

7   It should be noted that OECD negotiations is a discussion among developed countries, although, if adopted, the MAI would be a free-standing agreement open to accession by non-OECD countries.

8   In the draft MAI a special chapter is devoted to the financial services sector, which is deemed "unique in some respects" (OECD, 1997, p. 73).

9   However, there is a proposal to include an interpretative note saying that, in order to qualify as an investment, certain characteristics of an investment must be present, such as the commitment of capital or other resources, the expectation of gain or profit, or the assumption of risk (Schekulin, 1997, p. 12).

10   Since not all real estate and other property are used for a business purpose, a distinction may be necessary in this regard.

11   See, in particular, "Measures addressing developmental concerns".

12   For a distinction between "relative" and "absolute" standards, see UNCTAD (1996, p. 182).

13   Most BITs do not include provisions with regard to entry of FDI. This is also the case of the World Bank's Guidelines on the Treatment of Foreign Direct Investment. Such provisions were included, however, in BITs recently proposed by the United States and (only as "best efforts" obligations) in the Energy Charter Treaty (see UNCTAD, 1996).

14   The objective of ensuring "free access" is explicit in the proposed EC MFI, subject only to narrowly defined exceptions as, for instance, in the case of a vital defence industry.

15   An exception under discussion would refer to the "special share arrangements", under which a certain group of persons would be granted exclusive rights regarding initial privatization.

16   This is the case under the draft MAI.

17   The extension of the MIA provision on performance requirements to services is still under debate. NAFTA does not cover requirements in the field of services.

18   NAFTA also includes specific disciplines on performance requirements, which apply to all investments and not only to those originating in a NAFTA country. However, only a few BITs prohibit performance requirements (UNCTAD, 1996, p. 134).

19   NAFTA bans the linking of performance requirements to the receipt of subsidies. However, certain non-trade-related performance requirements are allowed, such as commitments to assist the training of workers and local research and development.

20   Under the GATS, the movement of personnel is to be allowed in order to ensure market access for a services supplier, as provided for in the lists of specific commitments (see Article XVI and the Annex on Movement of Natural Persons).

21   NAFTA also sets down conditions for the temporary admission of business people (chapter 16).

22   The WTO Agreement on Subsidies and Countervailing Measures only concerns goods (GATS does not cover subsidies) and does not prohibit all kinds of subsidies, but only those that are specific to and contingent on the use of domestic over imported goods or on export performance ("red light" subsidies), and those that may have adverse effects on the interests of other members ("amber light" subsidies). See Brewer and Young (1997, p. 188).

23   Thus, the European Union strongly advocated against a proposed amendment to the US National Competitiveness Act, which would have prohibited the United States Government from granting incentives to any one not a US citizen, national or legal alien (Graham, 1996, p. 42). In the EC proposal for an MFI, restrictive conditions for access to R&D incentives would be acceptable.

24   In the EC proposal, R&D subsidies would also be excluded from the general obligations.

25   As illustrated by the recent case of a Mercedes Benz plant established in the United States, following strong competition among a number of States. It should be noted that in accordance with the mandate granted by the Ministers of the OECD, the draft MAI is intended to apply to all government levels, including subfederal entities.

26   It has been observed that "... not unexpectedly, there appears to be more interest in provisions that would limit performance requirements and, in any case, the preliminary informal indications are that there will be very limited, if any, provisions in the MAI on investment incentives" (Brewer and Young, 1997, p. 192).

27   This issue is further considered below (subsection on balance of payments).

28   For instance, the Overseas Private Investment Corporation (OPIC) requires that an FDI project meet some criteria as far as the impact on host and home countries is concerned (e.g. positive developmental effects and the absence of negative environmental effects).

29   It should be noted that, given the proposed scope of the draft MAI, a rescheduling of the foreign debt required by a contracting party to handle a financial turmoil or for other reasons could become a kind of appropriation of property or expropriation (Schekulin, 1997, p. 13).

30   A possible qualification to the prior consent rule may be the right of a State to withhold consent in cases where the investor has previously submitted the dispute either to a national court or to international arbitration under another agreement (Baldi, 1997, p. 41).

31   This is in contrast with the approach followed, for instance, in GATS, where only specified sectors are subject to the negotiated disciplines.

32   All delegations have already submitted a preliminary list of specific reservations. Work is continuing in the

33 Under the MAI, as negotiated, this limitation would not affect tax policies or prevent special incentives to foster capacity-building, or for certain categories of enterprise not defined by nationality but by other attributes, for example small and medium enterprises. The treatment to be given to subsidies for R&D, which are specifically allowed under WTO disciplines, is still unclear.

34 See, for instance, article 66.2 of the TRIPs Agreement requiring developed member countries to promote the transfer of technology to least developing countries.

35 Many of these issues, such as those relating to RBPs, abuse of transfer prices and protection of the environment, cannot be deemed to be a concern of only developing countries, since they also attract considerable attention in developed economies.

36 Some developed countries have entered into cooperation agreements on notifications and exchange of information on competition law, without agreeing, however, on any common substantive principles or rules (UNCTAD, 1996, p. 147).

37 The draft MAI only proposes to discourage the lowering of labour standards in order to attract FDI.

38 Nevertheless, residency requirements would not be considered to be inconsistent with the obligations under the MAI.

39 According to the still unagreed draft text.

40 While FDI to developing countries quadrupled between 1986 and 1992, portfolio investments grew by 50 times during the same period (European Commission, 1995, p. 12).

41 A possible, albeit limited, approach suggested during OECD negotiations, is to permit an exception to the national treatment obligation for the acquisition or sales of assets of an initial maturity of, for instance, less than one year (Schekulin, 1997, p. 12).

42 It seems agreed, however, that no exceptions would be applicable to payment of compensation due in case of expropriation (OECD, 1997, p. 126)

References

AHNLID, Anders (1997), "Performance Requirements and Investment Incentives", *OECD: Multilateral Agreement on Investment, State of Play in April 1997* (Paris: OECD).

BALDI, Marino (1997), "Dispute Settlement", *Multilateral Agreement on Investment State of Play in April* (Paris: OECD).

BREWER, Thomas L., and Stephen YOUNG (1997), "Investment Incentives and the International Agenda", *World Economy*, Vol. 20, No. 2, March, pp. 175-198.

BRITTAN, Leon (1995), "Investment Liberalization: The Next Great Boost to the World Economy", *Transnational Corporations*, Vol. 4, No. 1.

CHAROLLES, Valérie (1997), "Treatment of Investors and their Investments: National Treatment, Most Favoured Nation Treatment and Transparency", in *Multilateral Agreement on Investment State of Play as of February* (Paris: OECD).

CORREA, Carlos (1994), "The GATT Agreement on Trade-Related Aspects of Intellectual Property Rights: New Standards for Patent Protection", *European Intellectual Property Review*, Vol. 16, No. 8 (August).

EUROPEAN COMMISSION (1995), *A Level Playing Field for Direct Investment World-Wide*, mimeo, COM(95)42, Brussels.

GANESAN, A.V. (1997), "Criteria to Test the Development Friendliness of International Investment Agreements", paper presented at Commission on Investment, Technology and Related Financial Issues, second session, 29 September to 3 October, Geneva.

GANESAN, A.V (1999), "Strategic Options Available to Developing Countries with Regard to a Multilateral Agreement on Investment", *International Monetary and Financial Issues for the 1990s*, Vol. X (New York and Geneva: United Nations).

GELLER, Paul (1997), "La propiedad intelectual en el mercado mundial: impacto del sistema de solución de controversias del ADPIC", *Temas de propiedad industrial y de la competencia*, No. 1 (Buenos Aires: Ediciones Ciudad Argentina).

GRAHAM, Edward (1996), "Investment and the New Multilateral Trade Context", in *Market Access After the Uruguay Round – Investment*, Competition and Technology Perspectives (Paris: OECD).

KARL, Joachim (1997), "Investment Protection", in *Multilateral Agreement on Investment State of Play as of February* (Paris: OECD).

KHANNA, Tejendra (1996), "Foreign Direct Investment: The Need for Selective Policies", background paper presented at the Seminar on the WTO and Developing Countries, Third World Network, 10-11 September, Geneva.

KHOR, Martin (1996), "The WTO and the Proposed Multilateral Investment Agreement: Implications for Developing Countries and Proposed Positions", TWN Trade & Development Series, No. 2 (Penang, Malaysia: Third World Network).

KUMAR, Nagesh (1996a), "A Multilateral Regime on Investments: A Note on Understanding the Developing Countries' Concerns", mimeo, UNU/INTECH, Maastricht.

KUMAR, Nagesh (1996b), "Intellectual Property Protection, Market Orientation and Location of Overseas R&D Activities by Multinational Enterprises", *World Development*, Vol. 24, No. 4.

MOHAMMED, Aziz Ali (1997), "Issues Relating to the Treatment of Capital Movements in the IMF", mimeo, IMF, Washington, D.C.

OECD (1997), "Multilateral Agreement on Investment – Consolidated text and commentary", mimeo, DAFFE/MAI/NM(97)2, Paris.

SAUVÉ, Pierre (1997), "Qs and As on Trade, Investment and the WTO", *Journal of World Trade*, Vol. 31, No. 4, August, pp. 55-79.

SCHEKULIN, Manfred (1997), "Scope of the MAI: Definition of Investor and Investment", *Multilateral Agreement on Investment State of Play as of February* (Paris: OECD).

SHELTON, Joanna (1997), "Opening Address", in *Multilateral Agreement on Investment State of Play as of February* (Paris: OECD).

SIKKEL, Marinus (1997), "Treatment of Investors and their Investments: Exceptions, Derogations and National Reservations", in *Multilateral Agreement on Investment State of Play as of February* (Paris: OECD).

SOUTH CENTRE (1997), *Foreign Direct Investment, Development and the New Global Economic Order – A Policy Brief for the South* (Geneva).

UNCTAD (1996), *World Investment Report 1996: Investment, Trade and International Policy Arrangements* (New York and Geneva: United Nations).

UNCTAD (1997), *Expert Meeting on Existing Agreements on Investment and their Development Dimensions* (New York and Geneva: United Nations), May.

WHEELER, D. and A. MODY (1992), "International Investment Location Decisions: The Case of U.S. Firms", *Journal of International Economics*, Vol. 33, pp. 57-76.

WITHERELL, William (1995), "The OECD Multilateral Agreement on Investment", *Transnational Corporations*, Vol. 4, No. 2 (Geneva: United Nations).

WOELLERT, Lorraine (1997), "Trade storm brews over corporate rights", *The Washington Times*, 15 December.

WORLD BANK (1985), *World Development Report 1985* (New York: Oxford University Press).

WORLD WILDLIFE FUND (1997), *Is the Multilateral Agreement on Investment Sustainable?* (Gland, Switzerland).

CAPITAL-ACCOUNT CONVERTIBILITY AND MULTILATERAL INVESTMENT AGREEMENTS: WHAT IS IN THE INTEREST OF DEVELOPING COUNTRIES?

Manuel R. Agosin*

Abstract

This paper deals with the recent efforts by developed countries to tighten international disciplines on various capital-account transactions. It discusses the OECD's draft Multilateral Agreement on Investment (MAI), the WTO Agreement on Financial Services, and efforts at the IMF to extend Fund jurisdiction to capital-account policies aimed at achieving full liberalization of international financial flows. The paper argues that the MAI is unsuitable to developing countries in that it is too broad (it covers all capital transactions, not just FDI), and it deals with investment only from the point of view of the interests of investors. Therefore, developing countries should seek to move discussions on investment to the WTO, where they have a say in shaping decisions. It also argues that the modality of liberalization of the WTO Agreement on Financial Services ("only what is specifically stated is liberalized") is more suitable to the interests of developing countries than the blanket liberalizations that the MAI would impose on them and than strict IMF enforcement of liberal policies toward capital flows. Unless the IMF takes a flexible view on the matter, it is bound to run into jurisdictional conflicts with the WTO and would force developing countries into accepting a greater degree of liberalization than that embodied in their WTO commitments.

* The author is indebted to Gonzalo Islas for his efficient research assistance and to Gerry Helleiner and Andrew Cornford for useful comments on earlier drafts.

I. Introduction and policy conclusions

One of the major international policy offensives of developed countries since the conclusion of the Uruguay Round has been to establish multilateral disciplines for foreign investment and capital movements. Efforts toward this end have been exerted in several fora, including the OECD, where negotiations have begun toward the establishment of a Multilateral Agreement on Investment (MAI) open for signature not only to OECD members but also to other countries; preliminary discussions at the World Trade Organization (WTO) aimed at the negotiation of a similar instrument, the Multilateral Framework for Investment (MFI); the recently concluded WTO Agreement on Financial Services; and attempts at the International Monetary Fund (IMF) to extend convertibility to the capital account and thus fully liberalize capital-account transactions.

This paper discusses these negotiations and the new disciplines that they are already imposing on, and would extend to, developing country policies. It also outlines the issues with which developing country negotiators will have to grapple in the coming negotiations. Among these are:

(i) What are the costs and benefits of an agreement on investment for developing countries? In other words, would an agreement on investment stimulate larger flows of foreign investment and enhance the quality of those flows? On the other hand, what obligations would such an agreement impose on developing countries?

(ii) In the above formulation, the term "investment" has been left deliberately vague. This is because there is dispute as to what kinds of flows any proposed agreement should cover. This is an issue of the utmost importance for developing countries and should command the attention of their policy makers.

(iii) Since there is considerable confusion with regard to the proliferation of efforts to establish disciplines on investment, it is important that developing countries choose the forum in which they will be negotiating. For example, disciplines on policies toward transactions in financial services have already been negotiated at WTO; discussions at the IMF on capital-account convertibility tread over some of the same ground. Developing countries may also be faced with the choice of signing an investment agree-

ment negotiated by OECD members or negotiating an investment agreement at WTO.

(iv) How will the development dimension of any agreement on investment be safeguarded? In other words, will the potential agreement include symmetry between the obligations of host countries and transnational corporations (TNCs)? As shall be discussed below, in some contexts, all international obligations fall on recipient countries, while obligations on corporations are left to the jurisdiction of national laws. The open issues in this regard are:

(a) Will the agreement include provisions for limiting such things as restrictive business practices or abusive transfer pricing?

(b) How can countries preserve the right, if they so wish, to screen investments or to seek and select investments that promise greater development returns?

(v) Will an agreement on investment include provisions regarding incentives?

While it does not pretend to provide governments with a fully articulated prescription, this paper takes the view that, given the nature of international financial transactions, developing countries ought to leave themselves as much freedom as they can to place prudential controls on the more volatile forms of capital movements, in particular portfolio capital and short-term flows.[1] This would, from the outset, preclude signing on to an instrument such as the MAI. Discussions on international regimes for FDI are inescapable, but they ought to be conducted at the WTO, where developing countries have a voice. In addition, developing countries should prod the IMF toward a flexible attitude on capital-account convertibility issues. The WTO Agreement on Financial Services gives them considerable room for manoeuver, which they would lose were the Fund to bring capital-account convertibility into its jurisdiction.

Even if one were to subscribe to the view that FDI is generally development-enhancing (as this author does), that does not necessarily mean that an international instrument limiting the control over investments that recipient governments can exercise is a good thing. International instruments commit governments not to use (ever again) certain policy instruments, and this can be dangerous. An analogy with trade might be apt here. One can subscribe to free trade without recommending that developing countries bind their tariffs at level zero. In fact, several governments that have embarked on far-reaching trade liberalization exercises have nonetheless bound their tariffs in WTO well above their actual levels, in case they may need to raise them in the future, say, for balance-of-payments purposes.

It follows from this discussion that developing countries, in the coming discussions on investment instruments, ought to leave themselves as many doors open as possible. Positive lists that make explicit what is liberalized are better than negative lists of what is excluded from blanket liberalization commitments. The right to impose prudential restrictions in order to safeguard macroeconomic stability and the stability of key macroeconomic prices (the exchange rate and interest rates) ought to be fought for. For example, when countries place restrictions on short-term capital flows, financial investors are tempted to enter capital into the recipient country as FDI. If FDI regulations include minimum stay requirements, this form of evasion becomes less attractive for short-term financial investors, without discouraging FDI, which anyhow, has longer-term horizons.[2]

It is extremely important that any international investment agreement impose minimum norms on the behaviour and practices of investors. Otherwise there will be a high probability that *domestic* regulations on business behaviour will weaken and that, in their anxiety to attract FDI, countries will engage in a sort of *race to the bottom*. The international framework ought to provide a minimum set of norms for TNCs, leaving recipient countries with the freedom to impose higher norms if they desire. This set of norms must necessarily include transfer pricing, restrictive business practices, and environmental and labour standards.

With regard to incentives, there are two apparently contradictory objectives that recipient countries ought to keep in mind. The first one is to limit incentive competition for investment, which only transfers the benefits of FDI from host countries to TNCs, without necessarily increasing FDI inflows. The second one is to safeguard the right to use tax incentives and subsidies to correct market failure. Incentive competition is, to some extent, already restricted by the subsidies agreement of the Uruguay Round, but only with respect to subsidies that affect export prices. The Subsidies Code does not apply to investments in import substituting or non-tradable sectors. Thus, there is a need to incorporate the issue into the discussions of a prospective investment agreement. On the other hand, market-failure-correcting subsidies ought to be permitted if they do not violate the WTO Subsidies Code (most of these subsidies in fact do not) and if they are also available to domestic investors.

II. An agreement for FDI: the OECD's or the WTO's?

Over the past couple of years, the issue of disciplines on countries that are recipients of foreign investment has been under active discussion at the OECD, and a draft agreement on the MAI has already emerged (see Ganesan and Correa in this volume). At the WTO, disciplines on FDI already exist in the General Agreement on Trade in Services (GATS) and in the Agreement on Trade-Related Investment Measures (TRIMs). In addition, the possibility of commencing negotiations toward the adoption of a Multilateral Framework on Investment (MFI) is currently under discussion at WTO.

Do developing countries really need a multilateral investment agreement to attract more FDI? The answer is "probably not". The most accepted theory suggests that FDI decisions by TNCs depend on three factors that must coalesce: (a) host countries must have locational advantages for TNCs; (b) companies must possess ownership advantages (e.g. technology, management skills, brand names, or other intangible assets), and (c) companies must have advantages in exploiting those assets within the internal structures of the firm, and difficulties in exploiting them at arm's length through sales on the market (see Dunning, 1993).

Indeed, the experience of the past two decades indicates that FDI flows to countries that offer important locational advantages. TNCs invest in developing countries with large markets, abundant and low-cost natural resources, skilled and low-wage labour; in countries that have stable legal environments and macroeconomic policies; and in countries with good infrastructure and reasonable regulations and tax rates.

Liberalization of investment regimes is clearly a necessary but insufficient condition for attracting FDI. Undoubtedly, countries that have very restrictive FDI regimes do not receive much of it. But opening up to FDI does not guarantee larger flows; nor does it enhance the prospects of obtaining flows with desirable properties.

Table 1

FDI FLOWS TO DEVELOPING COUNTRIES, 1991-1996

($ billion)

	1991	*1992*	*1993*	*1994*	*1995*	*1996*
All developing countries	34.9	42.2	66.1	78.8	88.2	120.3
of which:						
China	4.4	11.2	27.5	33.8	35.8	42.3
Hong Kong (China)	0.5	2.1	1.7	2.0	2.1	2.5
India	0.2	0.2	0.6	1.3	1.9	2.6
Indonesia	1.5	1.8	2.0	2.1	4.3	8.0
Korea, Republic of	1.1	0.7	0.6	0.8	1.8	2.3
Malaysia	4.0	5.2	5.0	4.3	4.1	5.3
Singapore	4.9	2.2	4.7	5.5	6.9	9.4
Taiwan Province of China	1.3	0.9	0.9	1.4	1.6	1.4
Thailand	2.0	2.1	1.7	1.3	2.0	2.4
Argentina	2.4	2.6	3.5	0.6	1.3	4.3
Brazil	1.1	2.1	1.3	3.1	4.9	9.5
Chile	1.0	0.9	1.4	2.6	2.5	4.8
Colombia	0.5	0.7	1.0	1.7	2.5	3.0
Peru	--	0.1	0.6	2.9	1.9	3.6
Mexico	4.8	4.4	4.4	10.9	7.0	7.5
Total of above countries	29.7	37.2	56.9	74.3	80.6	108.9
Share of above countries in total flows to developing countries *(per cent)*	85.1	88.2	86.1	94.3	91.4	90.5

Source: UNCTAD (1997).

China in the 1990s is a prime example. Its main attraction for TNCs is, of course, its enormous domestic market. Until the late 1970s, China was closed to FDI and, accordingly, had very small inflows. Since then, it welcomes FDI, but its investment regime cannot be described as liberal: there is still strict control over investment flows and approval is given case-by-case. Nonetheless, China has been the largest recipient of FDI among developing countries in the 1990s (see table 1).

The case of India is similar. Until the early 1990s, India had a rather restrictive FDI regime; as the decade progressed FDI was liberalized and very

large FDI flows became possible. But India, like China, possesses very attractive locational advantages for TNCs – a huge domestic market and abundant supplies of skilled and low-cost human resources.

As can be seen in table 1 above, during the 1990s between 85 and more than 90 per cent of all FDI flows to developing countries have gone to 15 countries, although a much larger number of developing countries have liberalized very significantly their FDI regimes since the mid-1980s. According to UNCTAD (1997, p. 132), the number of countries introducing changes to their regulatory regimes increased from 35 to 65 in the period 1991-1996. The number of changes in 1996 was 114, of which 98 were in the direction of liberalization. Most African countries place practically no limits on FDI, yet receive a very meagre share of total flows.

Thus, the evidence suggests that developing countries wishing to attract FDI need worry more about developing national assets that are attractive to potential investors (an educated labour force, a reasonable domestic infrastructure, a good telecommunications system, stable macroeconomic conditions, stable rules of the game, a predictable legal system) than about adopting and locking in very liberal investment regimes.

This suggests that a multilateral investment agreement that would foster the emergence of liberal regimes for investment and would encourage (or force) the locking-in of liberal investment norms is, at best, a secondary priority. Most developing countries have become convinced of the benefits of FDI and have already advanced toward a high degree of liberalization. They do not need the prodding of international negotiations on the issue. And most would probably be ill-served by locking in their current or even more liberalized regimes.

Some countries may, of course benefit from the "locking in" effect of an international regime. For countries characterized in the past by frequent and unpredictable changes in policies and rules of the game, signing on to a multilateral investment agreement might be viewed as a more binding commitment to liberal treatment of FDI than a mere liberalization of the investment regime, which, in the past, may have been frequently undertaken but also frequently reversed. This use of a multilateral agreement as a signal for a change in policy stance may be useful in attracting larger flows of investment to these countries. However, it cannot substitute for the harder task of asset and institution building. Moreover, other countries that are attractive locations for FDI clearly do not need to lock in their policy regimes. Such actions would only tie their hands in the future without bringing them any tangible benefit in the form of additional FDI inflows.

At some point in their development, it may be appropriate for countries to restrict FDI in order to develop indigenous managerial and technological capabilities in certain sectors (Bruton, 1989, and Helleiner, 1989). This was the path followed by the Republic of Korea. While it may not be feasible for many countries to implement productively policies

of this kind at their present stage of development, one need not discard them forever through "locking in".

A multilateral agreement does present some advantages over the current situation in which there coexist a large number of bilateral treaties signed between home and host countries of FDI. Each treaty has different characteristics and conditions. In this state of affairs, transactions costs for firms can be high and can discourage foreign ventures by small or medium-sized potential investors.[3] It must be recognized, however, that most of the bilateral treaties signed in the past have had scant effects on attracting investment.

A.   The OECD draft agreement

A detailed analysis of the OECD draft Multilateral Agreement on Investment (MAI) is of interest to developing countries because of the far-reaching disciplines it would impose on them and the degree of detail with which the issues are addressed (OECD, 1998). Unavoidably, a discussion under the auspices of WTO will use the negotiations in the OECD as a reference. Its examination is also useful for an understanding of the interests of developed countries in this matter and for determining how these interests differ form those of developing countries. Since OECD member countries are capital exporters, the draft MAI reflects basically the interests and concerns of TNCs and transnational banks, for whom the freedom to move capital internationally is critical for their profitability. The question arises as to whether unrestricted freedom in this domain is also in the interests of capital importers.

The negotiations on the MAI, which began in May 1995, were due to be concluded by May 1997. However, a consensus permitting the adoption of the treaty has not yet been reached.

The basic objective of the MAI is to prohibit all "discrimination" against foreign investors through the basic principle of national treatment. Although the MAI is addressed to OECD countries, the treaty will be open to ratification by any country that wishes to submit to its requirements. Due to its broadness and content the MAI is very different from the bilateral and regional treaties currently in force. As a first approximation, it is important to note that the MAI is a "top down" agreement: it covers everything unless something is explicitly excluded. This makes it quite different from the GATS, which is of the "bottom up" variety: whatever is not explicitly liberalized, remains restricted.[4] An investment agreement negotiated under the auspices of the WTO would follow the pattern of the GATS, in view of the fact that the GATS is already concerned with investment norms. A large variety of international services transactions take place through FDI, and this is fully recognized in the GATS.

With regard to definition, the MAI opts for the broadest definition. It includes within the purview of the draft agreement not only FDI but also any kind of asset or property controlled directly or indirectly by a foreign investor: enterprises, stock share holdings, bonds, loans, debt rights of any kind, contract rights, intellectual property rights, concessions, and all types of tangible or intangible property including leases, rents, mortgages, etc. Clearly, signing on to an agreement of this nature would involve the host country losing all possibility of controlling any item in the capital account of the balance of payments, and doing so at the pre-entry stage and in an indefinite time horizon.

It has been argued that countries may wish to enter lists of exceptions or exclusion at the time of signing the treaty, but this renders all aspects of balance-of-payments management policy subject to international negotiation. Moreover, as shall be discussed below, the "top down" nature of the MAI is in conflict with the WTO Agreement on Financial Services, which gives countries considerable leeway as to what they decide to liberalize.

The MAI enshrines two fundamental principles: national treatment (NT) and the most favoured nation (MFN) principle. NT ensures that foreign investors will receive equal treatment to that granted to national investors; the MFN principle ensures that, if a host country were to grant special advantages to foreign investors from a particular country, those benefits would be extended to all signatory countries. The novelty of the MAI is that these principles apply at the pre-investment phase and not merely after an investment has been approved. What this means in practice is unrestricted market access for foreign companies and foreign capital; in other words, that the right of signatory countries to screen investment applications is in fact derogated. In the case of developing countries, where development considerations are paramount in encouraging or regulating foreign investment, the application of NT and MFN to the pre-investment stage is tantamount to severely limiting their capability to use FDI as a tool of in-

dustrial policy. Even countries that have decided not to screen investment may not wish to tie their hands forever on this matter.

There are other ways in which the draft MAI would severely limit the use of FDI policy as an aspect of industrial policy. The MAI is quite explicit in its rejection of performance requirements. It prohibits host countries from imposing obligations with regard to the "transfer [of] technology, a production process or other proprietary knowledge to a natural or legal person in its frontiers", with the exception of those obligations stemming from court determinations related to competition laws or which are not inconsistent with the TRIPs Agreement (OECD, 1998, p. 20). It also prohibits requiring that firms "achieve a certain level of research and development in [the host country's] territory".[5] Other performance requirements that are explicitly prohibited include the employment of local personnel, the obligation of establishing joint ventures, and local content or export requirements.[6]

With regard to privatizations, the draft MAI forecloses the possibility that countries engaging in privatization policies may implement mechanisms that favour nationals. The only exceptions made are those that distribute shares among workers or management of the firms themselves. The same norms are applicable in the case of concessions (say, of infrastructure). Likewise, state-owned enterprises may not discriminate in favour of domestic firms in the granting of contracts.

The MAI is much less explicit with regard to incentives, because there has not been agreement in this area. Some countries have proposed the incorporation of a special chapter on incentives, which would establish the principles of NT and MFN in the sphere of incentives, understood as the concession of a specific fiscal benefit in connection with the establishment, acquisition, expansion, management, operation, or behaviour of an investment. Some countries have gone as far as proposing the elimination of all incentives that may distort investment decisions.

The exclusion of incentives from the proposed international disciplines on investment, together with complete freedom of entry and the severe limits proposed on performance requirements, clearly benefit TNCs and place recipient countries at a severe disadvantage. A battle of incentives for the attraction of FDI is already raging, and not only among developing countries. State governments in developed countries are also participating briskly. The adoption of a MAI will either exacerbate it or, at best, do nothing to curb it. This risks the loss of a good share of the benefits of FDI for recipient developing countries.

It is doubtful whether the granting of fiscal incentives does in fact attract additional foreign investment. However, countries that do not enter the contest are in danger of losing investment to other competing countries with similar locational advantages which do grant incentives. The end result is, probably, similar amounts of FDI in the aggregate and distributed more or less the same way as before the incentive war, but with sizeable transfers of resources from governments of poor countries to rich TNCs. Therefore, a balanced agreement on investment cannot fail to include the issue of incentives.

There is another aspect of the granting of incentives that is relevant to this discussion. While something must be done to curb the incentive war, developing countries need to retain the right to grant companies subsidies oriented toward the correction of market failures. In fact, both performance requirements placed on TNCs in the past and a certain variety of incentives granted to them (usually in conjunction with performance requirements) can be justified as (not always successful) attempts to correct for market failures.

These market failures occur in a few dimensions that are crucial to the development impact of investments. There is general agreement that subsidies to innovation are justified tools of development policy. In some cases, it may be entirely appropriate for a host country government to grant subsidies related to the R&D activities of a TNC, since they may involve the training of local technicians and engineers and this can have significant spillover effects on the domestic economy.

Some TNCs possess technological assets that are particularly attractive to host developing countries. However, FDI tends to flow to sectors with *current* locational advantages, not to those where the host country may have *potential future* locational advantages. Thus the attraction of specific TNCs with specific technological assets may be part and parcel of a development policy oriented toward the acquisition of comparative advantages. There is no reason why countries should foreclose this possibility.

The same argument can be made for other assets that specific TNCs may have. Examples are access to markets, product design, brand names, training of labour and management skills.

How is this issue to be handled? It would seem that the best way is to enable countries to practise these forms of development policy as long as it is done on a NT and MFN basis. In other words, if a market-failure-correcting incentive is available to a foreign firm, it should be multilateralized to firms from all home countries having the desired characteristics or performing the desired actions. The incentives should also be available to national firms meeting the specified requirements.

The draft MAI fails to incorporate any restriction or norms concerning the obligations of investors, be it with regard to restrictive business practices, transfer pricing, working conditions, environment, observance of national laws, or contribution to development. To be sure, these are sometimes difficult to make operational and are often captured by special interest groups. For example, the issue of environmental and social dumping or lack of regulations in these areas in developing countries have been often used as an excuse for the imposition of discriminatory trade restrictions against the exports of developing countries. However, the failure of the MAI to deal with these issues is conspicuous and reflects the fact that its drafters are more sensitive to the interests and needs of TNCs than to those of recipient developing countries.

The OECD's position in these matters is that obligations of investors are issues for national legislation, which ought to be applied to domestic as well as to foreign investors. On the face of it, this might seem an appropriate approach. However, in the absence of minimum standards, the lowest common denominator will prevail, as national governments in developing countries compete with each other to attract FDI. This is a clear case of putting host developing countries in a prisoner's dilemma, in which a race to the bottom will be almost unavoidable. Countries with high standards will tend to lose FDI to countries with low or no standards.

In the past, countries attempted to grapple with the problems posed by restrictive business practices through regulations and the imposition of performance requirements. Restrictions placed by parent TNCs on domestic users (including their own subsidiaries) of their licenses were tackled by regulations on what technology contracts could contain. Export restrictions on affiliates were dealt with by imposing export requirements (now banned). While the use of regulations and performance requirements was not always well conceived and often led to perverse results, the restrictions the MAI would impose on host governments in these areas, coupled with the absence of any restraints on companies, place developing host countries at a severe disadvantage.

An aspect of the draft MAI that may prove to be problematic for developing countries (in particular, the smaller ones that are in a weak bargaining position vis-à-vis powerful companies) is the provisions giving firms the right to sue a government allegedly in breach of its commitments under the MAI. Most international treaties are intergovernmental and leave it up to the governments of the parties to sort out their disputes. These provisions do nothing but reinforce the view that the draft MAI is indeed an unbalanced document which places all obligations on host governments and none on firms.

Thus the draft MAI responds to the interests and needs of TNCs and other multinational investors such as investment banks, large commercial banks and pension funds. Why should developing countries have any interest in it? For purely defensive reasons. Collectively, it is not in the advantage of developing countries to sign the agreement. However, individual countries may be tempted to "free ride" on the collective interest and may sign the agreement as a way of obtaining advantages in the attraction of investment. To the extent that a large enough number of countries acts in this manner, even countries that are extremely reluctant to sign will have no option but to do so, in order not to lose out on the competition for attracting FDI. Therefore, it is important that developing countries, in spite of their heterogeneity, develop a joint position and co-ordinate their actions closely with regard to an investment agreement.

The discussion on investment is unavoidable, given the pressures from the developed countries to include investment in the trade agenda and the importance that FDI and capital flows have acquired on the international economic scene. However, for developing countries, the OECD is not an appropriate forum, simply because they are not members and cannot have their needs and interests taken into account in the formulation of the new disciplines on investment. Therefore, they should strongly resist pressures to sign the OECD agreement and should seek to move the discussions to the WTO, where they are represented and where their voice can be fully heard. An instrument emerging from the WTO would apply largely to FDI, since other flows are already covered by the WTO Agreement on Financial

Services. Second, an instrument negotiated at the WTO can take into account more fully the interests of host developing countries. Third, an agreement reached under the auspices of WTO would apply to the entire membership and, therefore, individual countries would not be pressured into signing in order not to lose potential investors. Finally, a WTO instrument would be consistent with other WTO treaties, in particular the Agreement on Financial Services.

B.   WTO disciplines on investment

The WTO already incorporates some disciplines on investment issues. These relate to FDI in services and certain performance requirements that are prohibited under the TRIMs Agreement. In addition, on issues regarding intellectual property rights there has already been agreement at the multilateral level in the Agreement on Trade-Related Aspects of Intellectual Property Rights (TRIPs).

In the area of services, the GATS covers the supply of markets through foreign service suppliers. Some general principles (transparency and, subject to a once-off list of temporary derogations, MFN treatment) are applicable to all service industries. Market-access (in other words, NT at the pre-investment level for services transactions requiring FDI) and NT obligations depend on specific commitments contained in national schedules, which are to be progressively enlarged in coverage and depth in future negotiations. This is an attractive principle for an investment agreement in general. It works basically on the principle of a positive list ("only what is specified is liberalized, and in the manner specified"), rather than the negative list principle of the MAI ("everything is liberalized, with the exception of what is specifically excluded"). At the very least, countries ought to reserve the right of not offering a blanket liberalization at the pre-investment level.

Certain performance requirements are prohibited under the TRIMs Agreement, which deals with investment measures related to trade in goods. It forbids performance requirements inconsistent with Articles III (National Treatment) and XI (General Elimination of Quantitative Restrictions) of the General Agreement on Tariffs and Trade (GATT), including both mandatory restrictions and those linked with incentives. Although they are not the only ones, the forbidden performance requirements include local content, trade-balancing, and export requirements (Low and Subramanian, 1995; Agosin et al., 1996). In principle, there are a large number of acceptable performance requirements for those countries that wish to avail themselves of this tool of development policy, as long as GATT principles are observed.

The WTO has held preliminary discussions to begin negotiations toward the adoption of a Multi-lateral Framework on Investment (MFI). UNCTAD has also been holding informal expert group meetings and has launched a series of working papers on the subject. Although the negotiations have not yet got off the ground, it would seem appropriate for developing countries to seek to move the discussions from the OECD to WTO, or at the very least, to refuse to sign any agreement that emerges from OECD, on the grounds that they have not participated in its drafting.

III. Agreements having a bearing on capital flows

Undoubtedly, if approved and if developing countries were to sign it, the MAI would have large consequences for their ability to manage the capital account of the balance of payments. But even in the absence of a MAI, other agreements already signed or under discussion would have some of the same effects as the MAI in this regard. Here two inter-national instruments are discussed, one already in effect (the WTO Financial Services Agreement) and the efforts underway at the IMF to extend its jurisdiction from current to capital-account trans-actions ("capital-account convertibility").

A. The WTO Agreement on Financial Services

The WTO Agreement on Financial Services[7] was adopted in December 1997, after two years of negotiation. Because of failure of the United States to ratify the MFN clause for financial services, commitments made under the GATS in the area of financial services at the close of the Uruguay Round were temporary and due to expire at the end of 1997.

As already noted, the only two general prin-ciples of the GATS are transparency (requirement under which each member is obligated to reveal in a timely and complete fashion all measures that affect trade in services) and MFN treatment. The approach to market access (Article XVI) and NT (Article XVII) is for countries to include commitments in the sched-ules of liberalization by mode of service delivery. With regard to market access, unless a country specifies it in its schedule for each mode of delivery, certain categories of measures are expressly pro-hibited. These are limitations on:

- the number of suppliers;[8]

- the value of transactions or assets;

- the number of natural persons that may provide a service;

- the number of service operations or on the quality of service output;

- the type of legal entity through which a service can be supplied; and

- the size or share of the foreign capital interest.

The GATS recognizes four modes of delivery – cross-border transactions, establishment of market presence, movement of consumers to foreign markets, and cross-border movements of natural persons supplying services. These apply to financial services, for which the most relevant are cross-border trans-actions (as when a domestic bank borrows from a bank located in another country) and establishment of market presence through FDI.

Perhaps a couple of examples might be useful to illustrate the way the financial services agreement operates in practice. A country may explicitly grant market access to cross-border lending, in which case it may not impose restrictions on loans from foreign banks to national firms or banks. Similarly, a country may have committed itself to NT for foreign banks through market presence (the establishment of branches or subsidiaries). In this case it must treat the foreign bank in the same manner as it treats national banks in all aspects.

Under the agreement reached in December 1997, most countries made at most limited changes in their commitments, but the negotiations resulted in substantial additional liberalizations in some major cases. These countries include the European Union, Canada, Japan, and the Republic of Korea (for details, see Cornford and Brandon, in this volume).

Besides this positive-list approach, there are several other aspects of the WTO Agreement on Financial Services which provide space for policy intervention under certain circumstances. For example, there is latitude in the GATS for policies that may be needed in response to balance-of-payments crises (Article XII), to preserve the integrity and stability of the financial system (under the Annex on Financial Services), and to protect the financial sector from excessive competition on the part of foreign firms (under Article XVI and XVII) by inclusion of limitations regarding market access and NT in the schedule of commitments. Nothing in the Agreement limits a country's right to place prudential regulations on its banks, even though these regulations may formally violate NT. An example of such regulations is limiting the foreign borrowing of banks to the assets they can place with customers that earn foreign currency (in order to lessen exchange-rate risk). Government action in response to a banking crisis may include lender-of-last-resort operations, in which case governments retain considerable discretion as to the type, scale, and distribution of support they provide. However, it is not clear to what extent governments can discriminate between domestic and foreign firms.

With regard to the link between commitments to liberalize capital movements and financial services negotiations, it is clear that, under Article XVI of the GATS, *if a country makes a commitment* to grant market access with respect to cross-border transactions of which cross-border movements of capital are an essential aspect, then the country is committed to allow such movements. This is the case with bank lending and asset management services. In the case of the latter, granting market access to cross-border transactions in effect implies liberalizing portfolio inflows and outflows. But what is interesting about the GATS approach is that countries *need not make such commitments*. It is up to each country to decide whether they are prepared to enter into a specific commitment.

The appropriateness of liberalizing cross-border transactions in financial services such as banking services and portfolio flows will depend on the strength of banking regulations, the depth of domestic foreign exchange markets, and the strength of domestic firms producing tradable goods. Liberalizing access to foreign borrowing entails the introduction of new kinds of risk, including the risk of mismatches between assets and liabilities denominated in foreign currency. If banking supervision is weak, those enhanced risks could easily lead to a combination of foreign-exchange and banking crises, as evidenced by the Mexican crisis of December 1994 and the current Asian crisis. If domestic currency

and financial markets are shallow, liberalized cross-border financial transactions could provoke excessive exchange-rate and interest-rate fluctuations. If domestic firms are weak, such fluctuations could have very adverse effects on them and on the economy as a whole. Japanese or United States firms, say, can adapt rapidly to exchange-rate fluctuations by, for example, outsourcing or moving production facilities abroad, but for the generally much weaker firms in most developing countries such fluctuations can be devastating. They can bring to an untimely end their efforts to penetrate foreign markets or cause them to succumb to competition from imports.[9]

B.   The proposed amendment to the IMF's Articles of Agreement

In its meeting of 28 April 1997, the Interim Committee of the IMF "agreed that the Fund's Articles should be amended to make the promotion of capital-account liberalization a specific purpose of the Fund and to give the Fund appropriate jurisdiction over capital movements" (cited by Polak, 1998). At the Fund's annual meetings in Hong Kong, China, in September 1997, the Fund's Board of Directors endorsed this agreement and included it in its Hong Kong Declaration. The Fund is to assist countries in achieving an orderly and prudent liberalization of capital movements.

If implemented, this amendment would imply an enlarged role for the IMF. Up to now, the Fund has had formal jurisdiction over its members' current account, but it has not attempted to obligate recalcitrant countries to abandon restrictions, relying instead on disseminating "best-practice" policies in other countries and on technical assistance (Polak, 1998). Even though many developing countries have not formally accepted Article VIII (which commits them to current-account convertibility), most of them are de facto practising it. Polak (1998) argues that the Fund should follow a similar approach with regard to capital-account convertibility. If it attempts to force countries to open their capital accounts (to outward and inward flows), it might well fall into jurisdictional conflicts with other international agreements. As discussed above, the WTO Agreement on Financial Services allows countries to maintain restrictions on financial inflows and outflow unless they have explicitly liberalized them.

But beyond the issue of jurisdictional conflict, should the IMF insist that countries liberalize their capital account in all cases? It could do so, for example, by adding capital-account liberalization to the conditionality attached to the use of Fund resources, as it has already done in the case of the Korean bailout. From what has already been said above, the answer is "no". The Asian crisis, and before it the Mexican crisis, has revealed that the desirability of free capital movements is far from being a proven proposition.

While there are certain advantages to capital-account openness that have been well rehearsed in the literature[10], there are also costs. In developing country contexts, these are related to the volatility and unpredictability of certain types of capital flows, which tend to be excessive in certain circumstances and to dry up completely and even go into reverse in others. This leads to sharp swings in real exchange rates and to macroeconomic instability, both of which have adverse effects on outward-oriented development strategies. In fact, even current Fund practice seems to accept that temporary disincentives to short-term capital inflows, in the presence of very large supplies of foreign capital, can be beneficial to developing countries (Helleiner, 1997, p. 18; and Dornbusch, 1997, p. 32).

Most capital flows have a large degree of exogeneity from the point of view of recipient countries. In addition, portfolio flows and short-term lending tend to exhibit herd-like behaviour: when foreign portfolio investors wish to take positions in a country's assets (and international banks are desirous to lend to it), the amounts of foreign capital on offer to that country can be extremely large. In fact, given the contagion effects that are rampant in international financial markets, an "emerging market" country can see its foreign capital inflows swell simply because other countries are receiving large amounts of foreign capital. If the capital account is opened up indiscriminately, a country can suddenly experience very sharp capital inflows that are by nature reversible.

In fact, the inflows themselves sow the seeds of their subsequent reversal. Regardless of the policies pursued to deal with them, large inflows are bound to cause real exchange-rate appreciations, leading to large current-account deficits.[11] Both of these phenomena at some point scare off the foreign capital needed to finance the enlarged deficit and eventually lead to a stampede of investors to leave the country. This pattern, although not the detailed causes, has been identical in the case of the Mexican crisis of late 1994 and of the longer-lived Asian financial crises.

Thus, avoidance of real exchange-rate volatility and financial crisis seems to require the use of measures to discourage excessive, highly-liquid financial flows. Some observers have questioned the effectiveness of such measures in the long run, claiming that, in a highly globalized economy characterized by rapid financial innovation, agents eventually find ways to evade controls (Corbo and Hernández, 1996; Valdés-Prieto and Soto, 1997). However, there is strong evidence that reserve requirements on short-term and portfolio capital inflows in Chile and Colombia (which act essentially as a tax on short-term inflows) have succeeded for considerable periods of time in changing the composition of inflows toward long-term flows, or reducing the magnitude of inflows, or both (Agosin and Ffrench-Davis, 1996 and 1997; Larraín et al., 1997; Barrera and Cárdenas, 1997; Le Fort and Budnevich, 1997).

It has been argued that FDI itself can lead to greater volatility of the capital account, suggesting that policies toward FDI ought to take into account this adverse effect of TNC activities. TNCs are by nature international, and a large share of their profits are often derived from international financial transactions. TNCs have much greater opportunities and ability to move funds in and out of host countries than national companies and, "FDI can therefore be associated with higher, rather than lower, variability in capital flow ..." (Helleiner, 1997, p. 11). However, there is no reason to give better than national treatment to TNCs in this regard. Presumably, the finance departments of TNC affiliates would be as much subject to the disincentives or controls on short-term capital movements as any other domestic agent.

Another line of attack against the use of disincentives to, or controls on, short-term capital inflows has been to claim that, as regards their behaviour, it is impossible to distinguish between capital inflows such as FDI or long-term lending, on the one hand, and short-term flows, on the other. Claessens et al. (1995) claim that balance-of-payments categories have little to do with the stability of flows themselves, long-term flows being just as likely to be unstable as short-term flows. Part of the explanation for their result that FDI is just as likely to be volatile as short-term flows may stem from the fact that, for the countries that they chose, FDI flows are a very small percentage of total foreign financing, at least as reported by IMF statistics (which, by the way, sometimes seriously underestimate FDI). Fluctuations of small numbers tend to be larger than fluctuations of large ones. In the case of Chile, FDI flows, which have accounted for almost two thirds of total inflows in the 1990s, have been considerably more stable than either portfolio inflows or short-term credits (Agosin and Ffrench-Davis, 1997, p. 314).

Automatic and price-based disincentives are likely to be less distorting, more effective, and less prone to evasion or corruption than outright controls. Dornbusch (1997) argues in favour of a small tax on all cross-border payments, a sort of single-country Tobin tax.[12] A small tax on all transactions makes flows with short horizons particularly onerous and has no effect on long-term flows. The tax approach also has the advantage of flexibility, in that the tax rate can be adjusted upward or downward according to circumstances. The Chilean scheme of reserve requirements – and to a somewhat lesser extent, the Colombian system – functions in fact as such a tax.

Some observers argue that stronger bank supervision and regulation is enough to prevent the instability associated with recent episodes of international capital movements.[13] According to this view, countries would only need to reform their banking system before proceeding with full capital-account liberalization. However, a significant share of capital flows is not intermediated through the banking system. Many bank loans are arranged directly between large domestic firms (or even their foreign affiliates, as in the case of the Republic of Korea) and the international banks. In addition, unregulated portfolio flows are prone to pose particularly severe problems which are completely unrelated to the adequacy of banking regulations. Foreign portfolio investors tend to over-invest in the assets of emerging markets, only to head for the exits when their collective perceptions about those assets turn sour. Thus, flexible and non-dogmatic policies toward the capital account will remain essential, even after banking reform.

IV. Conclusion

Undoubtedly, controls on international capital movements introduce distortions and inflict microeconomic costs on countries applying them. However, such controls may be necessary in order to avert large macroeconomic costs in countries that are not ready to adopt full capital-account convertibility. Therefore, flexibility with regard to the capital account is superior to blanket liberalization. That is the reason developing countries should urge maximum understanding and flexibility on the part of the IMF in dealing with the issue. From the point of view

of developing countries, the worst outcome would be for capital-account convertibility to become another item in the list of conditions attached to the use of Fund resources.

It is also a reason for not signing on to the MAI (if it is ever approved by the OECD membership). Doing so will mean losing all control on capital-account transactions. As argued in this paper, this would have seriously adverse consequences on development, as it will leave developing countries without any defences with which to face increasingly volatile portfolio and short-term flows.

The MAI has other drawbacks for developing countries. Besides preventing countries from practising any kind of selectivity with regard to FDI, it places obligations only on host countries and none on investors. In particular, it is silent on complex issues such as abusive transfer pricing and restrictive business practices, it bans the use of performance requirements and has little to say on the issue of incentives. The interests of developing countries would be best served by moving the discussions on a multilateral investment treaty from OECD to the WTO, where they have a say in shaping any new international treaty. A new set of disciplines on investment negotiated under the auspices of the WTO would apply basically to FDI and would follow the pattern of the GATS (and the Agreement on Financial Services), which is more appropriate to tailoring liberalization to the needs of individual countries.

Notes

1   The term "prudential", which is borrowed from banking regulation and supervision, is not usually associated with international capital flows. However, given the volatility of certain kinds of capital flows and the widespread contagion effects that have recently become evident, national controls on international capital movements do, in fact, acquire a prudential nature. For a similar view, see M. Wolf, "The Last Resort", *Financial Times*, 23 September 1998, p. 16. The use of capital controls and disincentives for the purpose of improving the effectiveness of macroeconomic management, banking supervision and regulation, and corporate governance is discussed at length in UNCTAD (1998, pp. 101-105).

2   Avowedly, with the development of domestic stock markets in host countries and the growth of international mergers and acquisitions, the distinction between direct and portfolio investment is becoming more ambiguous.

3   Large TNCs have the resources and legal staff to deal with this problem.

4   These expressions are those of Ganesan, in this volume.

5   OECD (1998, p. 21). On this latter provision there is not full agreement as of yet.

6 The latter two are, of course, already prohibited by the TRIMs Agreement in the WTO.

7 For an in-depth analysis of this instrument, see the paper by Cornford and Brandon in this volume, as well as Brandon (1998) and Kono et al. (1997).

8 Nonetheless, these are explicitly considered acceptable in the case of the establishment of foreign banks, in order to prevent the problem of over-banking.

9 Following the liberalization of foreign bank lending in Chile in the late 1980s, sharp and quick real exchange-rate appreciation led to a decline of 5 percentage points in the share of manufacturing in GDP and caused a serious setback in the drive to diversify exports (see French-Davis et al., 1993; and Agosin, 1997).

10 These include access to cheaper sources of finance for investment, portfolio diversification for domestic savers, the decoupling of the time profiles of foreign exchange earnings and expenditures, the spreading over time of adjustment to foreign exchange shocks. For a discussion, see Devlin et al. (1996).

11 In principle, it is possible to fend off real appreciation through sterilized intervention in foreign exchange markets. In practice, however, no country faced with a foreign capital surge has been able to do so, even using sterilized intervention.

12 For a full discussion of the Tobin tax, see ul Haq et al. (1996).

13 This view is explicitly put forward in IMF (1995). It is implicit in arguments such as Krugman's (1998) that the Asian crisis is due mainly to the moral hazard problems arising from poor banking supervision and regulation, in conjunction with implicit government guarantees on deposits.

References

AGOSIN, M.R. (1997), "Export Performance in Chile: Lessons for Africa", *WIDER Working Paper,* No. 144 (Helsinki: World Institute for Development Economics Research/ United Nations University), October.

AGOSIN, M.R., and R. FFRENCH-DAVIS (1996), "Managing Capital Inflows in Latin America", in M. ul Haq, I. Kaul and I. Grunberg (eds.), *The Tobin Tax: Coping with Financial Volatility* (New York and Oxford: Oxford University Press).

AGOSIN, M.R., and R. FFRENCH-DAVIS (1997), "Managing Capital Inflow in Chile", *Estudios de Economía,* Vol. 24, pp. 297-326.

AGOSIN, M.R., D. TUSSIE, and G. CRESPI (1995), "Developing Countries and the Uruguay Round: An Evaluation and Issues for the Future", in UNCTAD, *International Monetary and Financial Issues for the 1990s,* Vol. VI (New York and Geneva: United Nations Publication, sales no. E.95.II.D.7).

BARRERA, F., and M. CÁRDENAS (1997), "On the Effectiveness of Capital Controls: The Experience of Colombia During the 1990s", *Journal of Development Economics,* Vol. 54, pp. 27-57.

BRANDON, J. (1998), "The WTO Financial Services Agreement – Characterizing the Results", Studies on International Monetary and Financial Issues for the Group of Twenty-Four, G-24/98/5, Washington, D.C., April.

BRUTON, H. (1989), "Import Substitution, in H. Chenery and T. N. Srinivasan (eds.), *Handbook of Development Economics,* Vol. II (Amsterdam: North Holland).

CLAESSENS, S, M.P. DOOLEY, and A. WARNER (1995), "Portfolio Capital Flows: Hot or Cold ?", *World Bank Economic Review,* Vol. 9, pp. 153-174.

CORBO, V., and L HERNÁNDEZ (1996), "Macroeconomic Adjustment to Capital Inflows: Lessons from Recent Latin American and East Asian Experience", *World Bank Research Observer,* Vol. 11, pp. 61-85.

CORNFORD, A., and J. BRANDON (1999), "The WTO Agreement on Financial Services: Problems of Financial Globalization in Practice", in UNCTAD, *International Monetary and Financial Issues for the 1990s,* Vol. X (New York and Geneva: United Nations).

CORREA, C. M. (1999), "Key Issues for Developing Countries in a Possible Multilateral Agreement on Investment", in UNCTAD, *International Monetary and Financial Issues for the 1990s,* Vol. X (New York and Geneva: United Nations).

DEVLIN, R., R. FFRENCH-DAVIS, and S. GRIFFITH-JONES (1996), "Surges in Capital Flows and Development: An Overview of Policy Issues", in R. Ffrench-Davis and S. Griffith-Jones, *Coping with Capital Surges* (Boulder, CO.: Lynne Rienner; and Ottawa: International Development Research Centre).

DORNBUSCH, R. (1997), "Cross Border Payments Taxes and Alternative Capital-Account Regimes", in UNCTAD, *International Monetary and Financial Issues for the 1990s,* Vol. VIII (New York and Geneva: United Nations Publication, sales no. E.97.II.D.5).

DUNNING, J.H. (1993), *Multinational Enterprises and the Global Economy* (London: Addison-Wesley).

FFRENCH-DAVIS, R., P. LEIVA, and R. MADRID (1993), "Trade Liberalization and Growth: The Chilean Experience, 1973-89", in M. R. Agosin and D. Tussie (eds.), *Trade and Growth: New Dilemmas in Trade Policy* (London: Macmillan).

GANESAN, A.V. (1999), "Strategic Options Available to Developing Countries with Regard to a Multilateral Agreement on Investment", in UNCTAD, *International Monetary and Financial Issues for the 1990s,* Vol. X (New York and Geneva: United Nations).

HELLEINER, G.K. (1989), "Transnational Corporations and Direct Foreign Investment", in H. Chenery and T.N. Srinivasan (eds.), *Handbook of Development Economics,* Vol. II (Amsterdam: North Holland).

HELLEINER, G.K. (1997), "Capital Account Regimes and the Developing Countries", in UNCTAD, *International Monetary and Financial Issues for the 1990s,* Vol. VIII (New York and Geneva: United Nations Publication, sales no. E.97.II.D.5).

IMF (1995), "Capital Account Convertibility, Review of Experiences and Implications for IMF Policies", *IMF Occasional Paper* No. 131 (Washington, D.C.), October.

KONO, M., P. LOW, M. LUANGA, A. MATOO, M. OSHIKAWA, and L. SCHUKNECHT (1997), *Opening Markets for Financial Services and the Role of the GATS* (Geneva: World Trade Organization).

KRUGMAN, P. (1998), "What Happened to Asia?", at http:// web.mit.edu/krugman/www/DISINTER/html.

LARRAÍN, F.R. LABÁN, and R. CHUMACERO (1997), "What Determines Capital Inflows? An Empirical Analysis for Chile", *Faculty Research Working Paper,* No. R97-18 (Cambridge, MA.: John F. Kennedy School of Government, Harvard University), April.

LE FORT, G., and C. BUDNEVICH (1997), "Capital-Account Regulations and Macroeconomic Policies: Two Latin American Experiences", in UNCTAD, *International Monetary and Financial Issues for the 1990s,* Vol. VIII

(New York and Geneva: United Nations Publication, sales no. E.97.II.D.5).

LOW, P., and A. SUBRAMANIAN (1995), "TRIMs in the Uruguay Round: An Unfinished Business?", paper presented at a World Bank Conference, 26-27 January 1995.

OECD (1998), *The MAI Negotiating Text* (as of 24 April 1998) mimeo, Paris.

POLAK, J.J. (1998), "The Articles of Agreement of the IMF and the Liberalization of Capital Movements", mimeo, Washington, D.C.

UL HAQ, M, I. KAUL, and I. GRUNBERG (eds.) (1996), *The Tobin Tax: Coping with Financial Volatility* (New York and Oxford: Oxford University Press).

UNCTAD (1997), *World Investment Report 1997* (New York and Geneva: United Nations Publication, sales no. E.97.II.D.10).

UNCTAD (1998), *Trade and Development Report, 1998* (New York and Geneva: United Nations Publication, sales no. E.98.II.D.6).

VALDÉS-PRIETO, S. and M. SOTO (1996), "New Selective Capital Controls in Chile: Are They Effective?", mimeo, Pontificia Universidad Católica de Chile, Santiago de Chile.

BANKING SUPERVISION IN DEVELOPING ECONOMIES

Christian Larraín*

Abstract

This paper seeks to assess the primary influences upon financial instability and banking oversight in developing economies, focusing on the microeconomic elements associated with both the quality of institutional management and deficiencies in monitoring within the market itself, as well as on institutional weaknesses in regulation and supervision. Six key characteristics that determine the weaknesses of developing economies' financial systems are examined: precarious public institutions; a lack of tradition in market operations and the excessive weight of public ownership in financial institutions; inappropriate accounting and portfolio classification systems; a high concentration of ownership in financial and goods markets; an expensive and inefficient financial system; and lack of international diversification in banking portfolios. Counter-measures in all these fields are proposed. First-generation reforms are essentially the opening of the financial system to foreign institutions, and the strengthening of prudential supervision. Second-generation reforms are in three areas: international diversification of the banking portfolio; regulation of financial conglomerates; and evaluation of the quality of bank management.

* The author thanks Gerry Helleiner and Guillermo Ramírez for helpful comments on an earlier draft.

I. Introduction

Any serious examination of the problems of supervising the banking industry in developing economies leads to the question of whether there are specific aspects of those economies that result in the need for an ad hoc regulatory and supervisory framework.

The response to this question is less than evident, particularly since banking crises are not restricted to the developing world. In fact, they have hit hard and often in developed nations as well, as demonstrated by the Savings and Loan scandals in the United States in the 1980s and a protracted period of financial instability associated with real estate loans in Japan that refuses to fade away. To one extent or another, the problems associated with credit exposure are a disconcerting common denominator in all of the world's banking crises.

Furthermore, one must legitimately ask whether a paradigm exists to classify an economy as "developing". In fact, the economic and financial literature has coined the concept of the "emerging economy" to refer to a group of some 20 to 30 economies that have recently experienced strong, consistent processes of economic reform combined with high, sustained rates of growth. These include such economies as Brazil, Chile, China, India, the Republic of Korea and Taiwan Province of China. It is difficult to compare the features of the financial systems in emerging economies such as Hong Kong (China) and Singapore – with their well-consolidated, highly competitive structures – with those of such developing economies as Honduras, Paraguay or Nigeria.

In that sense, there are a number of factors at the level of both market operations and public institutions that tend to be present to a varying extent in non-developed economies (emerging and developing) and that are unique to them. There is an abundant specialized literature on the problems of supervision in those economies, including the volatility of their markets, institutional weaknesses, inappropriate accounting standards, and errors in the design of financial liberalization programmes that have led to lending booms.

It would be beyond the scope of this paper to describe in depth the set of weaknesses that charac-

terize the operation of financial systems and supervision in emerging markets. Furthermore, a series of recent publications by the Bank for International Settlements (BIS), the International Monetary Fund (IMF) and the Inter-American Development Bank (IDB) have addressed the topic in detail (see BIS/ IMF, 1997; Goldstein and Turner, 1996), focusing on the problems stemming from the macroeconomic environment (for example, Gavin and Hausman, 1996), those born of the weaknesses in bank management (De Juan, 1996), as well as the issues involved in deficiencies in quality supervision.

This paper seeks to assess the primary factors behind financial instability and banking oversight in developing economies.[1] While recognizing the macroeconomic origin of many of the problems that affect the banking system in developing economies, this study focuses on the microeconomic elements associated with the quality of institutional management and with the deficiencies in monitoring effected by the market itself, as well as on those factors associated with institutional weaknesses characterizing regulation and oversight in these economies. In general, the aspects analysed here correspond to those that are directly or indirectly influenced by the regulatory framework and/or oversight practices.

The hypothesis proposed is that while there may be specific factors in the operation of financial markets that give rise to unique problems of supervision in developing economies, the institutional strength of regulatory agencies and the challenges posed to supervision will be of a different nature and scope depending on whether the reforms are "first" or "second generation".

Section II of this paper provides a description of the financial markets and the weaknesses in oversight in developing economies, understood in the broadest sense. Section III makes policy recommendations designed to strengthen supervision in those economies, distinguishing between first- and second-generation reforms. The former are primarily applied in recently privatized financial systems that are unsophisticated and where oversight is extremely precarious. Second-generation reforms are to be implemented in those cases of more developed and consolidated banking systems that, to a certain extent, have already moved along the learning curve in the operation of financial markets.

II. Problems of supervision in developing economies

The primary weaknesses of financial systems in developing economies are the following:

- precarious public institutions;

- a lack of tradition in market operations and an excessive weight of public ownership in financial institutions;

- inappropriate accounting and portfolio classification systems;

- a high concentration of ownership in financial and goods markets;

- an expensive and inefficient financial system;

- a lack of international diversification in banking portfolios.

These elements give rise to a series of problems that affect the stability of markets and weaken the quality of the oversight provided. These problems include high credit risk, continuous operations among related parties, a lack of market support for institutional monitoring, and inappropriate criteria for the entry and exit of financial institutions.

Obviously, in applying these stylized facts to specific economies, the relative bearing of each element will differ. For example, one can expect that in the most backward economies the most pressing problems will relate to basic asset supervision and related-party lending. In emerging economies with more consolidated financial systems it is likely that one of the most significant challenges will be posed by the lack of international diversification in the portfolio. For the more backward economies, given the precariousness of regulatory agencies, it is likely that the internationalization of their loans would bring more costs than benefits. These distinctions are significant when recommending policy. Despite their importance, these aspects are very often overlooked during analysis.

A. Precarious public institutions

The way in which faltering institutions are handled when they are on the verge of collapse has major implications for the long-term soundness and viability of deposit insurance and for the stability of the banking system as a whole.

As banks approach the breaking point of insolvency, they have less and less to lose if they adopt an aggressive strategy involving high risk loans in an attempt to put themselves back on a profitable footing. Supervision is therefore a powerful tool for controlling the negative incentives that influence undercapitalized banks.

Generally speaking, a supervisory agency's ability to take early and effective corrective action will depend on three factors (United States Department of the Treasury, 1991). First, it must be able to identify potential problems before they result in a loss that must be covered by deposit insurance. Second, once the problem has been identified, the supervisor must have the authority to impose corrective measures or to prevent the situation from deteriorating further. Third, once it has identified the problem and has the necessary regulatory powers, the agency must not hesitate to use its authority as appropriate.

Perhaps one of the most decisive features of the weaknesses in supervision in developing economies is the precariousness of their institutions. This problem is manifest at the three levels noted above: insufficient qualifications among the staff of regulatory agencies to identify the risks taken by private institutions; insufficient authority to take corrective action once problems have been identified; incorrect incentives for the supervisory authorities, that often cause them to hesitate when taking measures in cases of potential bank insolvency (Larraín, 1994).

As noted by Corrigan (1996), the essential component of the process of banking supervision is the oversight that takes place on site with a sample of individual loans. It helps to determine the current and future status of those loans and thus their potential for timely repayment. Such a review requires a high level of sophistication on the part of banking inspectors. This task is perhaps the weakest link in the supervision chain in developing economies, since without clarity on the future prospects of loans it is impossible to assess correctly a bank's condition.

These insufficiencies are to be found not so much at the level of senior officials at these institutions, but rather among those charged with field inspections and/or desk supervision. The causes for this phenomenon are varied, yet it is important to highlight the big gap in income between supervisory agency staff and equivalent positions in private industry. As a result, it is often quite difficult to acquire and retain sufficiently experienced and qualified staff. Since professionals with the required skills are quite often not available in the labour market, supervisory agencies are forced to resort mostly to in-house training.

Furthermore, the ability of these agencies to identify losses is of limited use unless they have sufficient power to enforce corrective action. Supervisors should have enough authority to impose sanctions if compliance with prudential regulations wanes. Depending on the institutions being supervised, such sanctions can include fines, dismissal from management posts in cases of imprudent practices, and restrictions on the activities that banks may undertake and – in extreme cases – liquidation (BIS/IMF, 1997).

This basic requirement is often not fully met in developing economies. The problem is that supervisory agencies are often given formal authority to take corrective measures with regard to faltering banks, but the administrative requirements as to the evidence they must gather in order to do so are so exacting that it is extremely difficult for them to compel a bank that is operating within the law and making a profit to increase its capital reserves or apply more prudent policies in specific areas.

The third requirement for prudential supervision is for supervisory agencies to act decisively in using their authority. There is a danger that the political and legal context will encourage banking supervisors to delay the liquidation of an insolvent institution or the application of corrective measures (Kane, 1989; Benston and Kaufman, 1988). The cost of failing to take timely measures can be high. When exit policies are weak and unstable banks are allowed to compete with solid ones, the former have an incentive to survive in the short term by competing aggressively. Clearly, this can debilitate financially secure banks and increase the cost of the solutions eventually required (Lindgren, 1996).

This area is also highly problematic in developing economies. Given the greater involvement of the government in such economies and the scope of banking ties with industrial conglomerates, considerable pressure may be applied to banking supervisors to delay corrective measures. The imposition of liquidation or penalty on a banking operation may generate not only illegitimate protests from powerful lobbies but may also lead to suit being filed against the supervisor (Goldstein and Turner, 1996).

B. Lack of market tradition in financial operations

Quite clearly, the solvency of the banking system does not depend solely on the role played by public regulatory agencies. Rather, it needs to be buttressed by responsible actions on the part of the bank management, as well as by monitoring by shareholders and depositors. In other words, market discipline is essential.

Despite the processes of financial liberalization that began earlier, one feature of many developing economies is that this process has taken off only in the course of the 1990s. Given the novelty of these reform and liberalization processes, the financial systems have not had the benefit of experience[2] that allows them to perform their risk-assessment role properly. This is compounded by a traditionally strong presence of the public sector in the system and a lack of monitoring by depositors themselves to help discipline bank management.

The initial conditions for financial systems have been identified in the literature as a determinant factor in the success of liberalization processes (Caprio et al., 1993). A bank's net worth, the initial composition of its assets and liabilities, the quality of available information and human capital, and the incentive system, all reflect pre-existing controls that condition banks' response to reforms. When the system is devoid of qualified bankers and when the incentives guiding banking operations revolve around governmental directives, an abrupt shift towards liberalization could generate significant losses (ibid.).

Liberalization has typically been associated with excessive expansion in lending. Increased confidence stemming from the reforms can engender overly optimistic expectations about the future. Free of lending restrictions, banks respond to new demands for types of loans that previously had been subject to controls (mainly consumer and real estate loans). The banks have only limited experience in establishing prudent lending limits since the restrictions that previously had been in place barred them from the lending levels that have become attainable since liberalization. If all the banks attempt to do the same, price bubbles will emerge for assets. The deterioration in the quality of the loans will become apparent only when the bubble bursts as a result of a domestic or foreign shock (BIS, 1996).

Regarding the Asian crisis, the IMF attributes an important part of imprudent lending to the limited experience of financial institutions in the pricing and management of risk, lack of commercial orientation, poor corporate governance and lax internal controls (IMF, 1997).

Where the tradition of bank monitoring by depositors and shareholders is weak, managers have little incentive to temper their behaviour. Bad management of pre-crisis situations aggravates these negative incentives, since bank stockholders and large holders of bank liabilities have not always been forced to pay for their risk-taking practices. Government intervention can harm incentives for disciplined management, for example by creating expectations of rescues among owners and creditors of financial institutions. Such face-saving measures include weak exit policies for troubled institutions and overly generous last-resort lender policies. Rojas-Suárez and Weisbrod (1996) conclude that the failure to punish shareholders was a key factor in the weaknesses of banking restructuring in Latin America in the 1980s.

The real problem is that governmental support has been *de facto* rather than *de jure*, and that it has normally exceeded the level explicitly insured. In fact, most developing economies offer only partial and limited formal coverage of banking deposits. In this vein, as Goldstein and Turner (1996) indicate, the problem lies in the discretionary nature of governmental support in coming to the aid of large creditors and/or bank owners to an extent far beyond the previously agreed levels. The signal this offers creates higher moral hazard in the banking sector.

C. *Accounting standards and asset classification systems*

Independent of the level of development attained by an economy, a realistic assessment of bank assets and an appropriate estimate of income and expenditures constitute fundamental aspects in determining banks' financial soundness. If most of the assets are in fact loans, an evaluation of the quality of the portfolio is crucial to ascertaining a bank's financial status. Typically, when the loan classification system fails, profits are overvalued and realistic provisions cannot be established to confront current or future losses. Furthermore, accrual of interest on non-performing assets cannot be suspended since very often bank managers are anxious to conceal the true state of their portfolio (Folkerts-Landau and Lindgren, 1997).

This is one of the most problematic aspects of banking system operations in developing economies. While a large number of countries do have "formal" asset classification systems, the main shortcoming is in the implementation of the regulations.

The quality of available information is typically poor. De Juan (1996) suggests that *in situ* supervision is essential in Latin America, given the lack of reliable bank financial statements. To review systematically and efficiently the portfolio classification prepared by a financial institution, a key instrument may be computer-based informational support on which a sampling mechanism can be based (Ramírez, 1991). But developing economies frequently lack historical data bases containing financial statements, borrower data bases and risk controls, and also lack computer systems to apply and cross-check this information. All of these are vital to guiding the *in situ* supervision process and focusing on those aspects presenting the greatest potential weakness and risk.

These problems are compounded by the practice of "evergreening", which is also a recurring problem in developing economies. In many countries, accounting standards for classifying uncertain or non-recoverable assets are not strict enough to prevent the banks that make bad loans from making themselves look good by lending more money to troubled borrowers. Where loan classification depends solely on the status of prior payments – more than on an evaluation of the debtor's exposure and the value of the collateral – it will be easier for bankers and their clients to collude in disguising losses through a series of restructurings and interest capitalizations (Goldstein and Turner, 1996). Various studies (Gavin and Hausmann, 1996; Rojas-Suárez and Weisbrod, 1996) show that information on bad loans reported in bank financial statements was a poor indicator of the true financial condition of banks in Latin America in pre-crisis periods.

Another important aspect is the currency mismatch that often affects banking systems in emerging economies. Normally, there are significant interest rate differentials, with the domestic rates in the developing economies being more attractive. In this context, there is a strong temptation for financial institutions to borrow in foreign currency and lend in domestic currency (Goldstein and Turner, 1996). The incentive to borrow abroad in hard currency is also present for non-financial-sector debtors, although this option is usually open only to the largest borrowers. In this context, an abrupt devaluation will generate significant losses, as witnessed in Mexico in early 1995.

The problem is not resolved solely by having banks maintain balanced positions in foreign currency. If borrowers are indebted in dollars but unable to generate hard currency, a devaluation can make them insolvent. From the bank's perspective, the devaluation can create a serious problem in terms of credit exposure. This was a significant factor in the financial crisis in Chile during the early 1980s. In Thailand too, financial institutions were recently weakened by the impact of currency depreciation on customers with foreign-currency liabilities (IMF, 1997).

D. Loans to related parties and conglomerates

The high concentration that characterizes developing economies creates a series of distortions in market operations. First, beyond the potential for abuse and fraud, an obvious conflict of interest emerges when a bank lends to individuals or corporations that are related to the bank through ownership or management. Banks tend to be overly optimistic about loans to related companies (Stiglitz, 1993).

In developing economies, there tends to be a high concentration of property ownership and an unequal distribution of income. The presence of large financial conglomerates with assets in both the real and financial sectors of the economy is a typical feature of those economies. In most developed countries, by contrast, the ownership of banks tends to be diversified and perverse managerial incentives are lower: executives oppose concealed transfers of resources from the bank to a related company in which a bank partner participates because, even if legal, they would be seen as contrary to the interests of the other owners and endanger their individual reputation (Larraín, 1996).

Loans to related parties have contributed to bank insolvencies in Argentina, Chile, Indonesia and Thailand, among others (IMF, 1997). The problem is not the absence of limitations and legal statutes. In Latin America, in particular, legislation has moved forward to establish caps on this type of lending. Studies by the BIS show that in developing economies legal limits are often more stringent than in developed economies (BIS, 1996). The real problem lies again in the practical implementation.

This problem tends to emerge at two levels. The most obvious is the inability of regulators to identify

or "map" the economic groups that own the banks. Although this is an essential element in enforcing the limits, the supervisory agencies in an overwhelming majority of developing economies are unable to comply with this basic requirement. The other is that banks tend to "disguise" these loans by reaching agreements with other banks to create cross loans. In other words, bank X lends funds to companies related to bank Y and bank Y lends to companies related to bank X. Another traditional mechanism for concealing operations with related parties is through branches in tax havens, which in turn provide loans to the related companies in the domestic economy. The approach used in the law to define related parties seeks precisely to identify the company that controls the conglomerate and, through exacting definitions and external indicators, to determine what types of companies can be deemed to belong to that conglomerate. This system, apparently legal and perfect, has proven to be disingenuous in practice. When the precise components for determining affiliation are known, it is not difficult to imagine ways to evade the law. Unlike the experience in some other spheres, the evidence shows that discretionary power here may be preferable to strict rules.

The problems associated with these conglomerates go even further. In developing economies there are numerous "de facto financial conglomerates" with a presence both in the banking sector and in such financial activities as stock brokerage, insurance brokering and investment funds. This situation poses a threat to the bank since the bankruptcy or insolvency of one of the financial companies associated with it can render the bank itself insolvent. This will endanger the stability of the entire system of payments in the economy and cause a contraction in lending. The risk of contagion stems from the presence of common controlling elements in the banks and other financial institutions and/or the fact that they share a corporate image, the use of common infrastructure, shared client bases, etc. In other words, a system of financial conglomerates appears to be in operation, even though their scope in law and/or consolidated supervision mechanisms have yet to be defined.

Similarly, a non-regulated parent company that controls banks can acquire financial institutions abroad, including in poorly regulated locations, thereby generating a grey area for effective consolidated supervision (Larraín, 1997). In fact, several Latin American conglomerates have internationalized across the region through their shareholders. This generates a non-covered risk of contagion for the domestic financial system should those institutions encounter difficulties in their international activities. Similarly, investments have been made by these conglomerates in tax havens such as the Cayman Islands, where supervision is practically non-existent.

E. Wide intermediation margins

In an increasingly globalized world of financial markets, the long-term viability and stability of banks require that they remain competitive internationally. This in turn requires efficient banking systems capable of evolving within a framework of "reasonable" margins for intermediation. In this sense, a bank sustained on the basis of oligopolistic revenues (something that is inherent to protected environments) becomes more vulnerable when confronted with unexpected financial events or increased international competition (Lindgren, 1996).

Before the eruption of the current Asian crisis, inefficiencies in financial systems, stemming partly from insufficient competition, may also have contributed to the scale of capital inflows because the spreads between lending and deposit rates in domestic financial institutions were wide compared to those of the industrial countries and contributed to relatively high lending rates which, combined with exchange rate policies, encouraged borrowers to seek funds abroad (IMF, 1997).

A series of studies shows that intermediation margins in developing and emerging economies tend to be considerably higher than in developed nations. This is particularly true in Latin America. According to a BIS (1996) study, net interest margins in 1990-1994 were, on average, above 5 per cent in Latin America. In more consolidated financial markets this margin rarely exceeds 3 per cent. The same study suggests that higher margins do not necessarily result from higher exposure and/or inflation, but are more closely linked to high operating costs. It is not unusual for these costs to amount to over 5 per cent of assets in Latin America, as compared to less than 2 per cent in more consolidated markets such as Germany, Singapore or Hong Kong (China).

The main explanation for that inefficiency is that banks in developing economies operate in a context that does not favour competition. Rates of concentration and oligopolization tend to be very high – in most cases as a result of inappropriate criteria regulating entry rather than as response to structural conditions. According to BIS data, banking concentration – measured as the market share of the five largest banks – was over 55 per cent in Brazil, Chile, Mexico and Venezuela, as compared to less than 40 per cent in Hong Kong (China) and Singapore, and less than 15 per cent in Germany and the United States (BIS, 1996). Regulations of market entry have often been used in a discretionary manner to discourage competition from foreign institutions. This has also had a negative impact on the transfer of technology and know-how.

Another factor contributing to the lack of competition and efficiency is government ownership. The BIS (1996) study noted earlier indicates that in 1994 the share of private ownership in financial institutions was just 58 per cent in Argentina, 52 per cent in Brazil, 77 per cent in Colombia, and 13 per cent in India, compared to 100 per cent in all of the consolidated, competitive financial systems. Normally, the lending policies of publicly funded banks emphasize targeted loans. This keeps banks from evaluating their exposure properly and causes them to operate with the strong implicit backing of the State. These factors generate unfair competition in the system and serve as an incentive for inefficiency.

F. Lack of portfolio diversification

Unlike the situation with respect to supervision of international banking conglomerates, where there are clear rules with regard to supervisory responsibility on the part of the country of origin and the host country, and for the reciprocal exchange of useful supervisory information, there are no international rules or recommendations from organizations such as the BIS on cross-border lending.

Nonetheless, a series of studies associated with the BIS indicates that one of the weaknesses in the banking system of developing economies is the absence of international portfolio diversification (BIS, 1996; Goldstein and Turner, 1996). Particularly in small economies with exports concentrated in a few commodities, international diversification is the ony way to isolate the financial system from shocks in the domestic economy. However, so far international lending in developing country bank portfolios is still very low, and where there is some international diversification, it is usually due more to direct investment by foreign banks than to cross-border lending. International portfolio diversification in these countries has been hampered by a lack of expertise in evaluating cross-border loans on the part of both the financial institutions and the supervisors; other factors are the scarcity of international currencies and/or restrictions on the free flow of capital.

When evaluating the benefits of increasing international diversification in bank lending, it is also important to recognize that these loans constitute new challenges for supervisors, particularly in terms of country risk. This risk is naturally different from the exposure associated with individual borrowers and includes both sovereign and transfer risk (Dale, 1984). If a bank is unable to recover its cross-border loans, this has a direct negative impact on its capital. This can lead to insolvency unless adequate reserves or diversification are in place. Thus, in the absence of a minimum of experience or expertise in a given country, the cost of international diversification may be higher than its potential benefits.

III. Strengthening prudential supervision in developing countries

Regarding the measures necessary to strengthen the stability and enhance the quality of oversight in developing economies, a distinction can be made between first- and second-generation reforms. First-generation reforms are essentially: the opening of the financial system to foreign institutions; the strengthening of prudential supervision; and the strengthening of the role of the market in monitoring banking institutions as a necessary complement to public-sector supervision. This "package" of reforms is of major relevance for poorer developing countries, where the primary weaknesses in financial stability have to be addressed effectively.

The second-generation financial reforms are: international diversification of the banking portfolio; regulation of financial conglomerates; and evaluation of the quality of bank management. Clearly, these measures are mainly relevant to financial systems that are already more complex – typically emerging markets – and where supervisory agencies have the necessary expertise to implement new supervisory instruments to cover new risks. It does not make much sense for economies that have yet to resolve their basic problems of supervision, such as having a good portfolio classification system or controlling limits on lending among related parties, to implement these types of reform, which are highly complex and

require a level of expertise in supervisory agencies that many developing economies simply lack.

Nonetheless, the first- and second-generation financial reforms should not necessarily be interpreted as being mechanically or strictly sequential; that is, finishing the first round is not a prerequisite to beginning the second. It is perfectly possible that second-generation reforms may be implemented alongside first-generation changes, depending on the characteristics of each specific market. For example, a supervisory law on consolidated financial conglomerates – a second-generation modification – can contribute to strengthening supervision and enforcement mechanisms for operations among related parties, a first-generation reform. Nor should second-generation reforms be interpreted as relevant to emerging markets only. Other developing economies may have reached an institutional strength that enables them to take additional steps, such as internationalizing their banks. Similarly, it is also quite likely that some basic problems in supervision will remain in emerging markets, as demonstrated by events in Indonesia, the Republic of Korea and Thailand.

A. *First-generation reforms*

1. *Improving the efficacy of prudential supervision*

(a) Strengthening institutions

One of the first tasks in improving the effectiveness of supervision in developing economies is institutional strengthening. This means taking action to improve supervisory agencies' ability to identify problems, reinforcing their power to take corrective action, and establishing clear rules that reduce stonewalling in implementing necessary measures.

Firstly, such change requires an improvement in the qualifications and experience of the staff working for the supervisory agencies. Supervisors will need resources to train their staff with regard to both *in situ* supervision and desk-based reviews. Staff members must also be able to understand new developments in the financial market. They need to be sufficiently familiar with bank operations to know where to look for and identify weaknesses below the surface. Supervision teams need to be skilled in evaluating lending systems, borrowers' ability to pay, the adequacy of provisioning, etc. (Folkerts-Landau and

Lindgren, 1997). Given that many of these skills cannot be acquired in the formal educational system, it is essential that the supervisory agencies themselves be capable of training their staff. This means providing the opportunity for a professional career, where meeting certain goals will lead to better job descriptions and pay. In this context, it is crucial that salaries at these agencies run not too far below those for similar work in the private sector. Banking supervision can significantly affect the progress of the industry and the property rights of bank owners. While it should be possible for interested parties to appeal rulings by supervisory agencies, the process is more effective if the supervisors themselves are not personally liable for damages caused by any actions legitimately performed in the course of their duties (ibid.).

Secondly, supervisors need to be granted real power to take corrective action in problematic situations. Usually, when a bank's financial standing begins to deteriorate, supervisory agencies have a range of options to choose from in order to remedy the problem. For example, following each inspection, examiners may meet with the bank's management, including the board of directors, to discuss the bank's operations, and thus solve some of the less serious problems. In more serious cases, regulators may have recourse to recapitalization plans, or they may block outward transfers of funds, limit the bank's exposure in certain types of operations, restrict the payment of dividends, limit growth, make staff changes at management levels or impose a freeze on bank operations (Larraín, 1994). To limit questioning by banks of decisions made by the regulators, these agencies must keep an updated log of the results of previous visits to each bank, as well as a copy of the commitments achieved in conversations with bank management. This way, corrective decisions by the authorities will be perceived to be less arbitrary.

In terms of the initial problem of the lack of incentives for regulators to take corrective action, it is essential that the law include automatic mechanisms to adjust equity. Banking legislation should establish clear rules that limit stonewalling by the supervisor in insolvency situations. This does not mean a law that seeks to cover each and every potential situation and defines regulators' responsibilities mechanically up to the very last detail. Rather, the law should define clear, objective measures to be taken by the regulator with regard to banks confronting problems of solvency. How drastic those measures will be depends on the financial institutions' degree of under-capitalization. Two good

examples of banking legislation that include the concepts expressed in the preceding paragraphs are the Chilean and United States laws.

In the United States, Prompt Corrective Action has been applied since 1993. This approach seeks to link supervision more directly to equity. For example, banks in "Zone 3" with sub-minimum capital are subject to penalties, such as restrictions on the payment of dividends and risk-intensive activities, or the possible removal of management, etc.; banks in "Zone 4" may be subject to more serious measures, such as intervention or closure.

The Chilean banking law of 1996 follows a similar approach. For banks that fail to achieve required minimum capital adjustments (corrected for non-provisioned losses), an automatic mechanism has been established to adjust equity by requiring shareholders to provide fresh resources without delay. For banks with severe problems of insolvency, defined as a Cook Index below or equal to 5 per cent, the law requires the board to call a "creditors' convention" as an alternative to straightforward intervention and/ or liquidation.

(b) Improving asset supervision capabilities

The ability to identify situations of bank insolvency in developing economies is limited because of insufficient ability to supervise assets. Therefore greater emphasis needs to placed on *in situ* supervision than on desk-based reviews. Given the poor quality of information in developing economies, supervisors have to complement reviews with on-site inspections so as to identify problematic situations early on (De Juan, 1996). Thus, if a bank has initially been classified simply as a "troubled" or "problem" bank and then fails within six months, it may be that it was not audited with sufficient frequency. Inspections should be conducted at least annually, although the larger banks – with greater systemic exposure – should at least be reviewed biannually.

A second requirement for improving the ability to supervise assets is improvement in sources of information. No information should be kept from the supervisor that influences an inspectors' ability to prioritize the components of an on-site review. Inspection information support systems must select the loan samples to be reviewed in the field. For that purpose, at least a bare-bones system must be devised to provide data on the status of borrowers in the financial system as well as a historical file of borrowers and their ratings. That file will grow as experience is gained in classifying assets (Ramírez, 1991).

To correct the problem of "evergreening", De Juan (1996) suggests that a loan should be classified as uncertain or non-recoverable whenever the borrowers' repayment ability is weak, even if he or she is up to date in the payments. In this case, banks should be required to provision up to the amount of the expected loss, the accrual of interest should be suspended and, most importantly, the bank should not be allowed to refinance loans to those borrowers. In the case of mismatches, a comparison should also be made of the borrower's ability to generate hard currency and the denomination of the debt, and the result must be incorporated into the portfolio classification and evaluation systems. In any event, sufficiently detailed supervision should be maintained to ensure that bank mismatches stay within reasonable limits as a percentage of equity.

(c)   Problems in lending to related parties

In addition to limiting operations eligible for transactions with related parties and establishing drastic penalties for those who break those limits, regulators also need some leeway in defining and establishing additional presumptions of wrongdoing as market operations become increasingly sophisticated in finding ways to dodge the law. In this sense, discretionary powers seem to have several advantages over firmly set rules.

Supervisory agencies need to create divisions capable of clearly identifying the composition of the primary conglomerates and their member companies. Without this ability, enforcement of the limits contained in the law is impractical. One of the most serious shortcomings among Latin American supervisory agencies is their tremendous ignorance of the morphology of these groups, so that private companies continually exceed the limits established by law. In addition, supervisors should ideally have a separate file or data base on borrowers related to each financial institution by ownership or management.

2.   *Strengthening market discipline*

A stable, solid financial system does not only require improvements in the area of official supervision, which will inevitably have shortcomings but, as a complement, also a strengthening of market discipline. The primary components of that added strength are: limited insurance for deposits, greater market transparency, and a credible mechanism for allocating losses among the private sector. Market monitoring as a complement to supervisory activities requires that depositors and investors perceive that they may lose their funds and savings should a bank become insolvent. In developing countries the State has traditionally stepped in when such problems have occurred. But this behaviour serves as a disincentive to market-imposed monitoring.

The first rule of market discipline is limited deposit insurance. The purpose of such insurance should be to protect only the small depositors, those who have neither the expertise nor the incentives to monitor the status of financial institutions (Folkerts-Landau and Lindgren, 1997). However, as noted earlier, the primary problem is the perception of implicit insurance that debilitates the credibility of this mechanism. In addition to limited deposit insurance, it is essential that in problematic cases the cost of insolvency be assumed by the banks' owners and, if necessary, by the non-guaranteed creditors. Unless the market has experienced this situation, it is unlikely that incentives for disciplining activities by banking institutions exist.

As part of a regulatory system that allows troubled institutions to normalize their situation early on – thereby reducing the potential of destabilizing effects on financial markets – it is important to have a private mechanism that can serve as an alternative to State support. In this vein, special supervisory measures, provisional administration and liquidation, and intervention of guarantee funds have the common denominator of involving the State and potentially leading to moral hazard. Furthermore, they tend to bring about strong noise or turbulence in the financial market. The experience in Latin America shows that, in practice, the problem of disorderly bankruptcy has typically been addressed by discretionary intervention in the troubled bank by the State, which nationalizes it, either temporarily or permanently, and absorbs the resulting losses.

An example of a private mechanism to resolve insolvency can be found in Chile's banking legislation. When there are severe problems of insolvency or ongoing lack of liquidity that have not been resolved through the markets' usual means (capital repositioning, sale of loan portfolios or mergers), the law allows creditors or depositors holding non-liquid liabilities (liquid assets are 100 per cent guaranteed) to reach an agreement with the troubled institutions that will allow them to swap the debt for equity in the institution. This safeguards the institution's continuing operation and serves as an alternative to straight liquidation. Under the agreement, subordinate bonds are automatically capitalized up to an amount that enables them to re-establish a Cook ratio of 12 per cent.

Furthermore, market discipline requires fostering transparency about the status of the institutions. For the market to operate in a framework of rewards and punishments, it needs to be able to distinguish between solid and potentially problematic banks as well as to demand appropriate risk premiums. Folkerts-Landau and Lindgren (1997) suggest that transparent information should permit a careful evaluation of the banks' exposure profile, its profitability and the capital available to cover those risks. This can be accomplished through annual and quarterly financial statements, with certain further information contingent upon unexpected events, such as an increase in provisions, expectation of significant losses or an increase in bad loans.

Nevertheless, public disclosure of information on the financial institutions should not involve a classification or rating by the authorities, since this may bring more costs than benefits. In other words, if the supervisor rates a given institution well and that bank subsequently has trouble, the public may seek to blame the supervisor. Similarly, a bad rating could, at some point, generate instability for a given institution. These arguments, of a general nature, can be particularly relevant in developing countries, given their strong dependence upon, and tradition of, public authorities stepping in to save banks.

3. Opening to foreign investment and access standards

One of the important challenges in modernizing financial systems in developing nations is the need for greater openness to foreign investment. A recent study by the IMF (Sorsa, 1997) shows that although openness to foreign banks is greater in emerging-market economies than in less consolidated developing economies, the "contestability" indicators suggest that even in many emerging-market economies foreign participation could bring benefits of higher competition, reduce the high margins and provide a broader range of services.[3]

As financial institutions from more developed countries physically move into developing econo-

mies, growing competition will emerge. This helps to overcome oligopolistic conditions, generating an increase in the supply of financial resources at a lower cost, to the direct benefit of credit users and depositors. Perhaps more importantly, their physical presence puts the host country in contact with different levels of knowledge and experience in the financial business, results in the transfer of technology and know-how, and will ultimately help to develop new skills.

Since foreign bank portfolios are less concentrated in lending to companies in the host country, and because they usually have access to external sources of liquidity and hard currency (from their headquarters on out), they will be capable of confronting a shock in the local economy better than the domestic banks. In addition, they will be less vulnerable to governmental pressure (Goldstein and Turner, 1996).

Despite claims that discretion in access criteria has been intended to ensure the solvency of the system and to protect local depositors, in practice it has been used in many developing countries to protect the domestic banking industry. However, there have also been cases in which indiscriminate access to the industry has generated destabilizing competition. The challenge, then, is to generate access standards with clear and objective rules that serve not to restrict competition but to filter out unscrupulous businessmen. Although access rules alone cannot guarantee that a bank will be well managed once it has been granted access to the industry, they can be an effective method for reducing the number of at-risk institutions that endanger the system's stability.

The essential criteria that must form the basis for the regulation of access to the financial industry are: the financial strength of the major shareholders; capital contributed by the financial institution; the presence of a critical mass of technical qualifications and experience; the honesty and integrity of the shareholders, board members and manager; and, in the case of foreign banks or foreign bank groups, the capacity of regulators in the country of origin to engage in effective supervision. With some differences, a similar set of criteria for the regulation of entry of financial institutions is described in detail in the BIS *Core Principles for Effective Banking Supervision* (1997). The principles noted here should serve as the foundation for clearly defined and explicit criteria for access to the financial industry. Once criteria are made objective through strictly defined access standards, there should be no impediment to licensing those who comply with the established requirements. The presence of clear, objective rules is better than fully discretionary instruments in preventing entrance requirements from serving, through their protectionist effect, to increase revenues for the domestic financial industry. Similarly, as the recommendations of the Basle Commission indicate, the presence of clear and objective criteria reduces the potential for political interference in the granting of licences, and ensures that strictly technical criteria prevail. The regulatory authorities should have the power to deny licences to those who do not meet the legal requirements.

B. Second-generation reforms

1. International diversification of the banking portfolio

Country-risk provisioning is a common instrument in developing countries because it allows banks to reduce their vulnerability to potentially adverse external events. This form of "provisioning" should go in parallel with the granting of credit to a particular country, independently of the specific risk characteristics of each individual country (Larraín, 1995). Different models exist for country-risk provisioning schemes, as, for example: that of the United States, which is highly dependent on the discretion of regulatory bodies; that of Britain, which is based on matrixes; that of Spain, which emphasizes private classification. It is crucial for developing countries to have such country-risk provisioning to complement individual loan assessments and classifications. For banks and regulators, however, the afore-mentioned schemes represent a great challenge in terms of evaluating risk.

Individual financial institutions should be required to compile pertinent information on their borrowers and the country context for lending, in such a way that a bank supervisor can evaluate risk situations. If a loan, for example, does not comply with required criteria, it should be given a poor rating. Likewise, international lending situations should be consistent with the banks' general international development strategies. This requires a strong system of internal controls and information gathering to ensure adequate management.

These criteria, which can also be applied in the case of domestic investments, are of fundamental importance to cross-border lending because regu-

lators typically have much less access to information internationally than domestically. In many cases, developing economies receiving such loans do not have adequate regulations on the provision of reliable information. The Chilean banking law of 1997 is a clear example of legislation intended to cover various risks that are associated with and originate from international banking.

2. Supervision of financial conglomerates

The operations of financial conglomerates are a significant part of the economic landscape in developing countries. As indicated above, their presence generates complications both domestically and internationally. The Basle Commission has proposed a series of minimum standards for the supervision of international banking conglomerates. Those worth highlighting include: the prime responsibility of the supervisor in charge of the home office, the need for simultaneous authorization by officials in the host country and the country of origin, and the need for continual exchange of information among regulators.

Although these recommendations seem like steps to an "ideal" regulatory scheme, it can be difficult to actually implement them in developing countries. One problem originates in the atmosphere within which bank shareholders make investments. That is, there are often controlling groups in banks that have diversified their investments via financial institutions in other countries, often through parent company ventures, rather than working through domestically regulated ones. In such cases, regulators in investment-receiving countries have not always had the full resources to apply or enforce the Basle recommendations, since in effect this form of internationalization is not based on foreign banks.

Moreover, thorny complications arise when countries make accords on supervisory cooperation and information exchange which do not comply fully with bank secrecy laws or other accords. In these cases, discrepancies affect not only bank shareholder investments but also bank lending. There are a few countries that have pertinent legislation on supervision agreements permitting their banks to operate in international markets. However, if these accords and agreements do not function properly, banks will be unable to invest internationally, and shareholders will be tempted to invest on their own in the international market.

Evidently, the participation of banks in the international market through unregulated pathways brings with it clear risks for domestic banks. These risks originate in market perceptions that such foreign involvement may, in the event of adverse foreign events, set off a chain reaction of collapse that spreads to local banks. In other words, although shareholders believe that they are internationalizing their investments and their exposure, they are in practice putting the financial system of their own country in jeopardy.

The often precarious situation of supervisory authorities makes it difficult for many countries to comply with the Basle consolidated supervision system. One cannot expect this to be possible with regard to the international operations of a conglomerate in countries where even domestic operations are not supervised adequately.

The obvious recommendation is that all countries should accept the Basle standards and that home countries with poor banking supervision should be blocked from investing internationally. The supervising authorities should be made aware of these recommendations in order to improve their functioning in this regard. A "second best" recommendation is that when it is inevitable that non-regulated international investments be made – either because the host country permits it or because it is not possible to prohibit such activity – a drastic "fire wall" should be erected to totally separate financial, commercial or any other kind of domestic banking from the bank operating in international markets. Doing so will define the boundaries of responsibility of the various bank actors.[4] This policy will also induce countries to protect their markets against unregulated banking groups.

Developed countries are frequently reluctant to sign banking or financial accords with developing countries. In such cases, one possibility is to exempt from the requirement for such an accord those investments abroad that, in accordance with protocols defined by regulators, are consistent with acceptable supervision and risk standards. For example, the recent Chilean law exempts investments in those countries which international risk classifiers have approved as acceptable for investment.

Domestically, the operation of conglomerates also presents significant challenges. Apart from the existence of two quite different operational structures (the "Anglo-Saxon" – or holding – type and the more "European" universal banking type), the achievement of a consolidated supervision system is challenging.

Perhaps the most complex problems arise with those conglomerate operational structures that have less than transparent control systems, often through domestically or internationally unregulated parent companies, that make the application of law difficult. Banking law requires the definition of a control threshold and/or minimum holding, beyond which a financial group is forced to submit to consolidated supervision. In practice, however, conglomerates can avoid regulation by changing control thresholds or by controlling conglomerate activity indirectly. Dealing with this problem, which is similar to regulating related parties, represents an enormous challenge for supervisory agencies.

There is no universally applicable formula for the supervision of conglomerates. One scheme that can be applied to mixed investment "groups" typical in developing countries – controlling both financial and industrial activities through relatively "murky" ownership ties – is based on the holding model. This scheme relies on regulated parent companies to separate out all the financial arms of their conglomerates, presenting themselves as umbrella-type organizations, to which it is possible to apply consolidated supervision. Such a regulated parent should be barred from investing in the industrial sector activity, in which shareholders can invest directly, erecting a "fire wall" that separates the activities of the financial conglomerate from the rest of the economy.

Another issue that needs to be dealt with in developing countries is the absence of any supervisory infrastructure to regulate companies that may seek to take advantage of synergies between different arms of a financial group. For example, members of a group may share a name or corporate image, despite the fact that the group is not under standard consolidated supervision, thereby increasing the risk of contamination for a bank within it. Likewise, clear regulations relating to the utilization of a network of bank branches by other businesses within the conglomerate, such as insurance companies, do not exist. It is crucial to make progress in regulating such operations, in order to avoid subsidies that can skew the level playing field of the financial system.

Developing countries have many gaps to fill if they are to build effective legal institutions for regulation and supervision of financial conglomerates. With the exception of Mexico, which has a comprehensive legal framework, and Chile and El Salvador, which are in the process of developing appropriate legislation, Latin American systems of financial supervision and law lag well behind that of more advanced parts of the world (Larraín, 1997).

3. Evaluation of management quality

The first line of defence against problems of bankruptcy is administrative competence (Folkerts-Landau and Lindgren, 1997). This principle has been included in recommendations by the BIS (1997), in the Principles quoted above, and in recent work by the IMF (1997). One of the weakest areas in bank supervision in developing countries is the afore-mentioned evaluation of management, despite the fact that it is one of the crucial elements in any pro-jection of a bank's future. Much more than reviews of quantitative financial indicators, management evaluation ought to be the principal basis for pre-dicting a bank's future, particularly during times of economic turbulence. A solid internal auditing sys-tem, effective use of all management information systems, strategic development plans and continuing development of human resources are essential for good management. In many developing countries, putting these essentials into practice can be difficult.

To endow bank examiners with the skills they need, the focus should be on preparing them to conduct evaluations in the following areas: capital, assets, market risks, profits and management. Flex-ible examiners who can see the big picture are preferable to specialists who analyse isolated trends within the bank.[5] Such preparations and skills tend to clash with institutional norms in the majority of developing countries, which lack the resources to employ inspectors who have the capacity to look beyond mere risk-management analyses.

These approaches are also fundamentally based on the idea that there can be compromise and coop-eration between a bank's board of directors and its management. An examiner should identify problems and reveal them to the board with all available evi-dence; recommend changes; and then leave the bank to choose the best route to overcome the problems.

This is especially difficult when a bank's financial indicators show a perfectly healthy outlook despite the existence of management problems. For example, a bank could be fulfilling minimum capital standards and showing high profits. However, a more thorough inspection could reveal that many of these positive indicators are the result of irregular profits and/or aggressive lending policies that do not comply with acceptable standards. If this were the case, the

bank would be undercapitalized. Given that manage-ment is responsible for defining appropriate policies for the bank's operation and establishing the neces-sary capital, such a bank would receive negative marks for capital reserves, investment quality and management, even if it had apparently complied with all minimum banking rules. In all of this, the attitude of the inspector is essential since the idea is not to interfere in the bank's decisions.

Likewise, in those countries that have a shortage of high-quality, professional boards of directors, it is crucial for banks to reinforce a sense of commit-ment within the institution and avoid working solely for controlling groups or their interests. A better link between examiners and board members, including ensuring that the latter have access to the conclusions of inspections even when serious problems are not detected, permits more input "from above" and can help boards in many cases become better supervisors. Such cooperation can also improve basic manage-ment, which can be discussed in periodic meetings between examiners and boards.

The application of a strategy emphasizing good management requires regulatory authorities to hire highly skilled and experienced personnel, who are provided with the necessary resources. These re-sources are not always readily available in developing countries – boards of directors in such countries do not have a tradition of commitment or precedents for allowing supervisory authorities to "interfere" in the general operations of their banks.

IV. Developing countries and international regimes for prudential supervision

The increasing international activity of banks of developed countries and the risks that have emerged from it have given rise to a series of agree-ments among these countries, involving recommen-dations for their national regulatory authorities. The most active forum for discussion of such issues is the "Basle Committee" formed by the member countries of the Group of Ten (G-10). The Basle Committee has reached agreements on appropriate capital adequacy ratios for banks, consolidated supervision of international financial conglomerates, and on the so-called "Core Principles for Effective Banking Supervision".[6]

This last document synthesizes approaches to the principal issues which the Basle Committee has addressed in the sphere of banking supervision, including licensing, mechanisms for prudential supervision, responsibilities of regulatory bodies and supervision of international conglomerates. The document was prepared by representatives of the G-10 countries in consultation with some non-member countries such as Chile, China and the Czech Republic, among others. This consultation was a new and positive development, permitting the broadening of its sphere of influence concerning minimum standards for banking to a wider range of countries.

The recommendations in the Basle document on core principles are an ideal framework for banking supervision, within the context of well-established and independent public institutions with the required authority and expertise, in economies where market discipline can play an important role. This context is not that of developing economies today. The Basle document makes little reference to the precarious nature of public institutions typical in developing countries, and results in a good proportion of their problems being matters of implementation rather than definition of principles. This is not to dispute these principles but to insist on greater discussion of the difficulties of implementing them.

Some of the issues dealt with have little relevance for the majority of developing economies (e.g. market risks and value at risk) and the recommended approach to some other issues (e.g. evaluation of the quality of management) is difficult to implement in those countries. Furthermore, there is great heterogeneity in the need for reform among the developing countries, which must somehow be incorporated into the discussions.

This section aims to contribute to the development of a position, for the developing and emerging countries, on the principal matters at issue in international banking supervision. Such a position should be based on a solid understanding of the specificity of the problems of supervision in developing economies and the most important courses of action to follow in matters of international policy.

Sections II and III above provide a framework for the developing country positions in international forums on banking supervision. Taking the "Core Principles" document as representative of the kind of approach now being taken in international forums, developing countries should aim at the following:

- The establishment of certain priorities that better reflect the needs of developing economies;

- Dealing in greater depth with certain areas, now touched upon only superficially but of great relevance to developing economies;

- The incorporation of other subjects pertinent to developing economies but totally absent in the current international discussion.

Below we consider some elements around which developing economies should shape their position with respect to banking supervision.

Capital adequacy

One of the most important and widely implemented advances in matters of international standards for banking is the 8 per cent capital requirement. Some point to the need for developing countries to establish capital requirements greater than the 8 per cent minimum, given the higher idiosyncratic risk of their economies relative to those of the G-10 countries. There are also proposals to increase capital requirements to compensate for the weaknesses in matters of portfolio classification and provisioning requirements frequently found in developing economies.

It is evident that, in the short term, raising capital requirements can increase systemic stability. In the long term, however, the international competitiveness of the financial sector of developing countries can be damaged, as long as the developed countries keep the 8 per cent, and that may reduce the long-term efficiency and stability of the system.

A better solution was incorporated into the recently approved Chilean legislation: it establishes a minimum requirement of 8 per cent but also gives incentives to the banks that have 10 per cent, giving them greater opportunity to open new international and domestic business. This approach provides a better balance between the social and private benefits of capital requirements. In any case, raising the capital requirements for all developing economies indiscriminately does not seem appropriate.

Financial conglomerates

There exist clear recommendations regarding minimum standards in the realm of international activities of conglomerates, but far more ambiguous standards are applied to the domestic operations of conglomerates.

In the majority of developing economies conglomerates are of a purely domestic nature. Only a few developing economies (for example, Chile) have banking conglomerates whose principal activity is internationally oriented. The main problem is that de facto conglomerates are created by investments by bank owners in other financial businesses, generating the risk of "contamination". This type of conglomerate is produced by structures of concentrated ownership in which it is not the bank itself that diversifies, making it very difficult for regulatory bodies to intervene and supervise in a consolidated manner. Given the lack of transparency in respect of locating the centre of power of such conglomerates, the regulatory body is faced with a "grey area" hampering its supervisory work. The elaboration of specific proposals for dealing with this problem should be requested by developing country authorities.

Consolidated supervision

Among the key agreed principles in the supervision of international conglomerates is the responsibility of the regulator in the country of origin for the consolidated supervision of the group, and the exchange of information between the parent and the host countries. The central idea is to ensure that no part of the conglomerate is left outside the ambit of supervision.

Even if it is not a widespread phenomenon, there are a few emerging-market economies in which banks have internationalized. In these cases the application of the principle of consolidated supervision faces several complications. In countries with a weak supervision capacity, ceding supervisory responsibility to the regulator of the head office may involve more costs than benefits. In many economies that have shown a weak supervision capacity at the domestic level, it is difficult to imagine their authorities providing adequate supervision at the international level. The principle of consolidated supervision can thus generate a problem of moral hazard that, if not offset somehow, may eliminate the net benefits of banking internationalization.

An obvious solution in such cases would be to prohibit the internationalization of the bank. Once again, however, the problem may arise from foreign investments undertaken by the owners of the domestic bank. Faced with the impossibility of forcing such internationalization to be done through the bank, the "second best" solution is to give wide powers for the local regulator to impose a "fire wall" that totally isolates the local bank from all kinds of direct or indirect financial or commercial ties with its owners' investments abroad.

Information exchange between regulatory bodies is frustrated, in numerous cases, by national regulations on banking secrecy that prohibit such exchange.

These problems are almost entirely ignored by documents elaborated in current international forums. The principles of consolidated supervision should be accompanied by many more implementation options than exist to date.

Internationalization

Organizations such as the World Bank, the Inter-American Development Bank and the International Monetary Fund, increasingly recommend internationalization as a tool for risk diversification in developing countries. Such internationalization usually involves foreign direct investment as well as international portfolio diversification. Following this recommendation is not without risk for many developing or emerging economies. As already pointed out, in order to generate more benefits than costs, internationalization must be backed by an adequate capacity for supervision, particularly in spheres that imply competencies different from those required in the corresponding domestic field, such as the analysis of country risk.

One obvious recommendation is to design an adequate legal framework that gives powers to the regulator to cover adequately the new risks of international operations. This framework must deal with matters such as appropriate provisioning for country risk limits relating to the need for diversification by project and by country, requirements for internal controls within the banks themselves, limits to their maximum exposure as a percentage of capital, etc. – all of which would facilitate a process of solid internationalization. Without an appropriate legal framework and the capacity for implementation on the part of regulatory bodies, internationalization may bring more costs than benefits to individual developing countries. In general, this set of issues is insufficiently dealt with in international forums.

Management evaluation

The quality of management is a central element in financial system performance. But recommendations for developing countries on how to improve it are particularly difficult, given the institutional weaknesses, insufficient expertise on the part of inspectors, and the lack of professionalism in boards of directors, which are often under the influence of economic groups and their interests. These factors must be addressed in international discussions of supervision.

Credits to related parties

Although most developing countries have legislation imposing severe limits on financial sector operations with related parties, there are very few countries that have managed in practice to establish an effective regime to control such operations. This is a central problem for developing economies, which are characterized by a high degree of concentration in ownership of assets. It is therefore essential for developing countries to bring the related problems to the attention of pertinent international forums. They may be able to benefit from relevant expertise in developed countries so as better to translate principles into effective practice.

Entry requirements

The "Core Principles" adequately describe the central criteria that must govern the regulation of access of new institutions to the banking industry. This constitutes a useful contribution for those countries that have not yet established such criteria within their domestic legislation.

Regarding the implementation of legislation in this sphere, one of the frequent problems in developing countries is the considerable discretion left to regulators. The absence of objective criteria is often used to restrict the access of foreign institutions purely as a result of pressure from domestic interest groups that enjoy great influence in many developing economies. On occasion, this discretion has also allowed indiscriminate access of banking institutions to the system, under the aegis of the application of liberal principles, and consequent potential weakening of the stability of the system. Greater effort at the international level to develop objective measures relating to the requirements for access to the banking industry would be welcomed by many developing countries.

Exit mechanisms

Although it is one of the key issues for the long-term stability of any financial system, there are no internationally accepted standards concerning exit. The continued presence of precarious institutions that do not resolve their problems – whether through liquidation, intervention, merger or some other mechanism – weakens the financial system. This is a prominent problem in developing economies, where

regulatory bodies are very susceptible to pressures from interest groups which seek to avoid adequate correction measures. The establishment of clear exit rules – including automatic mechanisms for asset adjustment, solutions permitting continuation of banking activity on the basis of private arrangements, or liquidation – would represent a tremendous advance for the stability of financial systems in developing economies.

Supervision of assets

A good system of asset supervision, including appropriate classification of portfolio and provisioning requirements, remains a high-priority objective in many emerging-market economies. This objective, although of crucial importance, has not received sufficient attention in current discussions of international standards. The main problem typically rests with implementation, including the absence of adequate systems of information. Unlike in developed countries, where the process works mainly on the basis of self-regulation, in developing countries regulatory bodies, emphasizing *in situ* supervision, are of key importance. This issue should be strongly emphasized by developing country representatives in international discussions.

Market risks

Recognizing the weaknesses of the capital adequacy ratio of 8 per cent, and the explosion of derivative instruments in developed countries, the Basle Committee has made great efforts to develop better measures of what is required to cover market risks. Its concept of "value at risk" aims at a common measurement standard so that institutions themselves can estimate their potential losses in any period of time. This new approach also comprises a series of qualitative standards that private institutions must address, such as an independent unit of risk control. Though the "value at risk" approach represents an important advance to complement the capital adequacy ratio of 8 per cent, its pertinence in developing economies is doubtful. Given the limited development of their financial markets, the exposure of developing country banks to market risks emanating from derivatives markets and other new instruments is generally far lower than that of banks in developed countries.

It should be taken into account that certain methods are too sophisticated to guide coverage of financial risks in developing economies, where priority should be on the development of simple techniques to limit the exposure of banks to exchange risks, and the incorporation of the exposure of debtors to the risk of devaluation in the evaluation of credit risks and the classification of assets.

V. Conclusions

There are six key characteristics that suggest weaknesses in the financial systems of developing countries: weak public institutions; lack of experience in the operation of financial markets and excessive emphasis on public ownership of financial institutions; inadequate accounting and risk-assessment standards; high concentration of ownership in financial institutions; expensive or inefficient financial intermediation; and lack of an internationally diversified banking portfolio.

These characteristics give rise to a series of problems that can affect market stability and weaken the quality of supervision in developing economies. They can also contribute to increased credit risk, a lack of market support in institutional monitoring, and inadequate standards for the entrance and exit of financial institutions. Although idiosyncratic events within financial markets generate specific obstacles to supervision in developing economies, the nature of the challenges in financial reforms is generally determined by the level of complexity and development in the financial market, and the ability and expertise of the supervisors.

First-generation reforms should be geared to an opening of the financial system to foreign institutions, strengthening the prudential supervision system, and reinforcing the market's ability to monitor banking institutions, thereby complementing the system of public supervision. This package of reforms is best applied to low- and middle-income developing economies, in order to overcome the deficiencies typical of their financial systems.

Second-generation reforms should go further and address the international diversification of the banking portfolio, the regulation of financial conglomerates, and the supervision of bank management. It is evident that these reforms are better suited to more complex markets – typically emerging markets – in which regulatory agencies have the expertise necessary to create fresh methods of supervision to cover new and changing risk situations. It is illogical to think that developing countries that have not created fundamental regulatory mechanisms, such as

basic systems of investment classification or loan controls, will be capable of implementing these types of reform, which require special expertise.

First- and second-generation financial reforms should not necessarily be implemented in a mechanical or strictly sequential fashion, in which finishing the first round is a prerequisite to beginning the second. It is perfectly possible for second-generation reforms to be implemented alongside first-generation changes, depending on the characteristics of each specific market.

The position of developing and emerging countries in international forums should be based on a solid understanding of the specific problems of supervision and the principal required courses of policy action in those countries. The recommendations in the Basle documents constitute general principles, useful as a reference to the elements of an ideal framework for banking supervision within a context of well-established markets and independent public institutions with the required authority and expertise. However, in the majority of developing and emerging-market countries the reality is quite different, with more severe weaknesses in the implementation of the agreed principles than in the areas of definition and legal frameworks. The main subjects on which the developing countries should concentrate as they develop their own positions in international forums are: capital adequacy, financial conglomerates, consolidated supervision, internationalization, management evaluation, credits to related parties, entry requirements, exit mechanisms, supervision of assets and market risks.

Notes

1   Unless otherwise noted, "developing economies" should be understood in the context of this paper to mean relatively less developed economies as well as emerging economies (the set of non-developed economies).
2   The benefits of competition emerge over time and along a learning curve. For an application to the financial system, see Arrau (1996).
3   This is not to deny that inadequate or inappropriate access standards have sometimes given rise to an excessive proliferation of financial institutions, as demonstrated in Argentina in the 1990s.
4   In many developing countries, constitutional regulations make it difficult to prohibit international investing through bank owners. Chile and El Salvador are two examples, among many, of such cases.
5   Nonetheless, examination teams specializing in highly complex subjects, like financial exposure or computer systems, can be useful.

6   Given its importance and international legitimacy, this document is the central reference for this paper, and it should be the base from which the developing countries continue to work.

References

ARRAU, Patricio (1996), "Competitividad de la Banca Chilena y su Proceso de Internacionalización", in L.H. Paul and F. Suárez (eds.), *Competitividad: El Gran Desafío de las Empresas Chilenas* (Santiago de Chile: Centro de Estudios Públicos).

BENSTON, George, and George KAUFMAN (1988), "Regulating Bank Safety and Performance", in W. Haraf and R. Kushmeider (eds.), *Restructuring Banking and Financial Services in America* (Washington, D.C.: American Enterprise Institute).

BIS (1996), *66th Annual Report* (Basle: Bank for International Settlements).

BIS (1997), *Core Principles for Effective Banking Supervision* (Basle: Bank for International Settlements).

BIS and IMF (1997), *Financial Stability in Emerging Market Economies*, Report of the Working Party on Financial Stability in Emerging Market Economies (Basle: Bank for International Settlements).

CAPRIO, Gerard, Izak ATIYAS, and James HANSON (1993), "Financial Reform: Lessons and Strategies", in S. Faruqi (ed.), *Financial Sector Reforms in Asian and Latin American Countries* (Washington, D.C.: The World Bank).

CORRIGAN, Gerald (1996), "Building Effective Banking Systems in Latin America: Tactics and Strategy", mimeo, Inter-American Development Bank, Washington, D.C., November.

DALE, Robert (1984), *The Regulation of International Banking* (Cambridge, United Kingdom).

DE JUAN, Aristóbulo (1996), "The Roots of Banking Crises: Microeconomic Issues and Supervision and Regulation", in R. Hausmann and L. Rojas-Suárez (eds.), *Banking Crises in Latin America* (Washington, D.C.: Inter-American Development Bank).

FOLKERTS-LANDAU, David, and Carl-Johan LINDGREN (1997), "Toward a Framework for Financial Stability", mimeo, IMF, Washington, D.C., September.

GAVIN, Michael, and Ricardo HAUSMANN (1996), "The Roots of Banking Crises: The Macroeconomic Context", in R. Hausmann and L. Rojas-Suárez (eds.), *Banking Crises in Latin America* (Washington, D.C.: Inter-American Development Bank).

GOLDSTEIN, Morris, and Philip TURNER (1996), "Banking Crises in Emerging Economies: Origins and Policy Options", *BIS Economic Papers*, No. 46 (Basle: Bank for International Settlements), October.

IMF (1997), *"World Economic Outlook"*, Interim Assessment (Washington, D.C.), December.

KANE, Edward (1989), *The Savings and Loans Insurance Mess: How Did It Happen?* (Washington, D.C.: The Urban Institute Press).

LARRAÍN, Christian (1994), "The Modernization of Bank Supervision", *CEPAL Review*, No. 54, December.

LARRAÍN, Christian (1995), "Internacionalización y Supervisión de la Banca en Chile", *Estudios Públicos*, No. 60 (Santiago de Chile).

LARRAÍN, Christian (1996), *Operación de Conglomerados Financieros en Chile: Una Propuesta*, Serie Financiamiento del Desarrollo (Santiago de Chile: ECLAC/UNDP).

LARRAÍN, Christian (1997), *Supervisión Consolidada de Conglomerados Financieros,* mimeo, Ministerio de Hacienda, Chile.

LINDGREN, Carl (1996), "Maintaining a Sound Banking System", mimeo, IMF, Washington, D.C., February.

RAMIREZ, Guillermo (1991), "Evaluación y Clasificación de Activos: La Experiencia Chilena", in G. Held and R. Szalachman (eds.), *Regulación y Supervisión de la Banca: Experiencias de América Latina y el Caribe* (Santiago de Chile: ECLAC-UNDP).

ROJAS-SUAREZ, Liliana, and Steven WEISBROD (1996), "Banking Crises in Latin America: Experiences and Issues", in R. Hausmann and L. Rojas-Suárez (eds.), *Banking Crises in Latin America* (Washington, D.C.: Inter-American Development Bank).

SORSA, Piritta (1997), "The GATS Agreement on Financial Services: A Modest Start to Multilateral Liberalization", *IMF Working Paper*, WP/97/55 (Washington, D.C.), May.

STIGLITZ, Joseph (1993), "The Role of the State in Financial Markets", *World Bank's Annual Conference on Development Economics*, Vol. 2 (Washington, D.C.).

UNITED STATES DEPARTMENT OF THE TREASURY (1991), *Recommendations for Safer, More Competitive Banks* (Washington, D.C.).

COPING WITH FINANCIAL CRISES: ARE REGIONAL ARRANGEMENTS THE MISSING LINK?

Percy S. Mistry

Abstract

Almost all recent financial crises have had powerful regional repercussions which have probably been amplified by the speed and intensity of the regionalization of trade and investment during this decade across every continent. But only in Europe have regional measures been devised or applied successfully to prevent contagion from getting out of hand. In the developing world, crisis management is an IMF monopoly. There has not been any serious and genuinely participatory global deliberation on whether the IMF should be playing such a role. On the other hand, developing countries individually do not have the resources or the capacity to withstand the shocks which such crises emit and which keep recurring in the absence of credible deterrents to speculative attacks or to market failure. This paper discusses the possible scope of additional self-help arrangements and institutions at the regional level. The countries of a region would have more influence and control over such institutions than they have over a global institution, but reciprocally they would also be placed under an obligation to take corrective action swiftly and decisively for the good of the neighbourhood.

Regional crisis management capacity - designed as an integral feature of the future multilateral institutional architecture - is found to be potentially useful in complementing national and global measures rather than substituting for them. Regional measures might be particularly appropriate in the context of short-term crisis management, by helping: (i) to augment national intervention capacity through credible arrangements which convey clear signals to markets of a resolute commitment to pooling and using regional reserves under pre-agreed conditions; (ii) to arrest the spread of neighbourhood contagion; (iii) to prevent the disruption of regional trade and investment flows when a crisis begins unfolding; (iv) to prevent the collapse of regional financial markets caused by panic selling; and (v) to avoid competitive devaluations.

Regional intervention can also be useful in crisis prevention. Measures and instruments which are being advocated for surveillance, transparency and enforcement at the global level might be better implemented through regional institutions or mechanisms in which member countries can participate more meaningfully than they can in the IMF. Moreover, in the medium- and long-term the construction of regional monetary and exchange-rate arrangements and of regional financial markets can help to reduce unsustainable disequilibria in foreign-exchange and financial markets and minimize the scope for intraregional currency speculation by reducing considerably the range of currencies available to attract it in the first place.

I.   Introduction

In the last two decades serious economic dislocations have been caused by five major financial crises: two in the 1980s and three so far in the 1990s. Occurring with increasing frequency, these include: (i) the developing country debt crisis of 1982 triggered by the Volcker interest rate shock, which persisted for a decade in Latin America and still impedes development in much of Africa; (ii) the equity market crisis of 1987, which led to a sharp drop in global asset values and consequent wealth effects, but from which recovery was quick as a result of prompt concerted action by the United States, European and Japanese authorities in propping up global liquidity and avoiding the prospect of a generalized solvency problem, with its deflationary consequences; (iii) the European currency crisis of 1992, which triggered a region-wide recession from which the United Kingdom did not recover until late 1994 and other major continental European economies began recovering only in 1996; (iv) the Mexican peso crisis of 1994, which caused immediate contagion in several emerging markets (the "tequila" effect) but was contained by the bailout led by the United States Treasury and the IMF; and (v) the Asian financial crisis of 1997, which began as a currency crisis but has since become a generalized financial and economic *débâcle* owing to market and crisis management failure at all levels – national, regional and global.

The Asian crisis is as much a "crisis of crisis management" as of financial ruction. Contrary to Latin America's experience, Asian Governments have been less adept at coping with unfamiliar crises than at managing years of success. Worse, the IMF's role has generated contention across a wide spectrum of liberal and conservative opinion about: (a) whether it has exacerbated the Asian crisis by turning what should have been a mild currency shock into a wider, deeper cataclysm (e.g. Sachs, 1997; Feldstein, 1998; Stiglitz, 1998); and (b) whether its prescriptions for Asia – especially for its financial systems – are fatally flawed (The Economist, 1997c, d, e, 1998g; Emmerson, 1998; FEER, 1998a; Wade and Venoroso, 1998a). Nor has its performance in the still evolving Russian financial *débâcle* escaped criticism (Bush, 1998). These controversies cannot be blithely dismissed. They raise doubts about whether it is in the global interest – as seems to be regarded as axiomatic in G-7 circles – for the IMF to strengthen its monopoly over crisis management in the developing world or in economies in transition. The belief that only the IMF should cope with financial crises in *developing* regions seems at odds with the reality that, since the 1970s, the *developed* countries have chosen to rely entirely on each other, often through regional arrangements, in coping with financial crises, and disregard altogether any prospect of their turning to the IMF in similar circumstances.

The IMF's monopoly over crisis management in the developing world has been acquired by default, not design, without serious and genuinely participatory global deliberation on whether it should be playing such a role. Its intrusion in such crises appears to be strongly supported by the United States Treasury's anxiety or perhaps more pointedly, the anxiety of the United States' financial services industry and its markets to avoid any loss of control in managing the evolution of the global financial system (Wade and Venoroso, 1998). As with all monopolies, the IMF's has inherent disadvantages, which have been highlighted extensively in the literature (see list of references). Would developing countries and the world be better served by additional self-help arrangements and institutions, instituted at the regional level, which could be triggered to bolster national intervention capacity, before the IMF needs to step in as a genuine lender of last rather than first (or second) resort?

It is interesting to note in this respect a crucial strategic difference between how the equity market collapse of 1987 was dealt with by developed country monetary authorities and how the Asian crisis is being managed by the IMF. In 1987, G-7 Governments responded to global asset value deflation with a significant loosening of liquidity and accompanying fiscal accommodation. That approach averted a systemic collapse, although it did require eventual monetary tightening in the recovery phase to bring post-collapse booms (which had been unleashed in Europe and the United States) under control. In Asia a decade later, the opposite approach has been taken: a sharp liquidity squeeze, with a sharp surge in local interest rates to prop up currencies, accompanied by early fiscal tightening, which was later reversed. Asia was asphyxiated with undue monetary tightness just when it was beginning to generate a powerful intraregional growth dynamic and gradually lessening its reliance on traditional export markets in Japan, the United States and Europe (Bergsten and Noland, 1993; Frankel, 1996, 1998; Fukasaku, 1995; Palmer, 1991; Streeten, 1988). As a consequence of the crisis management measures applied, that trend will be reversed to the medium-term detriment of Asia, as well as that of the United States and Europe – where the seeds of the next sterling and dollar crises, with accompanying financial turmoil, are now being sown.

During the period 1982-1998 there were also other mini-crises. These have not been trivial but neither have they (as yet) posed any threat of systemic disruption. Transitional problems in Central and Eastern Europe generated crises in several countries between 1990 and 1998. The most recent Russian financial crisis, which has been unfolding since June 1998 might have powerful regional repercussions in Eastern and Central Europe, where most countries have yet to achieve stability and sustainable growth. Added to the drag on the world economy, which is now being exerted by the Asian crisis, and the threat it poses to the balance sheets of several major European (principally German) banks, the rouble crisis might also prove to be the proverbial last straw tilting the balance towards a global recession.

In 1991 a balance-of-payments crisis over-whelmed India with spill-over effects on subregional currencies and financial markets. But recovery was relatively quick, although follow-up action on long overdue structural adjustments faltered after stability was restored. Since 1994, a relentless (if necessary) decline in the value of the South African rand – which was under speculative attack while this paper was being written – has had discernible effects in un-settling subregional financial and currency markets, although it has not yet led to a full-scale currency or financial crisis in the subregion.

II. The case for regional involvement in financial crisis management

In the 1990s, concern has grown about the impact of freer, more volatile capital flows – especially short-term debt and portfolio investment – along with the high incidence of speculative attacks involving "one-way bets" on currencies (Buira, 1996; Eichengreen et al., 1995; Eichengreen and Wyplosz, 1996; Ffrench-Davies and Griffith-Jones, 1995; Griffith-Jones, 1996; IMF, 1997a; Krugman, 1995; Obstfeld 1994). These have been blamed for exacer-bating if not creating financial crises – almost all of which have had powerful *regional* repercussions (the 1987 market meltdown had a *global* impact). Such effects have probably been amplified by the speed and intensity with which the regionalization of trade and investment has occurred during this decade across every continent (Cable and Henderson, 1994; de Melo and Panagariya, 1993; Frankel, 1998;

Greider, 1997; Mistry, 1996; Oman, 1994; Teunissen, 1998). That process has created closer intraregional economic and financial interdependencies, whose dimensions, and whose capacity for spreading contagion quickly and powerfully, have not been fully appreciated as yet.

Only in Europe[1] have regional measures been devised or applied to prevent contagion from getting out of hand (Currie and Whitley, 1994; Giovannini and Mayer, 1992; Kindleberger, 1984; Wallace, 1994) – unless, of course, the United States-led bailout in the Mexican crisis is construed as a regional measure, which to some extent it probably was. Japan's attempt to play a similar role in the early stages of the Asian crisis came to early grief partly because of United States and IMF opposition and because of its own unravelling economic and political situation (The Economist, 1997b, 1998g; Dornbusch, 1998; Khanna, 1998).

At this point perhaps an essential digression is in order. Discussion of regional measures of course raises the difficult question of what exactly is a region in the context of the propositions which this paper puts forward. That definitional issue has bedevilled the more general debate on "regionalism vs. multilat-eralism" for a considerable period of time (Bhagwati, 1993; Krugman, 1993; Mistry, 1996). Suffice it to say for the purposes of this paper that the term "re-gion" is deployed broadly and flexibly. Financial crises in the developing world are likely to be more credibly dealt with if the region in question included one or more of the major developed countries – especially reserve currency issuers – than a region which did not. The former are likely to present a more capable front – in restoring the confidence of global institutional investors and banks – to international financial markets, as was demonstrated in the 1994-1995 Mexican crisis (Ortiz-Martinez, 1998). This suggests the need for further movement in the process of regionalization, which is occurring simultaneously with globalization (Oman, 1994, 1998) towards the mixed North-South regionalism of the kind that took hold after the North American Free Trade Area (NAFTA) was formed. Of course the same idea had already been applied in the former European Com-munity, when countries which were still developing (e.g. Greece, Ireland, Portugal and Spain) were integrated with the developed nations of Western Europe (Wallace, 1994).

Seen from that angle, the chances of tackling regional financial crises successfully would be in-creased if, for example, in the Western Hemisphere crisis management and recovery measures involved active participation by the United States; those in Africa or Central and Eastern Europe engaged the European Union; and those in Asia involved Japan. This paper, especially in its discussion of the Asian crisis, regards the Asian region as a broad one: incorporating three subregions: i.e. ASEAN, Greater China (China, Hong Kong [China], and Taiwan Province of China) and North-East Asia (Republic of Korea and Japan). But, in doing so, it recognizes the possibility for greater cohesion and action _within_ these subregions as well. For example, China's willingness to support Hong Kong's currency peg in the face of speculative attacks in 1997 and 1998 (The Economist, 1997, 1998b, g; IMF, 1997b) was an interesting example of how swift, concerted subregional action can prevent damage resulting from speculative attack. In the final analysis, as far as financial crises are concerned, a region almost defines itself by the boundaries to which domino-effect contagion can spread. In the 1982 (debt) and 1997 (Asian) crises those boundaries became evident quite quickly in Latin America, Africa and Asia respectively.

Attempts in the early phases of these two crises to create a regional capacity for financial crisis containment in each case were deliberately derailed for reasons that have yet to be satisfactorily explained. In the 1982 debt crisis there were concerns on the part of creditor countries and banks (mainly in the United States) that the formation of regional debtors' cartels would complicate or detract from the debt strategies that eventually evolved – designed to favour almost exclusively the interests of creditors (Cline, 1995; Sachs, 1989). Analysis in retrospect suggests, however, that allowing debtor's cartels to emerge might have led to a more balanced distribution of "costs" between debtors and creditors who were equally culpable for the crises occurring, and may have brought the debt crises to an earlier end, at lower cost to debtor economies and to global welfare (Griffith-Jones, 1988). It would have been a useful counterweight to the creditors' cartels which immediately emerged, and which were explicitly supported by the IMF and World Bank acting as creditors with their own vested interests rather than as neutral, dispassionate intermediaries capable of striking the right balance between debtor and creditor interests in the process of crisis management (Mistry, 1994).

Moreover, there is evidence to suggest that a regional approach to economic and debt crisis management, and to the management of monetary policy and exchange regimes, in the subregions of Africa may have prevented some of the more egregious failures of post-debt crisis structural adjustment, especially in small fragmented national markets which failed to respond to supply-side stimuli because relative changes in key prices did not result in the desired switching effects (AfDB, 1993; Jayarajah and Branson, 1995; Mistry, 1996a).

Curiously, the _prima facie_ case for regional monetary arrangements in a globalizing world with open capital accounts seems even stronger than the case for regional development banks (RDBs). Yet the banks, by and large, enjoy support in the international community with little contention about their utility or value (Culpeper, 1997), while the creation of regional monetary arrangements raises objections and controversies, if not the spectre of a loss of discipline in the international financial system (The Economist, 1997a; Fischer, 1998; Summers, 1998). In the Asian crisis the reasons for suggested regional "self-help" initiatives being so swiftly and decisively derailed are opaque; though suspicions, both benevolent and malevolent, abound. Consequently, they have led to public speculation about "hidden agendas" being pursued by the United States Treasury and the IMF in taking command of, and monopolizing, the crisis management process before Asian Governments (once regarded as highly capable) could collaborate meaningfully in designing or influencing the stabilization and adjustment measures that were applied (The Economist, 1997c, d, e,1998d). In that sense, the lessons that should have been learnt from the 1982 debt crisis and the 1994 Mexican crisis (Buira, 1996; Eichengreen and Wyplosz, 1996; Griffith-Jones, 1996; Kenen, 1996; Ortiz-Martinez, 1998; Sachs et al. 1996) about the prevention of future financial crises were ignored. Over-anxiety on the part of the United States (and the IMF) to suppress any effective Asian regional initiative from emerging – especially one which excluded United States participation (Bergsten, 1997) – may well prove to have been myopic and costly (in terms of regional as well as global welfare) as events unfold over the longer term.

A dispassionate view might, nevertheless, suggest that turning to the IMF in the Asian crisis was a rational response on the part of the international financial community. After all, from a risk management perspective, there is lower risk incurred in relying upon an established crisis management mechanism (however imperfect) in the midst of a maelstrom than in attempting to devise a new mechanism which is untried and untested, with a high probability of being misdesigned when engineered under pressure. If such a regional mechanism failed to achieve its objectives, then it is not unreasonable to conclude that the costs of such failure might have been higher than the costs of possible crisis mismanagement by the IMF. But this argument, even if its validity is accepted at face value, does not lead to the conclusion that regional defences in Asia, or anywhere else, should not be devised and put in place once the present crisis has been contained and an environment for considered judgement restored.

What is significant from the viewpoint of contemplating regional intervention as a mezzanine bulwark for crisis containment, after national action has been taken but before global (i.e. IMF or World Bank) support is triggered, is that these crises (including the ERM *débâcle* of 1992) underscore the inherent vulnerability of most "non-reserve currency" countries – operating in a globalized financial world with open capital accounts – to currency shocks in the face of sudden changes in market perceptions or expectations about economic policies or fundamentals, and their risk weighting of uncertainty. Such vulnerability exists, although it may differ in degree, no matter how adroitly such countries manage their exchange rates, no matter whether countries are developed (ERM) or developing (Mexico and Asia), and no matter whether their exchange rates are fixed or floating. As Eichengreen and Wyplosz (1996) note:

> The dilemmas of exchange rate management are particularly acute for small, open developing economies. For them freely floating exchange rates are not tolerable because their markets are thin, their exchange rates would be volatile, and their trade and production would be severely disrupted. But fixed exchange rates are not viable either because they would be highly susceptible to speculative attack. As a practical matter such countries do not have available to them an exchange rate regime with the simplicity of a textbook model. In the short run, they will have to pursue a pragmatic policy that involves limited exchange rate management and the imposition of limited restrictions on capital movements. In the long run they will face strong pressure to contemplate monetary unification with a larger neighbour.

Until the world has moved towards a reduction in the number of currencies through the formation of larger regional currency blocs – a long-term development which is perhaps inevitable despite the opposition that could arise – financial crises will probably become more commonplace in a globalized

financial world of open capital accounts (Bayoumi and Eichengreen, 1994; Eichengreen, 1995; Greider, 1997; Obstfeld, 1994). Asymmetrical cost-risk ratios make short-term speculative attacks against non-reserve currencies unusually profitable unless effective deterrence in the form of credible and sustainable intervention capacity can be brought immediately into play (IMF, 1997a, 1998; Persaud, 1998). When such attacks succeed, and sometimes even when they do not, they invariably have secondary effects in destabilizing other financial markets which, unless quickly reversed, have even worse consequences for the real economy (Padoa-Schioppa and Saccomanni, 1994). The volume of funds now being traded in global foreign exchange markets, and available for speculative attacks, is so large as to overwhelm national intervention capacity, even when it is applied to support an exchange rate perceived as being in relative equilibrium (Mistry, 1997). Some augmentation of national capacity through regional pooling of reserves is an obvious remedy and one that has often been successfully applied.[2]

In such circumstances this paper asks whether it may not be opportune, indeed even necessary, for crisis containment and crisis management capacity to be developed and applied at the *regional* level before *global* defences are activated as a genuinely last (rather than first) resort. Such capacity already exists in Europe (Currie and Whitley, 1994; de Cecco and Giovannini, 1989; Giovannini and Mayer, 1992; Eichengreen et al., 1997). With monetary union, regional arrangements in Europe are, of course, much further advanced than in developing regions, but the question remains valid because of the short- and long-term "neighbourhood costs" of crisis mismanagement by international financial institutions throughout the developing world. These costs are not theoretical. They have actually materialized in Latin America, where they were prolonged for over a decade between 1982 and 1994. They are still being incurred across Africa as a result of official creditor failure to bring the debt crisis in that region to a decisive conclusion, despite the relatively low costs involved (Mistry, 1991, 1994, 1996b). And they are now materializing across Asia, where the costs are proving to be much larger than anyone could reasonably have anticipated or felt were necessary or desirable.

Regional crisis management capacity – designed as an integral feature of a future multilateral institutional architecture – could be useful in complementing national and global measures rather than substituting for them, as was the case in Europe with the OEEC and EPU (Kindleberger, 1984). In particular, when it comes to short-term crisis management, regional measures might be particularly appropriate in: (i) augmenting national intervention capacity through credible arrangements which convey clear signals to markets of a resolute commitment to pooling and using regional reserves under pre-agreed conditions; (ii) arresting the spread of neighbourhood contagion; (iii) preventing the disruption of regional trade and investment flows when a crisis begins unfolding; (iv) preventing the collapse of regional financial markets caused by panic selling; and (v) avoiding competitive devaluations. These five areas are examined in section III below.

Regional intervention can also be useful in crisis prevention – through the simple expedient of deploying at the regional level the same measures and instruments which are being advocated for surveillance, transparency and enforcement at the global level (IMF, 1998). Applying the concept of subsidiarity (i.e. devolving responsibility for dealing with an issue to the lowest level of governance capable of handling it) – which has been topical in the European context and which should apply with equal force elsewhere – such measures might be better implemented through stronger regional institutions or mechanisms in which member countries can participate more meaningfully than they can in the IMF; a global institution which has laboured to set itself up as the only "natural" disciplinarian even in managing local or regional crises.

Moreover, in the medium- and long-term the construction of regional monetary and exchange rate arrangements (similar but not identical to those evolved in Europe) and of regional foreign-exchange, securities and derivatives markets – which are broader, deeper, more robust, and more liquid than national markets in small countries can possibly be – can help to reduce unsustainable disequilibria in foreign-exchange and financial markets and minimize the scope for intraregional currency speculation by reducing considerably the range of currencies available to attract it in the first place (Bayoumi and Eichengreen, 1994).

III. Regional dimensions of financial crises and areas of regional action

In mid-1998, over a year after the Asian crisis broke out, explanations from academic, official, journalistic and market sources continue to differ on what caused the crisis, how it might have been contained, whether it was worsened by external intervention, how long it might last, and what the remedies might be for arresting and reversing the collapse of confidence in the economies concerned (see, for example, The Economist, 1997f, 1998a, d, g; FEER, 1998b; Goldstein, 1998; Krugman, 1998a; Radelet and Sachs, 1998; Reddy, 1998; Summers, 1998a; Stiglitz, 1998; Williamson, 1998; Wolf, 1998; IMF, 1997a, 1998a, b; World Bank, 1998).

This paper does not delve into issues concerning the causes and effects of Asia's collapse except to stress the sanguinity of earlier forecasts of recovery, and to draw on illustrative examples in making key arguments. The issues themselves have been dealt with at length (if not quite exhaustively or satisfactorily as yet) in the extensive literature which continues to emerge on the subject. The characteristics exhibited by financial crises affecting the developing world are noted mainly because of their relevance to the propositions this paper advances.

A. *Deploying reserves for effective intervention*

Financial crises in the developing world (and indeed even the 1992 ERM crisis in Europe) have demonstrated clearly the limitations of deploying national reserves and intervention capacity as immediate responses; even in countries deemed to have sufficient reserves to withstand currency shocks and destabilizing short-term capital outflows. That strategy failed in the United Kingdom and Italy (1992), in Mexico (1994) and in Thailand (1997), resulting in large and rapid reserve depletion, and leading to a loss of confidence and credibility in foreign-exchange and financial markets which triggered avoidable downward spirals (IMF, 1995, 1997a, b). It has since failed in Russia (1998) and South Africa (1998). What has become clear with the Mexican, European, Asian and other more recent financial crises is that it may no longer be possible for individual countries to attempt defending exchange rates successfully in the midst of a crisis, or even to support them credibly after large first-round corrections have occurred, without extra-national assistance; unless perhaps net reserve holdings are so large (as in Singapore, Hong Kong [China], and Taiwan Province of China) as to deter markets from making one-way bets on which they may be called. However, extra-large national reserve holdings are the exception rather than the rule and can be quite costly to maintain and deploy.

That raises two important questions. Should such extra-national assistance for credible intervention in exchange markets at the time of a crisis be provided automatically and immediately by external sources? If so, should it be provided by the IMF in its (mislabelled) role as international lender of last resort or by some other source? The IMF has not demonstrated in any of the financial crises between 1982 and 1998 the ability to act in "real time" or to mount a successful currency defence through intervention. Except in 1994, in no other financial crisis since 1982 has the IMF been able to forestall a liquidity crisis from becoming a solvency crisis. Its failure to act prophylactically has been the basis of several attacks by its critics. For that reason it is legitimate to ask whether the required extra-national assistance required to deal with a financial crisis might be more appropriately provided through a mezzanine regional line of defence first, which is designed to be more efficacious and can be justified on the grounds that regional concerted intervention, properly organized and executed, could be invaluable in preventing the high costs of neighbourhood contagion?

It should not be forgotten that, unlike the pound sterling, which collapsed after $2 billion in reserves had been spent defending it in September 1992, the French franc was defended successfully in the same month when Germany declared its willingness to use its own reserves to defend it. Speculators backed off. The same occurred when China signalled its intention in 1997 and 1998 to use its own reserves alongside those of Hong Kong (China) to defend the Hong Kong dollar peg. Those measures signalled a size of "pooled" intervention capacity, along with a degree of credibility and resolve, to markets to prevent them from taking one-way speculative bets. In both cases, these signals stabilized the situation and immediately ameliorated speculative pressures, without back-stopping reserves needing to be used, thereby arresting the process of spiral unravelling.

In a world of larger cross-border capital flows the need to deploy much larger amounts of usable reserves (if indeed reserves are to have any economic justification or financial value at all) to defend currencies under economically unjustifiable speculative attack – especially after exchange rates have been re-adjusted to approach "equilibrium" levels and essential macroeconomic policies have been appropriately realigned – has been recognized by almost every authority. A variety of proposals have been made for how this might be done (e.g. among others, Eichengreen, 1995; Helleiner, 1996; Kenen, 1996;

IMF, 1998). But outside common monetary arrangements, such as those in West and Southern Africa, the pooling and deployment of *regional* reserves in defence of the national currencies of members (especially in the developing world), under appropriate conditions and agreements, has been regarded as ineffectual at best, and dangerous at worst, even when those members are part of a regional integration arrangement. The reasons for such beliefs, however, remain obscure.

Many participants in the recent "debate" (The Economist, 1997a; Bergsten, 1997), which resulted in peremptory dismissal of Japan's proposal for an Asian facility of $100 billion, made at the 1997 Annual Meetings of the IMF and World Bank – coincidentally about the same amount that the Fund has since "packaged" for Thailand, Indonesia and the Republic of Korea with two thirds of those packages being funded regionally – suggested that the regional option must be eschewed. The ostensible reason for taking such a position was that regional facilities (or institutions) in the developing world would not be willing to apply harsh corrective discipline over their neighbours because "political" judgements would inevitably intrude into their decision-making. The IMF, on the other hand, could be relied on to be appropriately "harsh", taking only economic judgements into account in its remedial programmes and policy prescriptions.

Clearly there were no such fears about regional support facilities being acceptable and workable, if not *de rigeur,* in war-devastated Europe (cf. OEEC and EPU). Such an obviously biased view on why regional facilities would work in Europe but not in the developing world is curious and bears further examination. It assumes first that in the developing world, including the once "super-competent" Asia, politics will always prevent governments from using their reserves wisely in exercizing their self-interest because they are too polite (or supine) to be effective (The Economist, 1998c). By the same token it presumes that such a possibility does not exist in the developed world – a presumption which empirical evidence does not confirm. This concern about politics does, however, raise a question as to whether greater political sensitivity to ground-level realities in Indonesia, the Republic of Korea and Thailand, rather than adherence to disciplinary dogma, might have led the IMF to being more cautious, less "knee-jerk", and more effective than it was in designing its initial stabilization programmes. As events unfolded, it became apparent that the IMF attempted to mix into its early stabilization programmes too many structural reforms too soon and was forced to reverse on key issues – most embarrassingly in Indonesia (The Economist, 1997c, d, e, f, 1998a, d, g). As many credible voices have argued quite persuasively, the IMF may thus actually have exacerbated the crisis rather than arrested it, by conveying the message to markets and publics that Asian economies were structurally flawed to a much greater extent than they really were (Kissinger, 1998).

Second, such a view also assumes that the IMF has an automatic institutional right to a monopoly over crisis management in the developing world but not the developed world. Presumably it is assumed to possess the requisite institutional know-how, staff capacity and managerial wisdom always to apply the right remedies in a developing but not in a developed economy context. Such an assumption surely merits re-examination in the light of experience with the management of the 1982 debt crisis, the 1997 Asian crisis and the 1998 Russian crisis. Indeed the 1982 debt crisis suggested clearly that neither the IMF nor the World Bank possessed the "know-how" they were assumed to have (and often misrepresented themselves as having) to design, negotiate or help affected countries (especially in Africa) implement, successful structural adjustment programmes (Chhibber and Fischer, 1991; Corbo et al., 1992; Jayarajah and Branson, 1995; van der Hoeven and van der Kraaij, 1994). They were learning by doing; and at considerable cost to the economies they were experimenting with. Moreover, what they learnt in Latin America, and are still learning in Africa, does not appear to be particularly relevant to what is happening in Asia. Yet the IMF's prescriptions appear to be (dangerously) similar in all three regions; applying the same remedies to crises caused by public profligacy to those caused by private over-investment, over-saving and under-consumption. If such learning-by-doing has to occur in any event, might it not be much better, for political as well as economic reasons, for the learning to be done and experience accumulated at the national and regional levels, instead of being concentrated mainly at the global level?

Would a regional approach have fared better? In the case of Asia, the combined gross reserves of ASEAN, including Singapore, amounted to over $165 billion in July 1997, when the crisis hit Thailand (IMF, 1997) and net reserves were over $100 billion. If the reserves of China, Hong Kong (China), Taiwan Province of China, the Republic of Korea, and Japan were to be added to that sum, total Asian reserves available for defensive intervention would have been

in excess of $500 billion – assuming of course that all involved governments had agreed to intervene once they felt that the Thai baht had corrected to an appropriate level. That was a sufficiently credible amount to have forestalled further sustained speculative attacks. But, while large regional contributions were made to finance IMF-led rescue packages, monetary authorities in contributing Asian countries evaded exercizing the collective regional will to bring about changes in their neighbours' policies which they deemed to be necessary. They took cover under the IMF's umbrella instead.

That posture could be interpreted as substantiating the view that developing countries lack sufficient resolve to discipline themselves and to convey tough messages to one another – perhaps one of the downsides of having "Asian values" and policies of non-interference – leaving it to the IMF (again because of regional default and unwillingness) to play the role of disciplinarian, while using the region's money for credible financial support packages to be constructed. Or did the Asian countries involved simply find it more expedient to defer to United States Treasury and IMF pressure to leave crisis management to the IMF and eschew regional intervention?

In a regrettable (and avoidable) replay of the mishandled 1982 debt crisis, the events that have unfolded in Asia – regional contagion, disruptive political consequences, and large real economy dislocations by way of lost output and exports, corporate restructurings and bankruptcies, unnecessarily large reductions in asset values, continued vulnerability to repeated speculative attacks, and burgeoning unemployment – have been more damaging than anyone could have contemplated (FEER, 1998b). Most regional observers across a wide spectrum of opinion seem to agree that the degeneration of the Thai currency crisis into a region-wide economic *débâcle* was neither necessary nor desirable. In the aftermath of such events, it is not unreasonable to ask whether Asian Governments and the international community now need to reconsider whether coordinated regional action to stabilize foreign-exchange and financial markets more swiftly might not have been a superior alternative to IMF intervention as a way of preventing quite so much damage.

After the experience of Latin America and Africa in the aftermath of the 1982 debt crisis, was it wise or safe for Asia to relinquish its economic, political and security interests to global institutions – dominated by interests other than those of the region and in which Asian Governments did not have an adequate say – however well-meaning such institutions might be? Was it prudent to do, so especially when such institutions have not demonstrated any particular competence to suggest, beyond a reasonable doubt, that they have what it takes to address and resolve problems – which are quintessentially regional, rather than global or systemic in nature – in the way that they needed to be resolved? Would notions of subsidiarity and comparative advantage not imply that such problems should be addressed through regional measures, after national measures have proven demonstrably inadequate, before resorting to global agencies for support?

That, of course, raises the question of whether, with regional action, other structural problems such as financial system distress across Asia would have been attended to? Or would successful intervention only have led to premature complacency on the part of the Asian authorities concerned, resulting in the build-up of a larger and more damaging crisis later on – as seems to be the situation unfolding in Japan and South Asia at present? Counterfactuals are impossible to argue convincingly. It must be conceded, however, that the regional institutional infrastructure needed to "propose and enforce" policy changes and structural reforms is only in a nascent stage of being formed in Asia and Latin America and under two specific common monetary arrangements in West and Southern Africa. It really does not exist in other parts of the developing world. Yet, the increasing need for coordinated regional defence of currencies or financial markets which will arise in several developing regions (as emerging markets attempt to integrate into the global market) should, in itself, raise sufficient warning that serious structural problems exist in almost all developing regions which need to be attended to over an appropriate time-frame in a manageable way, through appropriately designed regional mechanisms and institutional machinery, and not just through global international financial institutions.

Mexico's experience in 1994/95 suggests that once an immediate crisis is overcome, with credible intervention and restored stability the spread of regional contagion can be arrested, and damage contained, before underlying structural problems are dealt with (Buira, 1996; Sachs et al., 1996; Ortiz-Martinez, 1998). Indeed, the crisis management experience gained so far suggests that early damage needs to be contained to avoid that problems which might otherwise be manageable (e.g. non-performing bank loan portfolios) become unmanageable. This happens when underlying asset (and collateral) values are permitted to collapse, leading to an eventual cessation of cash-flow generating (and debt-servicing) capacity, as liquidity to enterprises is squeezed and further credit is denied. Sceptics about the efficacy of regional action, on the other hand, can point to the experiences of: South Asia, where political complacency set in immediately after stabilization was achieved; and Japan, which has not until now, experienced a full-blown financial crisis, but has attended for seven years to problems that needed to be resolved in its domestic financial system (Lardy, 1998). These Asian examples could be construed as more valid comparators for suggesting that, without IMF pressure, Asian Governments might not have been inclined to attend to structural problems in financial systems had stability been immediately restored in currency and securities markets.

B. *Financial contagion*

The experiences of the 1982, 1994 and 1997 crises in developing countries, and the 1992 crisis in Europe, have differed in the neighbourhood contagion effects that they have had in currency, financial and property markets and, eventually, in causing regional economic implosion (Goldstein, 1998). In the 1982 debt crisis, contagion spread throughout Latin America, even in economies which were relatively sound and not excessively indebted at the time (e.g. Colombia and Venezuela). That happened because of a sudden and dramatic change of perception on the part of commercial banks, which collectively decided to stop new long-term lending and rollover of short-term facilities, seek immediate principal repayments, and reduce net exposure in all developing countries, especially in Latin America and Africa.

Asia escaped that fate in 1982. Early withdrawal by commercial banks from the Republic of Korea and Indonesia was reversed with swift corrective action being taken by their Governments with credible, swift IMF and World Bank support. However capital withdrawal from the Philippines was sustained, resulting in its suffering the same prolonged debt crisis (exacerbated by the unravelling of the Marcos Administration) as its Latin American cohorts. Financial and currency markets in the indebted countries were less developed and much less integrated, globally and regionally, at the time. Thus, while most were adversely affected, it was not as a result of herd behaviour on the part of private foreign institutional (or individual) investors but as a consequence of the economic implosion which followed, leading to a collapse of confidence on the part of global bank creditors and domestic investors.

In the Mexican crisis of 1994, immediate regional and emerging market-wide contagion occurred as foreign holders of high-yielding, currency-risk protected, short-term treasury bills in all developing countries manifested anxieties about the currency values and repayment capabilities of a number of other governments (especially in Central and Eastern Europe) which had also issued such paper (IMF, 1995). Such anxieties were heightened when the use of national reserves to prop up the peso failed; but they were contained, and reversed markets began to believe that the IMF rescue package, prompted by the United States, would work. The speed and manner in which that package was put together disturbed other G-7 Governments, which complained of indecent haste and lack of sufficient consultation. But it demonstrated the resolve of the United States Administration (though not of Congress) to prevent another region-wide or emerging-market-wide crisis. Also, the IMF was more familiar with the Mexican situation, having dealt with that country's problems intensively and continuously between 1982 and 1994 (Griffith-Jones, 1996, 1998a). The success of its intervention assured markets of the need (and the safety) of maintaining a sufficient flow of private liquidity to other emerging markets. Foreign and domestic investor sentiment in these markets was corrected and restored within a matter of months, i.e. by mid-1995, although many critics of the Mexican rescue package suggest that it might actually have set the stage for the ensuing *débâcle* in Thailand, and later on in Indonesia (Teunissen, 1996).

In Asia the contagion effects, after Thailand, built up more slowly. It took about three months before Indonesia was affected and six months before the Republic of Korea came to be seen as a problem (Khanna, 1998). Since then, contagion has spread more swiftly with more devastating effects (and repeated speculative attacks) on all financial, currency and property markets in the region; even in relatively strong economies which do not have the same problems: i.e. Hong Kong (China), Singapore, and Taiwan Province of China. Surprisingly, and fortunately, they have not yet encompassed China which, structurally, confronts more serious problems than Indonesia, the Republic of Korea or Thailand. China has a systemically fragile financial system, and the structural reforms needed for a successful transition to becoming a "normal" market economy are

unlikely to be smooth (The Economist, 1998h; Harding and Kynge, 1998; Hughes, 1998; Kynge, 1998; Lardy, 1998; Montagnon, 1998).

Region-wide contagion in Asia has been compounded and intensified by the rapid and simultaneous withdrawal from its financial markets of major actors, including (i) global commercial banks, which had stepped up short-term lending to private companies in Asia dramatically and non-transparently in 1996-1997; (ii) foreign private institutional investors concerned about currency and value losses on their equity investment portfolios and about the re-imposition of restrictions on capital account transactions; (iii) transnational corporate treasuries which had invested heavily in Asia in the form of both direct and portfolio investment; and (iv) domestic and regional private individual investors fearing substantial portfolio damage, accompanied by adverse political and ethnic repercussions.

Contagion in Asia has been exacerbated by a number of other factors. These include, first, the unexpected inability of Asian Governments to contain the currency crisis with swift, resolute action. Instead of behaving decisively, as was expected of them, they vacillated with uncharacteristic hesitation and weakness in their early responses (IMF, 1997b, 1998a; Goldstein, 1998). An inability to grasp the political nettle on the part of incumbent administrations required changes in governments for essential action to be taken; which of course led to political risk being added to the other risks perceived by private investors (FEER, 1998b). The forced change of government in every affected Asian country, except Malaysia, in 1997 and 1998 has also given rise to unfortunate speculation within Asia and throughout the developing world that (as was the case with the 1982 debt crisis in Latin America and Africa) the Asian financial crisis has been taken advantage of opportunistically by Western governments (using the IMF as their instrument) to bring about changes in political systems which, in their view, had outlived their usefulness; especially in Indonesia (Kissinger, 1998).

Second, the crisis was compounded by the United States' hesitation in the Thailand bailout for fear of a Congressional backlash at a time when legislation authorizing the United States' contribution to the recently negotiated IMF quota increase was being steered through for passage. This was followed by its over-compensating in inducing the IMF to seek more ambitious and immediate structural changes in the Republic of Korea and Indonesia than were politically achievable or justifiable. Third, the crisis did not abate but grew because of the failure of first-round IMF rescue programmes in Indonesia, the Republic of Korea and Thailand to have an impact (as they were neither large nor credible enough) on turning around market perceptions. They probably did more harm than good because of the haste, maladroitness, insensitivity and the humiliating (for Asian Governments and leaders) publicity with which they were conceived, negotiated and implemented. Fourth, it is possible that the Asian crisis is not receding quickly enough because of a growing sense on the part of the global investor community that what has come to be known in the international financial community as the "goldilocks scenario" (i.e. the "exactly-right" – neither too hot nor too cold – circumstances in which the longest post-1960s boom in global output and asset value growth has been sustained) might be coming to an end; with the Asian crisis being seen as the precursor of that prospect materializing.

Contagion in Europe spread instantaneously during the 1992 crisis. Its effects have been sufficiently documented in the media and literature to require being revisited here. Despite a large body of literature having been generated on contagion in each case, the speed and transmission mechanisms through which it has spread remain to be properly understood (Goldstein, 1998; IMF, 1998a). Most theoretical and anecdotal explanations advanced for contagion in the Mexican and Asian crises are incomplete and partial, if not misleading. In the Asian case, the contagion effect was significant because of interdependencies in Asian investor holdings, both portfolio and direct – i.e. cross-holdings on the part of Asian (including overseas-Chinese, Japanese and Korean) investor groups in trans-Asian industrial corporations, bank and non-bank financial institutions, and property development companies. These have not been researched as thoroughly as hindsight suggests they should have been. Through the 1990s these intra-regional ties have become closer, as suggested by relatively larger proportions of intra-industry and intra-company trade (and more rapid rates in the growth of such trade) in Asia than in other developing regions (Broinowski, 1990; Bundy et al., 1994; Fukasaku, 1995; Healey, 1991). But that reality does not seem to have been recognized in designing the crisis management measures that were applied, or in acknowledging the significant regional dimensions that the crisis was bound to have.

The financial crises affecting developing countries in the 1990s have invariably begun with a (first slow, then sudden) change in perception on the part of markets, usually triggered by a sense of impending (or actual) political failure, resulting in a creeping and/or sudden loss of market confidence in the ability of governments to manage the economy. A short period of growing market scepticism, when unallayed swiftly, has been followed by an early exit on the part of astute (or well-connected or well-informed) institutional (foreign and domestic) lenders and investors. The unwinding process gathers steam across all investor groups causing downward pressures on securities markets and exchange rates. When such pressures are not accommodated either by price adjustments in securities markets or exchange rates, or by successful intervention, they result in large, dramatic declines in currency values as a consequence of markets (and herd instincts) over-correcting and triggering a chain-reaction across imperfect emerging markets for equity, debt, derivatives and property, exacerbated by an accelerated outflow of short-term and portfolio capital, both foreign and domestic. The spectre of substantial portfolio losses being incurred by domestic investors triggers further sales of domestic assets (securities and property) and currency, as local capital seeks (with fewer means at its disposal than privileged foreign investors) to prevent further portfolio value erosion and create emergency liquidity. Contrary to widely held suspicions across Asia, the flight of domestic capital (which can rarely be arrested through the temporary re-imposition of capital controls because a parallel market develops almost overnight) is likely to have been at least as responsible for the continued downward pressure in currency and securities markets as the operations of global currency speculators and hedge funds.

Thus, what starts as a liquidity crisis can almost immediately become a solvency crisis when the chain-reaction triggered by a crisis in currency markets, spilling over into other financial (and asset) markets, is not interrupted quickly or effectively. The probability of that happening is high, not just because of government failure but also because national foreign-exchange and financial markets in most developing countries are still deficient. Despite their over-emphasized attractions (which are exaggerated when global institutional investors are in a mood to sell securities to their unsuspecting, often unsophisticated, domestic private client base), emerging markets are risky precisely because they are not sufficiently developed, resilient or robust. They do not provide enough local instruments for portfolio value hedging in tertiary derivative markets; they are also capable of becoming illiquid extremely quickly, when exit routes counted upon by portfolio managers in better times disappear (Mistry, 1997, 1998). In other words, taken individually, currency and financial markets in developing countries (and indeed even in some of the smaller developed ones) are narrow and shallow. They crack easily when they come under pressures which they are not equipped to withstand.

Apart from improving the ability of governments to recognize warning signals early and act swiftly, which often involves balancing difficult conflicts of political interests, what can be done on a regional basis to prevent contagion from spreading so swiftly? There are several possibilities. First, if intervention in foreign-exchange markets on a regional scale can be organized properly to augment national intervention capacity in the face of a speculative attack, contagion is unlikely to spread. Second, even if intervention in foreign-exchange markets is less successful than expected, regional lines of defence in other financial markets (i.e. in debt, equity and derivative markets) can be activated through organized direct intervention and sufficient liquidity support, as happened in 1987 throughout the OECD countries and as Hong Kong (China) successfully managed to do in 1998 (Ridding, 1998) to prevent asset values from falling too precipitately and declining well below realistic levels (judged by any yardstick used by the market), as has happened in the rest of Asia.

Again, such intervention is more likely to be successful and more credible to markets if it is backstopped by large pooled regional resources, rather than the much smaller amounts of national funds. Markets can pick off the currencies and securities markets of countries one at a time more easily than they can confront concerted action by a number of governments determined to prevent them from over-correcting and to arrest contagion. This can be achieved through regional arrangements which swiftly backstop, through compensating short-term inflows, sudden outflows of portfolio capital (foreign and domestic) that occur from equity or debt markets, coupled with national actions to bolster domestic liquidity for sufficiently long to stabilize markets followed by its later withdrawal.

Third, over the medium term, action can (and should) be taken to strengthen small, shallow national markets in debt, equity and derivatives by regionalizing such markets of developing countries: first subregionally, then pan-regionally to give them more width, depth and liquidity. Such a step would compel a greater degree of regional coordination and

harmonization in macroeconomic and macro-financial policies than is possible when dealing suddenly with crises in the neighbourhood. Policies changed under pressure in one country to cope with a crisis can drive policies in an inappropriate direction in neighbouring countries. Regionalization would also create an internal compulsion for establishing an institutional machinery through which benign regional peer group pressure can be applied on governments in a regular and "natural" way, ensuring that policy deviations in any single country are not permitted to go unchecked for too long, and certainly not to the point that compromises the interests of the region as a whole by necessitating intervention at the global level.

C. *Protecting regional trade and investment flows and financial markets*

Perhaps the strongest reason for advocating a larger (curative and preventive) role for regional mechanisms – as an integral part of the overall machinery that is activated to manage financial crises in developing countries – is to prevent the disruption of intraregional trade and investment flows that have a direct and immediate impact on regional output, not just in the short term but in the medium and long run as well. In Asia that phenomenon has been particularly strong. The spreading financial crisis has disrupted or severed normal lines of intraregional trade credit, and brought to a virtual halt flows of intraregional cross-border investment. Worse, it has resulted in unwinding many existing cross-border regional investments as equity holders in such investments attempt to cut their losses, restructure their balance sheets and reduce foreign holdings in order to focus on retaining market share and increasing cash-generation in home markets.

So far, the IMF's crisis management programmes in Asia have shown scant respect for accommodating this important dimension, focusing instead – as its programmes invariably do – on national policy measures and actions. Under such programmes, adjustments in tax rates, exchange rates, interest rates, along with public and private consumption "belt-tightening" restraints and sweeping reforms in fragile financial systems – are all aimed at improving national competitiveness and enhancing national debt-servicing capacity. This is invariably and unavoidably at the expense of immediate neighbours. Though rhetorical tribute is paid to eschewing beggar-thy-neighbour effects in the design of IMF programmes, what results in practice is precisely that.

Such an outcome is inevitable when a national government conducts bilateral negotiations with the IMF. In that negotiating context there is no mechanism or room for introducing legitimate regional concerns which might argue for taking a different tack, or for ensuring a degree of regional consistency in the conditionality imposed. In theory such concerns are supposedly accommodated by the IMF within its internal management circles as it negotiates programmes with several countries in the region at the same time. In practice the opposite usually happens, as the experience of Latin America and Africa during the debt crisis confirms. Bilateral negotiations conducted in an intense, pressure-cooker atmosphere – which crisis situations create by definition – usually preclude "extraneous" (i.e. non-national) issues from being recognized. Moreover, the inevitable bureaucratic dynamics in an international organization like the IMF invariably come into play in preventing a coordinated, consistent approach being taken to the design of programmes for highly interdependent and interlinked countries in any developing region.

Intraregional trade and investment flows among (and within the corporate boundaries of) interlinked East Asian companies – as opposed to North American, European or Japanese transnationals – as well as operations in Asia's financial markets, have been heavily supported by national or pan-regional Asian commercial and investment banks, and a plethora of Asian non-bank financial intermediaries, not all of which were originally unsound. Many of these, especially in Indonesia, Malaysia, the Republic of Korea and Thailand are now being wound up, merged, restructured and shrunk in size and lending capacity. The potential for creating large-scale, long-lasting damage to regional welfare in the process is considerable; especially if a "prolonged fit of absent-mindedness" and a "divided-we-rule" mentality (Morris, 1968, 1973, 1978) persists on the part of the institutions now involved in regional rescue operations for severely contaminated financial systems.

Unless specific actions and policies are undertaken to prop up intraregional lines of trade credit through the commercial banking system – i.e. through the Asian operations of global banks guaranteed by international financial institutions, as well as through special trade-finance support facilities administered by Asia's central banks and made available to importers and exporters through Asia's remaining national and pan-regional banks – the region's crisis will be unnecessarily prolonged.

Similarly, unless long-term financial facilities (both equity and debt) are made available to regional (as opposed to extraregional foreign) direct investors in existing cross-border Asian ventures to allow them to retain their holdings and allow sufficient room and time for workouts and corporate revival to occur, the result is likely to be both a reduction of Asia's productive base as well as a forced (and unnecessary) fire-sale of Asian assets to extraregional foreign investors, who risk being seen as having it in their own interests to reduce or impede the competitive threat posed by Asia in world export markets. Such facilities need to be made through Asia's regional and national financial markets in ways which enable them to resume functioning normally and recover from too precipitate and large a drop in the values of traded securities as well as in corporate and market capitalization. With the egregious over-corrections that have occurred in Asian equity markets, the market capitalization of many listed Asian companies is now a fraction of the marked-down value of their net assets.

Are the IMF and the World Bank Group the most appropriate sources for providing regional facilities to support sorely needed special finance for reviving intraregional trade and investment through Asia's financial markets? It is difficult to justify resort to global official institutions whose charters preclude them from providing facilities which discriminate between regional and extraregional traders and investors. That would be especially true for what might be perceived as facilities designed specifically to advance parochial (though no less legitimate) regional interests.

The desirability of the regional measures being suggested above may well raise a potential conflict between the non-discriminatory requirements of the World Trade Organization (WTO), at least in the agreement on financial services. Though that agreement contains some (rather ambiguous) provisions permitting extraordinary support for national financial institutions in times of crises, it does not contain similar provisions for discrimination in favour of regional institutions or measures. That raises the question as to whether the financial services agreement needs to contain sections and clauses similar to Article XXIV in the agreement on trade, with a view to permitting some latitude for appropriate regional monetary and financial arrangements, especially in the developing world.[3]

Europe would probably argue forcefully in its own case, but perhaps not as forcefully for Asia, that regional funds, monetary arrangements, financial markets and institutions are indeed needed to advance legitimate regional interests. They are needed even more to forestall anti-competitive predatory actions on the part of non-regional interests in emerging global industries, such as: financial services, airlines and other transport services, telecommunications and power, hospitality and tourism, semiconductors, textiles, consumer and industrial electronics, automobiles and intermediate products. Established enterprises in the developed world now have an unprecedented opportunity to carve out a long-term competitive advantage and bring under control what is often seen as "rampant" competition from Asia (with its allegedly adverse implications for the stability and security of protected labour, goods and services markets in Europe and the Western Hemisphere). This can now be easily achieved through entry at bargain-basement prices into the ownership and management of Asian enterprises in these industries.

The argument being made above about competitiveness holds particularly true for East Asia, with its demonstrated prowess in the world's export markets. But the more general underlying argument concerning the need for protecting and advancing legitimate regional interests, especially when they risk being compromised by financial crises, would hold for any region, whether developing or developed, and not just for Asia. It is an extension of the national interest argument which is invariably (often wrongly) accepted without question in international circles. The argument being made for regional interests to be respected and protected is predicated on two realities. The first is that, contrary to the trade and investment theories espoused in its favour, the present paradigm of multilateralism, and the institutional framework through which it is practised, serves the interests of only a few powerful, economically advantaged countries; it does not serve the legitimate interests of developing nations (Mistry, 1996). The second reality is that, because the present model of multilateralism is so flawed, a new form of regionalism (Hettne and Inotai, 1994; Hettne, 1998) is an essential intermediate step for improving global competition and welfare. Only when such regionalism takes hold, can a different and more genuine model of multilateralism evolve which represents more accurately the theoretical constructs on which it is based. Such multilateralism is likely to be based on interactions not among some 200 odd highly unequal nation-states, but among six to ten (emerging) regional blocs which are more equal in terms of their relative political and economic bargaining power and their overall weight in the global economy.

D.   *Avoiding competitive devaluations*

Another powerful reason for regional involvement and action, both in preventing financial crises and in managing them, is to avert the prospect of affected neighbouring countries resorting to competitive devaluations triggering other beggar-thy-neighbour policies, either in desperation or in a vortex created by action-and-reaction. Many credible observers suggest that an early factor that contributed to the Asian crisis was devaluation of the Chinese yuan by 40 per cent, which made the Chinese economy "super-competitive" relative to other East Asian countries exporting the same goods to the same markets, and lead to the accumulation of large trade surpluses (and reserves) mainly at the expense of its neighbours (Bergsten, 1997). Failure on the part of East Asian Governments to react and adjust quickly enough, in a measured fashion, to the decline of their competitiveness, completed with adherence to a dollar nominal peg when the dollar was appreciating against all other major currencies and especially against the Japanese yen, led to building up unsustainable disequilibria in Asian current accounts. These could not be financed indefinitely by hot portfolio capital and short-term borrowing from global commercial banks.

A further episode of competitive devaluation may have been triggered in November 1997 when, after the turmoil in Asian currency markets following sharp markdowns of the baht, ringgit and rupiah, Taiwan Province of China also let its currency slide, putting up only a minimal defence despite its ability to support its currency and with no real need for a rate realignment. That resulted in strong renewed pressures on the Hong Kong and Singapore dollars and started a run on the Korean won. This chain of events has been persuasively analysed (Bergsten, 1997), as has the need for regional mechanisms to dampen and quell such actions. The risk is considerable that a worst-case scenario of yet another round of Asian devaluations may occur if the decline of the Japanese yen is not successfully arrested (The Economist, 1998g). Should that not happen, China has threatened (and might be obliged) to devalue again, precipitating another currency shock throughout Asia and deepening as well as prolonging the Asian crisis. The impact of such a shock would not be confined just to Asia. In the wake of the August 1998 rouble crisis, a devaluation of the yuan would transmit tectonic tremors to South Asia, Latin America, Eastern and Central Europe and South Africa, as well and destabilize currency markets in the developed world. The impact of such an eventuality would be large in Asia and elsewhere as burgeoning trade deficits in Europe and the United States became unsustainable, conceivably triggering retaliatory, protective measures and reversing the progress that has been made in liberalizing global trade and finance over the last two decades.

Stabilizing Asian exchange rates at present levels almost certainly implies conveying to markets and potential speculators that: (i) credible intervention capacity does exist in Asia in terms of aggregate regional reserves, and (ii) all governments in the region will pool their reserves and utilize that capacity forcefully should such action become necessary, without having to resort to the IMF. If conveyed collectively and convincingly, such a message would not be lost on markets (Persaud 1998; Lipsky 1998). It might actually result in overcorrected Asian currencies reversing some of their excessive losses and appreciating back to new equilibrium levels, thus further easing market-induced pressures and creating the climate for appropriate adjustment measures. Such a turnaround might not occur as quickly as in 1995 subsequent to the Mexican crisis, but it would enable Asia to recover faster than the decade that it took for Latin America to recover as a result of the mismanagement of the debt crisis and the 15 years it has taken for Africa, where recovery is still uncertain.

IV. Regional financial crisis management: what arrangements?

The conclusion that emerges from the preceding sections, supported by widely-shared intuition in Asia as well as in developing countries more generally, is that *regional arrangements* for crisis management in the developing world are essential and need to be brought into play quickly and credibly at a "mezzanine" level, i.e. between national measures (which by themselves may be insufficient) and global (IMF) intervention to stabilize foreign-exchange and international financial markets. Such arrangements should be seen as complementing, rather than competing with or substituting for, arrangements at the national and the global level. They need to be coordinated closely with counterpart national and global arrangements on a continuing basis, not just when crises occur. Similar arrangements already exist in the developed world.

While far from perfect, as the European ERM crisis of 1992 and the equity market crisis of 1987 demonstrated, such arrangements among OECD countries have proven to be more efficacious in coping with such financial crises than the IMF was in 1982 or 1997. They have enabled developed countries to avoid recourse to IMF "discipline", which – if experience is any guide – involves two risks: (i) that the wrong prescriptions are applied for too long, and (ii) that prescriptions which might be correct for one set of circumstances are continued and become inappropriate when circumstances change.[4] Institutional inertia and/or obstinacy can result from an institutional monopoly (usually accompanied by institutional rigidity) determining the nature, direction, pace and intensity of policy reform. Such a monopoly exacerbates the risks of crisis mismanagement. Such risks are not contrived or fanciful. As already observed, they have materialized before and, in Asia, are materializing again.

What type of regional arrangements are needed to cope with financial crises?

It is tempting, but perhaps premature and overly ambitious, to be very specific at the outset about the institutional architecture, its decision-making characteristics, or the special facilities and instruments that are needed at the regional level to complement those that exist at the national and at the global level. Instead, we present below a few general ideas and concepts about the regional arrangements that might be considered, once stability has been restored, retrospectives have become clearer than opinions framed in the heat of a crisis, and the shortcomings as well as the large risks of relying too heavily on the existing framework and approach to crisis management have been more fully appreciated.

As indicated, the present approach relies excessively on the IMF despite the insufficiency of its funding, the limitations of a quota based approach to access, and the serious deficiencies in its "know-how", which prevent it from being as omniscient or as capable in managing crises as it is invariably assumed. Moreover, it is not obvious that the specific regional arrangements for different developing regions with different characteristics, and confronting different economic and financial circumstances, should be the same. To be effective they will probably need to vary quite substantially in form, function and financial capacity, even if the underlying principles on which they are founded have a degree of universality and consistency. They can be modelled on the "mutual support" institutions which already exist at the global level but which, at present, serve mainly the interests of their larger OECD share-holders. Several proposals for such regional monetary and financial support arrangements have emerged both before and in the aftermath of the Asian crisis. Others were mooted on various occasions between 1985 and 1995 in the context of Africa and Latin America.

As far as **East Asia** is concerned, the most important proposals have been the following:

(i) *An "Asian BIS":* A regional institution modelled on the Bank for International Settlements (BIS) to serve central banks in East Asia and the Antipodes. This idea was mooted by Governor Bernard Fraser of the Reserve Bank of Australia (Fraser, 1995) two years prior to the Asian crisis in a speech in which he noted that current global arrangements operating through the BIS did not suit Asia particularly well. Despite holding the largest part of the world's international reserves, East Asia as a whole had insufficient influence in the BIS, which was controlled by G-10, and the only Asian member in this Group was Japan. Moreover, the risk-weighting approach adopted by BIS tended to discriminate against Asian (and all non-OECD) banks in ways that were seen as inequitable. For that reason, a regional BIS clone was seen to be necessary which would work in ways that accommodated Asian re-alities. Governor Fraser went on to note that the IMF, as it was presently constituted, and its decision-making processes precluded it from acting quickly enough in crisis situations. For that reason he felt there was a case for "close neighbours to have their own mutual support arrangements to deal quickly with emergency situations" (op. cit.).

(ii) *An Asian Monetary Facility* (often misleadingly portrayed as an "Asian IMF" or "Asian Mon-etary Fund", "AMF") equipped with $100 bil-lion to be funded within the region and utilized for mutual assistance through regional inter-vention support. This proposal was made by the Japanese Minister of Finance (Mitsuzuka, 1997; The Economist, 1997a) at the 1997 Annual Meetings of the IMF and World Bank in Hong

Kong (China) just after the Thai baht crisis, but before the crises in Indonesia and the Republic of Korea erupted. The proposal, which might have been worthwhile and helpful if deliberated upon more carefully, was derailed quickly by the United States Treasury and IMF for fear that it would detract from the role (and power) of the latter and make it even more difficult to get the United States' contribution to the IMF's latest quota increase authorized by the United States Congress. Moreover, the hesitation of the Japanese authorities in the face of this opposi-tion, given the dramatic weakening of Japan's own economy shortly thereafter, coupled with reservations on the part of the Chinese, Hong Kong, Taiwanese, and Singaporean authorities to commit a portion of their reserves for neigh-bourhood support without linking such support, case-by-case, to IMF programmes, resulted in this proposal unfortunately being (prematurely and hastily) abandoned.

(iii) *New "AMF"-type regional arrangements* to "reinforce the efforts of the IMF", with the sug-gestion that the proposed AMF should be lodged under the Asia-Pacific Economic Cooperation (APEC) forum "as its logical institutional home" (Bergsten, 1997). This proposal was based on the conviction that the IMF would not, on its own, be able to convince countries heading for a financial crisis to act pre-emptively, as it failed to do in Thailand in late 1996. Nor would it have sufficient financial resources to intervene effectively on its own, and neither would the G-7, the United States or Japan. For those reasons, Bergsten felt that "the best prospect is (to rely on) neighbouring countries: because they are so likely to be hurt themselves by fallout from a crisis, their intervention is both legitimate and apt to be delivered forcefully".

(iv) *An APEC Standby Funding Arrangement* (also proposed by Bergsten) to support further IMF programmes in the region because "the current cases are only reminders that such crises in-evitably occur from time to time – international rescue packages will be required in the future as in the past – moreover the alternative to standby arrangements is ad hoc bailouts as cobbled together by the United States for Mexico and by Japan for Thailand". Bergsten went on to suggest that any APEC arrangement should be tied inextricably to IMF programmes testifying before a United States Congressional Committee that:

... the United States has a particular interest in lodging any 'Asian monetary fund' whether limited to new forms of multilateral surveillance ('peer pressure') or encompassing additional funding arrangements as well, in APEC. A central thrust of American foreign policy, including foreign economic policy, has been to avoid any institutional devices that – to use the words of former Secretary of State James Baker – 'would draw a line down the middle of the Pacific and threaten to divide East Asia and North America.' We have thus firmly, and successfully so far, rejected Malaysian and other proposals for an East Asian Economic Group or any other 'Asia only' devices.

(v) *Regional "General Agreements to Borrow":* Styled on the IMF's own GAB arrangements (superseded by the New Arrangements to Borrow, NAB), Asian Governments have been considering proposals advanced, *inter alia*, by Singapore to extend mutual assistance by entering into framework GABs among the central banks of neighbouring countries in Asia. These would enable member countries to draw, to a limited pre-agreed extent, on additional resources from neighbouring countries in the event that such resources are necessary to augment national reserves in mounting a credible and successful intervention defence. Reciprocally, under such arrangements, countries would be obliged to accept mutually enforced financial and monetary discipline under enhanced surveillance and information-sharing arrangements.

(vi) *Enhanced regional surveillance arrangements:* Although all of the four proposals above have been mooted, the only one taking any shape at present involves enhanced information-sharing and surveillance arrangements among the central banks of the ASEAN member countries. This was the only concrete outcome of several meetings held among ASEAN countries to consider prospects for the Japanese and Malaysian proposals to set up an AMF, culminating in the Manila meeting in December 1997, which dropped the idea of an AMF but agreed to strengthen mutually supportive surveillance. Several regular meetings have since been held at the level of senior central banking officials in improving existing surveillance mechanisms. But these appear to have been aimed more at information-sharing on transactions involving portfolio capital flows and the activities of

known speculative funds in ASEAN currency markets in order to provide earlier warning signals. There has been less emphasis on surveillance over the health of Asian banking and financial systems and over the management of monetary and exchange-rate policies of the different Asian countries. These issues, however, are gradually becoming a more important part of the regional information-sharing and surveillance agenda.

As is obvious from the foregoing, most of the proposals that have been made (and, up to now, rejected) for regional institutions and mechanisms in Asia focus on crisis prevention and on enhancing the ability to contain crises in their early stages before they become full-scale *débâcles* of the type which unfolded in Latin America and Africa in 1982 and in Asia in 1997/98. There is a clear need for the more ambitious of these proposals (e.g. an Asian monetary support facility, if not quite an Asian equivalent of the IMF) to be revived and reconsidered. It is critical that large-scale intervention capacity utilizing pooled reserves be created in a manner which enables such capacity to be activated quickly by regional actors. Whether the creation of such capacity also requires the creation of a regional institution like the IMF to manage is questionable since another plurilateral bureaucracy may not be in the best interests of its users.

Obviously some type of secretariat (incorporating both research capacity as well as operational capacity to lend either directly to national central banks or for open-market operations in currency and financial markets) is essential to support such a facility. But it needs to be lean and have an established reputation in international financial markets, operating in the way that the monetary authorities of both Hong Kong (China) and Singapore have demonstrated is possible. Indeed, such a secretariat could be lodged in either of these two authorities or in both, i.e. in Singapore for the ASEAN countries and in Hong Kong (China) (or Tokyo operating as an independent entity under the Bank of Japan) for the North-East Asian countries, including China, with close day-to-day communication, coordination and interaction between these centres. Had such a facility existed in late 1997, it might have proven instrumental, if not decisive, in preventing the Asian currency crisis from becoming a full-blown *débâcle*.

Contrary to the presumption that was made emphatically in successful but probably short-sighted attempts to derail the AMF idea, such a facility would not necessarily have denied the IMF the space it needed to bring about more fundamental transformations in Asia's financial systems, if Asian authorities had been disinclined (even after deploying their own collective reserves) to act on these as expeditiously and decisively as they should. The mere existence of such a facility would almost certainly have avoided the economic trauma that has been caused unnecessarily (and unwittingly by the IMF and the United States authorities) by over-exaggerating Asia's problems in international financial markets. Operated properly, the facility would have permitted the requisite initial correction in Asian currencies without precipitating the free fall that occurred in all financial and asset markets in its aftermath.

The question of how such a facility ought to have been set up and how it might have (or should be) operated will not be discussed here. Suffice it to assert that there is sufficient global experience with such facilities to learn from best practices and apply them to the circumstances confronted. Proposals similar to the ones for Asia elaborated on above have also been advanced for Latin America (in the context of Mercosur arrangements being extended to embrace regional monetary as well as trade arrangements) and for parts of Africa. A recent study by the African Development Bank (AfDB, 1993) proposed an exchange-rate stabilization fund for the Southern African Development Community, both as a reaction to the extreme currency instability that many countries of the region experienced between 1985 and 1995 and in anticipation of Mexico- and Asia-type of problems occurring also in South Africa.

But as yet no regional proposals have been advanced for coping with the fallout of currency crises in other financial and asset markets (e.g. property) when values collapse, confidence disappears completely, and they both trigger a wider financial and economic crisis. At the national level, Malaysia instituted public "buying support" actions to prop up falling values in securities markets, while Hong Kong (China) took a number of actions to prevent the floor from falling out of its unusual property market and even intervened in the stock market. Almost all Asian countries have taken a number of measures to prevent a collapse of their banking markets, while resorting to orderly mergers and shutdowns which address the problem without leading to runs on liquidity caused by depositor panic. Could these actions at the national level be bolstered by supportive regional action to prop up values and prevent regional contagion?

The case for regional intervention in these markets could be justified by the degree of regional cross-holdings – particularly in Asia but increasingly also in Latin America – in all such markets. However, the resources required and the operating (as well as legal) difficulties involved in intervening in each of these fragmented national markets suggest that, for the time being, attention should be focused primarily on strengthening regional intervention capacity in currency markets and preventing breakdown in such markets from wreaking havoc across the board. Japan's experience in propping up property and share prices artificially through the banking system has not been salutary and much remains to be learned from that experience.

In the long run, the answer lies in regionalizing small, fragmented, illiquid national asset markets, as has been suggested for Africa (Mistry, 1994, 1996, 1998; World Bank, 1990). Widening and deepening these markets on a regional basis is likely to make them more resilient and robust than they would be if left to operate nationally (which is true even for the smaller capital markets of Western Europe). That in turn would render such markets considerably less vulnerable to large swings in value caused by the inward or outward movement of relatively small volumes of funds from international markets.

Unfortunately the second-best option of re-imposing capital controls temporarily in one form or another – with the Chilean example being cited most often – is invariably being advanced in a number of quarters as the answer to these problems and is being reconsidered by the IMF and the World Bank. While there may be some validity in reconsidering the speed and sequencing of capital-account liberalization in developing countries which have not yet liberalized and which have critical weaknesses in their domestic financial systems (Bhagwati, 1998; Fischer and Reisen, 1993; Stiglitz, 1998), it would be much riskier to reimpose controls in countries which have already liberalized their capital accounts. Such options are second best because the genie of globalization and capital-account opening has now been let out of the bottle. From the practical viewpoint of market operators in both the financial and real worlds it has become almost impossible to suggest putting it back in without the risk of suffering disproportionate costs and consequences. There is little chance – Chile's experience notwithstanding – for capital controls, even temporarily re-imposed, to work efficaciously, particularly in markets characterized by non-compliance cultures, as most emerging markets are. There is a much higher probability (and risk) that the re-imposition of such controls in countries which have already opened their capital accounts would create even greater distortions and more trauma as parallel markets re-emerged for currency and securities transactions to counteract the effect of such controls. The net result would be a negative sum game, especially if played in the midst of a currency, or a more generalized financial, crisis.

V. Conclusions

Regional arrangements to cope with financial crises are not just necessary but imperative. They reflect the stake that any neighbourhood or region has, or should have, in protecting its own social, economic and political interests, as well as in maintaining or improving its competitiveness and its general welfare. Such arrangements are necessary also to: (i) create and reflect a measure of regional cohesion which enhances credibility in global markets; (ii) develop the political capacity that is necessary for countries within a region to exert effective peer group pressure over policy corrections in good time without incurring the risk of intraregional political ruction or embarrassment; and (iii) develop a collective "neighbourhood watch" capacity for limiting damage.

When such crises occur in *developing* countries, the damage to financial systems and economies is invariably concentrated in a region. It is not limited to just one country, nor is it immediately spread across the world at large. But when such crises occur in the developed world, the implications and consequences are usually transmitted around the globe very quickly. Yet in the latter case there is almost complete insulation from recourse to global institutions, except, of course, when the developing countries which are affected as by-standers are compelled to seek assistance. Thus there is an odd and striking asymmetry in the insistence of players in global financial markets and OECD Governments that: (i) a global institution – the IMF – must be resorted to immediately by developing countries even though the impact of a financial crisis in the developing world is likely to be concentrated regionally; and yet (ii) have regional and other arrangements in the developed world constructed specifically so as to bypass submission to the same institutional discipline, when the impact of financial crises in OECD countries is much more likely to be global.

For that reason, first-recourse reliance by developing countries and regions to *global* facilities

and institutions for dealing with what are essentially *regional* issues and problems is logically unsound from the viewpoint of the countries affected as well as that of the global economy. Automatic or forced recourse to the IMF transfers the responsibility for damage limitation and agenda from the governments of the region (which is where such responsibilities belong) to extra-national and extraregional institutions, forces and influences, which may not necessarily have the same objectives, outlook or interests. On the contrary, they may have quite different interests and agendas (hidden or transparent), which may even conflict with those of regional damage limitation and quick recovery in the post-crisis phase. Therefore, the absence of suitably designed regional arrangements (except in Europe) in the current panoply of institutions, facilities and instruments which exist to combat such crises reflects a serious gap in the international financial system.

It is a vacuum which global institutions cannot and should not be required, nor perhaps even permitted, to fill, at least not until other immediate options have been exhausted. In coping with financial crises, especially in the developing world, there can be little question that mezzanine regional mechanisms have a significant role to play. That role may be as large if not larger than the role that global institutions such as the IMF are being required to play in managing financial crises even though they may not be best placed or suited to doing so. Most developing countries are becoming regionally interdependent even faster than they are becoming globally intertwined.

Of course there are exceptions to this general rule: e.g. (i) countries which constitute regions themselves, such as Brazil, China, India, or (ii) small entrepot economies such as Hong Kong (China) and Singapore. But even in these exceptional instances, regional influences and regional contagion still have powerful spill-over effects. The economies of both China and India are being affected by the Asian crisis, albeit to a lesser extent than the "ASEAN-4" (Indonesia, Malaysia, the Philippines and Thailand) or the Republic of Korea. By the same token, the island entrepots of Singapore and Hong Kong (China) have been affected to an even greater extent than the two larger countries but are, for the present at least, weathering the storm with greater resilience than the ASEAN-4 and the Republic of Korea.

Taking those realities into account, it would seem to make more sense for developing countries to rely on regional defences first. Instead, they are now compelled to resort first to global defences simply because their regional defences and mutual support arrangements through institutions such as the BIS are either too weak and unformed, or simply do not exist. Their weakness and vulnerability as a result of such regional arrangements not being in place have now been evidenced by the economic *débâcles* of 1982 and 1997. Both these crises were made much worse and prolonged unnecessarily as a result of crisis mismanagement by global agencies.

Those experiences suggest that developing countries are ill-advised to risk continued reliance on non-regional institutions and mechanisms in which they have little influence or control. Left to become the victims rather than the beneficiaries of crisis management by international financial institutions, developing countries witness a loss of management and directional control over a corrective agenda which is invariably imposed on them without sufficient local knowledge or sensitivity, and often at the urging of the more powerful shareholders of global agencies which have their own agendas. Yet, most developing countries do not have the resources or the capacity, on their own, to withstand the shocks which such crises emit and which keep recurring in the absence of credible deterrents to speculative attacks or to market failure. The only way for them to cope, therefore, is to resort to the creation of regional mechanisms over which they have some influence and control, but which reciprocally also place them under an obligation to take corrective action swiftly and decisively for the "good of the neighbourhood".

Precisely what such regional arrangements should be, what amounts should be involved, and what management arrangements are necessary, depends on the particular characteristics, needs and circumstances of the countries in each region. A comprehensive set of regional arrangements – with institutional capacity to match – would need to encompass the following functions and capacities: (i) surveillance and early-warning capacity coupled with the institutional ability to exert peer group pressure in inducing essential policy changes and course corrections, swiftly and effectively; (ii) the capacity to avoid repeated rounds of competitive devaluations from occurring in neighbouring countries and preventing countries from adopting beggar-thy-neighbour policies to exit from a crisis likely to engulf the region; (iii) sufficient intervention capacity in currency and financial markets – after necessary adjustments in currency or asset values have occurred – to stabilize those values at adjusted levels, restore market confidence and forestall the prospect of

further free-falls in currency or financial markets; (iv) the ability to provide sufficient post-stabilization liquidity, risk management instrumentation and long-term (equity and debt) finance (which could come from existing regional development banks) to prevent financial systems and economic engines from running into liquidity problems at critical junctures in the stabilization and adjustment processes; and (v) the collective capacity to induce essential longer-term structural changes in financial markets and institutions, and to promote greater capacity for self-regulation and prudential behaviour on the part of private firms as well as national regulatory authorities.

Such arrangements can mirror, to a certain extent, the global arrangements which now exist but which have their own weaknesses and inadequacies. They can be tied, for institutional and administrative convenience to the institutional structures which already have been created in the regional development banks. Regional arrangements also need to be framed to work in tandem with counterpart arrangements at national and global levels in order to work most effectively. But, there can be little doubt that the answer to the question posed in its title is decidedly in the affirmative.

Notes

1 In post-war history such regional arrangements began under the Marshall Plan with the establishment of the Organization for European Economic Cooperation (OEEC) and the European Payments Union (EPU) (Kindleberger, 1984). Under the Marshall Plan recipient countries had full authority to manage the funds received from the United States and, in effect, to discipline one another with the EPU playing an integral role in that process. Regional monetary arrangements in Europe, of course, have been evolving through time with the creation of the European "snake" right up to the crisis faced by the European exchange rate mechanism (ERM) in 1992 (Giovannini and Mayer, 1992) and now to full monetary union (EMU).

2 This was the case in France during the 1992 ERM crisis when Germany made publicly known its intent to use its reserves to defend the French franc and in 1997 when China expressed willingness to use its reserves jointly with those of Hong Kong (China) to defend the peg of the Hong Kong dollar to the United States dollar.

3 I am grateful to Gerry Helleiner for making this point when reviewing an early draft of this paper.

4 This latter risk was pointed out in the external review undertaken of the IMF's ESAF programmes, where the authors argued that the macroeconomic restraint prescribed for the early stabilization phase of the programmes was correct but became inappropriate for the post-stabilization and recovery phase. The review urged the IMF to take greater account of these changing requirements (Helleiner, 1998).

References

AfDB (African Development Bank) (1993), *Economic Integration in Southern Africa* (Abidjan).

AsDB (Asian Development Bank) (1993), *Sub-regional Economic Co-operation* (Manila).

AZIZ, U. (ed.) (1990*), Strategies for Structural Adjustment: The Experience of Southeast Asia* (Washington, D.C.: IMF).

BALINO, T.J.T., and Cottarelli, C. (eds.) (1994*), Frameworks for Monetary Stability: Policy Issues and Country Experiences* (Washington, D.C.: IMF).

BAYOUMI, T., and B. EICHENGREEN (1994), "One Money or Many? Analysing Prospects for Monetary Unification in Various Parts of the World", *Princeton Studies in International Finance,* No. 76 (Princeton, N.J.: Department of Economics, Princeton University).

BERGSTEN, F. (1997), "The Asian Monetary Crisis: Proposed Remedies*", Statement before the US Congressional Committee on Banking and Financial Services*, 13 November, Washington, D.C.

BERGSTEN, F., and M. NOLAND (eds.) (1993*), Pacific Dynamism and the International Economic System* (Washington, D.C.: Institute for International Economics).

BHAGWATI, J. (1993), "Regionalism and Multilateralism: An Overview", in J. de Melo and A. Panagariya (eds.), *New Dimensions in Regional Integration* (Cambridge, United Kingdom: University of Cambridge Press).

BHAGWATI, J. (1998), "The Capital Myth" *Foreign Affairs*, Vol.77, No.3 (May/June).

BROINOWSKI, A. (1990), *ASEAN into the 1990s* (London: Macmillan).

BUIRA, A. (1996), "The Mexican Crisis of 1994: An Assessment", in J. Teunissen (ed.), *Can Currency Crises be Prevented or Better Managed? Lessons from Mexico* (The Hague: Fondad).

BUNDY, B.K., S.D. BURNS, and K.V. WEICHEL (eds.) (1994), *The Future of the Pacific Rim: Scenarios for Regional Cooperation* (Westport, Conn.:Praeger).

BUSH, J. (1998), "Forget the IMF; listen to the locals", *The Times*, London, 19 August.

CABLE, V., and D. HENDERSON (eds.) (1994), *Trade Blocs? The Future of Regional Integration* (London: Royal Institute for International Affairs).

CALVO, G.A. (1996), "The Management of Capital Flows: Domestic Poliocy and International Cooperation", in G.K. Helleiner (ed.), *The International Monetary and Financial System: Developing Country Perspectives* (New York: St. Martin's Press).

CHHIBBER, A., and S. FISCHER (eds.) (1991), *Economic Reform in Sub-Saharan Africa*, Proceedings of a World Bank Symposium (Washington, D.C.: The World Bank).

CLINE, W.R. (1995), *International Debt Re-examined* (Washington, D.C.: Institute for International Economics).

CORBO, V., S. FISCHER, and S.B WEBB (eds.) (1992*), Adjustment Lending Revisited: Policies to Restore Growth*, Proceedings of A World Bank Symposium (Washington, D.C.: The World Bank).

CULPEPER, R. (1997), *The Multilateral Development Banks (Vol. 5): Titans or Behemoths* (Ottawa: North-South Institute, and Boulder, Colorado: Lynne Rienner).

CURRIE, D., and J. WHITLEY (1994), "European Monetary Integration and Prospects for Monetary Union", in V. Cable and D. Henderson (eds.), *Trade Blocs? The Future of Regional Integration* (London: Royal Institute for International Affairs).

DE CECCO, M., and A. GIOVANNINI (eds.) (1989*), A European Central Bank? Perspectives on Monetary Unification after ten years of the EMS* (Cambridge, United Kingdom: University of Cambridge Press).

DE MELO, J., and A. PANAGARIYA (eds.) (1993), *New Dimensions in Regional Integration* (Cambridge, United Kingdom: University of Cambridge Press).

DORNBUSCH, R. (1998), "On the Edge: Japan could topple as reforms slip and debt mounts", *Far Eastern Economic Review*, 26 February.

THE ECONOMIST (1997), "Rumpus in Hong Kong", 27 September, p. 16.

THE ECONOMIST (1997a), "An Asian IMF?", 27 September, p. 114.

THE ECONOMIST (1997b), "Japan to the Rescue", 11 October, pp. 131-132.

THE ECONOMIST (1997c), "The IMF and SE Asia", 25 October, pp. 120-121.

THE ECONOMIST (1997d), "The Asian Crash: Beggars and Choosers", 6 December, pp. 87-88.

THE ECONOMIST (1997e), "New Illness, Same Old Medicine", 13 December, pp. 95-96.

THE ECONOMIST (1997f), "Burying the Asian Miracle", 20 December, pp. 96-97.

THE ECONOMIST (1998), "Why did Asia Crash?", 10 January, p. 88.

THE ECONOMIST (1998a), "East Asia: Which Way to Safety?", 10 January, pp. 82-83.

THE ECONOMIST (1998b), "The Hong Kong Dollar: Off the Peg?", 14 February, p. 90.

THE ECONOMIST (1998c), "ASEAN's Failure:The Limits of Politeness", 28 February, pp. 73-74.

THE ECONOMIST (1998d), "Survey of East Asian Economies", 7 March, pp. 9-10.

THE ECONOMIST (1998e), "Asian Exports: Missing Link?", 9 May, pp. 111-112.

THE ECONOMIST (1998f), "Indonesia Awakes: SEAsia starts to wonder", 6 June, pp. 75-76.

THE ECONOMIST (1998g), "Asia Trembles Again", 20 June, pp. 105-106.

THE ECONOMIST (1998h), "China: Reforms on Ice", 18 July, pp. 75-76.

EICHENGREEN, B. (1995), *International Monetary Arrangements for the 21st Century* (Washington, D.C.: The Brookings Institution).

EICHENGREEN, B., A. ROSE, and C. WYPLOSZ (1995), "Exchange Market Mayhem: The Antecedents and Aftermath of Speculative Attacks", *Economic Policy*, Vol. 21 (October).

EICHENGREEN, B., A. ROSE, and C. WYPLOSZ (1997), "Is there a Safe Passage to EMU? Evidence from the Markets", in J. Frankel and A. Giovannini (eds.*), The Micro-Structure of Foreign Exchange Markets* (Chicago, Ill.: University of Chicago Press).

EICHENGREEN, B., and C. WYPLOSZ (1996), "What Do Currency Crises tell us about the future of the International Monetary System?", in J. Teunissen (ed.), *Can Currency Crises be Prevented or Better Managed: Lessons from Mexico* (The Hague: Fondad).

EMMERSON, D.K. (1998), "Americanising Asia", *Foreign Affairs*, Vol. 77, No. 3 (May/June).

FEER (*Far Eastern Economic Review*) (1998), "Is the IMF Prescribing the Right Medicine?", *The Crash of '97* (Hong Kong [China]: FEER Publications).

FEER (1998a), "A Poor Grade for the IMF", *The Crash of '97* (Hong Kong [China]: FEER Publications).

FEER (1998b) *Asia 1998* (Hong Kong [China]: FEER Publications).

FELDSTEIN, M. (1998), "Refocusing the IMF", *Foreign Affairs*, Vol. 77, No. 2 (March/April).

FFRENCH-DAVIES, R., and S. GRIFFITH-JONES (1995), *Coping with Capital Surges: The Return of Finance to Latin America* (Boulder, Co.: Lynne Rienner).

FISCHER, S. (1998), "The Asian Crisis and the Changing Role of the IMF", *Finance and Development*, Vol. 35, No. 2 (June).

FISCHER, B., and H. REISEN (1993), *Liberalising Capital Flows in Developing Countries: Pitfalls, Prerequisites and Perspectives* (Paris: OECD, Development Centre Studies).

FRANKEL, J.A. (1996), *Regional Trading Blocs in the World Economic System* (Washington, D.C.: Institute for International Economics).

FRANKEL, J.A. (ed.) (1998), *The Regionalization of the World Economy* (Chicago, Ill.: University of Chicago Press, and National Bureau of Economic Research).

FRASER, W.B. (1995), "Central Bank Cooperation in the Asian Region*", Reserve Bank of Australia Bulletin*, October, pp. 21-28.

FUKASAKU, K. (ed.) (1995), *Regional Co-operation and Integration in Asia* (Paris: OECD).

GALBRAITH, J.K. (1993), *A Short History of Financial Euphoria* (New York: Whittle Books, Penguin).

GIOVANNINI, A., and C. MAYER (eds.) (1992), *European Financial Integration* (Cambridge, United Kingdom: University of Cambridge Press).

GOLDSTEIN, M. (1998), *The Asian Financial Crisis: Causes, Cures and Systemic Implications* (Washington, D.C.: Institute for International Economics).

GREIDER, W. (1997), *One World, Ready or Not: The Manic Logic of Global Capitalism* (New York: Touchstone, Simon & Schuster).

GRIFFITH-JONES, S. (ed.) (1988), *Managing World Debt* (London: Harvester-Wheatsheaf).

GRIFFITH-JONES, S. (1996), "How Can Future Currency Crises be Prevented or Better Managed", in J. Teunissen (ed.), *Can Currency Crises be Prevented or Better Managed? Lessons from Mexico* (The Hague: Fondad).

GRIFFITH-JONES, S. (1998), "Regulatory Challenges for Source Countries of Surges in Capital Flows", in J. Teunissen (ed.), *The Policy Challenges of Global Financial Integration* (The Hague: Fondad).

GRIFFITH-JONES, S. (1998a), "How to Protect Developing Countries from Volatility of Capital Flows", paper presented to the Meeting of the Commonwealth Expert Group on Protecting Countries Against Destabilising Effects of Volatile Capital Flows (July).

GUITIAN, M. (1998), "The Challenge of Managing Global Capital Flows", *Finance and Development*, Vol. 35, No. 2 (June).

HARDING, J., and J. KYNGE (1998), "China: Slow-burning Remedy", *Financial Times*, 31 July.

HEALEY, D. (1991), *Japanese Capital Exports and Asian Economic Development*, Development Centre Studies (Paris: OECD).

HELLEINER, G. (ed.) (1996), *The International Monetary and Financial System: Developing Country Perspectives* (New York: St. Martin's Press).

HELLEINER, G. (1998), "The East Asian and other Financial Crises: Causes, Responses and Prevention", paper presented at the UNCTAD Seminar on The East Asian and Other Financial Crises, 1 May, Geneva.

HETTNE, B. (1998), "The New Regionalism: Security and Development", in J. Teunissen (ed.), *The Policy Challenges of Global Financial Integration* (The Hague: Fondad).

HETTNE, B., and A. INOTAI (1994), *The New Regionalism: Implications for Global Development and International Security* (Helsinki: UNU/WIDER).

HUGHES, N.C. (1998), "Smashing the Iron Rice Bowl", *Foreign Affairs*, Vol. 77, No. 4 (July/August).

IMF (1995), *International Capital Markets* (Washington, D.C.), August.

IMF (1997), *International Financial Statistics*, July.

IMF (1997a), *International Capital Markets* , November.

IMF (1997b), *World Economic Outlook*, Interim Assessment, December.

IMF (1998), *Toward a Framework for Financial Stability*, January.

IMF (1998a), *World Economic Outlook*, May.

IMF (1998b), "The Asian Crisis: Causes and Cures", *Finance and Development*, Vol. 35, No. 2 (June).

JAYARAJAH, C., and W. BRANSON (1995*), Structural and Sectoral Adjustment: World Bank Experience 1980-92*, An Operations Evaluation Study (Washington, D.C.: The World Bank).

KENEN, P.B. (1993), "Reforming the International Monetary System: An Agenda for the Developing Countries", in J. Teunissen (ed.), *The Pursuit of Reform: Global Finance and the Developing Countries* (The Hague: Fondad).

KENEN, P.B. (ed.) (1994), *Managing the World Economy: Fifty Years after Bretton Woods* (Washington, D.C.: Institute for International Economics).

KENEN, P.B. (1996), "How Can Future Currency Crisis à la Mexico Be Prevented", in J. Teunissen, (ed.), *Can Currency Crises be Prevented or Better Managed? Lessons from Mexico* (The Hague: Fondad).

KHANNA, V. (1998), "The Great Asian Bust: Twelve Months of Meltdown", *Business Times On-Line*, http://www.asia1.com.sg/ biztimes/special/ melt06.html, 30 June.

KINDLEBERGER, C. (1984), *A Financial History of Western Europe* (Boston, MA: Allen & Unwin).

KISSINGER, H. (1998), "The Asian Collapse: One Fix Does Not Fit All Economies*"*, mimeo, Washington, D.C.

KRUGMAN, P. (1991), *Geography and Trade* (Leuven, Belgium: Leuven University Press; and Cambridge, MA: MIT Press).

KRUGMAN, P. (1993), "Regionalism versus Multilateralism: some analytical notes", in J. de Melo and A. Panagariya (eds.), *New Dimensions in Regional Integration* (Cambridge, United Kingdom: University of Cambridge Press).

KRUGMAN, P.(1995), *Currencies and Crises* (Cambridge, MA: MIT Press).

KRUGMAN, P. (1998), "What Happened to Asia?", at http://web.mit.edu/krugman/www/ DISINTER.html (January).

KRUGMAN, P. (1998a), "Will Asia Bounce Back?", at http://web.mit.edu/krugman/www.suisse (March).

KYNGE, J. (1998), "China Considers Restructuring Methods", *Financial Times*, 16 July.

LARDY, N.R. (1998), "China and the Asian Contagion", *Foreign Affairs*, Vol. 77, No. 4 (July/August).

LINCOLN, E.J. (1998), "Japan's Financial Mess", *Foreign Affairs*, Vol. 77, No. 3 (May/June).

LIPSKY, J. (1998), "Asia's Crisis: A Market Perspective", *Finance and Development*, Vol. 35, No. 2 (June).

MISTRY, P.S. (1991), *African Debt Revisited: Procrastination or Progress?* (The Hague: Fondad).

MISTRY, P.S. (1994), *Multilateral Debt: An Emerging Crisis?* (The Hague: Fondad).

MISTRY, P.S. (1996), *Regional Integration Arrangements in Economic Development* (The Hague: Fondad).

MISTRY, P.S. (1996a), "Regional Dimensions of Structural Adjustment in Southern Africa", in J. Teunissen (ed.), *Regionalism and the Global Economy: The Case of Africa* (The Hague: Fondad).

MISTRY, P.S. (1996b*), Resolving Africa's Multilateral Debt Problem: A Response to the IMF and World Bank* (The Hague: Fondad).

MISTRY, P.S. (1997), "Global Financial Integration in Capital Markets", paper presented to a Fondad Conference at the Ministry of Foreign Affairs, 18-19 November, The Hague.

MISTRY, P.S. (1998), "The Challenges of Financial Globalisation", in J. Teunissen (ed.), *The Policy Challenges of Global Financial Integration* (The Hague: Fondad).

MITSUZUKA, H. (1997), Statement by the Minister of Finance, Government of Japan at the 1997 Annual Meetings of the International Monetary Fund and World Bank, Hong Kong (China) 23-27 September.

MONTAGNON, P. (1998), "China quandary over speed of reform", *Financial Times*, 10 August.

MORRIS, J. (1968), *Pax Brittanica: The Climax of an Empire* (Middlesex, United Kingdom: Penguin Books).

MORRIS, J. (1973), *Heaven's Command: An Imperial Progress* (Middlesex, United Kingdom: Penguin Books).

MORRIS, J. (1978), *Farewell the Trumpets: An Imperial Retreat* (Middlesex, United Kingdom: Penguin Books).

OBSTFELD, M. (1994), "The Logic of Currency Crises", *NBER Working Paper No. 4640* (Cambridge, MA: National Bureau of Economic Research).

OMAN, C. (1994), *Globalisation and Regionalisation: The Challenge for Developing Countries* (Paris: OECD).

OMAN, C. (1998), "The Policy Challenges of Globalisation and Regionalisation", in J. Teunissen (ed.), *The Policy Challenges of Global Financial Integration* (The Hague: Fondad).

ORTIZ-MARTINEZ, G. (1998), "What Lessons does the Mexican Crisis Hold for Recovery in Asia", *Finance and Development*, Vol. 35, No. 2 (June).

PADOA-SCHIOPPA, T., and F. SACCOMANNI (1994), "Managing a Market-Led Global Financial System", in P.B. Kenen (ed.) *Managing the World Economy: Fifty Years after Bretton Woods* (Washington, D.C.: Institute for International Economics).

PALMER, N.D. (1991), *The New Regionalism in Asia and the Pacific* (Lexington, MA: Lexington Books).

PERSAUD, A. (1998), "Market Mechanisms for avoiding the next currency crash: Lessons from Asia", paper prepared for a *Meeting of the Commonwealth Expert Group on Protecting Countries Against Destabilising Effects of Volatile Capital Flows*, July.

PORTES, R., and D. VINES (1997), "Coping with International Capital Flows", *Economic Paper No. 30* (London: Commonwealth Secretariat), April.

QUIRK, P. (1994), "Capital Account Convertibility: A New Model for Developing Countries", in T.J.T. Balino and C. Cottarelli (eds.), *Frameworks for Monetary Stability: Policy Issues and Country Experiences* (Washington, D.C.: IMF).

RADELET, S., and J. SACHS (1997), "Asia's Reemergence", *Foreign Affairs*, Vol. 76, No. 6 (November/December).

RADELET, S., and J. SACHS (1998), "The Onset of the East Asian Financial Crisis", mimeo, Harvard Institute for International Development, January.

REDDY, Y.V. (1998), "Asian Crisis: Asking the Right Questions", address delivered at the India International Centre, 1 May, New Delhi (available on BT Internet Explorer).

RIDDING, J. (1998), "Hong Kong: Playing With Fire in an Attempt to Hit Speculators", *Financial Times*, 17 August.

SACHS, J. (ed.) (1989), *Developing Country Debt and the World Economy* (Chicago, Ill.: University of Chicago Press, and National Bureau of Economic Research).

SACHS, J. (1997), "IMF: Power Unto Itself", *Financial Times*, 11 December.

SACHS, J.D., A. TORNELL, and A. VELASCO (1996), "Financial Crises in Emerging Markets: The Lessons from

1995", *NBER Working Paper No. 5576* (Cambridge, MA: National Bureau of Economic Research).

SCHADLER, S. (1994), "Capital Movements and Surveillance", in T.J.T. Balino and C. Cottarelli (eds.), *Frameworks for Monetary Stability: Policy Issues and Country Experiences* (Washington, D.C.: IMF).

STIGLITZ, J. (1998), "Boats, Planes and Capital Flows", *Financial Times*, 25 March.

STREETEN, P. (ed.) (1988), *Beyond Adjustment: The Asian Experience* (Washington, D.C.: IMF).

SUMMERS, L. (1998), "Emerging from Crisis: The Beginnings of a New Asia", prepared remarks presented at the Economic Strategy Institute, 12 February, at http://www.econstrat.com/econstrat/summers.htm.

SUMMERS, L. (1998a), "Go with the Flow: The Asian Crisis", *Financial Times*, 11 March.

TEUNISSEN, J. (ed.) (1992), *Fragile Finance: Rethinking the International Monetary System* (The Hague: Fondad).

TEUNISSEN, J. (1993), *The Pursuit of Reform: Global Finance and the Developing Countries* (The Hague: Fondad).

TEUNISSEN, J. (1996), *Can Currency Crises be Prevented or Better Managed? Lessons from Mexico* (The Hague: Fondad).

TEUNISSEN, J. (1998), *Regional Integration and Multilateral Cooperation in the Global Economy* (The Hague: Fondad).

VAN DER HOEVEN, R., and F. VAN DER KAAIJ (1994), *Structural Adjustment and Beyond in Sub-Saharan Africa* (London: James Currey).

WADE, R., and F. VENOROSO (1998), "The Asian Crisis: The High-Debt Model vs. the Wall Street-Treasury-IMF Complex", *New Left Review*, No. 228 (March/April).

WADE, R., and F. VENOROSO (1998a), "The Asian Financial Crisis: The Unrecognized Risk of the IMF's Asia Package", mimeo.

WALLACE, W. (1994), *Regional Integration: The West European Experience* (Washington, D.C.: The Brookings Institution).

WILLIAMSON, J. (1992), "International Monetary Reform and the Prospects for Economic Development", in J. Teunissen (ed.), *Fragile Finance: Rethinking the International Monetary System* (The Hague: Fondad).

WILLIAMSON, J. (1998), "Learning from East Asia's Woes", paper presented at a Conference of the Bangladesh Economic Association and International Economic Association, 30 March - 1 April, Dhaka.

WILLIAMSON, J., and C.R. HENNING (1994), "Managing the Monetary System", in P.B. Kenen (ed.), *Managing the World Economy: Fifty Years after Bretton Woods* (Washington, D.C.: Institute for International Economics).

WOLF, M. (1998), "Capital Punishment: The Emerging Washington Consensus on the Asian Crisis is Not Wrong, But Too Limited", *Financial Times*, 17 March.

WORLD BANK (1990), "Sub-Saharan Africa: From Crisis to Sustainable Growth: A Long-Term Perspective Study of Sub-Saharan Africa", *Proceedings of a Workshop on Regional Integration and Co-operation, Background Papers*, Vol. 4 (Washington, D.C.).

WORLD BANK (1993), *The East Asian Miracle: Economic Growth and Public Policy*, Policy Research Report (Washington, D.C.).

WORLD BANK (1997), *Private Capital Flows to Developing Countries: The Road to Financial Integration*, Policy Research Report (Washington, D.C.).

WORLD BANK (1998), "East Asia's Financial Crisis: Causes, Evolution, Prospects", Chapter 2, in *Global Development Finance 1998* (Washington, D.C.).

YORK, R.C. (1993) *Regional Integration and Developing Countries* (Paris: OECD).

YOSHIDA, M. et al. (1994), "Regional Economic Integration in East Asia: Special Features and Policy Implications", in V. Cable and D. Henderson (eds.), *Trade Blocs? The* *Future of Regional Integration* (London: Royal Institute for International Affairs).

THE WORLD BANK'S NET INCOME AND RESERVES: SOURCES AND ALLOCATION

Devesh Kapur

Abstract

This paper analyses the proposals by the World Bank's management to address the problem of the Bank's net income and reserves. It questions the emphasis in these proposals on raising net income primarily by augmenting loan charges, and argues that several factors other than the supposed financial "subsidy" implicit in the Bank's current loan pricing policies are important in explaining the institution's predicament. These include the structure of loan pricing, which gives little weight to incentives and adverse selection and moral hazard; a common pool problem wherein net income has been deployed in a manner that concentrates benefits, especially political benefits accruing to non-borrowing shareholders, whereas costs are spread amongst all shareholders, but especially on IBRD borrowers; and excessive attention to the revenue side of the Bank's balance sheet with limited attention to expenditures. The paper further argues that proposals made by the management will further weaken the link between financial burden and political control, with adverse consequences for the institution's governance. Finally, it proposes several alternatives aimed at addressing the problem in a manner whereby the burden will be shared more equitably among the four major constituencies: non-borrowing shareholders, IBRD borrowers, IDA borrowers, and staff and management.

I. Introduction

For more than a year the management of the World Bank has been flagging attention to looming problems facing the Bank's net income – its levels and trends – and the widening gap between the level of net income and the demands being placed upon that income (World Bank, 1997). The issue acquired a new urgency with the Asian crisis, and in May 1998 management proposed several steps aimed at addressing the problem of falling income and rising demands (World Bank, 1998). These proposals have sought to raise net income principally by augmenting loan charges and by modifying the uses of net income.

Four questions arise:

(i) How serious is the issue of declining net income and reserves, and are the consequences likely to be as adverse as is being projected?

(ii) What explains the decline in net income?

(iii) If the outlook for net income is to be reversed, how should the proposal by the management be evaluated?

(iv) Finally, is there an alternative framework for the allocation of net income in a manner that would meet the Bank's development objectives while being equitable in its burden sharing?

This paper argues that several factors other than the stated financial "subsidy" in current loan pricing policies are important in explaining the institution's predicament. These include the structure of loan pricing, which gives little weight to incentives and adverse selection and moral hazard; a common pool problem wherein net income has been deployed in a manner that concentrates benefits, especially political benefits accruing to non-borrowing shareholders, whereas costs are spread amongst all shareholders, but especially on IBRD borrowers; and excessive attention to the revenue side of the bank's balance sheet with limited attention to expenditures. The paper further argues that the proposals by the management will further weaken the link between financial burden and political control, thereby aggravating the institution's governance problems. Finally, the paper discusses several alternatives which address the problem in such a way that the burden would be shared more equitably among the four major constituencies: non-borrowing shareholders; IBRD borrowers; IDA borrowers; and staff and management.

II. Net income and reserves: what are the issues?

The IBRD's equity (or reserves), the "free" money available to the institution, can increase either by an injection of paid-in capital or by additions to retained earnings. In practice, the cost of additions to paid-in capital is borne largely by the larger, non-borrowing shareholders. Retained earnings, on the other hand, can only increase from successive annual allocations from net income, which depends both on the level of income and the percentage of this income that is transferred to reserves. The former depends in part on revenues stemming from loan charges whose cost is borne by the borrowers and, to a more limited extent, on income generated by the Bank's portfolio of liquid assets. But net income is also a function of expenses, including administrative (see chart 1).

There have been debates on the level and allocation of net income – and in this context on capital increases, the level of reserves, loan charges and administrative expenses – within the institution for almost four decades. A higher level of net income increases the institution's capacity to absorb higher lending risks; higher levels of reserves imply better financial health for the institution. Both benefit all members. Furthermore, high reserves also benefit the borrowers in the long term by reducing the Bank's overall cost of funds and therefore lending charges.

However, funding higher reserves – and by implication the distribution of net income – through higher loan charges has long been a contentious issue among the institution's shareholders with fault lines running not only along a North-South cleavage but also among the borrowing countries. In the former case, the major shareholders have understandably pushed for higher reserves both to reduce their risk of contingent liabilities, and to reduce paid-in capital increases in any future capital replenishment. During the 1980s another justification for higher loan charges was to provide adequate provisions for non-accruals. This rationale revealed the fissures in the Bank's self image as a financial cooperative, since the burden was largely shouldered by one group – the borrowers who had continued to service their Bank debt in a timely way. The other use of net-income favoured by non-borrowing shareholders of the Bank has been transfers to IDA. Pressures in this direction grew particularly over the past decade, as the Bank's financial health improved on the one hand and donors' budgetary commitments to IDA flagged on the other.

Chart 1

DETERMINANTS OF NET INCOME

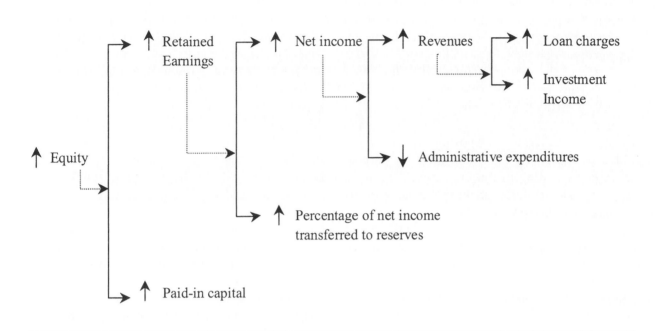

Borrowers have been primarily interested in reducing their borrowing costs, and have opposed increases in loan charges and pushed for a reduction of reserves and net income. Loan charges that are too low blunt the Bank's efforts to get the higher-income and creditworthy borrowers to go to the market. On the other hand, high loan charges make no difference in the demand for Bank loans by less creditworthy borrowers whose demand for IBRD loans is price-inelastic. And although higher loan charges can increase net income and reserves, their structure also matters. Altered loan charges, and interest rates in particular, only have a gradual effect on the level of reserves while adding front-end fees on loans has a more rapid impact. The latter, however, shifts the burden to current borrowers and consequently has implications for intertemporal equity.

Borrowers have not been united on these issues. IBRD-only borrowers have generally pressed for net income to be used to lower future loan charges rather than to supplement IDA, to which they lack recourse. Blend countries, particularly the giants, China and India, have been fence-sitters, but as they are phased out of IDA lending their position is likely to shift.

A short historical detour may help to understand why the net income issue has assumed renewed salience. In 1991, with high projections of future net income, the Executive Directors approved a framework to guide the annual process of net income allocation. First priority was accorded to a targeted reserves-to-loans ratio (which gradually rose to 14.25 per cent by 1995, before subsequently declining to 14 per cent in 1997); the second priority was placed on reducing borrower costs by prefunding waivers of loan interest charges up to 25 basis points for the following fiscal year to all borrowers which serviced all of their loans within 30 days of their due dates during the prior six months. The framework also identified two other uses for the residual net income. One was to support high-priority development activities. The other was to accumulate funds temporarily in a "Surplus Account", adding to the institution's financial strength pending future use of these funds. Both were indicative of the changing nature of "burden sharing" in the funding of development activities.

At the time of its creation, the principal rationale for creating the surplus account was new uncertainty about the risk scenario and it represented a compromise between strongly divergent views within the Board on the level of reserves. The insistence by most of the G-7 shareholders on a higher level of reserves appeared to be prompted by two concerns: first, the pressures on the Bank by the G-7 to lend more to Eastern Europe, particularly Russia, and to loosen its negative pledge clause to the same end; second, the perception on the part of both the major shareholders and the management of the Bank that achieving any increase in paid-in capital would be extremely difficult in the near future. A surplus account (with a moveable cap) could thus be seen as a device to squirrel away funds that could later be added to equity. At the same time, the surplus account, by adding to the institution's earnings capacity, also stemmed growing pressures on its administrative budget.

Given the inverse relationship between the size of the administrative budget and net income, the debates on the use of net income also brought into relief long simmering dissension on what should be included in or funded out of the administrative budget. The Bank began making grants from net income in 1964, beginning with IDA. Later on, auditors argued that since grants made to organizations not affiliated with the Bank were "expenses" they should be treated as a part of the cost of doing business and included under the administrative budget. Thus, from FY1982 onwards the Bank made two types of grants: one, the "special grants programme" (SGP), included in the administrative budget; and the other made from net income.

Beginning with an annual allocation for international agricultural research in 1971, the SGP steadily increased in scope and size over the next quarter century; it remained concentrated on two broad areas: international agriculture (slightly over three fifths) and health (about one fifth).[1] In the 1990s, additional special-grant-like programmes were added – the Institutional Development Fund and the Consultative Group to Assist the Poorest (CGAP). Together, the three constitute the "Special Programmes" and account for one twelfth of the administrative budget – an allocation of around $110 million in FY1998.

The inclusion of the Special Programmes "above the line" in the balance sheet was unfortunate. Much of the expenditure for these programmes is for global public goods – but by including them within administrative expenses, the Bank's costs of doing business have been inflated. As a consequence,

borrowers have to pay for the Bank's providing global public goods "above the line". And as will be note below, they also pick up the tab for the Bank's provision of public goods "below the line", i.e. out of net income.

In the 1990s, after the Bank had rebuilt healthy reserves and a surplus, its net income emerged as a tempting target to fund a range of worthy causes. The Bank began using part of its net income to fund humanitarian efforts[2] and, under pressure from the large shareholders, to fund activities in non-members. Trust funds for technical assistance to the former Soviet Union, for investment activities in the Gaza strip, and to jump-start the reconstruction effort in Bosnia-Herzegovina without waiting for financial normalization and membership, were three prominent examples.[3]

The Heavily Indebted Poor Countries (HIPC) Initiative represents another new and significant claim on net income. The IBRD borrowers' negotiating stance towards the HIPC Initiative is noteworthy in what has been left unresolved – and the price paid as a result. At least some of the earlier loans that are now to be written-off under the Initiative had been undertaken as a result of political pressure by the major powers and/or personal agendas of Bank staff. For years, many IBRD borrowers (as well as some non-borrowers) had privately expressed skepticism regarding some of this lending. However, presumably based on the belief that "what goes around comes around", none had ever gone on record against such lending. While there can be no doubt as regards the need for a new approach to the debt problem, the HIPC Initiative does not have any repercussions for non-borrowers. With the Bank's contribution coming out of net income, the burden of the Initiative falls substantially on the IBRD borrowers. For this the borrowers have only themselves to blame: having weakly exercised their responsibility for decision making as shareholders, it was perhaps proper that IBRD borrowers share the financial implications of their silence.

Although allocations from net income have been ostensibly for the benefit of the Bank's membership as a whole, there is little doubt that particular foreign policy interests of some of the Bank's largest shareholders, rather than intrinsic merits or benefits to the institution's membership as a whole, have played an increasingly important role. Traditionally, the large shareholders would have funded their interests through direct claims on their own budgetary resources, but in the strained political and fiscal environment of the 1990s, the cost would be shared by all of the Bank's members.[4]

III. Current trends in net income and reserves

The dire predictions of the Bank's management with regard to trends in net income notwithstanding, the problem needs to be put in perspective. The definition of the problem – declining net income as an aberration that needs to be rectified – is itself questionable. The issue can easily be turned on its head by arguing that the increase in net income during the decade 1987-1997 was the aberration, not its current decline. The IBRD's net income was artificially buoyed through much of the 1980s, by purportedly high returns on its investments, which in fact were achieved by transferring currency risk to the borrowers. Another source of buoyant net income was high-interest fixed-rate loans, at a time – the 1990s – when global interest rates (and the Bank's borrowing costs) were declining. Other than the paid-in portion of the 1988 General Capital Increase (GCI), which moderately boosted the Bank's equity, from the mid-1980s to the mid-1990s, borrowers disproportionately bore the costs of the Bank's financial policies while their benefits, in the form of higher net income and reserves, were shared by all.

Even before the onset of the Asian crisis, and the additional demands on the institution, the IBRD's net income was already coming under stress due to the cumulative effect of several factors: the expiry of lucrative fixed-rate loans; low world interest rates that reduce the return on the Bank's equity; excessive administrative costs as well as costs incurred in yet another round of internal restructuring; and the adoption of single currency loans by some borrowers. The consequences of these effects were projected to lower the reserves-to-loans ratio to about 13 per cent by 2002 (from around 14 per cent in FY1998). Additionally, the decline in dollar net income is also the product of currency fluctuations and the Bank's political paralysis in addressing the root of the problem. Despite being a multilateral institution, and unlike the IMF which moved to the SDR more than two decades ago, the Bank continues to maintain its accounts in United States dollars, which leads dollar net income to decrease when the dollar appreciates and vice versa. The appreciation of the dollar over the past two years has therefore adversely affected net income and to that extent is a temporary phenomenon.

The problem was magnified by a strategic inability to manage growing demands on net income. This weakness has led to a lowering of the share of net income transferred to reserves. A striking example is that even as management was lamenting the trends in net income, it was sanguine about transfers from net income to partially pay for the capital increase of the Multilateral Investment Guarantee Agency (MIGA). A higher reserves-to-loans ratio both provides greater protection against higher portfolio risks as well as greater "free resources" to augment net income.[5] Even so, while a projected decline in the reserves-to-loans ratio is a matter of concern as it adversely affects the institution's income generating capacity, there are no unequivocal criteria for an appropriate level of reserves as Bank Presidents have privately acknowledged in the past.[6]

Since the onset of the Asian crisis and the sharp increase in Bank lending the projections have turned bleaker. Even though dollar net income will improve marginally, if current policies remain unchanged the reserves-to-loans ratio is set to decline to 11.8 per cent by 2002 with quite modest amounts allocated to reserves. Consequently the pressures to boost net income and to modify the principles for the allocation of net income (so as to increase the amounts transferred to reserves) have mounted.

IV. Measures to increase net income and reserves

The crux of the problem facing the Bank is that reserves need to be augmented, which also implies a focus on net income, given the links between the two. This section examines the measures proposed by the Bank's management to increase reserves and the extent to which they align incentives with fairness.

A. *Reducing administrative expenses*

The proposals of the Bank's management on increasing net income have focused almost exclusively on the revenue side. The option of cutting expenditures has been categorically rejected by management as "simply not possible" (World Bank, 1998, para. 23). The management argues that there is an "increase in the implicit subsidies to borrowers as the spread on loans covers a declining share of administrative expenses", and assumes that administrative costs are a given (ibid., para. 34). The fact that the World Bank (unlike commercial banks) is a price setter in its lending rate, not a price taker, sharply reduces its incentives to cut costs. For a long time, the institution has had a "soft budget" (Kapur et al., 1997). One indication of this is the doubling, in real dollars, of administrative costs per project committed between the mid-1970s and the mid-1990s, while project effectiveness has fallen or, as in more recent years, remained stagnant (table 1). It should be emphasized that these increases are not just due to salary increases per staff person.

Table 1

ADMINISTRATIVE COSTS AND EFFECTIVENESS OF WORLD BANK PROJECTS

	1975-1977	1985-1987	1995-1997
Administrative costs/project *(1997 $ million)*	2.3	3.7	4.4
Share of satisfactory projects *(Per cent of all projects)*	85	68	69

Note: Data for the percentage of satisfactory projects is the average for the periods 1974-1980, 1981-1989 and 1990-1995. While actual figures for the years in question are likely to differ the trends are clear and would not affect the inferences drawn.

Why has the Bank been so blasé about its budget at a time when its member States had to curb their budgets drastically? Despite substantial rhetoric and some effort, administrative costs of the Bank increased during much of the 1990s, while lending stagnated. Between 1986 and 1996, the Bank's administrative budget (including IDA) increased by 95 per cent while lending increased by just 28 per cent. The increase in expenditures was most apparent in areas removed from direct lending. Corporate management expenditures – which are weakly linked with direct lending but closely linked with management and major shareholder prerogatives – increased by 142 per cent during that period (from

$56.5 million to $136.5 million – 10 per cent of the administrative budget) and continued to increase in 1997-1998 (see Appendix).[7]

The standard answer has been that, on the one hand, fixed costs rose with the increase in the number of borrowers and, on the other, variable costs increased because projects have become more "complex" due to a more sophisticated understanding of the development process. But the answer is quite unconvincing if one compares administrative expenses of the World Bank to the European Investment Bank (EIB) (table 2). It is highly questionable that an almost fivefold difference between the two institutions can be attributed solely to their very different clientele.

Table 2

ADMINISTRATIVE COSTS: A COMPARISON BETWEEN THE WORLD BANK AND THE EUROPEAN INVESTMENT BANK

(FY1996)

	World Bank	*EIB*
Administrative expenses *($ million)*	733	181
Outstanding loans *($ billion)*	110	132
Administrative expenses *($ million)* per $ billion in loans outstanding	6.7	1.4

Administrative expenses have also increased substantially because non-borrowing shareholders have insisted on introducing mounting safeguards together with increases in reviews, consultations, conditions and the like. Many of these were introduced through the backdoor of IDA replenishments, but soon became Bank-wide policies (Kapur et al., 1997). Complexity, however, is not an exogenous variable. Over time a vested bureaucracy grew in the Bank, insisting on the virtues of ever more safeguards but paying little attention to costs – a pass-through loan pricing system weakened the incentives to do so. Furthermore, as the Bank's advice to its borrowers has so frequently emphasized, ever mounting safeguards and regulations creates their own political economy dynamic which can skew bureaucratic incentives within the Bank itself. Recent reports suggest that this fear is unfortunately not unfounded (New York Times, 16 July 1998).

In addition, the Bank's internal administrative practices have been an important cost-driving factor. Personnel policies made it exceedingly difficult to fire staff – and on the rare occasions when the Bank did so, the handshake was golden. It is regrettable that the Bank's shareholders have not chosen to seek any equivalence between the personnel policies of the institution and what the institution regularly asks of its borrowers in its lending advice and conditions. The Executive Directors seem to have been far more concerned with having personnel from their countries than with reducing costs. Complex and expensive compensation policies for expatriate staff have encouraged abuse, whether with regard to schooling or home travel allowances. Add to it staff costs to administer all these allowances.

Equally, it has to be said that sheer administrative incompetence, manifest for instance in the myriad of reorganizations, plays a not unimportant role in ratcheting up the Bank's cost. The shareholders' reluctance to shield the institution from outside carping has not been unimportant in providing a cloak of legitimacy for perennial reorganizations. Built-in structural features of the Board – ranging from frequency of rotation of Executive Directors to widely varying agendas – make its task of oversight difficult. While asymmetric information between principals and agents always strengthens the agent's hand, the problem is particularly acute in the case of the Bank where differing interests among principals, and the inherent ambiguities in ascribing specific outcomes on the ground to specific institutional actions, further strengthen the agent's hands. No matter the nature of the "compact" between management and the Board, there is no effective enforcement mechanism and it is difficult to imagine that a credible mechanism can be instituted. It is not that the Board is unaware of these realities. But sadly its response in recent years often confuses strategic oversight with a tendency to micromanage, simply adding to costs.

There is however, no ambiguity about the cost, in terms of human, financial and institutional effectiveness, that has resulted. Perpetual reorganizations

in the Bank have engendered distrust and cynicism and lowered morale – hardly the sort of organizational culture that enhances institutional effectiveness.[8] For borrower countries these costs have been twofold. For one, there are the direct administrative costs of the Bank, which translate into reduced net income and higher loan charges. For another, there are the substantially greater transactions costs in availing of an IBRD loan. These are more insidious and an important reason for the stagnation of lending during most of the 1990s despite the presumed financial subsidy in IBRD loans. Unless struck by a crisis, countries with access to markets have themselves "rationed" their intake of Bank loans, suggesting that the transactions costs of Bank loans more than outweighed their financial attractiveness. In any case, both financial and transaction costs are borne entirely by the borrowers. The management should provide a detailed analysis of the transaction costs involved in World Bank lending and how these compare with alternatives. Such an analysis is a precondition for a serious assessment of "subsidies" in the loan terms of the IBRD.

It is obvious that net income could increase significantly if the Bank and its shareholders found the political will to reduce its excessive administrative expenses. Is that possible? If administrative costs were cut by an additional 10 per cent, cost savings of about $560 million over four years would meet more than four fifths of the revenues projected from the proposed front-end fee (projected at $690 million over the same period).[9] It should be noted that the cuts should be applied to the total of the administrative expenses of IBRD and IDA since savings in IDA administrative expenses can by applied to a reduction in transfers from the IBRD's net income. Although the budget compact seemed to indicate that costs were already being pared to the bone, the reality is that cuts came on top of rapid budgetary growth in the 1990s. There are several ways where these cuts can be implemented without affecting the volume and quality of lending (see suggestions in the appendix).

Borrowing countries have usually opposed, or at best been reluctant in their support for, tighter budgets of multilateral development banks (MDBs). The roots of this attitude lie in a collective action problem. Private reservations aside, no developing country is individually willing to publicly cross swords with the management of a MDB on the budget, fearing that its programmes will be singled out to bear the burden of cuts. A second, and more parochial, reluctance stems from a fear that budget cuts would adversely affect their nationals employed in the institution. This has been a myopic strategy since in the end developing countries have to bear a large part of the burden in any case.

B. Raising equity through additions to paid-in capital

In the past when the shareholders deemed that the reserves needed strengthening, a capital increase was always integral to the proposals put forward by management. During this decade, however, it has been apparent that the major shareholders would not countenance a capital increase. This was evident during the contentious discussions around the last General Capital Increase approved in 1988 when the Bank's major shareholders, pointing to increasing budget difficulties at home, insisted that the paid-in component be reduced to just 3.0 per cent. Barely three years later, even as their fiscal problems worsened, the OECD countries accepted a 30 per cent paid-in contribution to a new multilateral development bank: the European Bank for Reconstruction and Development (EBRD). The creation of the EBRD, and the rapid agreement amongst the major OECD countries on a much larger budgetary outlay ($3.45 billion as compared to $2.25 billion in the case of the General Capital Increase of the IBRD in 1988) for an institution most of whose functions could potentially have been replicated by the IBRD at a smaller cash outlay were a strong portent of the relative priorities of the Bank's major shareholders, which were reinforced by subsequent events.

Despite the recent spurt in lending following the Asian crisis the IBRD continues to enjoy a comfortable "headroom" and does not need a capital increase to augment its lending capacity. Additional paid-in capital would, however, boost equity and result in more equitable burden sharing. A small capital increase – between $15 and $25 billion, but with 20 per cent paid-in (the maximum permissible under the Articles) – would not only ensure that the burden of providing global public goods is shared in a more equitable manner, but also strengthen the fraying links between power and financial burden.

Reserves play a fundamental role in affecting the tenor of governance of the World Bank, a crucial point that management's proposals completely ignore. Unlike in the United Nations system, in the Bretton Woods institutions the unequal distribution of power was initially expressly linked to an unequal

financial burden, both direct (in the form of paid-in capital in the IBRD), and indirect (the contingent liabilities inherent in callable capital). But over time, especially since the mid-1980s, both the direct and the indirect burden has waned, while the distribution of power has remained constant. For instance, in real dollar terms, the Bank's largest shareholder's capital contributions to the IBRD were greater before 1949 than today. As far as indirect contributions go, contingent liabilities are minuscule not only because of the historical track record of IBRD debt servicing but also because rising reserves and substantial loan-loss provisions make a call on capital ever more improbable.[10]

And that is the crux of the matter. As the Bank's financial strength grew and took firmer roots, the cost of "ownership" fell: easier borrowings and comfortable equity reduced the need for additional paid-in capital; higher reserves and the track record on defaults diminished the risks to the callable part of subscribed capital. One consequence of these financial trends was that the influence that came with ownership became less expensive, indeed almost costless – and therefore more attractive. This reality has been manifest in the greater intensity of disputes centred on even slight changes in capital share and the use of net income by the major shareholders for expressly partisan purposes – analytically equivalent to a common pool problem. Thus transfers from IBRD net income to IDA allow major shareholders to retain voting shares over IDA while reducing their financial outlays. Using net income to augment a capital increase in MIGA serves a similar though even more questionable purpose: in effect the IBRD's borrowers are paying for the non-borrowers to retain their voting power in MIGA. It stretches credulity to argue that the much larger transfers from the Bank's net income for Bosnia-Herzegovina and Gaza compared to those for countries such as Liberia, Somalia or Rwanda are driven more by humanitarian or developmental than by political concerns.

In earlier years the Bank's management was more cognizant of the reality that higher reserves reduce the financial burden on rich country shareholders: first, by reducing the need for future injections of paid-in capital and thereby shifting the burden of raising equity to borrowers; second, since reserves serve to absorb risk, by reducing contingent liabilities (the non-paid-in part of subscribed capital). In the1970s, McNamara quietly ran down reserves in the belief that this was an effective strategy in urging obdurate shareholders to agree to a capital increase. The present Bank management clearly does not see this as a possibility, thereby ignoring that placing the entire burden of augmenting the reserves-to-loans ratio on borrowers will further reduce the possibility of a capital increase.

While it is true that a capital increase takes time, a decline in the reserves-to-loans ratio in the interim period will have no important repercussions. Further, in the past a substantial fraction of paid-in capital has not been "usable" because of restrictions put in by many countries, especially the Bank's borrowers. This must change and a "no restrictions" clause should be a condition of participation in the capital increase.

C. Rationalizing loan pricing

The time has come for the Bank's members to accept greater variance in the Bank's loan pricing policies.[11] Borrowers who have viewed the institution as a financial cooperative have long opposed this. While it is important to preserve a cooperative spirit, it is also important that incentives, adverse selection and moral hazard issues receive greater attention; otherwise the cooperative spirit will increasingly come under stress. The growing discrepancy between political power and financial obligation in the case of rich country shareholders in the Bank is skewing incentives and thereby encouraging moral hazard. Equally, however, the structure of loan charges should not create incentives for moral hazard among borrowers or management.

As already noted, the proposals of the Bank's management focus on revenue increases. In the following, these proposals will be examined in greater detail.

Proposal 1: *Increase the contractual loan spread by 30 basis points.*

Borrowers should not approve an undifferentiated increase in loan charges by 30 basis points (from 50 to 80 basis points above the Bank's funding cost). Instead, loan pricing should discriminate among borrowers on the basis of differences in country risk. In assessing its portfolio risk, the Bank places each borrowing country in a risk category (of which there are seven). Although these risk categories have an impact on net income, they do not at present affect a country's borrowing costs from the Bank. This should change since loan-loss provisions (which

reduce net income) are a function of a country's portfolio risk classification and the volume of its borrowing. Not only is the current practice inequitable across borrowers, penalizing countries that manage their economies better than others, but it also socializes the costs of additional Bank lending to certain countries in response to political pressures by the major shareholders. Loan pricing policies should recover the loan-loss provisions set aside from net income to cover loans to specific borrowers. In practice such price discrimination would be quite modest. For instance, the proposed 30 basis point loan cost increase could instead be broken into 5 basis point increments (over the base of 50 basis points over LIBOR) for each higher risk classification (assuming the seven country risk classifications the Bank currently uses). Such a change would:

* result in additional income for the Bank (albeit less than if the blanket 30 basis point increase were put into effect);

* reward those borrowers who manage their economies better than others;

* protect all borrowers against the effects of excess lending to a single borrower as a consequence of the political interests of the major powers;

* protect the interests of smaller borrowers, since risks to the Bank are more apparent in the case of large borrowers.

Proposal 2: *Charge a 1 per cent front-end fee.*

The proposal for a front-end fee should be rejected. Such a charge builds up cash balances rapidly and reduces pressures to cut expenditures. Consequently, such a fee-structure helps an incumbent administration and passes the buck onto future managers.

Proposal 3: *Maintain the current commitment fee.*

The proposal should be supported. Delays in the implementation of approved projects by borrowers create opportunity costs and financial costs for the Bank and all its members. A commitment fee serves as a negative incentive to borrowers, pushing them to implement projects and programmes rapidly.

Proposal 4: *Eliminate for the short-term (FY1999 and 2000) the 25 basis-point interest-rate waiver.*

The World Bank offers a 25 basis-point interest-rate waiver to borrowers that service their debts on time. The proposal, which supposedly would raise about $450 million over the two years, should not be accepted in its present form. This is not to say that the principle of reducing the waiver should be rejected out of hand. Given current financial realities, IBRD borrowers should be willing to accept a reduction in the interest-rate waiver between 10-15 basis points, but only under the following conditions:

(i) cuts in administrative expenditures by at least 10 per cent;

(ii) an agreement on a capital increase, thereby increasing the contribution of shareholder equity, and especially contributions by major shareholders;

(iii) an agreement with IDA borrowers on the share of net income transferred to IDA and a firewall between IBRD and IDA on conditions arising from an IDA replenishment.

The latter two conditions are discussed in greater detail below.

Proposal 5: *A surplus balance of $250 million should be created at the beginning of each fiscal year, before any consideration is given to granting an interest rate waiver.*

This proposal should be opposed, although a conditional acceptance, as in the case of proposal 4 should not be ruled out. The record shows that such discretionary funds are liable to be grabbed for politically expedient purposes and borrowers will find this impossible to oppose since there will always be some borrowers supporting it. The Bank's members should realize both the political inevitability and the opportunity cost of such outcomes. Given this inevitability, borrower interests are best served by a firmer "hands-tying" strategy wherein all borrowers agree *ex ante* to the priorities guiding the use of such funds instead of leaving these resources in a discretionary fund such as a "surplus". In a rapidly changing global environment, discretion is indeed important. But where power is unequal, the interests of the weak are likely to be better served by rules than by discretion.

Proposal 6: *Defer cash payments to IDA and to the Heavily Indebted Poor Countries.*

This proposal should be accepted.

V. Uses of net income

IBRD borrowers have proposed that the use of net income be restricted to post-conflict assistance, African capacity building, and soft-loans and debt relief for poor countries. Unfortunately these proposals do not adequately take account of the principles of net income allocation. Several alternatives are outlined below.

(i) All grant-like allocations should come out of net income, rather than being included in part (as in the case of "special programmes") in administrative expenses. An all-encompassing trust fund should be created to handle all grant allocations. An annual lump-sum transfer from net income to this trust fund, which in turn allocates grants to IDA or the Consultative Group on International Agricultural Research (CGIAR), would make the administrative budget more transparent.

(ii) Since the World Bank is a global institution, its net income should be allocated to truly global public goods. The Bank has never done any substantive analysis that would help its members rank global public goods in order of their relative contribution to global welfare. It is well documented that investments in global research systems have very high rates of return (see for instance, Bell, Clark and Ruttan, 1994). Investments in the CGIAR system, for instance, have had one of the highest rates of return of Bank investments. An even stronger case could be made for tropical disease research, which is a genuine "global public good". Investment in tropical disease research is completely consistent with the Bank's overriding purpose of poverty alleviation given the differentially adverse impact of tropical disease on the poor. Further, such an investment is politically non-controversial in that allocations to such research will not drive out existing private sector efforts. A long-term commitment of allocation of net income (between $50 million and $100 million) for research on three or four major tropical diseases would arguably have a higher rate of return for global welfare than virtually any existing use of net income by the Bank. Such programme could be administered in collaboration with WHO, through an arrangement similar to that to be found in the National Science Foundation whereby money is allocated to the most promising research proposals. The practical difficulties of achieving a consensus can be reduced by periodically appointing independent commissions of experts to make recommendations on priorities with the members agreeing *ex ante* to abide by these recommendations.

(iii) The "subsidiarity" principle should apply to the purposes for which the Bank's net income can be deployed. Wherever the locus of a problem – and potential benefits – are clearly of a regional nature, regional multilateral institutions should bear the burden first. Only where regional multilateral institutions are evidently weak, should global institutions fill the breach. This principle would suggest that conflict, which is usually regional in nature, should be first addressed by regional institutions. In post-conflict assistance the lead agency should be the relevant regional institution: the IDB and Caribbean Development Bank in Central America, the EBRD in Bosnia-Herzegovina, and the Asian Development Bank in Cambodia. Only where the regional institutions are weak and financially stretched can a case be made for use of World Bank net income in post-conflict resolution. Given the limited resources of the African Development Bank, Africa is the only region where exceptions are currently warranted.

(iv) If, as likely, non-borrowers are unwilling to come up with additional resources in the form of paid-in capital, they should at least agree to desist from imposing unfunded mandates and using the Bank's net income for parochial political ends. Any new conditions, mandates and requirements must first be costed out and implemented only after equivalent budget cuts have been made. Only when there is an explicit recognition of opportunity costs will the institution and its shareholders actually realize what the trade-offs really are. The United States

Congress has adopted this budgetary principle; and it is not clear why what is deemed as good budgetary policy in the Bank's largest shareholder should not be good for the Bank.

(v) The needs of IDA borrowers are imposing increasing costs on IBRD borrowers. Transfers from net income for IDA as well as for the HIPC debt-relief facility reduce reserves and thereby the Bank's income-generating capacity. Equally, if not more, detrimental to the interests of IBRD borrowers are the institutional compromises made to secure successive IDA replenishments since the 1980s. These compromises have institution-wide repercussions, resulting in substantially higher transaction costs for Bank borrowers. The IDA borrowers should recognize the new realities of burden sharing and reach an agreement with IBRD borrowers on a ceiling on the share of net income that will be transferred to IDA, and accept that any requirements agreed to as part of an IDA replenishment will apply only to IDA borrowers and not IBRD borrowers.

VI. Conclusions

When presenting its proposals for raising the World Bank's net income, the management of the institution warned that "structural weaknesses which, if not remedied in a timely fashion, are likely to adversely affect the financial integrity of the institution and eventually to impair its capacity to deliver on its development mandate" (see IBRD, 1998). While this paper concurs to a considerable degree with the prognosis, it disagrees with the prescriptions, particularly that the solution lies in increasing net income through higher loan charges. The proposals put the onus on regaining structural stability on one group: IBRD borrowers. Successful structural adjustment – whether in a country or an organization – requires at least a modicum of equitable sharing of the costs of adjustment. In the Bank's case all stakeholders – non-borrowing countries, staff and management, and IDA-borrowers, in addition to IBRD borrowers – must share in the costs of adjustment, if fairness is to be regained and if the problems are not to recur. The proposals of the Bank's management therefore need substantial modifications.

Appendix

Some suggestions for reducing administrative costs

1. *Reduction of the administrative costs of frontline activities by 5 per cent and of backline activities by 15 per cent so as to achieve overall reductions by 10 per cent.*[12]

The 5 per cent cut would be imposed on frontline activities 1-4, as defined in a review undertaken by an external consultancy firm for the Strategic Compact: activities directly delivering products and services; those providing support or advice to product or service teams directly required for the delivery of specific products or services to clients; activities or systems which directly service core client needs, including knowledge dissemination to clients; direct country and product strategy work including direct country economic work. The 15 per cent cut would be all other activities. Each of the two groups has a weight of 50 per cent in total administrative costs.

Some backline activities need to be trimmed even more drastically. The expenditures on the Bank's governance structure (Executive Directors, Board of Governors, Administrative Tribunal, and Inspection Panel) now consume more than $80 million, about 6 per cent of total administrative costs. Expenditures on the Executive Office have increased two-and-half fold between FY1995 and FY1998 (from $4.5 to $11.3 million). The external relations budget is officially $26 million. But the Bank's budgeting department estimated that in 1996, based on submissions by different vice-presidents, the regions and other central vice-presidencies spend an additional $31 million on public relations. How justifiable is an expenditure of about $60 million on external affairs? How much of this expenditure really helps the poor? Do the borrowers really want to pay for World Bank advertisements on radio and television in the United States or for advertisements in the *Financial Times* for programmes promoting cultural understanding amongst the youth of the world? Even the *World Development Report* should not be seen as outside the pale of budgetary review. In principle, the report encapsulates both cutting-edge thinking as well "the" consensus on some facet of the development process. In practice, it is not at all self-evident that an annual expenditure of $4-5

million for this purpose is the optimal use of Bank resources. To be sure, this problem is not peculiar to the World Bank. But alternatives are rarely examined let alone pursued. For example, if the Bank and the UNDP (where the Human Development Report is produced) published their flagship publications every two years, and devoted the resources saved to building up research capabilities in developing countries, would the outcome be any worse?

2. *Radical overhaul of expatriate staff benefits policies.*

Instead of the numerous education and home-leave allowances, a modest salary mark-up to expatriate staff for these purposes should be sufficient. It is pointless checking whether a staff member and his family spend their vacation in their home countries or wiggle their toes in the Potomac or whether they travel home annually and, if so, in business or economy class. These micro-checks have become an institutional pathology, whether internally or with respect to its borrowers. Just the administrative and opportunity costs of these practices far exceed any potential benefits. It should be noted that staff benefits policies have been particularly profligate in the case of support staff. On the basis of salaries alone, most expatriate support staff in the Bank earn substantial rents (the difference between what they earn at the Bank and what they would earn in their home countries) – add-in the benefits and the total rents skyrocket.

3. *Elimination of tax reimbursement to member countries for their nationals serving on the Bank's staff.*

Currently, this imposes a burden of $60 million on the institution; virtually all of it goes to one country. Given the sea change in burden sharing, the merits of the original rationale (if there was one) no longer exists. It is one thing for member countries to plead political inability to contribute additional funds to the Bank. It is quite another to continue to insist that the institution's members reimburse them for the privilege of employing their nationals.

4. *Ensuring that frequent flyer miles would accrue to the institution, not the individual staff member.*

That alone could reduce travel costs by at least 5 per cent as well as reduce incentives to pad-up travel budgets.

5. *Substantially greater outsourcing of Bank activities – from information technology to printing and publishing to use of consultants – to lower-cost suppliers based in developing countries.*

Multinational companies do this routinely because they have to respond to market pressures. But in the Bank's case, the absence of market discipline means that only budgetary pressure is likely to force such shifts.

Notes

1   The criteria for the SGP emphasize multi-country benefits, multi-donor support, and independence of the recipient institution from the World Bank Group. In FY1998, funding for the SGP accounted for about 5 per cent of the Bank's budget (around $80 million).

2   Examples include grants to the World Food Programme in 1984/85 to support relief efforts for the famine in sub-Saharan Africa and in 1993 to fund relief operations in Rwanda.

3   The Bank committed $30 million for the study on the former Soviet Union mandated by the G-7. It committed $140 million to the Trust Fund for Gaza through 1995, funded by transfers from IBRD surplus earmarked for IDA; a $150 million Trust Fund for Bosnia-Herzegovina was created from the surplus account.

4   Indeed the World Bank's authorized history had warned of these impeding problems and unsurprisingly these have now come to pass (see Kapur, Lewis and Webb, 1997).

5   Although in the Bank's early years the "comfort factor" that those high levels of reserves signaled to markets helped lower its borrowing costs, this has not been the case for the last three decades. Unless there is a sharp year-to-year decline or reserves are at very low levels markets pay little attention to the IBRD's reserves.

6   Thus Black admitted that "since this [level of reserves] is a psychological matter, it cannot readily be given precise quantitative expression", while for Woods "the question [of the adequacy or inadequacy of the reserves] was not susceptible of a mathematical determination. It was a question of judgement".

7   Corporate management expenditures include the Board and Executive Directors offices, Development Committee, the Executive Office, the Secretary's department, the Inspection Panel, OED, the Administrative Tribunal, the Ombudsman and Appeals, and External Affairs.

8   This is evident, for instance, from the staff surveys.

9   Revenue projections from the proposed front-end fees are from the table on p. 14 of the 2 July 1998 paper, "IBRD income dynamics: a follow up note".

10   A commentary in the *Financial Times* of 15 June 1998 on the World Bank's net income notes, as if it were still a fact, that "the rich industrial nations provide much of its capital". This is true notionally, but not in terms of cash outlays.

11   Currently the only form of price discrimination is that loans to higher income borrowers have a shorter maturity profile.

12   For definitions see annex B.9 in "Implementing the Strategic Compact, Vol. 2", May 1997.

References

BELL, D., W. CLARK, and V. RUTTAN (1994), "Global Research Systems for Sustainable Development: Agriculture, Health and Environment", in V. Ruttan (ed.), *Agriculture, Environment and Health: Sustainable Development in the 21st Century* (Minneapolis: University of Minnesota Press).

KAPUR, D., J. LEWIS, and R. WEBB (1997), *The World Bank: Its First Fifty Years. Volume 1: History* (Washington, D.C.: The Brookings Institution).

WORLD BANK (1997), "Allocation of FY1998 Net Income", R97-175 (Washington, D.C.), 16 July.

WORLD BANK (1998), "IBRD Income Dynamics", R98-134 (Washington, D.C.), 27 May.

LAX PUBLIC SECTOR, DESTABILIZING PRIVATE SECTOR: ORIGINS OF CAPITAL MARKET CRISES

Lance Taylor*

Abstract

A principal message of this paper is that external financial crises are not caused by an alert private sector pouncing upon the public sector's foolish actions, such as running an unsustainable fiscal deficit or creating moral hazards. Such crises are better described as private sectors (both domestic and foreign) acting to make high short-term profits when policy and history provide the preconditions and the public sector acquiesces. This conclusion emerges from a review of balance-of-payments crises in the Southern Cone around 1980, Mexico in 1994/95, East Asia in 1997/98, and Russia in 1998, in light of existing theories – speculative attack models and moral hazard – and a synthesis of ideas proposed by Salih Neftci and Roberto Frenkel. The standard theories do not explain history well. The Frenkel-Neftci framework supports a better description of crisis dynamics in terms of five elements: (1) the nominal exchange rate is fixed or close to being pre-determined; (2) there are few barriers to external capital inflows and outflows; (3) historical factors and the conjuncture act together to create wide financial "spreads" between returns to national assets and borrowing rates abroad – these in turn generate capital inflows which push the domestic financial system in the direction of being long on domestic assets and short on foreign holdings; (4) regulation of the system is lax and probably pro-cyclical; (5) stock-flow repercussions of these initially microeconomic changes through the balance of payments and the financial system's flows of funds and balance sheets set off a dynamic macro process which is unstable. Policy alternatives are discussed in terms of these five conditions and the present global macroeconomic environment, in particular the destabilizing interventions of the International Monetary Fund in East Asia.

* This paper draws heavily on the results of a project on International Capital Markets and the Future of Economic Policy, Center for Economic Policy Analysis, New School for Social Research, with support from the Ford Foundation. Comments by Alice Amsden, Jane D'Arista, Thorsten Block, Ha-Joon Chang, Sandy Darity, Roberto Frenkel, and Gerry Helleiner are gratefully acknowledged.

I. Tolstoy was wrong (about international capital markets, at least)

Everyone knows the epigraph to *Anna Karenina*, "Happy families are all alike; every unhappy family is unhappy in its own way". Tolstoy may well have been right about families, but the extension of his judgement to economies hit by capital market crises distinctly fails. Their causes and unhappy consequences in Latin America, Asia and Eastern Europe over the past 20 years have many elements in common.

Most of these boom and bust episodes took place with the fiscal house in order. They pivoted around the government's withdrawal from regulating the real side of the economy, the financial sector, and especially the international capital market. This premeditated laxity created strong incentives for destabilizing private sector financial behaviour, on the part of both domestic and external players. Feedbacks of their actions to the macroeconomic level upset the system.

At best, the past decades may be transitions toward a more "mature" public/private relationship in the developing world; at worst, they presage long-term stagnation or systemic collapse. The latter outcomes become ever more likely if the current incentive structure for private sector international financial transactions in both poor and rich countries remains unchanged.

To consider how the system can be rebuilt in a more stable fashion, we have to understand why the crises happened in the first place. That is not an easy task. A plausible place to begin is with the models economists have designed to explain events such as Latin America's "Southern Cone" crisis around 1980, European problems with the ERM in 1992, Mexico and the "tequila" crisis in 1994, events in East Asia in 1997/98, and the Russian crisis of summer 1998. We start out in section II with a review of mainstream work – accounting conventions, crisis models, "moral hazards" and other abstract niceties. Then we go on to a narrative proposed by people who operate close to macro policy choices and micro financial decisions. Reviews of Latin American (section III) and Asian and Russian (section IV) experiences show that the overlap between mainstream models and the reality they are supposed to describe is slight; the practitioners' framework fits history far better. In section V, this framework is used as a basis for

suggestions about reasonable policy lines to follow in the wake of the recent disasters.

II. Existing theory

This section discusses existing crisis theories. It begins with relatively innocuous but important accounting conventions, and goes on to present mainstream models and a more plausible alternative.

A. Accounting preliminaries

A proper macroeconomic accounting framework is essential for disentangling the causes of financial crises; this subsection is devoted to laying one out. Table 1 presents a simplified but realistic set of accounts for an economy with five institutional sectors: households, business, government, a financial sector, and the rest of the world.

How each sector's savings originate from its incomes and outlays is illustrated in the top panel. Households in the first line receive labour income W, transfers from business J_b (that is, dividends, rents, etc.) and from government J_g, and interest payments ζ_h on their assets held with the financial system. They use income for consumption C_h, to pay taxes T_h, and to pay interest Z_h to the financial system. What is left over is their savings S_h. To keep the number of symbols in table 1 within reason, households are assumed to hold liabilities of the financial system only. That is, their holdings of business equity are "small" and/or do not change, and they neither borrow nor hold assets abroad. The last two assumptions reflect a major problem with the data: it is far easier to register funds flowing into a country via the capital market than to observe money going out as capital flight by numerous less than fully legal channels. Repatriation of such household assets is implicitly treated as foreign lending to business or government in the discussion that follows.

Similar accounting statements apply to the other sectors. Business gets gross profit income Π, and has outlays for transfers to households, taxes T_b, and interest payments to the local financial system (Z_b) and the rest of the world. The latter payment, eZ_b^*, amounts to Z_b^* in foreign currency terms converted to local currency at the exchange rate e. Business savings S_b is profits net of these expenditures. It will be lower insofar as interest payments Z_b and eZ_b^* are

Table 1

MACROECONOMIC ACCOUNTING RELATIONSHIPS

Generation of savings

Household:
$$S_h = W + J_b + J_g + \zeta_h - C_h - T_h - Z_h$$

Business:
$$S_b = \Pi - J_b - T_b - Z_b - eZ_b^*$$

Government:
$$S_g = T_h + T_b - C_g - J_g - Z_g - eZ_g^*$$

Financial system:
$$0 = Z_h + Z_b + Z_g - \zeta_h$$

Foreign:
$$S_f = e[M + Z_b^* + Z_g^* - E]$$

Resource balance
$$S_h + S_b + S_g + S_f = W + \Pi - (C_h + C_g) + e(M - E)$$

Investment-savings balance
$$(I_h - S_h) + (I_b - S_b) + (I_g - S_g) = S_f$$

Accumulation

Household:
$$(I_h - S_h) = \Delta D_h - \Delta H_h$$

Business:
$$(I_b - S_b) = \Delta D_b - e\Delta D_b^*$$

Government:
$$(I_g - S_g) = \Delta D_g - e\Delta D_g^*$$

Financial system:
$$0 = \Delta H_h - (\Delta D_h + \Delta D_b + \Delta D_g) - e\Delta R^*$$

Foreign:
$$0 = S_f - e(\Delta D_b^* + \Delta D_g^*) + e\Delta R^*$$

Spreads

Interest rate:
$$\Sigma_i = i - [i^* + (\Delta e / e)^E] = i - (i^* + \hat{e}^E)$$

Capital gains:
$$\Sigma_Q = (\Delta Q / Q)^E - [i^* + (\Delta e / e)^E] = \hat{Q}^E (i^* + \hat{e}^E)$$

high. As discussed later, firms in Asia are said to suffer from constricted saving possibilities because their debt/equity ratios are high. Standard stabilization programmes that drive up interest rates and currency values and thereby Z_b and eZ_b^* can easily lead to heavy business losses (negative values of S_b), culminating in waves of bankruptcy.

Government savings S_g is total tax revenue net of public consumption C_g, transfers to households,

and interest payments at home (Z_g) and abroad eZ_g^*. For simplicity, the financial system is assumed to have zero savings, so that its interest income flows from households, business and government just cover its payments to households. Finally, "foreign savings" S_f in local currency terms is the exchange rate times the foreign currency values of imports (M) and interest payments less exports (E). The implication is that the rest of the world applies part of its overall savings to cover "our" excess of spending over income.

This interpretation shows up clearly in the "resource balance" equation or the sum of all the savings definitions. Total savings result from the excesses of income from production $W + \Pi$ over private and public consumption $C_h + C_g$, and of imports over exports. Or, in other words, S_f equals total income minus total outlays and the sum of domestic saving supplies.

Likewise, the "investment-savings balance" shows that the sum over sectors of investment less savings must equal zero. Much of the macroeconomic drama in recent crises results from large shifts in these "financial deficits". They show up in each sector's accumulation of assets and liabilities in the penultimate panel of the table.

Households, for example, are assumed to finance their deficit ($I_h - S_h$) by running up new debt ΔD_h with the financial system, partially offset by their greater holdings of the system's liabilities or the increase ΔH_h in the "money" supply.[1] Business and government both cover their deficits by new domestic (the ΔD terms) and foreign (the ΔD^* terms) borrowing.

The accounts for the financial system and the rest of the world are slightly less transparent, but essential to the following discussion. The former's flow balances show that new money creation ΔH_h is backed by increases in domestic debt owed by households, business, and government, as well as by increases in the system's foreign reserves $e\Delta R^*$. In the foreign balance, reserve increments and foreign savings are "financed" by increases in the foreign debts of business and government $e(\Delta D_b^* + \Delta D_g^*)$.

How the "spreads" in table 1's last panel enter the analysis is taken up below. What we can do now is say something about how the public sector was supposed to be the prime culprit for "old" financial upheavals, e.g. the debt crisis of the 1980s. As will be seen shortly, this assertion is far from the truth, but it is so widely accepted that we must discuss it on its own terms.

B.   Mainstream crisis models

The first post-World War II wave of developing economy crises in which external financial flows played a significant role took place around 1980. The countries affected included Turkey in the late 1970s, the Southern Cone in 1980/81, Mexico and many others in 1982, and South Africa in 1985. The Southern Cone collapses attracted great attention. They teach significant lessons about how market deregulation by the public sector and private responses to it can be extremely destabilizing.

The academic models underlying the belief that the public sector "caused" the early crises are built around a regime shift (or "transcritical bifurcation" in the jargon of elementary catastrophe theory). They emphasize how gradually evolving "fundamentals" can alter financial returns in such a way as to provoke an abrupt change of conditions or crisis – a ball rolls smoothly over the surface of a table until it falls off.

An early model of this sort was set out by Hotelling (1931). It describes speculative attacks on commodity buffer stocks. Hotelling set up a dynamic optimizing model that shows (obviously incorrectly) that prices of exhaustible resources should rise steadily over time at a rate equal to the real rate of interest. Suppose that the government tries to stabilize such a price with a buffer stock. So long as the potential capital gain from holding the commodity lies below the return to a risk-free alternative, speculators will let the government keep the stock. But when the gain from the potentially trending (or "shadow") price exceeds the alternative return, they will buy the entire stock in a speculative attack and let the observed market price go up steadily thereafter.

The regime change is triggered when the profit from liquidating the "distortion" created by the buffer stock becomes large enough – investors choose their moment to punish the government for interfering in the market. Similar sentiments underlie balance-of-payments crisis models of the sort proposed by Krugman (1979) and pursued by many others.[2] They assert that expansionary policy when the economy is subject to a foreign exchange constraint can provoke a flight from the local currency.

In a typical scenario, the nominal exchange rate is implicitly assumed to be fixed or have a predetermined percentage rate of devaluation $\hat{e} = \Delta e / e$. Moreover, the local interest rate i exceeds the foreign rate i^*. Under a "credible" fixed rate regime, the *expected* rate of devaluation $\hat{e}^E = (\Delta e / e)^E$ will equal zero. From the last panel of table 1, the interest rate "spread" $\Sigma_i > 0$ will favour investing in the home country.

Now suppose that the government pursues expansionary fiscal policy, increasing the fiscal deficit $I_g - S_g$. If the household and business sectors do not alter their behaviour, the investment-savings balance in table 1 shows that foreign savings S_f or the external current account deficit has to rise. A perceived "twin deficit" problem of this sort lies at the heart of traditional IMF stabilization packages that have thrown many countries (now including those in East Asia) into recession.[3] The external imbalance can lead to crisis via several channels. We describe two:

The first is based on the recognition that the government has to issue more debt, i.e. in the "accumulation" panel of table 1, ΔD_g or ΔD_g^* must rise when $I_g - S_g$ is increased. Assume that the government is credit-constrained in external markets so that ΔD_g expands. To maintain its own balances, the financial system can "monetize" this new debt so that ΔH_h goes up as well. If the domestic price level P is driven up by money creation (which does not always happen), then the real value of the currency eP^* / P (where P^* is the foreign price level) will appreciate or decline in absolute value. Imports are likely to rise and exports to fall, leading to greater external imbalance. With more borrowing ruled out by assumption, foreign reserves will begin to erode.

Falling reserves suggest that the trade deficit cannot be maintained indefinitely. When they are exhausted, presumably there will have to be a discrete "maxi"-devaluation – a regime shift which will inflict a capital loss on external investors holding liabilities of the home country denominated in local currency. At some point, it becomes rational to expect the devaluation to occur, making $\hat{e}^E$ strongly positive and reversing the spread. A currency attack follows. As with Hotelling's commodity stocks, the economically untenable fiscal expansion is instantly erased.

A second version of this tale is based on the assumption that the local monetary authorities raise "deposit" interest rates to induce households to hold financial system liabilities created in response to greater public borrowing. In the financial system balance in the first panel of table 1, ζ_h will increase so that interest rates on outstanding domestic debts have to go up as well.

The spread Σ_i immediately widens. Foreign players begin to shift portfolios towards home assets, so that from the foreign accumulation balance in table 1 reserves begin to grow. If the monetary authorities allow the reserve increase to feed into faster growth of the money supply, we are back to the previous story. If they "sterilize" a higher ΔR^* by cutting the

growth of household (ΔD_h) or business (ΔD_b) debt, then interest rates will go up even further, drawing more foreign investment into the system. From the foreign accumulation balance, pressures will mount for the current account deficit S_f to increase, say via exchange appreciation induced by inflation, or else a downward drift of the nominal rate as the authorities allow the currency to gain strength. A foreign crisis looms again.

C. Moral hazards

The notion of moral hazard comes from the economic theory of insurance. The basic idea is that insurance reduces incentives for prudence: the more fire insurance I hold on my house, the more arson becomes an intriguing thought. Insurance companies frustrate such temptation by allowing homeowners to insure their properties for no more than 75 per cent or so of their market valuations.

In the finance literature, moral hazard has been picked up in diverse lines of argument. Writing in an American context, the unconventional macroeconomist Minsky (1986) saw it as arising after the 1930s as a consequence of counter-cyclical policy aimed at moderating real/financial business cycles. At the same time, "automatic stabilizers" such as unemployment insurance were created as part of the welfare state. As is always the case, these bits of economic engineering had unexpected consequences.

One was a move of corporations towards more financially "fragile" positions, leading them to seek higher short-term profitability. In the absence of fears of price and sales downswings, high risk/high return projects became more attractive. This shift was exemplified by increased "short-termism" of investment activities, and the push towards merger and acquisition (M&A) activity in the 1970s and 1980s.

Second, the intermediaries financing such initiatives gained more explicit protection against risky actions by their borrowers through "lender of last resort" (LLR) interventions by the Federal Reserve. The resulting moral hazard induced both banks and firms to seek more risky placements of resources. Banks, in particular, pursued financial innovations. Among them were the elimination of interest rate ceilings on deposits and the consequent creation of money market funds which effectively jacked up interest rates in the 1970s, the Saving and Loan (S&L) crisis of the 1980s, the appearance of investment funds and "asset securitization" at about the same time, and the later emergence of widespread derivatives markets and hedge funds.

To an extent all these changes were driven by gradual relaxation of restrictions on external capital movements (D'Arista, 1998). When Eurocurrency markets began to boom in the 1970s, the higher deposit rates they paid put pressure on United States regulators to lift interest rate ceilings. Meanwhile, without reserve requirements off-shore banks (and off-shore branches of American banks) could lend more cheaply in the domestic market, leading to further deregulation. The United States took the lead in pushing for new regulatory mechanisms, e.g. the "Basle" standards for capital adequacy adopted in 1988.

Unfortunately, these changes introduced a strong pro-cyclical bias into regulation – just the opposite of the sort of system that should be in place. In an upswing, banks typically have no problem in building up equity to satisfy adequacy requirements. In a downswing, however, unless they already have the capital, they can easily be wiped out. As will be seen, such regulatory structures helped exacerbate financial crises in developing countries.

So far, moral hazard looks sensible; it can be used to underpin plausible historical narratives. Extensions out of context begin to stretch verisimilitude. Deposit insurance, for example, certainly played a role in the S&L crisis in the United States. In the Garn-St. Germain Act of 1982, depositors were allowed to have any number of fully-insured $100,000 accounts with an S&L. With their prudential responsibilities removed by the Act, S&L managers were free to engage in any high-risk, high-return projects they saw fit – which they immediately proceeded to do.

However, a frequently stated extension of this observation to developing country markets makes less sense. For example, deposit guarantees have been accused of worsening the Southern Cone crises, but in Chile they had been abolished precisely to avoid moral hazard! Similarly, for the Republic of Korea Krugman's (1998) assertion that the government provided implicit guarantees for banks and industrial corporations holds no water. He argues that Korean conglomerates or *chaebols* engaged in reckless investment and had low efficiency as proven by their low profitability. But as Chang et al. (1998) point out, profitability was low only *after* interest payments, not *before*. Moreover, over the 1980s and

1990s the government did not bail out any *chaebols*; in the period 1990-1997 three of the 30 biggest ones went bankrupt. The government did have a history of stepping in to restructure enterprises in trouble, but that left little room for moral hazard – managers knew they would lose control over their companies if they failed to perform.

Despite such shaky empirical antecedents, moral hazard is given a central role in mainstream crisis models. Dooley (1997), for example, argues that developing country governments self-insure by accumulating international reserves to back up poorly regulated financial markets. National players feel justified in offering high returns to foreign investors, setting up a spread. Domestic liabilities are acquired by outsiders (or perhaps nationals resident in more pleasant climes or just engaging in off-shore manipulations) until such point as the stock of insured claims exceeds the government's reserves. A speculative attack follows.

The leitmotif of an alert private sector chastizing an inept government recurs again. This time it encourages reckless investment behaviour. All a sensible private sector can be expected to do is to make money out of such misguided public action.

D.   *A more plausible theory*

A more realistic perspective is that the public and private sectors generate positive financial feedbacks between themselves first at the micro and then at the macro level, ultimately destabilizing the system. This line of analysis is pursued by Salih Neftci (1998), a market practitioner, and Roberto Frenkel (1983), a macroeconomist. Both focus on an initial situation in which the nominal exchange rate is "credibly" fixed (setting the $\hat{e}^E$ terms equal to zero in table 1's equations for spreads), and show how an unstable dynamic process can arise. A Frenkel-Neftci (or FN) cycle begins in financial markets, which generate capital inflows. They spill over to the macroeconomy via the financial system and the balance of payments as the upswing gains momentum. At the peak, before a (more or less rapid) downswing, the economy-wide consequences can be overwhelming.

To trace through an example, suppose that a spread Σ_i (e.g. on Mexican Government peso-denominated bonds with a high interest rate but carrying an implicit exchange risk) or Σ_Q (e.g.

capital gains from booming Bangkok real estate, where $\hat{Q}$ is the growth rate of the relevant asset price) opens. A few local players take positions in the relevant assets, borrowing abroad to do so. Their exposure is risky but small. It may well go unnoticed by regulators; indeed for the system as a whole the risk is negligible.

Destabilizing market competition enters in a second stage. The pioneering institutions are exploiting a spread of (say) 10 per cent, while others are earning (say) 5 per cent on traditional placements. Even if the risks are recognized, it is difficult for other players not to jump in. A trader or loan officer holding 5 per cent paper will reason that the probability of losing his or her job is close to 100 per cent *now* if he or she does not take the high risk/high return position. The future, meanwhile, can take care of itself. Personal discount rates are ratcheted up by the spread; the caution that an exposed position may have to be unwound "sometime" becomes a secondary consideration.

After some months or years of this process, the balance sheet of the local financial system will be risky overall, short on foreign currency and long on local assets.[4] Potential losses from the long position are finite – at most they amount to what the assets cost in the first place. Losses from short-selling foreign exchange are in principle unbounded – who knows how high the local currency-to-dollar exchange rate may finally have to rise?

In a typical macroeconomic paradox, individual players' risks have now been shifted to the aggregate. Any policy move that threatens the overall position – for example cutting interest rates or pricking the real estate bubble – could cause a collapse of the currency and local asset prices. The authorities will use reserves and/or regulations to prevent a crash, consciously ratifying the private sector's market decisions. Unfortunately, macroeconomic factors will ultimately force their hand.

In a familiar scenario, suppose that the initial capital inflows have boosted domestic output growth. The current account deficit S_f will widen, leading at some point to a fall in reserves as capital inflows level off and total interest payments on outstanding obligations rise. Higher interest rates will be needed to equilibrate portfolios and attract foreign capital. In turn, S_b will fall or turn negative as illiquidity and insolvency spread *à la* Minsky, threatening a systemic crisis. Bankruptcies of banks and firms may further contribute to reducing the credibility of the exchange rate.

A downturn becomes inevitable, since finally no local interest rate will be high enough to induce more external lending in support of what is recognized as a short forex position at the economy-wide level. Shrewd players will unwind their positions before the downswing begins (as Mexican nationals were said to have done before the December 1994 devaluation); they can even retain positive earnings over the cycle by getting out while the currency weakens visibly. But others – typically including the macroeconomic policy team – are likely to go under.

The dynamics of this narrative differs from that of standard crisis models: it does not involve a regime shift when a spread Σ_i or Σ_Q switches sign from positive to negative. Rather, movements in the spread itself feed back into cyclical changes within the economy concerned that finally lead to massive instability. Reverting to catastrophe theory jargon, the standard models invoke a "static" instability, like a buckling beam. More relevant to history are "dynamic" or cyclical instabilities that appear when effective damping of the dynamic system vanishes. A classic engineering example is the Tacoma Narrows suspension bridge: opened in July 1940, it soon became known as "Galloping Gertie" because of its antics in the wind; its canter became strong enough to make it disintegrate in a 41-mile-per-hour windstorm in November of that year. Despite their best efforts, economists have yet to design a system that fails so fast.

Finally, a soupçon of moral hazard enters an FN crisis, but more by way of pro-cyclical regulation than through "promised" LLR interventions or government provision of "insurance" in the form of international reserves. After a downswing, some players will be bailed out and others will not, but such eventualities will be subject to high discount rates while the cycle is on the way up. In that phase, traders and treasurers of finance houses are far more interested in their spreads and regulatory acquiescence in exploiting them than in what sort of safety net they may or may not fall into some way down the road.

III. Latin American crises

All these theories can be put to empirical test. One effective technique for doing so is through history-based narratives. This approach is unabashedly "anecdotal", but it often allows a fuller appreciation of country situations than the most sophisticated econometrics. The following case studies should prove instructive.

A.   What really happened in the Southern Cone?

The financial crises around 1980 in the Southern Cone, especially in Argentina and Chile, are important empirical referents for both mainstream models and the FN narrative just sketched. As it turns out, the former elide much of the relevant history. That is, public and private sector actions clearly interacted to derail the external finances. Capital market upheavals originated in a domestic cycle, rather than as the consequence of an overnight change of heart (or the sign of a spread) of market players.[5]

In the mid-1970s Argentina and Chile were going through similar political and economic phases. *Peronista* and *Unidad Popular* governments had been succeeded by military dictatorships in the midst of domestic economic upheavals. Initially, macroeconomic policy did not deviate significantly from the traditional stabilization recipes that both countries had repeatedly applied since the 1950s (and which the IMF built into its standard practice). Price controls were lifted, wages were repressed, and the currency was devalued. After that, a crawling peg was adopted, aimed at holding the real value of the currency stable in the face of ongoing inflation. Fiscal adjustment was based mainly on reduction of the government wage bill. Real wages fell dramatically in both countries and employment dropped in Chile. The fiscal adjustment was deep and permanent in the Chilean case, and less significant and lasting in the Argentine. An innovation in economic policy was domestic financial reform: the interest rate was freed and most regulations on financial intermediaries were removed.

Both economies had been isolated from international financial markets in the first half of the 1970s and did not have sizable external debts. Their external accounts had already been balanced by the stabilization packages. The orthodoxy of the military administrations gained credibility with the IMF and international banks despite the fact that both economies still had high inflation rates (160 per cent and 63.5 per cent per year in 1977, in Argentina and Chile respectively). The high real domestic financial yields that followed market deregulation attracted capital inflows even before controls were relaxed. Confronted with these pressures, the authorities initially gave priority to controlling the domestic monetary supply and attempting to curb inflows with tighter regulations.

In the second half of the decade, first Chile and shortly afterwards Argentina implemented new and similar policy packages. Liberalization of the exchange market and deregulation of capital flows were added to the domestic financial reforms. Trade liberalization programmes were launched simultaneously. Exchange-rate policy was the anti-inflation component of the package. Nominal rates were fixed by announcing predetermined paths for monthly devaluations, converging to a constant rate (the "tablitas"). The stylized facts about the outcome of these manoeuvres are as follows:

From that moment at which the exchange-rate regimes were established, both countries suffered persistent real appreciation. The inflation rate fell, but was systematically higher than the sum of the programmed rate of devaluation plus the international rate of inflation.

The launching of the packages was followed by injections of funds from abroad. In each country, the monetary base, bank deposits, and credit grew swiftly, as did the number of financial intermediaries. There was rapid appreciation of domestic financial and real asset prices. Domestic demand, production and imports all expanded. The import surge, caused by trade opening, currency appreciation, and expansion in domestic demand, steadily widened the trade deficit. The current account deficit showed a more gradual increase because the external debt was small. At the outset, capital flows were higher than the current account deficit and reserves accumulated (see the foreign accumulation balance in table 1). No attempt was made to sterilize the inflows, so the money supply expanded.

The evolution of the external accounts and reserves marked a clear cycle. There was a continuous but gradual increase in the current account deficit, which after a time exceeded the level of inflows. Reserves reached a maximum and then contracted, inducing monetary contraction overall. However, the cycle was not exclusively determined by this mechanical element – the size of capital flows was not an exogenous datum. Portfolio decisions regarding assets denominated in domestic currency, and dollars were affected by the evolution of the balance of payments and finance. Both played a crucial role in boom and bust.

The domestic interest rate reflected financial aspects of the cycle. It fell in the first phase and then turned upwards. Because the exchange-rate rule initially enjoyed high credibility, arbitrage between domestic and external financial assets and credit led at the beginning to reductions in the domestic interest rate and the expected cost of external credit (which became negative in both countries). Lower interest rates helped spur real and financial expansion. It led to increased financial fragility in Minsky's sense: more players took positions in which their interest obligations were not covered by expected income flows in at least some time periods.

In the second phase, rising domestic interest rates and episodes of illiquidity and insolvency appeared, first as isolated cases and then as a systemic crisis. What explained the increase in nominal and real interest rates? Along the lines of table 1, the nominal domestic interest rate can be expressed as the sum of the international interest rate, the programmed rate of nominal devaluation, and a residual (the spread Σ_i in the notation of the table) accounting for exchange and financial risks.

Changes in the interest rate were driven by Σ_i. Risk rose in Chile and Argentina in conjunction with financial fragility. But, more importantly, the increase was driven by the evolution of the external accounts. Persistent growth of the current account deficit – and at some point the fall in reserves – reduced the credibility of the exchange-rate rule. Higher interest rates were needed to equilibrate portfolios and attract foreign capital. This dynamic proved to be explosive in both countries. There were runs on Central Bank reserves, leading finally to the collapse of the exchange-rate regime. The resulting devaluations deepened the financial crisis.

Fiscal deficits and public guarantees on bank deposits did not play significant roles. Both were present to some extent in Argentina, but Chile had a fiscal surplus and deposit guarantees had been eliminated with the explicit goal of making the financial system more efficient and less risky. Neither balance-of-payments attack models nor moral hazards had any relevance to these primordial developing country capital market crises. So much for received theory.

Important destabilizing factors included the rudimentary nature of the financial systems concerned and weaknesses in banking supervisory norms and practices. These are generic background features of capital market liberalization attempts in Latin America and elsewhere. If such packages had been postponed until financial systems were robust, diversified and well monitored, then they never would have been implemented, either in the 1970s or 20 years thereafter.

B.   Mexico

For example, Mexico in the 1990s was no more financially sound than were the Southern Cone economies two decades earlier, even though it had been an active laboratory for economic policy moves. The main success was an anti-inflation programme which took advantage of favourable initial conditions created by a previously orthodox phase. The great failure, of course, was the financial crisis of 1994.[6]

The roots of the disaster of 1994 trace back to well before the debt crisis of 1982. Mexico then was faced with the problems unleashed by loan-pushing on the part of commercial banks and the country's too-ready acceptance of foreign credits to undertake expansionary policies aimed at putting into concrete the jump in national wealth which the massive oil discoveries in the mid-1970s had brought about. At least during the 1970s growth was rapid, but more disquieting developments included real currency appreciation with inflation rates that rose to 100 per cent per year, capital flight, and a massive accumulation of external debt. Arguably, the 1982 crisis is well described by the mainstream models dicussed above, although one should not discount the importance of loan-pushing by foreign banks. When they retrenched, they led the speculative attack (as we shall see, loan-calling by international banks was also a powerful component of the East Asian crisis 15 years later on).

After the crisis broke in August 1982, Mexico was forced to transform an external current account deficit of about 5 per cent of GDP into a 3 per cent surplus within less than a year to compensate for the loss of "fresh money" in the form of new loans that the commercial banks had cut off. The economic team achieved the current account adjustment, using the time-tested tools pioneered in the Southern Cone three decades earlier. They induced a recession by devaluing the peso and cutting the fiscal deficit and monetary emission. Such actions usually cause stagflation, as they certainly did in Mexico; GDP growth averaged out at zero between 1982 and 1988, while by 1987 prices were rising 160 per cent per year.

During the 1987/88 presidential transition, stagflation was attacked in two ways. A success was the implementation of an exchange-rate-based inflation stabilization programme. Despite IMF opposition, in 1987/88 an "Economic Solidarity Pact" aimed at stabilizing prices combined a pegged nominal exchange rate with a wage freeze, trade liberalization and more austerity. This heterodox package did brake inflation, but at some cost. Real wages were reduced once again, and $10 billion in foreign reserves built up after 1982 was spent on supporting the fixed exchange rate and bringing in imports. The output growth rate, however, did not improve.

The authorities tried to stimulate growth by resorting to extreme market friendliness. They privatized state-owned industries, further liberalized foreign trade by dismantling export subsidies and an import quota system which had been built up over decades, and – most importantly for the present discussion – removed restrictions on inflows of direct and portfolio investment. The push to sign the North American Free Trade Agreement was the capstone of all these efforts. The macroeconomic outcomes were disquieting, on at least eight counts:

First, foreign capital came in, letting the trade balance shift from a small surplus in 1988 to a deficit of about $20 billion in 1993; the current account deficit was around 6 per cent of GDP in 1993 and 9 per cent in 1994. Output growth rose to 4.4 per cent in 1990, but tailed off thereafter. The foreign credits were largely short-term, in part because of quirks in the Basle standards discussed below in connection with the Asian crisis.

Second, along the lines suggested by the FN model, capital inflows were enticed by a Mexico/United States interest rate spread Σ_i exceeding 10 per cent (and an internal Mexican real interest rate of about 5 per cent). Perhaps an even stronger incentive took the form of capital gains on the stock market. The share price index rose from around 250 in 1988/89 to over 2500 early in 1994, setting up a large capital gains spread Σ_Q. In the second half of 1994 the index fluctuated erratically, as unnerving political events and interest rate reductions of a few percentage points around mid-year made Mexico a less attractive place to invest. Lustig and Ros (1993) suggest that the financial actors who determined movements of funds across the border comprised bulls (mainly foreign), bears (mainly Mexican), and "sheep" who wobbled in-between to generate a teeter-totter market with multiple equilibria – a boom in the early 1990s, an unstable intermediate balance in 1994, and then a crash.

Third, there was substantial internal (peso) credit expansion, as banks accepted inflated securities as collateral for loans. Between 1987 and 1994 commercial bank credit doubled, with loans for consumption and housing increasing by 450 per cent and 1000 per cent respectively. The M_2 money multiplier also doubled, owing to a reduction in reserve requirements and elimination of quantitative credit controls. Regulation was pro-cyclical, with a vengeance. After the crash, an upward spike in nominal interest rates decimated bank balance sheets – bad debt within the system now amounts to around 15 per cent of GDP. Local banks were not aided by Mexico's 1995 "rescue" package, which largely protected foreign creditors. How to refinance bad peso debt remains to this day a flaming political issue.

Fourth, while it lasted the external capital inflow had to enter the economy via the widening trade deficit already noted – as shown by the foreign savings generation and accumulation equations of table 1, there was no other channel. The deficit was engineered partly by a steadily appreciating real currency value, and partly by trade liberalization. The value of the peso in terms of both consumer and producer prices fell by about 45 per cent between the mid-1980s and 1994, with most of the drop prior to 1991. One reason for depreciating the nominal exchange rate more slowly than price growth was to restrain inflation, but Mexican authorities were also pushed towards a powerful peso by the outward-shifting supply curve in the foreign exchange market. In the midst of radical trade liberalization, allowing the peso to strengthen so markedly was a perilous policy to pursue.

Fifth, in contrast to external financial investment, real capital formation within Mexico did not rise much above 20 per cent of GDP, despite increases in the early 1990s from the extremely depressed levels of the previous decade. From the side of demand, low domestic absorption was the basic cause of slow growth. Private investment was not robust for several reasons: real interest rates were high; profit margins of companies in the traded goods sector were held down in real terms by the strong peso; and public investment, which historically had "crowded in" private projects, was cut back as part of the liberalization/ austerity programme. For both consumption and investment spending, the import content shot up.

Sixth, investment fell back from historical levels, but private (both household and business) savings dropped even more from roughly 15 per cent to 5 per cent of GDP in the 1990s, despite high interest rates. The resulting incremental increase in the private sector's financial deficit (or the sum of $I_h - S_h$ and $I_b - S_b$ in table 1) was immediately reflected into a bigger "twin" trade deficit supported by the strong peso/high interest rate/trade liberalization policy mix already discussed. As in Chile before its financial crash early in the 1980s, somehow the allegedly beneficial effects of public sector thrift did not transmit themselves to private firms and households.

Seventh, while the game lasted, foreign money kept pouring in, blind to devaluation risk. The foundation for this house of cards was the ever-increasing stock of external debt, much of it short-term. It began to crumble when stock prices stopped rising after the first few months of 1994, while American interest rates continued to increase. The collapse came with Mexico's devaluation at the end of that year. It spread rapidly when investors began to compute the volume of short-term obligations due in 1995. The sum was $50 billion, as compared to Mexico's $6 billion in reserves. In terms of its international exposure, the economy was highly illiquid.

Finally, beyond the financial system's "locational" imbalance, one can argue that other "mistakes" in policy, such as reduced interest rates in anticipation of the September 1994 presidential election, worsened the situation by deterring capital inflows. A far more important point is that the balance of international financial power strongly influenced the endgame. When inflows slowed, the Mexican authorities issued a new instrument, peso-denominated "*Tesobonos*" which were indexed to the peso/dollar exchange rate. Asset-holders switched en masse from non-indexed government debt to the *Tesobonos*, apparently on the belief that they could be cashed in for dollars freely. After the crisis hit in December, the United States Treasury/IMF bail-out loans were made conditional on *Tesobono* convertibility. An alternative (permitted under article 6 of the IMF charter) would have been for Mexico to redeem *Tesobonos* in pesos and impose controls to deter dollar flight. But that option was denied by Washington. The result was that *Tesobono* holders on Wall Street were bailed out, while Mexico incurred tens of billions of dollars of additional debt to pay them off. The widely circulated assertion that *Tesobonos* were dollar-denominated was a follow-up public relations move by the United States financial community to cover its players who had guessed wrongly in increasing their Mexican exposure.

Such a public relations "spin" cloaks but does not erase the basic contradiction: By the early 1990s, Mexico had come as close as practical politics permit toward adopting a fully orthodox package of fiscal, monetary and external adjustments. The fiscal account was in surplus and barriers to external transactions had been removed. Yet the foreign account was heavily in deficit because private savings had collapsed and hot money was flowing in.

All that an orthodox stabilizer could try to do to overcome such problems would be to increase the fiscal surplus (cutting back aggregate demand still more, and thereby private incentives for capital formation and capacity growth), raise interest rates (drawing in more short-term external capital but amplifying macroeconomic pressures towards further recession, a stronger currency and a greater trade deficit), or depreciate the value of the peso (dealing a capital loss to foreign investors and daring them to pull out – as they did in December). The private sector was the principal source of macro imbalance, abetted by the government's insistence on full capital market liberalization, abandonment of reserve requirements and other supply-side restrictions on credit expansion, and the maintenance of an overvalued currency.

C. Summing up

Briefly, the Latin American experiences show that foreign capital market crises are intimately related to external liberalization exercises, coupled with lax financial regulation at home. A fixed or predetermined exchange rate seems central to the existence and persistence of spreads wide enough to draw substantial capital inflows, which are especially volatile when they are short-term. They generate macroeconomic changes which play a fundamental role in driving investors' expectations. Their responses in turn feed in destabilizing fashion into local performance. Big public deficits and moral hazards had at most secondary significance in generating the Latin crisis events.

IV. East Asian crises

With their importance varying from country to country, the same factors carry over to the pan-East Asian crisis of 1997/98. That Asia's typhoon was not foreseen is not surprising – in the past, many if not most, such gales have struck without warning.

This one has already provoked an enormous retrospective literature. In Rakshit's (1997a) words, "... economists, proverbially adept at explaining why their forecasts go wrong, have drawn attention to quite a few sources of crisis ...". Here, we argue that the most relevant sources are just the ones that we (and the Latin Americans) have already met.[7]

A.   Background on East Asia

There are marked differences in institutional structure between East Asian and Western (especially Anglo-American) capitalism, as numerous scholars have pointed out. In terms of an "ideal type" *à la* Singh (1998), one can point to four major Asian departures (especially prior to a liberalization phase that got under way around 1990):

First, especially in the "Northern tier" of Japan, the Republic of Korea and Taiwan Province of China, relationships between business and government were historically close and mutually interactive. "Administrative guidance" was the state's chosen means for microeconomic intervention, as opposed to legislation and/or judicial proceedings, such as American anti-trust actions.

Second, corporate finance was largely channelled through banks, especially a "main bank" for each enterprise or conglomerate. Such durable relationships are said to allow business executives to take a long planning view because they are not threatened by hostile stock market takeovers. As discussed later, one implication of reliance on bank finance is that, depending on the specific country concerned, corporations have carried high debt/equity ratios. Representative values are in the order of 3.0 in the Republic of Korea (as also for Japan in the 1960s), and 1.0 in Malaysia and Thailand. The aggregate ratio in the United States fluctuated between about 1.5 during the stock market slump in the late 1970s to about 0.35 now. In Asia, corporate debt loads depended on industrial policy, as the banks and the state coordinated provision of cheap, directed credits to targeted manufacturing sectors. Had cross-border capital movements not been strictly controlled, this sort of intervention would not have been possible.

Third, just as capital markets were far from open, product markets and investment decisions by firms were regulated. "Excess competition" in the sense of overinvestment by firms and extreme cost/price cycles in sectors subject to economies of scale were avoided by the planning authorities. One corollary is that, besides major investment decisions, import and export trade had to be regulated by the state. The goal was "strategic" as opposed to "close" integration with the world economy.

Finally, social tensions never spilled over into high inflation rates, and growth was relatively stable. Communist transitions in China, Indo-China and North Korea aside, the region did not experience macroeconomic earthquakes after World War II, in sharp contrast to Latin America. This is one reason why the events of 1997/98 were an enormous psychological shock to both economic policy makers and the general public.

Of course, not all the economies (not even Japan and the Republic of Korea) followed the "Asian" model slavishly. Differences between the Northern and Southern tiers were significant. In Thailand and Indonesia, Japanese firms (collaborating closely with the Japanese Government) played a big role in steering industrialization after the mid-1980s. Aside from sporadic efforts at industrial intervention in specific sectors, local governments remained passive. The state took a more explicitly developmentalist stance in Malaysia, but again in collaboration with Japanese multinationals. All the Southern countries, nonetheless, retained trade barriers or "distortions" in support of their various versions of industrial policy.

The model changed somewhat over time. Asian intraregional trade as a share of total trade grew from less than 40 per cent in the 1960s to over 50 per cent in the 1990s, with the volume concentrated around the continent's Pacific rim (the corresponding intra-trade share for Latin America is around 20 per cent). Trade restrictions were gradually relaxed. Capital market regulations were removed much more abruptly in the 1990s, more or less simultaneously with decontrol of national financial systems. The Southern Cone experience, forgotten a decade later on, might have suggested the dangers that these deregulatory moves entailed.

The region's macroeconomic environment was also evolving. The Plaza Accord of 1985 marked a big transition when it set off substantial yen appreciation against the dollar. Japanese companies (along with those in the Republic of Korea and Taiwan Province of China) began to seek cheaper platforms for manufactured exports. The Southern tier was the natural place to go, especially as its economies pegged their currencies more or less tightly to the falling dollar.

Credit was relatively cheap in Japan, and after its stock market and real estate bubbles burst in 1990, the trade surplus soared as the real economy stagnated (that is, in terms of table 1, S_f was strongly negative). Much of the resulting Japanese acquisition of foreign claims (negative values of ΔD_b^* and ΔD_g^*) took place in the Southern tier.

Some of this flow took the form of foreign direct investment from Northern tier companies, in effect turning the Southern countries into subcontractors for third country export markets. By the mid-1990s their economies were encountering skilled labour shortages and chronically inadequate infrastructure. Beginning in 1996, export growth dropped substantially (to 10 per cent from the 20 per cent annual rate observed earlier in the decade). Part of this collapse can be attributed to exchange-rate changes. The Chinese devalued the yuan by 35 per cent in 1994. The dollar rose by 50 per cent against the yen after 1996, strengthening Southern tier rates because of their dollar pegs and adding to the pressure. This latter shift was especially damaging because Japan was still the region's major trading partner.

The other capital flows into South-East Asia were "financial" in nature. North Asian, European and American players all invested heavily in short-term notes, in part because the Basle capital adequacy standards encouraged banks to lend in that fashion. They also masked transactions by using off-balance sheet accounting and derivatives. (Both this ploy and reasons for short-term lending are discussed in more detail below.) To a degree, the Americans may have been animated by moral hazard induced by the bailout of Wall Street's exposed position in Mexico in 1995, but the same cannot be true of the Asians and Europeans. All were attracted by ample spreads and South-East Asia's growth cachet.

According to published, and presumably perused, Bank of International Settlements (BIS) estimates, consolidated bank claims on Indonesia, Malaysia, the Republic of Korea and Thailand were $202 billion at the end of 1995 and $248 billion a year later – an annual increase of 23 per cent. In mid-1996 about 70 per cent of claims against the Republic of Korea and Thailand had maturities of one year or less. The figures for Indonesia and Malaysia were 62 per cent and only 47 per cent respectively. As will be seen, the assets used as collateral for all this short-term borrowing were far from being rock solid. Insofar as their prices were high as a consequence of speculative booms or were linked closely to nominal exchange rates that

had been stable for a decade, their valuations were at risk.

Beginning in 1995, there were disturbing signs in East Asia: a breakdown of traditional regulatory regimes, a major hiccup in export-led growth, substantial short-term borrowing backed by a shaky asset base, and exchange rates drifting out of line. Not enough bad news to back a strong forecast of crisis, perhaps, but in retrospect it is surprising that more people were not scratching their heads.

B. Thailand

Thailand was the most "Latin" of the rapidly growing Southern tier economies. Its FN cycle beginning in 1993 bears an uncanny resemblance to events in Mexico and the Southern Cone. Early in that year, Thai companies were permitted to borrow in international capital markets. Together with lax financial regulation, this move led total credit to the private sector to leap from 39 per cent of GDP in 1992 to 123 per cent in 1996 – a bigger increase than even Mexico's. A public sector fiscal error of commission was nowhere to be seen, but the government surely erred in omission by suddenly allowing businesses to borrow as much abroad, and with such a short maturity structure as they did. The oldest story in the trade is about inexperienced financial players who seek high short-term returns and thereby set off a chain of events leading to a crash.

Over-expansion was most evident in loans for real estate investment, although the property market was beginning to slow down already in 1993. Prices fell drastically in early 1995, and the stock market crashed in mid-1996. The busts landed around two thirds of the country's financial and securities firms into serious trouble, exacerbated by the fact that they had neither hedged their future exchange risks with forward contracts nor attempted to assure future earnings flows in foreign currency. Belief in the immutability of the baht/dollar exchange rate was apparently universal. In terms of the spread equations in table 1, a zero value for $\hat{e}^E$ created levels of Σ_i and (before the real estate and stock markets crashed) Σ_ρ, which were very appealing to foreign lenders. Thai financial intermediaries borrowed from them, mostly at short term. They may have thought they were hedged because much of their relending within the country was short term also. But a portfolio balanced in maturities was no protection against foreign-exchange risk.

By 1997, the economy as a whole had around $60 billion in short-term obligations and $40 billion in reserves – not quite up to Mexican or (as we will see) Korean standards, but still a substantial liquidity imbalance. The current account deficit abruptly widened from just under 6 per cent of GDP in 1992-1994 to over 8 per cent in 1995/96 when exports levelled out. Via the savings-investment balance, the internal reflection of this jump in S_f was an increase in the private sector's financial deficit, while the government maintained a small fiscal surplus. The adjustment took the form of a 2 per cent increase in the investment share of GDP, although the quality of the underlying projects may not have been high.

The crisis per se was triggered by the conjuncture: Japanese hints at an interest rate increase, the collapse of a leading financial house (Finance One) and growing fears of a maxi-devaluation, which cut expected spreads. In July the baht was allowed to float and promptly sank as bulls metamorphozed into bears and the sheep stampeded. The IMF arrived with a package in August, which had only temporarily favourable effects (as discussed in more detail later). The East Asian crisis was under way.

An interesting question to ask in retrospect is whether the Thai authorities should have intervened, say in 1995, as the IMF was then advising (Rakshit, 1997a). The problem is that at that stage they were already complicit in the upswing. Higher interest rates or a devaluation could easily have had an adverse impact on foreign investors' confidence, hastening the baht's downfall. The end of the export boom in 1996/97 added considerably to the problems besetting the financial firms and precipitated the downswing. With hindsight, it is fair to say that had the authorities slowed the economy in 1995, they could well have provoked a much deeper crisis in 1997.

C. Initial contagion

Thailand's troubles instantly focused the minds of the international financial community, as had Mexico's 30 months previously. Investors began to look at indicators, such as ratios of debt coming due within one year to international reserves, debt/equity ratios in the business sector, and the currency composition of foreign liabilities – all readily available data that had somehow previously been ignored. In Wade's (1998) words, "... *all* the South-East Asian currencies suddenly looked vulnerable, since all the

economies had a significant overhang of short-term debt".

Banks, especially Japanese banks, began to call loans. In 1996 there had been a net capital flow of $93 billion into the five most affected economies.[8] There was a net outflow of $12 billion in 1997, with the most volatile item being commercial bank credit which shifted from an inflow of over $50 billion in 1996 to an outflow of $21 billion the following year. The overall turnaround of $105 billion was close to the five countries' total reserves of $127 billion and exceeded 10 per cent of their combined GDP (about two percentage points higher than the impact of the 1982 debt crisis on the GDP of Latin America). It was a supply shock with sharp contractionary effects on the macroeconomy.[9] Taking advantage of the short-term nature of their credits, the banks ran from their borrowers before they had a chance to default, making default itself or a massive international bail-out a self-fulfilling prophecy.

D. Republic of Korea

Why did the Southern tier crisis jump North? Taiwan Province of China devalued by 12 per cent in October 1997 despite its ample stock of international reserves ($83 billion at the end of that year, or about nine months' imports), and there was a run on the Hong Kong stock market. The exchange rate held, however, after short-term interest rates went up by about three percentage points. Wobbles in both Taiwan Province of China and Hong Kong (China) were transitory, but redirected investors' concerns toward the Northern tier in general and the Republic of Korea in particular. The main source of the latter's vulnerability appears to have been a badly designed attempt at liberalizing the country's entire economic system, with (misplaced) emphasis on financial markets.

The Republic of Korea's fundamentals in 1997 were far sounder than those of its neighbours to the South. The won was overly strong, but even so the current account deficit was only about 3 per cent of GDP. The fiscal budget was largely in balance and gross public debt amounted to only 3 per cent of GDP. There was little significant inflationary pressure. The main substantive change from the past was government emphasis on "deregulation", undertaken in part because of the intellectual convictions of the policy team but also in response to international (especially American) pressure.

In one key area, the government abandoned its traditional role of coordinating investments in large-scale industries to avoid excess competition. It allowed excess capacity to emerge in sectors such as automobiles, shipbuilding, steel, petrochemicals and semiconductors, which eventually led to a fall in export prices and a run up of non-performing loans.

Second, in the name of financial liberalization, the government failed to monitor foreign borrowing activities, especially by newly licensed merchant banks. These entities were very loosely regulated, and proceeded to acquire $20 billion in external debt. They operated with a large maturity imbalance: 64 per cent of their liabilities were short-term and 85 per cent of assets long-term.

The activities of the merchant banks and a general bias in the local regulatory system toward short-term international borrowing (administrative controls on long-term loans were more strict, etc.) were instrumental in a rapid buildup of $150 billion of external debt, with 60 per cent of the obligations having less than one year to maturity and over 25 per cent at 90 days. The major similarity with the Mexican and South-East Asian crises rests here: the government allowed the private sector to act in a destabilizing manner while holding its fiscal house in order.

Third, the authorities were sold on the idea that inflation control was the most important objective of macro policy and that the exchange rate should be the principal anchor. The predictable real appreciation damaged export performance.

Finally, the government committed "mistakes" and suffered a run of bad luck as its economic troubles worsened. It dithered over the fate of the third largest car manufacturer, Kia, unnecessarily undermining confidence. As the crisis deepened, it wasted $10 billion (one third of foreign reserves) trying to defend an indefensible exchange rate, exacerbating the foreign exchange shortage. External events also came into play. South-East Asia's slump reduced demand for exports from the Republic of Korea and dealt a blow to financial companies that had been speculating in that region's capital markets (see more details later). The entrance of new semi-conductor manufacturers from Taiwan Province of China drove down the prices of memory chips, which accounted for nearly 20 per cent of Korean exports when their prices were high. But the main problem was a failure of oversight by a government priding itself on deregulation.

With panic in the air in late 1997, foreign investors could easily find reasons to worry about the Republic of Korea. The growth rates of exports and GDP had slowed in 1996, there was industrial overcapacity, and interest on debt obligations was crippling the business sector's savings (the ratios of operating income and financial expenses to sales in 1996 were 6.5 per cent and 5.8 per cent respectively, leading to a very low aggregate value of S_b). The country had historically enjoyed stunning export growth and a high credit rating; its authorities (in contrast to those in the other "miracle" exporters, China and Taiwan Province of China) had never felt the need to carry a big stock of international reserves. At the end of 1996 they stood at $34 billion, around one third of the total of the short-term external obligations the country had built up. The run against the won got under way in October 1997, and the IMF was called in by the government one month later.

E. Derivatives, asset prices, balance sheets and bank incentives

Before going on to discuss how IMF and other international interventions transformed the regional bust into a pandemic, it makes sense to take up four issues bearing on how it unfolded: the uses and misuses of derivatives; changes in the quality of remaining national assets (how their prices changed, and whether Asian enterprises are especially vulnerable because of high debt burdens); how bad debt can be dealt with; and incentives for short-term lending by international banks.

Financial "derivative" contracts – swaps, forwards and options, in the first instance – have their vices and virtues. Among the latter is the ability they give financial players to reduce risk (from price volatility, at least) on their own positions by diversifying it to the broader market. Had Asian financial houses successfully hedged their exchange risks with forward contracts in currencies, for example, the crisis might well not have happened.

The most notable vice of derivatives is that they can be used to *hide* risk (in the broad sense of the word) in financial transactions. Obscurity is deepened by the recent practice of placing many commitments "off" as opposed to "on" balance sheets (Neftci, 1998).[10] An example is a "special purpose vehicle" (or SPV). A bank can transfer some its stock to an SPV, setting up a corresponding counter-claim on its own balance sheet. The SPV can issue short-term paper in international credit markets, using the stock as collateral (if the SPV defaults, the creditor will get the underlying stock); the SPV then uses the foreign exchange to take a position the bank desires. Fundamentally, the bank itself has assumed the foreign liability; yet it will never show up on its balance sheet.

"Total return swaps" (or TRS) added derivative complications to such manoeuvres, helping to accelerate the Asian contagion. This is not the first time that new financial vehicles have worsened downswings (remember the margin calls in the 1929 Great Crash), but how the present crop can be dealt with is a contemporary regulatory problem. The following example is due to Neftci (1998):

During 1995-1997 interest costs of long-term floating rate liabilities of banks in the Republic of Korea went up as a result of tighter credit conditions in Japan, various scandals, and the weakening of the historically close relationship between the state and the *chaebols*. At the same time, Indonesian companies were seeking funding but lacked the credit standing of the Republic of Korea.

Double swaps were set up between Indonesian companies and international investment banks on the one hand, and between those banks and Korean banks on the other. The Indonesian companies paid an interest of 340 basis points above LIBOR (LIBOR +340bp)[11] to the international banks, which in turn swapped the underlying paper to the Korean banks at LIBOR+280bp (both differentials narrowed over time as more players entered). The counter-swap took the form of Korean liabilities at LIBOR+75bp. Payments on these obligations were made regularly, every six months or once a year. As part of the package, the Korean banks committed themselves to compensate the international banks for the loss if the Indonesian companies went bankrupt.

The upshot, apparently, was that Indonesian borrowers got credit market access while the Korean banks made a high return. All went well until the companies defaulted and the Korean banks could not get credit in international markets to compensate the international banks for their bankruptcy loss; indeed, they themselves began to default, mainly to their Japanese backers. In this way, part of the Indonesian crisis was transmitted to the Republic of Korea and then to Japan. Meanwhile the international banks had to absorb their Indonesian losses.

What the swaps did, finally, was to create highly opaque loan books. The TRS also failed to diversify

Indonesian risk, which is what derivatives are supposed to do in the first place. Just how much of the Asian crisis can be attributed to off-balance sheet transactions and improper use of derivatives is a question that cannot properly be answered, in part because appropriate accounting procedures are still being developed. What is known is that total transactions of this sort were large, in tens of billions of dollars.

Turning to internal asset markets, two issues deserve discussion: changes in asset prices (and returns) and their effects on balance sheets. With regard to the former, when the currency in each country started to depreciate, the local share price index dropped in percentage terms more or less in proportion (Rakshit, 1997b).[12] Short-term interest rates rose universally (sometimes to dramatic double or even triple digit levels), but were obviously unable to stem the depreciation of real currency values caused by departing capital.

What were the implications for business balance sheets? As noted above, corporations in some Asian economies have debt/equity ("gearing" or "leverage") ratios that are high by Western standards. A "representative" ratio in the West might be in the range of 0.5 to 1.5, with banks and their regulators becoming dubious about loans to firms when their ratios significantly exceed unity. The ratios in Asia have gone up since the crisis because of falling asset prices and depreciating currencies. The interest rate increases also cut into corporate cash flow.

Standard economics in the form of the Modigliani-Miller (1958) theorem suggests that such problems are of second order – finance is a veil and the performance of business enterprises is independent of their liability structure.[13] This assertion is not completely true, as Minsky's work demonstrates. But it is not completely false either. The distinction between debt and equity is in part a matter of convention, and conventions can change.

In Anglo-American finance, for example, equity is beginning to look more like debt as rebelling stockholders call for assured dividend pay-outs. Similarly, debt can be made to look like equity if obligations to pay interest are relaxed One common method is to sell public debt to the non-bank private sector to pay for restructuring of weak balance sheets in the financial sector. The United States dealt with its S&L crisis in this way (putting the public debt off-balance sheet for the Federal Government, incidentally). To clean up its banking system's non-performing assets to the tune of a third of GDP after the crisis in the early 1980s, Chile did the same thing via the central bank, which refinanced with the government, which then re-refinanced abroad with the help of international institutions. For debt denominated in the local currency, how to set up such a package (a task which inevitably has to be undertaken by the government) is a political question. The Chileans and Americans apparently had no problems. The Japanese Government is encountering political difficulty in cleaning up the remnants of the bubble economy, and the Mexican Government faces a similar problem with its post-1995 banking system bad debt – the obligations amount roughly to 10 per cent and 15 per cent of GDP respectively. In both cases the public does not want to pay off the financiers.

Another way to deal with a debt overhang is for the government to step in and organize moratoria on domestic repayments and enforce rollovers of short-term loans. This route was taken by the Government of the Republic of Korea in 1972 to deal with a domestic debt crisis.

Finally, there is the option of running a controlled inflation to shrink the real value of debtors' obligations and force real interest rates below zero. On the financial side, banks have to monetize growth in some asset, e.g. give credits to the private sector to cover bad debt. On the cost side, there would have to be some agreement about margins versus nominal wage growth. The inflation and forced rollover strategies would almost certainly have to be accompanied by re-imposition of tough controls to restrain capital flight.

For the Asian economies, the harder question is what to do about foreign currency debt. Here, international support is needed. As discussed in the following subsection, initiatives along such lines have been strikingly unsuccessful to date.

A final financial point worth mentioning concerns incentives for short-term lending by international banks. At present, the Basle capital adequacy provisions for all foreign bank loans of less than one year's maturity require only 20 per cent backing, as opposed to 100 per cent for loans to non-OECD members with more than one year's maturity. This provision was apparently introduced to protect the inter-bank market, but for this purpose a low backing ratio for loans of three-month (or even one-month) maturity would probably be enough. As it stands, the provision offers considerable encouragement to OECD bankers to make short-term loans to developing economies. This regulatory bias has certainly been as important as some sort of generalized moral hazard in affecting the volume and profile of international bank loans.

F. *The IMF in action*

So far, we have been describing an international financial crisis perpetrated by the private sector, operating under lax and ultimately complicit public supervision. The remaining actor on the stage is a public institution, the International Monetary Fund. Its interventions during the crisis made a bad situation far worse.

With regard to the substance of the stabilization policies it convinced countries to adopt, the Fund's behaviour was completely predictable (even up to the ploys it utilized: first junior staff/"hard cop" then senior staff/"soft cop" negotiators on successive missions). With regard to economic restructuring, it went well beyond its traditional mandate. We briefly review the first topic, and then go on to raise questions about the second one.

The Fund's speciality is running a recession to improve the balance of payments by cutting imports. The well-known twin deficits rationale for its "financial programming" exercises was sketched briefly above and can be developed fully in terms of accounting balances like those in table 1 (Taylor, 1994). A familiar policy package always materializes: reduction of the fiscal deficit by expenditure reductions or tax increases; tight monetary policy; closing down ailing banks and other financial institutions; financial liberalization, including removal of restrictions on entry of foreign banks; and trade liberalization. In exchange, the Fund disburses credits from time to time as the specific conditionality requirements attached to its package are satisfied.

Beyond trade balance improvement, such interventions are supposed to restore the confidence of foreign investors so that they start lending again to crisis-afflicted countries. In East Asia, the Fund's moves failed resoundingly in this regard. In the words of Rakshit (1997b):

> ... following the announcement of the IMF bailout, for the country concerned there was an immediate improvement in stock and currency markets which generally pulled up markets in neighbouring nations as well. However, the

upswing did not last for more than a few days and soon currencies and share prices tended to resume their downslide. Quite clearly, after a more serious scrutiny the market recorded disappointment with the IMF package(s).

Why such dismal results? Several factors may be mentioned. One is that, as observed previously, East Asian economies are tightly linked in terms of trade and asset ownership. Contractionary effects in one spread readily to all others. Moreover, the trade-improving impacts of devaluation in one country will be dampened by its import dependence on its neighbours.

Furthermore, because of conditionality restrictions, the bulk of the credit attached to the bail-out packages was not in fact disbursed. As Helleiner (1998) observed in May: "It is striking that the amounts quickly supplied to Mexico during its crisis far exceeded the amounts slowly being made available to the East Asian countries ... Only about 20 per cent of the financial package put together for East Asia has so far been disbursed". Given the contractionary impact of the international banks' capital strike in 1997, it is no surprise that GDP growth rates have fallen in tandem all over the region and are expected to be strongly negative in 1998.

Fund interventions may even have worsened the contagion. As Sachs (1998) observed: "... instead of dousing the fire the IMF in effect screamed fire in the theatre". Investor confidence plummeted instead of being bolstered by the Fund's orthodox shows of force; outsiders can recognize a depressed economy and social unrest when they see them. The ultimate outcome may have been to transform a short-term "liquidity" crisis to one of "solvency", in which an economy can never stabilize its external debt to GDP ratio because its output growth rate has been driven below the real rate of interest.

All of this is depressing but no surprise. The contractionary and distributionally perverse effects of IMF programmes are achingly familiar in Africa and Latin America. A novelty in East Asia is how much worse the impacts can be when the package is applied jointly to a set of closely linked economies. The even more disquieting issue, however, is that the Fund is doing its very best to dismantle the Asian economic model discussed above by insisting on wholesale restructuring of economic systems (witness the exceptionally heavy-handed interventions in Indonesia and the Republic of Korea). Why? And what will be the outcome?

To answer the first question requires walking a fine line between explanations based on interests and a conspiracy theory. On the side of the interests, there is at least some agreement among the OECD (or rich) countries that steps should be taken to liberalize the world economy in several dimensions: revision of the IMF articles to require member nations to remove all controls on capital markets, liberalization of trade in financial services and suppression of industrial policy interventions under the auspices of the WTO, and the OECD's own multilateral investment accord (recently blocked, for the moment, when the United States representative objected to other countries' attempts to incorporate environmental and labour standards into the document). These initiatives all respond to a need felt on the part of international banks and transnational corporations to have relatively unfettered market access worldwide.

On the more conspiratorial note, American administrations always have close ties with Wall Street, but they are particularly strong (for both the Treasury and State departments) in the one now in office. Moreover, there are close personal and professional ties among high-level people in Treasury and the IMF. As an institution, the Fund itself has recently ventured much more aggressively than before into wholesale rearrangement of economies. In this sense, its East Asian packages are a natural follow-on to the restructuring exercises it and the American Government continue to support in the post-socialist corner of the world, most notably in Russia.

How the Asian story will end is completely unclear. Except for Poland, post-socialist rebuilding attempts have on the whole been failures, but then those economies were in very poor condition from the start. The Asians, on the other hand, had been successful for decades prior to 1997. A complete remake along Anglo-American lines will certainly not happen; well-entrenched institutions are not readily removed. The real danger is that a long period of stagnation will ensue before the IMF and the Americans give up on the effort as a bad job. Military interventions aside, the staying power of the United States in external sanitizing exercises has never been great; more pressing political concerns always arise at home. But even a few years of unfettered market trumphalism is a prospect that few Asians care to contemplate.

G. *Summing up*

Just as in Latin America, the FN framework provides a useful way to reflect on what happened in Asia. As its real/financial cycles peaked, the region's fundamentals were shaky. Immediately after, the situation was rendered far worse by the flight of the international banks and the interventions of the IMF; new derivative-based financial instruments and off-balance sheet operations by all parties accelerated the contagion. Massive attempts on the part of the Fund to restructure Asian economies will undoubtedly fail. But in so doing, they may doom the region to stagnation for an extended period of time.

V. The Russian crisis

Economic historians will need many years to sort out the tumultuous changes in Russia during the 1990s. It is certainly far too early to disentangle all the causes of the summer 1998 currency crisis. But its economic aspects do share striking similarities with the boom-bust episodes we have just discussed. As was true elsewhere, Russia had minimal restrictions on international financial transactions; a pegged exchange rate at a "strong" level; wide spreads between returns available domestically and costs of raising funds abroad; and a financial system long in rouble assets and short in dollars.

Russia's previously tightly controlled capital account had been thrown open when economic restructuring began in 1992, facilitating capital flight (funded by a consistent trade surplus and foreign capital inflows) to the tune of $20-30 billion per year. The nominal exchange rate was roughly stabilized as an anti-inflation anchor. The result was that from 1993 to 1998 the real exchange rate appreciated by a factor of between three and five - depending on which price indexes are used in the calculation. Finally, there was virtually no financial regulation, so that balance sheet mismatches were unconstrained.

Money emission had been cut back sharply in the fight against inflation; ratios of money and bank credit to GDP were therefore very low by international standards. The government was paying high interest rates on its short-term bonds. Equity prices rose sharply as of 1996. Both interest rate and capital gains spreads were large, and foreign investors poured in. As the relevant intermediaries, Russian financial institutions took on unbalanced positions. In particular, banks borrowed heavily abroad to speculate on the government's short-term liabilities. They did not hedge their positions, although some foreign investors are rumoured to have hedged with Russian banks, which presumably ploughed the resulting dollar assets back into roubles. The Russian players were effectively bankrupted by the devaluation in August 1998. The collapse of the banking system resulted in the virtual disappearance of the already under-monetized domestic payments mechanism.

The main contrast with Mexico and East Asia was that owing to a drastic fall in tax collection there was a large fiscal deficit that supported the bond market. The strict monetary policy was the other side of the coin, in a Muscovite rerun of early "Reaganomics". The resulting high interest rates and strong rouble were part and parcel of the debacle, stimulating the acceleration and then speculative reversal of capital inflows.

What were the orthodox policy options available after the crisis? Prior to its dismissal in August, the Kiriyenko Government was apparently planning to deal with the banking collapse by allowing some big banks to be taken over by their Western creditors. The idea was that one or more Western banks would be temporarily licensed to run a retail banking network (for example, taking over a bankrupt bank and expanding it). The Western bank(s) could receive a fee for services, perhaps paid directly by the IMF. Such a move could, in principle, restore confidence in the banking system, maintain the payments mechanism, prevent a run, and encourage financial deepening. This proposal appears to have been politically infeasible – witness the fall of Kiriyenko.

Another set of concerns centred around the fiscal position, a direct cause of the crisis. For the public sector (central government, local governments, off-budget sheet funds) to be at least in balance, it would have had to run a "primary" surplus (before interest payments) of 4-5 per cent of GDP. Even such stringency would leave unresolved the government's arrears in public sector wages, pensions and debts to firms. Fiscal balance may have been desirable, but it seemed most unlikely that any Russian Government would be able to attain it, given the depression, difficulties in raising revenue, and pressures to boost expenditures.

A third possibility was to introduce a currency board, as implemented in Argentina in the early 1990s and Estonia and Bulgaria more recently, and as suggested by George Soros. But apart from technical difficulties and the very high cost, Russia quickly opted not to abandon its monetary autonomy.

The final option was a fudge. The IMF and the Russian authorities could have agreed on a set of conditions that would not be fulfilled – a familiar feature in IMF-Russian government agreements in the past. Both parties showed enough common sense not to pursue that option.

In late 1998, it looked as though the Russian authorities would try to resolve their problems by their own means. One step might be to impose controls on trade and international payments. A significant tariff surcharge on imports, say 20 per cent, might be introduced. Together with a depreciated exchange rate, this would generate substantial rouble revenues quickly. On the export side, the main problem is that throughout the 1990s hard currency earnings were usually not repatriated, contributing to the enormous capital flight that Russia experienced. A requirement that a politically feasible 75 per cent of export earnings be paid directly to the Central Bank appeared to be the remedy at hand. In addition, wide capital controls could be introduced and foreign exchange only made available to authorized importers at an administratively determined exchange rate. Such moves would short-circuit the "hot money" flows that were the major cause of the crisis. Indeed, capital controls of this form would be like those imposed by France and the United Kingdom in the immediate post-War period.

In many ways the situation in Russia in 1998 was worse than in Western Europe in the late 1940s – purely physical destruction was, less but social and institutional dislocations were far greater. There was an advanced process of state collapse, economic life suffered from criminal activities, and there were corrupt links between business and political *élites*. But in a desperate situation, desperate measures of the nature just outlined should be judged by two main criteria: the preservation of democracy and the pursuit of long-run economic goals. How such measures may fare in satisfying these ends is something only the future can tell.

VI. Policy alternatives

The principal message of this paper is that financial crises are not made by an alert private sector pouncing upon the public sector's fiscal or moral hazard foolishness. They are better described as private sectors (both domestic and foreign) acting to make high short-term profits when policy and history provide the preconditions and the public sector acquiesces. Mutual feedbacks between the financial sector and the real side of the economy then lead to a crisis. By global standards, the financial flows involved in a Frenkel-Neftci conflagration are not large: $10-20 billion annually (the United States routinely absorbs around 10 per cent of the inflow) over a few years is more than enough to destabilize a middle-income economy. The outcome is now visible worldwide.

A number of policy issues are posed by the experiences reviewed herein. It is convenient to discuss them under three headings: steps that may be taken at the country level to reduce the likelihood of future conflagrations; actions both an afflicted country and the international community can take to cope with a future crisis, when and if it happens; and how the international regulatory system might be modified to enhance global economic comity and stability.

A.   Avoiding Frenkel-Neftci cycles

Rather than a formal model, Neftci and Frenkel provide a framework which can be used to analyse crisis dynamics. There are five essential elements: (1) the nominal exchange rate is fixed or close to being pre-determined; (2) there are few barriers to external capital inflows and outflows; (3) historical factors and the conjuncture act together to create wide spreads of the form Σ_i and Σ_Q in table 1 – these in turn generate capital movements which push the domestic financial system in the direction of being long on domestic assets and short on foreign holdings; (4) regulation of the system is lax and probably pro-cyclical; (5) macroeconomic repercussions via the balance of payments and the financial system's flows of funds and balance sheets set off a dynamic process which is unstable.

To some extent, national policy makers can prevent these components from coming together explosively.

1.   The exchange rate

There are often very good reasons to have a pegged nominal rate (or one that is limited to fluctuations within a narrow band). It is anti-inflationary, which has been crucially important to

Latin American stabilization packages, beginning with Mexico's in the late 1980s. It can also enhance export competitiveness, as happened when countries in South-East Asia pegged to the falling dollar after the Plaza Accord.

Problems with a pegged rate arise when it contributes to wide spreads and (especially) when it is overvalued. In the formulas of table 1, for example, a positive value of $\hat{e}^E$ can reduce Σ_i and Σ_Q; this is a good argument for a thoughtfully designed crawling nominal depreciation. An even better argument is that such an exchange-rate regime can help avoid real appreciation, which in turn can widen the trade deficit, bring in capital inflows or induce reserve losses, and kick off an unstable macro cycle.

2. Barriers to capital movements

Without international assistance, it is virtually impossible to prevent capital from fleeing the country in a crisis; it is much more feasible to construct obstacles to slow it down (at least) as it comes in. In the recent period, Chile and Colombia have had some success with prior deposits and taxes on inflows, especially short-term ones. In the not very distant past, Asian economies had fairly effective restrictions on how much and how easily households and firms could borrow abroad. In non-crisis times, acquisition of foreign assets can also be monitored. The key task is to prevent a "locational" mismatch in the macro balance sheet, with a preponderance of foreign liabilities (especially short-term) and national assets. Local regulatory systems can certainly be configured toward this end.

If imbalances are detected, the relevant authorities can direct or encourage players to unwind their positions. Such guidance is routine (and usually undertaken by the private sector) in well managed markets for securities and derivative contracts written on them. At the very least, exposed players can hedge, although when push comes to shove hedging in thin markets for developing country currencies can be more notional than real. In the TRS example discussed above, the international banks presumably thought they had hedged their Indonesian exposure through the merchant banks of the Republic of Korea. At the end of the day, they had not.

3. Spreads

In many instances, one does not have to be a financial genius to recognize a wide-open spread.

Under a fixed exchange-rate regime, it is easy to see a 10 per cent differential between local and foreign short-term interest rates, or a similarly sized gap, between the growth rate of the local stock market index or real estate prices and a foreign borrowing rate. Such yields are an open invitation to capital inflows that can be extremely destabilizing. Whether policy makers feel they are able to reduce interest rates or deflate an asset market boom is another question, one that merits real concern.

Another source of potential spreads is through off-balance sheet and derivative operations. Here, local regulators can be at a major disadvantage. They do not necessarily know the latest devices, and most (but one hopes not all) of the "really smart guys" will be on the other side inventing still newer devices to make more money. Staying up-to-date as far as possible and inculcating a culture of probity in the local financial system are the best defences here.

4. The regulatory regime

There is of course a serious question as to whether many developing country regulatory systems can meet such goals, especially in the wake of liberalization episodes. Another difficulty arises with timing. It is very difficult to put a stop to capital flows *after* the financial system has reached a locationally unbalanced position; at such a point interest rate increases or a discrete devaluation can easily provoke a crash. The authorities have to stifle an FN cycle early in its upswing; otherwise, they may be powerless to act.

5. Unstable dynamics

Each balance-of-payments crisis is *sui generis*: to produce a set of formal descriptions, one would have to write a separate model for each episode in each country. Many components, however, would be the same. The simplest classification is in terms of disequilibria between stocks and flows, along with more microeconomic indicators. Here are some examples:

(a) Flow-flow

One key issue here is identifying the internal "twin(s)" of an external deficit. In the country examples discussed above, the financial deficits were in the hands of the private sector, business or households. The follow-up question is how they are being paid for. Are rising interest obligations likely to cut into savings and investment flows? Are flows cumulating to produce locational or maturity mismatches in balance sheets? Another precursor of crisis is the relationship between the volume of capital inflows and the current account deficit. If the former exceeds the latter reserves will be rising, perhaps lulling the authorities into a false sense of security. It will rudely vanish when interest payments on accumulating foreign debt begin to exceed the amount of capital flowing in.

(b)   Stock-flow

Have some asset or liability stocks become "large" in relation to local flows? East Asia's short-term debt exceeding 10 per cent of GDP was a typical example; it was a stock with a level that could change rapidly, with sharply destabilizing repercussions. Rapid expansion of bank credit to the private sector as a share of GDP while booms got under way in the Southern Cone, Mexico and Thailand might have served as an early warning indicator, had the authorities been looking. The causes included monetization of reserve increases and growth of loans against collateral assets, such as securities and real estate with rapidly inflating values.

(c)   Stock-stock

Besides lop-sided balance sheets in the financial sector, indicators such as debt/equity ratios and the currency composition of portfolios (including their "dollarization" in Latin America recently) become relevant here. They can signal future problems with financing investment-savings differentials of the sort presented in table 1.

(d)   Microeconomics

Micro-level developments go along with the evolution of these macro changes. Investment coordination across firms may be breaking down, leading to excess competition, real estate speculation and luxury consumption.

The problem with indicators such as those mentioned above is that they often lag behind an unstable dynamic process. By the time they are visibly out of line, it may be too late to attempt to prevent a crisis; its management becomes the urgent task of the day.

B.   *Coping with crises when they strike*

Once a country enters into a payments crisis, it cannot cope with it on its own. International assistance has to be called in. Again, each situation follows its own rules, but there are a few measures that appear to be imperative, while others should be avoided.

1.   *Necessary measures*

The contrast between the Mexican and Asian "rescues" is striking: the first happened (at least as far as foreign creditors were concerned) and the second did not. Very slow disbursement of funds by the IMF may well have crippled the Asian effort permanently, pushing fundamentally healthy economies from illiquidity into insolvency. The first and most obvious necessary measure that emerges from experience is to disburse rescue money fast. In Helleiner's (1998) words: "Finance that is supplied only on the basis of negotiated conditions and which is released only on the basis of compliance with them ... is *not* liquidity". East Asian economies became highly illiquid in 1997. By mid-1998, their position had not significantly improved, despite more than six months of Fund psychotherapy accompanied by liquidity transfusions on a homeopathic scale.

In fact, the transfusions might not even have been required if the rescuers had "bailed in" the countries' creditors in the sense of forcing them not to call outstanding loans instead of bailing them out. By appealing to G-7 regulatory authorities if need be, the IMF presumably has enough clout to prevent international creditors – especially large international banks – from closing out Asian borrowers overnight. Such a procedure should be built into rescue protocols before the next crisis strikes.

After a crisis, countries also often have an ample load of "bad debt", typically non-performing assets of the banking sector. Domestic refinancing via a bond issue to the non-bank private sector, an administratively enforced credit rollover, and price inflation are three ways of dealing with the problem. The latter two would almost certainly require re-imposition of tight controls on outward capital movements, which the international community would have to abet.

Distributional questions also come to the fore. Asian nations are big and visible. But what about small, poor, raw material or assembled goods exporters in sub-Saharan Africa, Central America, the Pacific and the Caribbean? Several have been hit by rapid reversals of private capital inflows. Presumably they merit international help as much as the Republic of Korea or Thailand. They are not getting it.

Within all afflicted countries, income generation and employment problems are critical. The authorities can repress their peoples, up to a point, but ultimately will have to offer them a degree of social and economic support. Such an effort goes diametrically against the emphasis in Fund-type packages. As Singh (1998) puts it:

> To provide such assistance effectively and on an adequate scale will require not only considerable imagination but also a large expansion in government activity and often direct intervention in the market processes. Such emergency safety net programmes may include wider subsidies, food for work schemes, and public works projects. How to pay for these measures within the limits of fiscal prudence, let alone within IMF fiscal austerity programmes, will be a major issue of political economy for these countries.

2. What should be avoided

The most obvious "don't" is further liberalization of the capital accounts of the affected countries. If the single most apparent cause of crisis was a door three quarters open, the last thing one wants to do is move it the rest of the way. As already noted, there is agreement among many rich countries that deregulated external financial markets are upon them now, and should be extended to poor countries as rapidly as possible. Given the experience of the past few years, this recommendation looks ill-timed at best.[14]

Similar observations apply to the timing and extent of the types of reform the Fund is imposing on the East Asian economies. The best guess is that they will not take. Economic engineering is an imprecise art, likely to give rise to large and largely unforeseen consequences, and societies are rarely amenable to massive change. But these observations do not seem to deter Washington from trying to remake the world in its own perceived self-image. It should not.

C. Changing the global regulatory system

The foregoing observations lead naturally to five suggestions for restructuring international financial arrangements.

First, recent experiences demonstrate that the global macroeconomic/financial system is not well understood. "What have been miracle economies" one month turn into incompetent bastions of "crony capitalism" the next. Under such circumstances, an immediate recommendation is for humility on the part of the major institutional players (Eatwell and Taylor, 1998). There is no reason to force all countries into the same regulatory mould; international institutions should whole-heartedly support whatever capital market, trade and investment regimes that any nation, after due consultation, chooses to put into place.

Second, international agencies should support national regulatory initiatives. A lot of information was available from the BIS and other sources about the gathering storm in Asia; it was not factored into either the private or public sector's calculations. If national regulators were made more aware of what is happening in their countries, perhaps they could take prudent steps to avoid a pro-cyclical bias in their decisions.

Third, the Fund seems unlikely to receive large additional sums of money to allow it to serve as a (conditional) lender of last resort. It will therefore have to become more of a signaller to other sources of finance, e.g. central banks and the BIS. That opens room for new forms of regional cooperation, such as Japan's summer 1997 proposal for an Asian bail-out fund, which died after being opposed vigorously by the United States Government and the IMF. Such institutional innovations should be thought through seriously, and very possibly put into place.

Fourth, specific changes in international regulatory practices may make sense. One obvious modification to the Basle capital adequacy provisions is to permit 20 per cent as opposed to 100 per cent backing on loans to non-OECD countries for maturities of (say) only three months or less, as opposed to one year at present. Such an adjustment should substantially reduce incentives for banks to concentrate their lending to developing countries in the short term.

Finally, there is no independent external body with power to assess the IMF's actions. More transparency (especially regarding relationships between the American Government and the Fund) and independent evaluations of the IMF are sorely needed in light of its largely unsuccessful economy-building enterprises in post-socialist nations and now in East Asia.

Notes

1 The " Δ " term signifies a change over time, e.g. $\Delta H_h = H_h(t) - H_h(t-1)$, where $H_h(t)$ and $H_h(t-1)$ are money stocks at the end of periods t and $t-1$ respectively.

2 The following discussion concentrates on first-generation speculative attack models. Second-generation models make the fundamentals sensitive to shifts in private expectations, thereby allowing extrinsic, random "sunspot" shocks to generate multiple equilibria. The mathematical complications are intriguing to the professorial mind but add little to attempts to understand historical crises.

3 Pieper and Taylor (1998) present a fairly up-to-date review. In various numbers of its *World Economic Outlook*, the IMF is up-front about attributing crises in both Latin America and Asia to "incompatibilities" between macro policies and the exchange-rate regime as well as "excessive regulation" and "too little competition" in the financial sector.

4 There may also be problems with maturity structures of claims, especially if local players borrow from abroad at short term. Nervous foreign lenders may then compare a country's total external payment obligations over the next year (say) with its international reserves. Such ratios proved disastrous for Mexico in 1995 and several Asian countries in 1997. A maturity mismatch in which local players borrow at short term abroad and lend at long term at home may be less significant – a property developer will default on his or her loan if the real estate market crashes, regardless of whether it is formally of short or long duration.

5 The following discussion draws heavily on Frenkel (1998) and ultimately on the model in Frenkel (1983). The latter paper was written before Argentina's exchange crisis of 1981. It is available only in Spanish, but Taylor (1991), and Williamson and Milner (1991) provide English glosses, emphasizing cyclical implications.

6 The narrative for Mexico draws on Griffith-Jones (1997), Lustig and Ros (1993, 1998), and Pieper and Taylor (1998).

7 This section draws on many sources, most notably Chang (1998), Chang et al. (1998), Corbett (1998), Neftci (1998), Rakshit (1997a, 1997b), Singh (1998), and Wade (1998).

8 They were Indonesia, Malaysia, the Philippines, the Republic of Korea and Thailand.

9 In terms of table 1, $\Delta D_b + \Delta D_g$ contracted sharply, with an impact in the foreign accumulation balance amplified by devaluation, or a higher value of the exchange rate e. Either reserves had to shrink ($\Delta R^* < 0$) or the current account deficit S_f had to decline. Both effects are contractionary, the former by cutting money supply growth and driving up interest rates, and the latter by forcing the private and public sectors to reduce investment relative to savings, cutting effective demand.

10 The standard convention is that claims must be included on balance sheets if they (or their antecedents) have been acquired with hard cash. An example would be an automobile on a household's balance. Off-balance-sheet would be contingent contracts on the underlying asset, like collision insurance for example. For both the household and the insurance company, the policy sets out specific transactions that must occur if the car crashes. They will then show up on income statements and thereby balance sheets in due course.

11 LIBOR, the "London interbank offered rate", is the benchmark for international floating rate transactions. A "basis point" or bp is 0.01 of one per cent, i.e. 340bp = 3.4 per cent.

12 The exception is Hong Kong (China), where the stock market dropped in October. The currency-board rules held the exchange rate constant, but credit contraction forced short-term interest rates to rise by over 300 basis points.

13 Let D and E be a firm's debt and equity, Z its value, r its rate of return, and Π its profit flow. Then $Z = \Pi/r = D + E$, with the last equality imposed by assumption (in practice, asset values of firms only equal their debt plus equity loads by a fluke). If i_d and i_e are the returns to debt and equity respectively, then $rZ = r(D + E) = i_dD + i_eE$. Rearranging gives $i_e = (r - i_d)(D/E) + r$. That is, the "required" return to equity (dividend payments, capital gains, etc.) rises linearly with the gearing ratio. This relationship does not fit the data badly. Of course it presupposes that $r > i_d$, or the firm's gross rate of return exceeds the interest rate at which it borrows; otherwise, it would technically be insolvent.

14 To borrow a thought from Polanyi (1944), the recommendation is highly ideological as well. The Utopian character of liberal arguments – anything falling short of full deregulation is never enough – comes out strikingly in this instance.

References

CHANG, Ha-Joon (1998), "Korea: The Misunderstood Crisis", *World Development*, Vol. 26, No. 8 (August).

CHANG, Ha-Joon, Hong-Jae PARK, and Chul Gyue YOO (1998), "Interpreting the Korean Crisis: Financial Liberalization, Industrial Policy, and Corporate Governance", *Cambridge Journal of Economics*, Vol. 22, No. 6 (December).

CORBETT, Jenny (1998), "The Asian Crisis: Competing Explanations", mimeo, Center for Economic Policy Analysis, New School for Social Research, New York.

D'ARISTA, Jane (1998), "Financial Regulation in a Liberalized Global Environment", mimeo, Center for Economic Policy Analysis, New School for Social Research, New York.

DOOLEY, Michael P. (1997), "A Model of Crises in Emerging Markets", mimeo, Department of Economics, University of California at Santa Cruz.

EATWELL, John, and Lance TAYLOR (1998), "International Capital Markets and the Future of Economic Policy", mimeo, Center for Economic Policy Analysis, New School for Social Research, New York.

FRENKEL, Roberto (1983), "Mercado Financiero, Expectativas Cambiales, y Movimientos de Capital", *El Trimestre Economica*, Vol. 50, pp. 2041-2076.

FRENKEL, Roberto (1998), "Capital Market Liberalization and Economic Performance in Latin America", mimeo, Center for Economic Policy Analysis, New School for Social Research, New York.

GRIFFITH-JONES, Stephany (1997), "Causes and Lessons of the Mexican Peso Crisis" (Helsinki: World Institute for Development Economics Research).

HELLEINER, G. K. (1998), "The East Asian and other Financial Crisis: Causes, Responses, and Prevention", mimeo, UNCTAD, Geneva.

HOTELLING, Harold (1931), "The Economics of Exhaustible Resources", *Journal of Political Economy*, Vol. 39, pp.137-175.

KRUGMAN, Paul (1979), "A Model of Balance-of-Payments Crises", *Journal of Money, Credit, and Banking*, Vol. 11, pp. 311-325.

KRUGMAN, Paul (1998), "What Happened to Asia?", mimeo, Department of Economics, Massachusetts Institute of Technology, Cambridge, MA.

LUSTIG, Nora, and Jaime ROS (1993), "Mexico", in L. Taylor (ed.), *The Rocky Road to Reform* (Cambridge, MA: MIT Press).

LUSTIG, Nora, and Jaime ROS (1998), "Economic Reforms, Stabilization Policies, and the Mexican Disease", in L. Taylor (ed.), *After Neoliberalism: What Next for Latin America?* (Ann Arbor, Michigan: University of Michigan Press).

MINSKY, Hyman P. (1986), *Stabilizing an Unstable Economy* (New Haven, Connecticut: Yale University Press).

MODIGLIANI, Franco, and Merton H. MILLER (1958), "The Cost of Capital, Corporation Finance, and the Theory of Investment", *American Economic Review*, Vol. 48, pp. 261-297.

NEFTCI, Salih N. (1998), "FX Short Positions, Balance Sheets, and Financial Turbulence: An Interpretation of the Asian Financial Crisis", mimeo, Center for Economic Policy Analysis, New School for Social Research, New York.

PIEPER, Ute, and Lance TAYLOR (1998), "The Revival of the Liberal Creed: The IMF, the World Bank, and Inequality in a Globalized Economy", in D. Baker, G. Epstein and R. Pollin (eds.), *Globalization and Progressive Economic Policy: What are the Real Constraints and Options?* (New York: Cambridge University Press).

POLANYI, Karl (1944), *The Great Transformation* (New York: Rinehart).

RAKSHIT, Mihir (1997a), "Learning and Unlearning from the Thai Currency Crisis", *ICRA Bulletin: Money and Finance* (New Delhi), Vol. 1, No. 3, pp. 24-46.

RAKSHIT, Mihir (1997b),"Crisis, Contagion, and Crash: Asian Currency Turmoil", *ICRA Bulletin: Money and Finance* (New Delhi), Vol. 1, No. 4, pp. 8-44.

SACHS, Jeffrey (1998), "The IMF and the Asian Flu", *The American Prospect,* No. 37, pp. 16-21.

SINGH, Ajit (1998), "'Asian Capitalism' and the Financial Crisis", mimeo, Center for Economic Policy Analysis, New School for Social Research, New York.

TAYLOR, Lance (1991), *Income Distribution, Inflation, and Growth* (Cambridge, MA: MIT Press).

TAYLOR, Lance (1994), "Gap Models", *Journal of Development Economics,* Vol. 45, pp. 17-34.

WADE, Robert (1998), "The Asian Debt-and-Development Crisis of 1997-9?: Causes and Consequences", *World Development*, Vol. 26, No. 8 (August).

WILLIAMSON, John, and Chris MILNER (1991), *The World Economy* (New York: New York University Press).

GLOBALIZATION, ECONOMIC POLICY AND GROWTH PERFORMANCE

Paul Mosley

Abstract

Many recent contributions to the literature on globalization and growth have argued that the two go together, and that developing countries can best hope to converge on the living standards of developing countries if they adopt policies of small government, openness and macroeconomic stability. The latest such contribution, in the May 1997 World Economic Outlook *of the IMF, takes the argument further by claiming that all three policies are needed together, and that any one in isolation will not be helpful.*

This paper subjects this "new Washington consensus" to critical analysis. A general conclusion is that: contrary to the proposition above, there is no one single set of "good" or "sound" policies capable of bringing about convergence in every developing country; rather, "good policy" takes on a different meaning in each developing or transition economy contingent upon the latter's structure, its stage of development and the external shocks to which it is subject. In particular, policy response varies by region: as regards the three policies commended by the IMF, government size is generally completely insignificant, openness is more positive in middle-income countries, and growth impact is inversely related to inflation in most regions except Africa.

Another conclusion is that there are many important alternatives to the policies advanced by the standard "Washington Consensus". These alternatives may be relevant to bringing about convergence both in middle-income and in poorer developing countries. In particular, measures to combat endogenous distortions, such as financial repression, performance-related protection and anti-poverty measures, are positively related to growth, especially in poorer countries; and the stability of policy is important, as well as its stance.

These results appear to be resilient to changes in estimation method and time period. The right inference appears to be that "Washington Consensus" policies, which compensate for policy-induced distortions, need to be accompanied by other policies, particularly in low-income countries, which compensate for endogenous distortions caused by risk and deficiencies in institutions and infrastructure. This conclusion has implications for the conditionality imposed by aid donors.

I.　The "open economies converge" consensus

A number of recent contributions to the growth literature have emphasized the positive role played by the forces of globalization in enabling poor countries to converge on the living standards of rich ones. These include Sachs and Warner (1995), Aziz and Wescott (1997), IMF (1997), World Bank (1997), Dollar and Burnside (1997) and Edwards (1998), and their general message is well captured by Sachs and Warner's claim (1995, p. 3) that "open economies converge, and closed ones do not". In other words, if developing countries were to adopt a consistent policy package conducive to the preservation of an open economy, that would, according to all the authors cited above, at least be a necessary condition for convergence.

There is some disagreement within the "Washington Consensus" concerning exactly what the ingredients of this consistent policy package are, with Sachs and Warner placing primary emphasis on measures of trade policy openness and Aziz and Wescott (1997, p.18) arguing that three separate elements are needed in combination: "trade openness, macro stability, and a relatively low degree of government involvement in economic activity". But the IMF's *World Economic Outlook* of May 1997 seeks to summarize the state of play by arguing that:

> A key lesson seems to be that the pressures of globalization, especially in the past decade or so, have served to accentuate the benefits of good policies and the costs of bad policies. Countries that align themselves with the forces of globalization and embrace the reforms needed to do so, liberalizing markets and pursuing disciplined macroeconomic policies, are likely to put themselves on a path of convergence with the advanced economies, following the successful Asian newly industrialized economies. These countries may expect to benefit from trade, gain global market share, and be increasingly rewarded with larger private capital flows. Countries that do not adopt such policies are likely to face declining shares of world trade and private capital flows, and to find themselves falling behind in relative terms.
>
> (IMF, 1997, p. 72)

In the following it will be argued that, contrary to this proposition, there is no one unique set of "good" or "sound" policies. The meaning of "good policy" differs across regions and countries, de-pending on their structure, stage of development and the external shocks to which they are subject.

II.　Critique

Before any serious critical comment on the "new Washington Consensus" is made, it is appropriate to explore the extent of consensus and divergence within the large literature on policy and growth, and to emphasize the limitations attaching to all of it, not least the present study. The literature consists essentially of cross-section studies of over a hundred different developing countries, the data for many of which are suspect, especially as they relate to the very important agricultural and informal components of GNP. Both these inaccuracies in the data and structural changes over time may prejudice the ability of any studies using the cross-section method to give a true picture. In any case, they should be seen as guides to the strength of correlation between the available data, and "not as behavioural relationships that suggest how much growth will change when policies change" (Levine and Zervos, 1996, pp. 426-427). Within that role, they can nonetheless perform a valuable function in screening out beliefs and relationships that fit the data from those that do not; and that is the spirit in which we try to use them here.

The literature on policy and growth begins with studies of the effects of adjustment in the 1980s and then expands greatly in the 1990s as these evaluations merge with "new growth theory" studies, in which technical progress is driven by human capital and individual policy influences on growth are given more prominence. From the hundreds of published studies of this kind, we summarize in table 1 those which bear on the elements of policy mentioned by the IMF "liberalizing markets", "pursuing disciplined macroeconomic policies" and "other necessary reforms" which we shall interpret, following Aziz and Wescott (1997), as a restriction on the share of government in total output. The inferences which emerge from table 1 are as follows:

(i)　Growth correlates with "composite openness" as measured by an average of the different available openness measures (Edwards 1998). However, the strength of the correlation found varies according to both the index of openness chosen, since the different available indices of openness do not correlate well with one another and the character of the non-policy variables

Table 1

POLICY IMPACTS ON GROWTH

Investigator	Sample and time period	Regression coefficient on growth of:				Other variables in regression[a]
		(1) "Openness"	*(2)* Inflation	*(3)* Government share	*(4)* (1) to (3) combined	
Fischer (1991)	All available countries 1960-1988		-3.55** (3.19)			o, i, p
Levine and Renelt (1992)	101 countries 1960-1989			-0.59 (0.15)		o, i, p, n, country and political dummies
Easterly (1993)	38 countries 1970-1985	-0.015 (0.71)				o, p, I
Easterly et al. (1993)	80 countries 1970s and 1980s	-0.009 (0.64)				o, p, M2, s
Mosley et al. (1995)	19 African countries 1980-1993		-0.001 (0.71)			o, i, h, r
Sarel (1996)	87 countries		-0.02** (4.02)[b]			o, n, s
Aziz and Wescott (1997)	76 countries	-0.02 (0.13)	-0.18 (0.1)	-0.17 (0.12)	0.17** (0.098)	o, i, n, e
Dollar and Burnside (1997)[c]	56 aid recipients	1.61** (2.76)		-8.25 (1.43)	0.24** (2.87)	o, M2, various political dummies
Edwards (1998)[d]	53 countries	0.07** (2.8)				o, h

Note: *, **, *** indicate that estimations are significant at the 90, 95 and 99 per cent confidence level, respectively.

   a Code for other variables in regression: o = initial income level; i = investment as percentage of GDP; h = human capital indicator (mean years of education); p = primary school enrolment rate; e = secondary school enrolment rate; M2 = M2 as share of GDP; n = population growth rate; s = indicator of external shocks; r = real interest rate.

   b Coefficient on *inflation in excess of 8 per cent;* the coefficient on inflation alone is 0.0016, positive and insignificant.

   c Regression coefficients from an equation not containing an interaction term.

   d "Openness" is an average of five openness indicators used by other authors.

selected for the regression set, with the inclusion or non-inclusion of external shocks having a particularly important bearing on the results obtained. In particular, if openness is measured in terms of the foreign exchange premium or the share of trade in GDP, the impact of openness on growth does not show up as significant, especially if external shocks are included in the regression set (Easterly et al., 1993, table 5).

(ii) In most multi-country samples inflation has a negative impact on growth; but not, apparently,

Table 2

CONDITIONAL PROBABILITY OF HIGH GROWTH IN THE EVENT OF "HIGH-QUALITY POLICY COMPLEMENTARITY": ANALYSIS BY COUNTRY GROUP

	High growth	*Medium growth*	*Low growth*
All countries			
(Aziz and Wescott estimate)	0.89	0.11	0
(Our estimate)	0.55	0.27	0.16
Low-income	0.25	0.50	0.25
Middle-income	0.80	0.10	0.10
Africa	0.33	0.33	0.33
Latin America	0.60	0.40	0
East Asia	1.00	0	0
South Asia	0.20	0.80	0
Eastern Europe and Central Asia	0	0.25	0.75

Source: World Bank (1997), appendix tables 1 (for GDP per capita level and growth rates), 2 (for inflation rates) and 13 (for government share); Sachs and Warner (1995, pp. 72-95) for openness index.

Note: The definition of "high quality complementarity", established by Aziz and Wescott is as follows : either two or all three of the following policy variables are more than half a standard deviation "better" than the mean value: openness (as measured by the ratio of trade to GDP), inflation variance, ratio of government share to GDP. "High" and "low" growth are similarly measured as growth rates more than half a standard deviation above and below the mean for the period 1985-1995, with growth performance between these two limits being classified as "medium".

in Africa (Mosley et al., 1995) and not, apparently, at lower levels of inflation.

(iii) There is little evidence suggesting that government size has any independent influence, positive or negative, on the growth rate.

(iv) Although most studies prior to Aziz and Wescott (1997) examine the *separate* influence of different policy variables and ignore complementarities, there is an interesting class of exceptions which come from the literature on aid and adjustment in relation to growth. But here too there is controversy, with Dollar and Burnside (1997) claiming that the effectiveness of overseas aid in relation to growth is contingent on the level of a composite index of "good policy" – comprising budget deficit, inflation and openness – and Mosley and Hudson (1997) being unable to replicate this result in relation to Africa only. Studies of the effectiveness of

adjustment, such as World Bank (1992) and Elbadawi (1992), also find the returns to "adjustment" – a composite indicator very similar to "good policy" – to be much weaker in Africa than elsewhere.

The existing literature, therefore, although able to report some success with respect to openness and inflation, has had some difficulty in identifying the effects of individual policy variables, which are robust with respect to sample, definition of the specified policy variable, time period and estimation method. The IMF background paper (Aziz and Wescott, 1997, p. 12) in particular acknowledges this, and puts its faith in the claim that *complementarities* between the three elements of policy specified in table 2 are what matters:

> Are such policies (those examined in table 1) individually *sufficient* to promote fast growth? The answer is no ... and that at least a moderate degree of policy success is necessary in several

areas to achieve fast growth. This points at least tentatively toward a possible complementarity among these policies – that a good policy produces the desired outcome only in the company of other mutually reinforcing good policies.

(Aziz and Wescott, 1997, p.12)

In attempting to test whether this claim is right, we begin by accepting the variable definitions and methodology adopted by Aziz and Wescott (1997) and used as the basis for the IMF's policy advice quoted above. We have been able, however, only to replicate the general sense and not the exact detail of the result reported by Aziz and Wescott in their table 6 and as the top line in table 2 below: although there are 18 countries which, on their criteria, exhibit "high-quality complementarity" (i.e. high scores on two of the three performance criteria listed in table 1), we find that only a small majority of countries had high growth performance over 1985-1995, and that three countries (Burundi, Mali and Hungary) had low growth performance. If we split the sample by region, we find that the tendency of high policy complementarity to produce high growth was highest in East Asia, lowest in Africa and Eastern Europe, and in general lower in low-income than in middle-income countries.

We now extend the analysis in table 2 to examine the separate influence of the three policy components highlighted by Aziz and Wescott: openness, macro stability and small government (see table 3). As before, the benefits of "good policy" are reflected in better growth performance only in the middle-income group; indeed, in Africa, countries with *higher* inflation and a *higher* government share in the economy have markedly better growth performance than countries with low inflation and smaller government. Therefore, far from a strong anti-inflation effort and low government share having "complementarity" with openness, it would appear that in low-income countries they actively *detract from,* just as in middle-income countries they more often than not assist, the process of convergence. However, table 3 also suggests that the influence of government share is weak throughout all country groups; except in East Asia, it neither adds much to nor subtracts much from country performance.

Again, these results echo those listed in table 1 by suggesting low growth impact for policy variables (in particular government share) in poorer countries. The question which must now be tackled is why this is so. Following on from this, it will be useful to ask

whether alternative policies exist which have greater effectiveness in boosting economic performance in low-income countries. However, some methodological problems have to be resolved before:

- *First,* the period examined by Aziz and Wescott (1997) – 1985-1995 – is short compared to most studies of long-term growth (for example, those listed in table 1).

- *Second,* it uses a very strange proxy for openness, namely the share of trade in GDP, which has no connotations of "good" or "bad" policy, being dependent as much on country size and factor endowments as on policy quality. As discussed earlier, there are many different measures of openness, nine of which are compared and eventually combined in Edwards (1998). These do not intercorrelate well: for example, some authors treat the Republic of Korea as a classically outward-oriented economy, while others treat it as a semi-closed government-controlled economy. But whichever measure of openness is used, it should not be the trade dependence ratio, a high level of which is consistent with a high level of trade distortions.

- *Third,* the inflation variable – the standard deviation of inflation – may be a consequence as much as a cause of slow growth, and takes no account of the non-linearity problem discussed above.

- *Fourth,* it is not clear what the rationale is for the complementarities on which Aziz and Wescott's argument depends. This fourth point requires a little more discussion.

We can begin from first principles. Economic growth may improve either because of an increase in the amount and quality of the factors of production available to the economy, or because of an increase in the efficiency with which they are used (for example, an increase in the utilization of existing resources), given the level of existing factors of production. How can the policies prioritized by the IMF be expected to do either of these things?

Government share: There is no presumption in economic theory (nor any evidence from the data in tables 1 and 2) that a high or low share of government economic activity is associated with the level of efficiency with which resources are allocated. As the World Bank has stated (1983, p. 50), "the key factor in determining the efficiency of an enterprise is not

Table 3

GROWTH RATES BY DIMENSION OF POLICY QUALITY, 1985-1995

Policy criterion	Average per capita GDP	Openness	Inflation	Government share	All criteria
South Asia:	350				
good policy		2.5	2.3	2.3	2.5
bad policy		2.2	n/a[a]	n/a[b]	2.2
CP		*33*	*20*	*20*	*20*
Sub-Saharan Africa:	490				
good policy		1.1	-0.5	-0.6	-0.1
bad policy		-1.0	0.8	0.8	0.0
CP		*75*	*40*	*20*	*33*
East Asia:	800				
good policy		6.0	5.0	5.4	6.0
bad policy		2.2*	n/a[a]	2.3*	2.2
CP		*100*	*100*	*20*	*100*
Eastern Europe and Central Asia:	2220				
good policy		0.1	-1.4	-6.7	0.1
bad policy		-7.2*	-6.6*	-5.6	-7.2
CP		*0*	*0*	*0*	*0*
Latin America and Caribbean:	3320				
good policy		1.2	1.1	1.2	2.2
bad policy		-1.1*	0.5	-0.8	1.1
CP		*40*	*20*	*55*	*60*
Low income:					
good policy		1.5	0.5	0.4	0.8
bad policy		-0.9	0.8	0.8	0.6
CP		*58*	*32*	*20*	*25*
Middle income:					
good policy		3.6	2.5	1.9	3.5
bad policy		-2.1	..	2.5	-0.4
CP		*59*	..	*27*	*80*
All developing countries:					
good policy performance		2.5	2.0	1.2	2.1
medium or bad policy performance		-0.9	-1.0	1.6	0.2
CP		*49*	*36*	*22*	*55*

Source: As for table 2. *CP* is the percentage value of the *conditional probability* that growth performance will be "good" (more than half a standard deviation above the mean) if the policy variable mentioned at the head of this column is also "good" in this sense.

    a   There are no countries with average inflation above 20 per cent over the 1985-1995 period in the South Asia and East Asia regions.

    b   There are no countries with government recurrent expenditure share in excess of 15 per cent over the 1985-95 period in the East Asia region.

whether it is publicly or privately owned, but how it is managed". There are multiple sources of both market and government failure in developing countries (see, for example, Stern, 1989, p. 616), and the issue is what mechanisms exist to combat both and thereby increase the efficiency of resource allocation. Government share is a poor proxy for such mechanisms.

Inflation: There are two theoretical arguments as to why a country's stabilization and inflation performance may matter for economic growth. The first is that the inflation rate acts as a proxy for the variance of inflation (and sometimes for the instability of the economy more generally), such that high inflation rates lead investors to feel uncertain about the level of returns on their potential investment, and deter them from investing (i.e. they prevent the production possibility curve from moving outwards). The second argument is that the inflation rate acts as a proxy for the government's control over the economy: as Fischer (1993, p. 5) puts it, " a government that is producing high inflation is a government that has lost control", the implication being that nobody will willingly invest in a country with such a government. In each of these senses there is indeed a risk that increasing globalization (in the sense of higher mobility of capital) will increasingly penalize high-inflation countries by redirecting capital movements away from them; and there is some empirical evidence for this, at least in the middle-income countries (table 2; Fischer, 1993, p. 13). However, we note in each case that it is the unpredictability of inflation, rather than inflation itself, which is the villain of the piece. The "loss of control" argument can be expected to become relevant at high rates of inflation (say 20 per cent plus) rather than to imply a continuous linear relationship between inflation and growth; and there is still the apparently perverse relationship between inflation and growth in Africa to be sorted out. Our hypothesis is that in Africa, since the 1980s, inflation has been acting as a proxy for something which really does matter for efficiency and growth, namely the real exchange rate and the willingness of governments to remove controls on it. Where they failed to do so (especially in the CFA zone of Francophone Africa until 1994) there was a catastrophic loss of competitiveness – leading to seriously negative growth rates – but very low inflation, since the exchange rate was being used as a nominal anchor. In other words, growth prospects were damaged by a botched anti-inflation policy. The implication is that any attempt to analyse the effects of inflation on economic performance needs to take into account both the causal mechanism through which it operates and the potential costs of alternative methods of stabilizing it.

Openness: This is a measure of incentives to increase productivity, analogous to contestability in the theory of the firm: as discussed earlier, the share of trade in GDP as measured by Aziz and Wescott does not act as an effective proxy for such incentives. The Sachs and Warner (1995) measure of openness does attempt to measure these incentives, admittedly by sometimes rather ad hoc measures but often by reference to a measure of policy-induced market distortion, usually the foreign-exchange premium on the black market. In what follows this latter measure of openness will be used. However, much depends not only on how *strong* is the incentive given to improve efficiency, but also on how *consistent* it is. Moderate but steady liberalization may have more impact, because it sends a credible signal, than drastic liberalization which risks later reversal.

Complementarities: The Aziz and Wescott analysis is purely empirical and gives no reasons why the three policy factors it assesses (openness, low inflation and a low government share) should be expected to be complementary. Openness and low inflation may be expected to be complementary if greater openness increases competitiveness whose full implications for the profits of potential investors can only be assessed if inflation becomes lower and therefore more stable; however, it is not easy to see where a lower government share, as such, comes into the equation. It is possible to visualize strong incentives to increased productivity with both a high and a low government share in the economy, and of course it is also possible to visualize weak incentives to higher productivity at both high and low levels of government intervention. The share of government in the economy might be complementary with the degree of policy-induced distortion if the degree of such distortion increases with government size; but there is little evidence, empirical (see tables 1-3) or theoretical, for such a claim. More broadly, the degree of complementarity between instruments may reflect the sequence in which they are deployed. Although sequencing is still more of an art – both political and economic – than a science, the experience of the last two decades has taught a range of useful empirical lessons in this respect: devalue before undertaking domestic fiscal reform, liberalize the internal capital market before the external capital account, etc.

Alternative policies and factors affecting efficiency: Over and above the inefficiencies analysed above, caused by policy-induced distortions in particular markets, there exist of course other in-efficiencies due not to the actions of government but to intrinsic imperfections in the economy – for example, imperfect information, economies of scale and externalities. We shall refer to these imperfections as endogenous distortions. Many government interventions, especially in the context of less developed countries, consist not of policy-induced distortions but of perfectly legitimate attempts to counteract endogenous distortions. Successive Chief Economists of the World Bank have drawn attention to two specific channels by which the latter has been successfully achieved: temporary wage-price controls and tax-based incomes policy as devices to extract an economy from a high-inflation equilibrium, as portrayed by Bruno (1993, chapter 8), and regulatory intervention to reduce the element of asymmetric information in domestic financial markets, as portrayed for the case of East Asia by Stiglitz and Uy (1996). It is a commonplace of contemporary discussion on development that these and other measures to offset policy-induced distortions are subject to all the perils of "government failure" – corruption, incentive distortions and the like – and an important issue for empirical investigation is how these perils can be circumvented. One highly promising option consists of subjecting all interventions intended to combat endogenous distortions to a performance contract – for example, tariff protection or agricultural input subsidies provided on a temporary basis and continued if, and only if, such protection leads to an improvement in performance in the sense of an improvement in productivity, competitiveness or exports. In each of these cases the risk that government intervention in the market may be damaged by "government failure" is offset by building an efficiency-based contest for access to rents into the process of allocating them.

Inequality of income may be seen as a special case of an endogenous imperfection which policy needs to combat. In countries where income is highly unequal and as a consequence a large proportion of the population is below the poverty line, the domestic market for consumer goods is depressed and those who live at the margin of subsistence are constrained by considerations of protecting their livelihood from investment in fixed capital (and also from the hiring of labour, which reduces poverty by the indirect route of the labour market). As a result, investment and growth are depressed (other things remaining equal) in high-inequality countries, and stimulated in low-inequality countries. There is now substantial empirical evidence of this effect: for example, low-inequality countries such as those of the Far East

invariably lie above a regression line relating growth to inputs of the orthodox factors of production, and high-inequality countries such as Brazil, Peru and South Africa invariably lie below (Barros, 1993, table 1).

We may summarize the discussion in this section as follows. "Good policy", as understood by the IMF's researchers in terms of stabilization and the correction of policy-induced distortions, explains a part of the inter-country variance in growth between countries, but only a small part, particularly in low-income countries. This is exactly what we should expect from considerations of theory, which draw attention to the role played by policy components which correct endogenous distortions, by non-policy influences upon production and by external shocks in explaining growth and convergence. Before proceeding to a test of the significance of policy factors in explaining growth differences, therefore, we need to incorporate the orthodox factors of production, external shocks and policy variables not considered by the IMF analysis; we also need to correct for the methodological problems associated with the IMF approach, in particular related to time period and to openness and inflation proxies.

III. Reconstruction and alternative ideas

In the light of the discussion in the preceding section, we perceive a priori four groups of forces tending to speed or slow down convergence between countries, and not simply the elements of "good policy" adverted to by the IMF. The first is the strength of policy-induced distortions, as identified by the Fund; the second is the effectiveness of government actions to offset endogenous micro-economic distortions; the third is inputs of the conventional factors of production, both those analysed by "old growth theory" (such as labour and capital) and those introduced by new growth theory, such as human capital and skills; and the fourth is the impact of adverse shocks, such as terms of trade, which poorer countries cannot in the short term protect themselves against on account of imperfections in the capital market. We will now use regression analysis to assess, as well as we can given the available data, the relative impact of these four sets of factors in the developing world during the 1980-1995 period.

The data

Table 4 sets out the empirical proxy variables used for this purpose in the regression analysis. Some of them are fairly straightforward, but others are controversial; we may note in passing the following variables used in the estimation whose proxy variable is debatable:

Policy uncertainty: This is proxied by means of an average of standard deviations of the inflation rate, exchange rate, public capital expenditure and interest rates (the central bank discount rate) over the period 1980-1995. *Ex post* instability is thus used as a surrogate for *ex ante* uncertainty: inescapable perhaps, but not ideal.

Effective protection of industry (weighted and unweighted): The average effective protection rate as estimated from World Bank country economic memoranda over the period 1980-1995 is used as an independent variable both raw and weighted by the growth rate of industrial total factor productivity over the period 1980-95. The logic of doing this is to make an estimate of the extent to which protection was *performance-related,* as we argued above it should be in order to induce growth. But, of course, productivity may rise for reasons other than the performance incentive embedded in the protection: to this extent, the weighted effective protection indicator is flawed. We will return to this issue below, in the discussion of the results.

Agricultural input subsidies (weighted and unweighted): The average rate of agricultural input subsidy, again as estimated from World Bank country economic memoranda over the period 1980-1995, is used as an independent variable both unweighted and weighted by the growth of agricultural productivity, by analogy with the method used to estimate "performance-weighted" effective protection above. The merits and flaws in of this approach are the same as those of performance-weighted protection.

Openness: In response to the critique above, we use the Sachs and Warner measure of openness rather than the share of foreign trade to national income.

Inflation: In response to the evidence that growth responds to this in a non-linear way, this is measured as the excess of inflation over 8 per cent.

Complementarities between policy instruments: We measure these as the product of the three policy variables highlighted by the IMF analysis (openness, inflation and government share), squared so as to emphasize the interaction between the terms. To pick up the effects of sequencing we introduce an additional complementarity variable in which the value of the openness dummy is increased if real devaluations have preceded macroeconomic stabilization and it liberalization of the current account of the balance of payments has preceded liberalization of the capital account), and is left the same if they have been introduced at the same time or in the "wrong" sequence.

Regression analysis: developing countries as a group

In table 5 we present regression estimates of the impact of different influences on growth over the 1980-1995 period analysed by the IMF. We introduce groups of variables step by step according to the type of influence which they represent, and we draw the following preliminary conclusions:

Equation 1: As a first analytical step, the "Washington Consensus" policy variables (openness, inflation and government share) are set out as the only right-hand-side variables in the first line of table 4, alongside the actual regressions adopted by Aziz and Wescott (1997). Between them they explain only 8 per cent of the variance in growth. Inflation, with the expected negative sign, is the only one of the three variables to show statistical significance; this significance increases when, in equation 5, the inflation variable is rendered as "inflation in excess of 8 per cent", acknowledging the likely non-linearity of the relationship. As will be recalled, the Aziz and Wescott study (1997, p. 4) was careful to concede that many regression studies had found "that the effects of traditional Washington Consensus-type policy variables, if they are significant at all, are not robust with respect to specification, and therefore do not merit great attention".

Equation 2: This adds into equation 1 the standard "new growth theory" variables, base-year income (to incorporate catching-up effects), investment, and primary and secondary school enrolments. All these variables are significantly correlated with growth rates and have the expected sign except secondary education (the regression coefficient on which is unexpectedly *negative).* Within the "Washington Consensus" variables, the level of openness now becomes significant in addition to the inflation rate. The correlation coefficient (the percentage of growth explained by the right-hand-side variables) rises from 8 per cent to 33 per cent.

Table 4

EMPIRICAL PROXIES USED IN REGRESSION ANALYSIS

Expected determinant of growth	Corresponding variable used in regression analysis	Comments
IMF "good policy" variables:		
Openness	Sachs and Warner measure of openness	Source: Sachs and Warner (1995, pp. 65 ff.)
		Attempts to measure degree of policy-induced distortion, unlike IMF (1997), which is purely ratio of trade to GDP
Inflation	Annual increase in consumer price index 1980-1995 less than 8 per cent	Source: World Bank (1997, appendix table 2)
Government share	Government consumption as a share of total income	Source: World Bank (1997, appendix table 14)
Complementarity	Product of openness, inflation and government share, squared	
Sequencing	Complementarity variable, with value of openness term doubled if real devaluations have always preceded reductions in budget deficit during 1980-1995	
Orthodox factors of production:		
Investment rate	Average investment/GDP ratio 1980-1995	Source: World Bank (1997, appendix table 13)
Initial income level	Per capita GDP in 1960	Source: World Bank (1997, appendix table 1)
Human capital input	Average of primary and secondary school enrolments from 1960-1995	Source: UNICEF (1998, table 8)
External shocks and other external influences on the economy	1995 terms of trade (1987 = 100)	Source: World Bank (1997, table 3)
"Non-orthodox "policies:		
Policy stability	Policy stability index	Average of standard deviations of: inflation interest rates
Measures to counteract endogenous distortions in agricultural sector	Efficiency-adjusted agricultural protection index	Rate of agricultural subsidy multiplied by growth rate of agricultural total factor productivity, 1980-1995
Income distribution	Gini coefficient of inequality	Source: World Bank (1997, table 5)
Measures to counteract endogenous distortions in industrial sector	Efficiency-adjusted effective protection index	Rate of effective protection multiplied by growth rate of industrial total factor productivity, 1980-1995

Table 5

RESULTS OF REGRESSION ANALYSIS: ALL COUNTRIES IN SAMPLE

Regression coefficients on independent variables

Equation	Estimation	Constant	"Washington consensus" Openness	Inflation rate	Government share	Complementarity	Standard "new growth theory" 1960 per capita income	Investment/GDP ratio	Primary school enrolments	Second. school enrolments	Mean enrolments (1)	Heterodox policy variables Real interest rate	Effective protection rate	Effective protection rate[a]	Agric. Subsidies (2)	Agric. Subsidies weighted (3)	Policy instability (4)	In-equality (5)	Terms of trade 1995 (1980 = 100)	r²	F-stat (prob)	Functional (prob)	Heteroskedasticity (prob)
0	OLS	*0 (0.09)*				*0.17* (2.10)*	*-0.18 (1.15)*	*0.33* (3.15)*		*0.1 (0.89)*										0.46			
1	OLS	-0.88 (0.91)	1.72 (1.67)	-0.008* (2.45)	0.001 (0.54)															0.084	2.54 (0.06)	35.66 (0.00)	1.60 (0.20)
2	OLS	-6.43** (3.56)	1.83* (1.97)	-0.006* (2.41)	-0.0022 (0.09)		-0.0011 (1.40)	0.18** (3.38)	0.076** (2.62)	-0.07 (2.15)			-0.16 (0.016)		0.10 (2.30)					0.39	7.41 (0.00)	1.81 (0.01)	7.02 (0.03)
3	OLS	-3.58 (1.38)	2.02* (1.94)	-0.007* (2.33)	0.004 (0.15)		-0.002* (2.48)	0.22** (3.53)			0.021 (1.17)			0.05** (6.05)		0.02 (2.02)			-0.053 (0.09)	0.33	5.64 (0.00)	0.008 (0.92)	5.94 (0.002)
4	OLS	-2.71 (1.02)	0.73* (1.95)	-0.024** (4.75)	0.33 (0.006)		-0.001* (2.09)	0.04* (1.91)	0.58 (0.56)			-0.025** (4.60)		0.039** (4.90)			-0.048* (1.97)	-0.057* (1.59)		0.69	13.97 (0.00)	14.18 (0.00)	6.66 (0.01)
5	OLS	-0.03 (0.013)	0.80 (1.19)	-0.022** (4.40)	0.0064 (0.35)		-0.001* (1.90)	0.05* (2.22)				-0.024** (4.58)		0.036* (4.29)			-0.015 (1.66)	-0.06* (2.45)		0.69	15.55 (0.00)		
6	2SLS	-4.15 (0.16)	0.84 (1.06)	-0.028** (2.78)	0.068 (0.02)		-0.004 (0.90)	0.04 (1.40)	0.25 (1.60)			-0.067* (3.50)		0.026* (4.00)			-0.082* (2.14)	-0.17 (0.07)		0.41			
7	OLS	1.48 (0.55)				-0.15×10^{-4} (2.19)	-0.001* (2.22)	0.049 (1.09)				-0.018** (2.59)		0.039* (4.41)			-0.018* (1.87)	-0.08** (3.02)	-0.0011 (0.03)	0.63		9.55 (0.003)	3.07 (0.03)

Source: As for table 3. Number of observations: 87 in all cases.
Note: Row 0 (in italics) is the regression with policy interaction effects estimated by Aziz and Wescott (1997, table 7). For definitions of all variables, see table 4.
a Efficiency adjusted.
Codes:
(1) Average of primary and secondary school enrolments.
(2) Average rate of subsidy on fertilizer and (if applicable) other agricultural inputs.
(3) Average rate of subsidy multiplied by rate of growth of agricultural total factor productivity, 1980-1995.
(4) Policy instability index (for details of calculation see table 4).
(5) Gini coefficient of income inequality.

Table 6

COMPLEMENTARITY BETWEEN POLICY INSTRUMENTS

Complementarity variable	*Coefficient*	*t-ratio*
(1) As in equation 7	-0.000018	2.43
(2) As (1) with government share deleted	-0.000018	2.41
(3) As (1) with inflation deleted	+0.000054	0.44
(4) As (1) with openness deleted	-0.000017	2.43
(5) As (1) with sequencing term added	-0.000025	3.02

Note: Dependent variable: growth of per capita income, 1980-1995 in equation (7), table 5. All independent variables except "complementarity" are as in that equation.

Equation 3: This adds into equation 2 an estimate of external shocks (the trend in the terms of trade) and two "heterodox" policy terms: the unweighted rate of effective protection and the unweighted rate of agricultural subsidy. Terms of trade and effective protection are insignificant but agricultural subsidies are just significant in an unorthodox direction (i.e. higher subsidy is now associated with higher growth). The coefficients on the other variables are virtually unaltered.

Equation 4: This adds into equation 3 on an experimental basis all the other "heterodox policy" variables mentioned in table 3. Of these new variables, policy instability is negative and significant, equality of income distribution is positive and (just) significant, and the real interest rate is *negatively* significant, a result consistent with orthodox IS/LM analysis and with the support for "economically rational" financial repression expressed by Stiglitz and Uy (1996), but inconsistent with the "Washington Consensus" approach. Finally, the level of effective protection shows much higher significance when weighted by the growth of productivity than in its raw state (equation 3).

Equation 5: This deletes from equation 4 all the insignificant right-hand side terms (and corrects the inflation variable for the likely non-linearity of response) in order to produce an experimental "best fit equation" for later analysis.

Equation 6: The estimation here is by two-stage rather than by ordinary least-squares in order to counteract any bias. When inflation is instrumented by the M2 definition of the money supply and investment by business profits, the regression results are as in the sixth row of the table, with investment and 1960 per capita income losing their significance but with other results substantially unaltered.

Equation 7: An attempt is made here to come to grips with the claim of Aziz and Wescott that "complementarity matters", in particular between inflation, openness and government share. A "complementarity term" consisting of the squared sum of inflation, government share and the negative of openness – in effect, a loss function – is substituted for the separate values of those policy variables as they appear in the previous specifications of the equation. If complementarity matters, the significance of the complementarity term in equation 7 should be in excess of the significance of the separate policy terms in equation 5: the impact of the whole should exceed the impact of the sum of the parts. It does not, however: the significance of inflation on its own in equation 5 is in fact greater than the significance of the "complementarity term" in equation 7. If we experiment further by deleting stepwise the individual components of the complementarity term and then by adjusting for the sequence in which reforms were implemented, we get the results summarized in table 6.

The results are revealing. If government share or openness is deleted from the "complementarity" loss function, the coefficient on this loss function and its significance scarcely change, implying that complementarity between these policy instruments and the others is actually quite small. If inflation (in excess of 8 per cent) is deleted from the loss function the results change drastically: the sign of the coefficient goes from negative to positive and the coefficient itself loses significance, implying that in the absence of inflation restraint (beyond a moderate value) openness and restraint in the size of government, by themselves, have little value. Finally, if the complementarity term is corrected for sequencing by adding a premium in those cases where reforms were carried out in the "correct" sequence (devaluation before budgetary cuts and liberalization of the current account before the capital account of the balance of payments) the coefficient increases in size and gains significance, suggesting that what matters is not only sticking to, and combining, the conventional elements of reform but also getting them into a coherent order.

Regression analysis subdivided by country group

Recalling the analysis in section 2, we now wish to see whether the basic pattern of results represented above changes when the sample is subdivided by country groups. Accordingly, we next estimate the "best fit" equation (equation 5 of table 5) separately for Central Asia and for middle-income and low-income countries, defined as those with a per capita income of less than $800 (essentially most of Africa and South Asia, with a few others, including Haiti, Bolivia, Cambodia, Laos and Viet Nam). The results are set out in table 7.

From table 7 it is clear that the growth response of different country groups to the different policy and non-policy stimuli which we analyse is by no means uniform. As was already apparent from tables 2 and 3, the response of growth to the "Washington Consensus" components of good policy, controlling for other influences on growth, tended to be weaker in poorer countries. This is particularly true with regard to inflation which has the expected negative significance in middle-income countries, and in the sample as a whole, but is *positively* though insignificantly associated with growth in low-income countries and in Africa, which contains most of those countries. (One may speculate that the high rates of inflation experienced in Latin America and in Eastern Europe, both of which sparked off significant nega-

tive coefficients, did more harm than the relatively modest rates of inflation experienced elsewhere.) Sachs and Warner's measure of "openness" is likewise more significant in middle- than in low-income countries, whereas the government share of GDP is insignificant everywhere.

As regards the "orthodox new growth theory" variables at the left-hand end of the table, this investigation finds little that departs from the previous findings. Investment rates are everywhere positive and significant, primary school enrolments are positive and significant in Latin America and Eastern Europe but not elsewhere, and particularly not in low-income countries, reflecting the finding of Levine and Renelt (1992) and 1960 per capita income (the "convergence term") is everywhere negative, as theory would predict, but not always significant. Two reasons for the apparent lack of convergence are the prominence of African countries (most of which have showed no tendency towards convergence) in the sample and the absence of a mass of high-income, low-growth observations on the industrialized countries from the countries examined.

It is the estimates of the effect of "other policy variables" at the right-hand end of the table which most obviously suggest a departure from the conclusions of previous work. For whereas several writers suggest that "growth rates among developing countries are mainly determined by factor endowments and other non-policy factors rather than by policy variables" (Aziz and Wescott, 1997, p. 4), our interpretation is that policy does matter for growth, but at least as much the policy variables which seek to compensate for endogenous distortions as those which compensate for policy-induced distortions, provided that they are effectively administered. There is, however, inter-country variation in policy effects of this type. The effective protection rate (adjusted for productivity growth) is a significant influence on growth in the low-income country group and in the sample as a whole, but not in the middle-income country group; and financial repression (the inverse of the real interest rate) is a significant influence on growth in the sample as a whole, but only in Asia of the respective country groups. This suggests that complementary policies, including regulation and anti-monopoly policy in the financial sector, may have been more effectively implemented here than elsewhere in the developing world. Policy instability is a negative influence on growth everywhere but significant particularly in Africa and Eastern Europe, the two areas where policy is particularly volatile, often under the impetus of pressure from aid donors.

Table 7

RESULTS OF REGRESSION ANALYSIS: ANALYSIS BY COUNTRY GROUP[a]

Regression coefficients on independent variables:

	Constant	"New growth theory" variables:			"Washington Consensus" variables:					Other policy variables:		r²
		1960 per capita income	Investment rate (Per cent GDP)	School enrolments (Primary)	Openness (Sachs and Warner measure)	Inflation (Per cent p.a. 1980-1995)	Government share of GDP	Effective protection rate adjusted	Real interest rate	Gini coefficient of income inequality	Index of policy instability	
Whole sample (n = 87)	-2.70 (1.21)	-0.001* (1.95)	0.041* (1.96)	0.007 (0.41)	0.80 (1.09)	-0.025* (5.05)	0.006 (0.34)	0.029** (5.30)	-0.026** (4.91)	-0.016* (1.83)	-0.048* (2.17)	0.68
Sub-Saharan Africa only (n = 29)	-5.67 (1.42)	-0.0041 (0.12)	0.08 (0.04)	-0.028 (0.037)	1.19 (1.15)	0.01 (0.51)	0.15 (1.04)	0.033* (2.24)	-0.031 (1.03)	0.051 (0.68)	-0.0038* (1.69)	0.66
Asia and Middle East only (n = 20)	0.90 (0.40)	-0.001 (0.024)	0.024* (2.10)	-0.011 (0.45)	-0.21 (0.78)	-0.008 (0.70)	-0.006 (0.67)	0.029** (4.06)	-0.0035 (0.41)	-0.006* (2.11)	-0.036 (0.95)	0.89
Latin America and Caribbean only (n = 20)	-2.31 (0.26)	-0.0068 (0.38)	0.03 (0.27)	0.08* (1.97)	1.34 (0.53)	-0.0079* (2.34)	-0.007 (0.74)	0.038 (1.30)	-0.007 (0.74)	-0.045* (1.86)	-0.014 (1.12)	0.56
Eastern Europe and Central Asia only (n = 18)	-8.12 (0.22)	-0.001 (0.47)	0.023* (2.14)	0.10 (2.43)	1.38 (1.77)	-0.045* (2.45)	0.036 (0.42)	0.037 (0.98)	0.019 (0.89)	-0.011 (1.59)	-0.027* (2.04)	0.80
Low income countries only (n = 38)	2.09 (0.62)	-0.0074 (1.27)	-0.046 (0.57)	0.02 (0.72)	-0.56 (0.51)	-0.022** (4.29)	0.011 (0.60)	0.021* (2.72)	-0.027** (4.96)	0.053 (1.22)	-0.13** (3.71)	0.77
Middle income countries only (n = 49)	-5.14 (1.43)	-0.003 (1.10)	0.065* (1.99)	-0.018 (0.62)	1.10 (1.05)	0.01 (0.53)	0.19 (1.27)	0.036* (2.26)	-0.028 (0.88)	0.022 (0.30)	-0.013 (0.40)	0.66

Source: As for table 2.

a   Dependent variable: growth rate of per capita GDP, per cent p.a. 1980-1995.

As with inflation, the implication is that instability is an influence which becomes significant only when a threshold is crossed, and that minor low-level variations in the independent variable have little significance for growth. Finally, the Gini coefficient of inequality is significant at least at the 10 per cent level in areas other than Africa, where it is thoroughly insignificant. This may reflect the inability of relatively high levels of equality to give a significant boost to consumer demand in economies which are poor and of small size (such as Ghana and the United Republic of Tanzania); or it may simply represent a data problem.

Are the findings robust?

Several authors, notably Levine and Renelt (1992), Barros (1993) and Sala-I-Martin (1997), have lamented the inability of findings from growth regressions to stand up when exposed to variations in diagnostic tests, estimation procedure, sample composition or time period. We therefore subject both of our main findings – the apparently low significance of some of the "Washington Consensus" policy variables and the apparently high significance of some of the "heterodox" policy variables – to sensitivity analysis of this sort.

Estimation procedure: Growth may influence, as well as be influenced by, both policies and factors of production; in particular, investment and primary education enrolments may be increased by growth (because growth makes them more affordable), as may the real interest rate (because growth influences the demand for loanable funds). To see whether this possible simultaneous causation makes any difference to the results, we used a two-stage least-squares estimation procedure. No significant changes in the measured impact of the policy variables emerged from this, although several coefficients diminish in magnitude and the Gini coefficient of income inequality loses its significance as an explanatory variable.

Sample composition and diagnostic tests: As indicated earlier, policy effects, both "Washington Consensus" and "heterodox", appear not to be within-sample stable: in particular, we have noticed major differences between country groups in the responsiveness of growth to inflation, interest rates and protection. As shown in table 8, a formal Chow-test confirms that these differences are significant, though for Africa only at the 10 per cent level.

Table 8

TESTS FOR WITHIN-SAMPLE STABILITY OF STRUCTURAL RELATIONSHIPS

Sample subdivision	F-statistic for Chow-test *(Probability level)*
Africa	1.69 (0.11)
Asia	6.32 (0.00)
Latin America and Caribbean	3.38 (0.01)

The Chow-test measures the probability that the structural relationships for each country group considered in table 7 are the same as the overall relationship for all developing countries (as specified in row 4 of table 5). This probability is set out in brackets in the second column, and is very low (11 per cent or less) for all of the three country groups examined. The inference that we draw is that the response of national economies to policy variables in particular vary according to circumstances (especially infrastructural resources) which condition the responsiveness of those countries, and that it would be a mistake to assume the same policy response everywhere.

There remains the question of the consistency of these findings with those reported by other authors and for other periods. We can take these two questions together, since most other authors use a period earlier, and sometimes longer, than the 1980-1995 period used in this exercise. In relation to "orthodox policy variables", inflation, openness and government share, the findings of other authors were summarized in table 1. Table 9 now completes the picture by summarizing the findings of different authors in relation to "heterodox" policy variables such as financial repression, performance-related protection and income distribution. There is considerable consistency at the aggregate level. Most authors that have examined a range of periods between 1960 and 1995 report a significant response of output to greater income equality, to reduced policy instability, and to measures to remove endogenous imperfections in various markets, including financial markets, if and only if these are accompanied by measures to increase efficiency.

We therefore believe that the central results of this study – of the variation in the influence of

Table 9

SUMMARY OF FINDINGS CONCERNING IMPACT OF POLICY ON GROWTH

("Heterodox" variables only)

Policy variable investigator	*Period*	*Real interest rate*	*Effective protection* [a]	*Income inequality*	*Policy instability*
This study	1980-1995	-	+	-	-
Rodrik (1990)*	1978-1986				-
Barros (1993)	1960-1985		(+)	-	
Levine and Renelt (1992)	1960-1989	(1)			
Mosley et al. (1995) *(Africa only)*	1980-1991	-			(-)

Source: First line from this study, table 4; other lines from studies listed in the references, as follows:
Notation: + significant positive impact; - significant negative impact; ( ) insignificant impact as specified. All impacts, unless specified *, are measured as partial regression coefficients in a "new growth theory" relationship containing, at least, initial income, investment and some measure of human capital development.

Note: (1) Levine and Renelt (1992) examine money supply rather than interest rates.

a Performance-adjusted.

"Washington Consensus" policies between regions and the significance of other policies – emerge as reasonably robust from this set of sensitivity tests for the years and countries for which we have data. It remains to examine the implications of this conclusion for policy action, especially in developing countries.

IV. Conclusions and implications

On the basis of this investigation we conclude that the IMF's prescription for a successful strategy for growth, "openness toward international trade, macroeconomic stability, and limited government intervention in the economy" (IMF, 1997, p. 92) needs to be both modified and supplemented. It needs to be modified inasmuch as openness to international trade (in low-income countries) and limited government intervention (everywhere) do not correlate with growth. It needs to be supplemented not only by taking note of the contribution to growth by the standard factors of production, but also by broadening the list of policies which may be relevant to achieving convergence so as to include measures aimed at correcting endogenous distortions in income dis-

tribution and in the capital market. The stability of policy also appears to be important, conceivably more important than liberalization itself. In this context we find the Fund's opposition to "protectionist trade policies such as high tariffs" (IMF, 1997, p. 92) and its earlier warning that "globalization will accentuate the costs of bad policies" (ibid., p. 72), of which protection is certainly seen as an example, over-deterministic and not necessarily helpful to the poorest countries (Helleiner, 1996 b, p. 11). These "bad policies" have already made a notable contribution to the fastest economic growth rates recorded in human history – in East Asia and other countries modelled on this template (e.g. Mauritius) – and it is unwise, as our analysis confirms, to claim that "globalization will always punish them". It has not done so in the past, and there is no evidence that it is bad policy in this sense which globalization is currently punishing in East Asia. Obviously, interventionist policies such as financial repression and performance-based protection become effective only if accompanied by safeguards which enable them to provide an incentive to efficiency, as recently emphasized by the 1997 *World Development Report* (World Bank, 1997). Such safeguards exist – the organization of contests, service provision by the private and non-governmental organization sector as well as by the public sector, performance-based contracts between the protector and the protected – and can be adapted to local environments (World Bank, 1993, chapter 2).

It is crucial to the argument that "good policy" and "bad policy" should be seen as *relative* to the economy's resources and state of development, and not as absolutes. Just as high levels of (performance-based) protection and financial repression were appropriate for the East Asian countries in the 1960s and became less appropriate once those economies had become more internationally competitive in manufactures in the 1980s, so, on the evidence of the eight column in table 7, the same may be true of sub-Saharan Africa in the 1990s, which is not to say that such policies will always be needed. In Africa, which has the poorest institutional and physical infrastructure and hence the highest level of endogenous distortions, policies which effectively compensate for those distortions are more important as a complement to prudent macro policy than in an environment with better infrastructure and worse macroeconomic fundamentals such as Eastern Europe, where, on the evidence of table 7, the payoff to orthodox stabilization is greater.

This argument has considerable relevance to aid donors and recipients, most of whom are in the poorer part of the developing world. In one of the few papers before the IMF's to argue for the significance of policy complementarities, Dollar and Burnside of the World Bank (1997, pp. 19-21) argued that overseas aid would be effective only if a complementary cluster of "good policies", which they defined as an open economy, a low budget deficit and low inflation, were all implemented at the same time. However, this conclusion is vulnerable to criticisms very similar to those already deployed here in relation to the IMF analysis. The set of "good policies" examined by Dollar and Burnside omits government share from the set of policy variables examined by the IMF, and adds the budget deficit. This procedure gets rid of one of the problems associated with the IMF analysis (the irrelevance of the "government share" variable; see table 5 above), but leaves two others: firstly, the results are sensitive to changes in specification (for example, budget surplus and inflation are intercorrelated, and openness loses significance when middle-income countries are omitted from the analysis (Dollar and Burnside, 1997, p. 23; compare table 7 above); hence, at a minimum, the degree of complementarity between policy instruments varies between country groups. Secondly, alternative definitions of "good policy", in particular the "heterodox"

policy variables considered in table 5 above, are not examined. Aid effectiveness appears to be more sensitive to credibility of policy stance – i.e. the measured short-term effect of policy on growth – than to the conventional measures of "good policy" suggested by Dollar and Burnside (Mosley, 1996). The lesson which we draw is that aid policy, like development policy more generally, needs to avoid reliance on the idea of one standard, complementary package of "good" economic policies which will ensure success wherever implemented. On the evidence presented above and indeed by Dollar and Burnside themselves, donor conditionality needs to be sensitive to differences in initial conditions between recipient countries, and to incorporate those "heterodox" policies which have proved themselves to be effective, rather than to be premised on one inflexible set of "pro-globalization" policies.

More broadly, whether or not the aid relationship is involved, the design of both macro and micro policies in a developing country needs to be sensitive to a country's existing level of market and institutional development and its vulnerability to external shocks, as well as its social and political objectives. A greater willingness by international financial institutions to accept these limitations on policy prescription might increase the credibility of their advice and hence their ability to assist developing countries to maximize the gains from globalization.

References

AZIZ, J., and R.WESCOTT (1997), "Policy complementarities and the Washington Consensus", mimeo, International Monetary Fund, Washington, D.C.

BARROS, A. (1993), "New growth theory: A survey", *Journal of International Development,* Vol. 5, September.

BRUNO, M. (1993), *Crisis, Stabilisation, and Economic Reform: Therapy by Consensus* (Oxford: Oxford University Press).

DOLLAR, D., and C. BURNSIDE (1997), "Aid, policies and growth", mimeo, World Bank, Washington, D.C.

EASTERLY, W., M. KREMER, L. PRITCHETT, and L.SUMMERS (1993), "Good policy or good luck? Country growth performance and temporary shocks", *Journal of Monetary Economics,* Vol. 32, pp. 457-483.

EDWARDS, S. (1998), "Openness, productivity and growth: What do we really know?", *Economic Journal,* Vol. 108, pp. 383-399.

ELBADAWI, I. (1992), "World Bank adjustment lending and economic performance in sub-Saharan Africa in the 1980s", *Working Paper,* No. 1000 (Washington, D.C.: World Bank Country Economics Department).

FISCHER, S. (1993), "Macroeconomic factors in growth", *Journal of Monetary Economics,* Vol. 32.

GULHATI, R., and R. NALLARI (1991), "Successful stabilisation and recovery in Mauritius", *Occasional Paper,* No. 6

(Washington, D.C.: Economic Development Institute of the World Bank).

HELLEINER, G. (1996a), "Linking Africa with the world: A survey of options", mimeo, Africa Economic Research Consortium, Nairobi.

HELLEINER, G. (1996b), "Towards autonomous development in Africa: External constraints and prospects", mimeo, Canadian International Development Authority, Toronto.

INTERNATIONAL MONETARY FUND (1997), *World Economic Outlook,* Washington D.C., May.

LEVINE, R., and D. RENELT (1992), "A sensitivity analysis of cross-country growth regressions", *American Economic Review*, Vol. 82, pp. 942-963.

LEVINE, R., and S. ZERVOS (1993), "What have we learned about policy and growth from cross-country regressions?", *American Economic Review, Papers and Proceedings,* Vol. 83, May, pp. 426-430.

MOSLEY, P. (1996), "The failure of aid and adjustment policies in sub-Saharan Africa: Counter-examples and policy proposals", *Journal of African Economies,* Vol. 5, September, pp. 406-443.

MOSLEY, P., and J. HUDSON (1997), "Has aid effectiveness increased?", *University of Reading Discussion Papers in Development Economics,* No.3.

MOSLEY, P., T. SUBASAT, and J. WEEKS (1995), "Assessing *Adjustment in Africa*", *World Development,* Vol. 23, September, pp. 1459-1473.

SACHS, J., and A. WARNER (1995), "Globalization and economic reform in developing countries", *Brookings Papers on Economic Activity*, No. 1, pp. 1-117.

SALA-I-MARTIN, X. (1997), "I just ran two million regressions", *American Economic Review,* Vol. 87, May, pp. 178-183.

STERN, N. (1989), "Development economics: A survey", *Economic Journal,* Vol. 99, September.

STIGLITZ, J., and M. UY (1996), "Financial markets, public policy and the East Asian miracle", *World Bank Research Observer,* Vol. 11, August, pp. 249-276.

UNITED NATIONS CHILDREN'S FUND (UNICEF) (1998), *State of the World's Children* (New York: United Nations).

WORLD BANK (1983), *World Development Report 1983* (New York: Oxford University Press).

WORLD BANK (1992), *Report on Adjustment Lending III* (Washington, D.C.: World Bank Country Economics Department).

WORLD BANK (1993), *The East Asian Miracle* (New York: Oxford University Press).

WORLD BANK (1997), *World Development Report 1997* (New York: Oxford University Press).

UNITED NATIONS CONFERENCE ON TRADE AND DEVELOPMENT

Palais des Nations
CH-1211 GENEVE 10
Switzerland
(http://www.unctad.org)

International Monetary and Financial Issues for the 1990s

Volume VI (1995)   United Nations Publication, Sales No. E.95.II.D.7
ISBN 92-1-112375-5

Manuel R. Agosin, Diana Tussie and Gustavo Crespi
Developing Countries and the Uruguay Round: An Evaluation and Issues for the Future
Dani Rodrik
Developing Countries After the Uruguay Round
Ann Weston
The Uruguay Round: Unravelling the Implications for the Least Developed and Low-Income Countries

Volume VII (1996)   United Nations Publication, Sales No. E.96.II.D.2
ISBN 92-1-112394-1

John Williamson
A New Facility for the IMF?
Ariel Buira and Roberto Marino
Allocation of Special Drawing Rights: The Current Debate
Chandra Hardy
The Case for Multilateral Debt Relief for Severely Indebted Countries
Azizali F. Mohammed
Global Financial System Reform and the C-20 Process
Raisuddin Ahmed
A Critique of the World Development Report 1994: Infrastructure for Development
Dipak Mazumdar
Labour issues in the World Development Report: A Critical Assessment
Ann Weston
The Uruguay Round: Costs and Compensation for Developing Countries

Volume VIII (1997)   United Nations publication, Sales No. E.97.II.D.5
                                                                              ISBN 92-1-112409-3

G. K. Helleiner
   Capital Account Regimes and the Developing Countries
Rudi Dornbusch
   Cross-Border Payments Taxes and Alternative Capital-Account Regimes
Guillermo Le Fort V. and Carlos Budnevich L.
   Capital-Account Regulations and Macroeconomic Policy: Two Latin American Experiences
Louis Kasekende, Damoni Kitabire and Matthew Martin
   Capital Inflows and Macroeconomic Policy in Sub-Saharan Africa
Yung Chul Park and Chi-Young Song
   *Managing Foreign Capital Flows: The Experiences of the Republic of Korea, Thailand, Malaysia
   and Indonesia*
Devesh Kapur
   The New Conditionalities of the International Financial Institutions
Aziz Ali Mohammed
   Notes on MDB Conditionality on Governance
Matthew Martin
   A Multilateral Debt Facility - Global and National
Peter Murrell
   From Plan to Market: The World Development Report 1996 - An Assessment

Volume IX (1998)   United Nations publication, Sales No. E.98-II-D.3
                                                                              ISBN 92-1-112424-7

José Maria Fanelli
   *Financial Liberalization and Capital Account Regime: Notes on the Experience of Developing
   Countries*
Tony Killick
   Responding to the Aid Crisis
Jeffrey D. Sachs
   External Debt, Structural Adjustment and Economic Growth
Jacques J. Polak
   The Significance of the Euro for Developing Countries
Hannan Ezekiel
   The Role of Special Drawing Rights in the International Monetary System
Ngaire Woods
   *Governance in International Organizations: The Case for Reform in the Bretton Woods
   Institutions*
Charles Abugre and Nancy Alexander
   Non-Governmental Organizations and the International Monetary and Financial System
Devesh Kapur
   The State in a Changing World: A Critique of the World Development Report 1997

Other selected UNCTAD publications

Trade and Development Report, 1996

United Nations Publication, Sales No. E.96.II.D.6
ISBN 92-1-112399-2

Part One		Global Trends
	I	The World Economy: Performance and Prospects
	II	International Capital Markets and the External Debt of Developing Countries
Part Two		Rethinking Development Strategies: Some Lessons from the East Asian Experience
	I	Integration and Industrialization in East Asia
	II	Exports, Capital Formation and Growth
	III	Responding to the New Global Environment
Annex		Macroeconomic Management, Financial Governance, and Development: Selected Policy Issues

Trade and Development Report, 1997

United Nations Publication, Sales No. E.97.II.D.8
ISBN 92-1-112411-5

Part One		Global Trends
	I	The World Economy: Performance and Prospects
	II	International Financial Markets and the External Debt of Developing Countries
	Annex	Issues Involved in Trade Disputes that Have Arisen Concerning the National Treatment Provision of the WTO Agreement
Part Two		Globalization, Distribution and Growth
	I	The Issues at Stake
	II	Globalization and Economic Convergence
	III	Income Inequality and Development
		Annex: Trends in Personal Income Distribution in Selected Developing Countries
	IV	Liberalization, Integration and Distribution
	V	Income Distribution, Capital Accumulation and Growth
	VI	Promoting Investment: Some Lessons from East Asia

Trade and Development Report, 1998

United Nations Publication, Sales No. E.98.II.D.6
ISBN 92-1-112427-1

****

These publications may be obtained from bookstores and distributors throughout the world. Consult your bookstore or write to United Nations Publications/Sales Section, Palais des Nations, CH-1211 Geneva 10, Switzerland, fax: +41-22-917.0027, e-mail: unpubli@un.org, Internet: http://www.un.org/publications; or from United Nations Publications, Two UN Plaza, Room DC2-853, Dept. PERS, New York, N.Y. 10017, U.S.A., telephone:+1-212-963.8302 or +1-800-253.9646; fax: +1-212-963.3489, e-mail: publications@un.org.

African Development in a Comparative Perspective

In September 1996 UNCTAD launched the project *Economic Development and Regional Dynamics in Africa: Lessons from the East Asian Experience.* Building on earlier research on the role of policies in successful economic development in East Asia, the project aimed to identify development strategies for Africa to promote investment and exports, as well as to stimulate regional growth dynamics. It examined selected African development problems, including reasons for poor supply-side response to policy reforms, the lack of export diversification and difficulties in building up domestic capacity in the private and public sectors; it considered the applicability of East Asian type policies to solving these problems. The studies listed below were prepared under the project and provided the background for the International Conference on African Development in a Comparative Perspective, held in Mauritius, 24-25 September 1998:

No. 1   *Capital accumulation and agricultural surplus in sub-Saharan Africa and Asia*
Massoud KARSHENAS (School of Oriental and African Studies, University of London, UK)

No. 2   *Informal economy, wage goods and the changing patterns of accumulation under structural adjustment – Theoretical reflections based on the Tanzanian experience*
Marc WUYTS (Institute for Social Studies, The Hague, Netherlands)

No. 3   *A comparative analysis of the accumulation process and capital mobilization in Mauritius, the United Republic of Tanzania and Zimbabwe*
L. Amedee DARGA (Straconsult, Curepipe, Mauritius)

No. 4   *Africa's export structure in a comparative perspective*
Adrian WOOD and Jörg MAYER (Institute of Development Studies at the University of Sussex, UK; and Macroeconomic and Development Policies, UNCTAD, Geneva)

No. 5   *How African manufacturing industries can break into export markets with lessons from East Asia*
Samuel WANGWE (Economic and Social Research Foundation, Dar es Salaam, Tanzania)

No. 6   *Trade policy reform and supply responses in Africa*
Charles Chukwuma SOLUDO (University of Nigeria, Nsukka, Nigeria)

No. 7   *The role of policy in promoting enterprise learning during early industrialization: Lessons for African countries*
Lynn K. MYTELKA and Taffere TESFACHEW (Division on Investment, Technology and Enterprise Development, UNCTAD, Geneva)

No. 8   *Financing enterprise development and export diversification in sub-Saharan Africa*
Machiko K. NISSANKE (School of Oriental and African Studies, University of London, UK)

No. 9   *Thinking about developmental States in Africa*
Thandika MKANDAWIRE (UN Research Institute for Social Development, Geneva)

No. 10   *The relevance of East Asian institutions designed to support industrial and technological development in Southern African countries*
Martin FRANSMAN (Institute for Japanese-European Technology Studies, University of Edinburgh, Scotland)

No. 11   *Trade in the Southern African Development Community: What is the potential for increasing exports to the Republic of South Africa?*
Friedrich von KIRCHBACH and Hendrik ROELOFSEN (UNCTAD/WTO International Trade Centre, Geneva)

No. 12   *Movements of relative agricultural prices in sub-Saharan Africa*
Korkut BORATAV (University of Ankara, Turkey)

No. 13   *The impact of price policies on the supply of traditional agricultural export crops – Africa vis-à-vis the rest of the developing world*
Alberto GABRIELE (Macroeconomic and Development Policies, UNCTAD, Geneva)

Proceedings of the International Conference on East Asian Development: Lessons for a New Global Environment, Kuala Lumpur, Malaysia, 29 February - 1 March 1996,

UNCTAD/GDS/MDPB/2

United Nations Conference on Trade and Development, Geneva
and Institute of Strategic and International Studies, Kuala Lumpur

Session 1	Regional and National Dimensions of East Asian Development
Session 2	Government-Business Relationship and Industrialization
Session 3	Policy Initiatives for Marginalized Sectors
Session 4	Policy Options in a Globalizing Environment
Session 5	Policy Lessons

UNCTAD Discussion Papers

No. 111, January 1996	Charles GORE	Methodological nationalism and the misunderstanding of East Asian industrialization
No. 112, March 1996	Djidiack FAYE	Aide publique au développement et dette extérieure: Quelles mesures opportunes pour le financement du secteur privé en Afrique?
No. 113, March 1996	Paul BAIROCH & Richard KOZUL-WRIGHT	Globalization myths: Some historical reflections on integration, industrialization and growth in the world economy
No. 114, April 1996	Rameshwar TANDON	Japanese financial deregulation since 1984
No. 115, April 1996	E.V.K. FITZGERALD	Intervention versus regulation: The role of the IMF in crisis prevention and management
No. 116, June 1996	Jussi LANKOSKI	Controlling agricultural nonpoint source pollution: The case of mineral balances
No. 117, August 1996	José RIPOLL	Domestic insurance markets in developing countries: Is there any life after GATS?
No. 118, September 1996	Sunanda SEN	Growth centres in South East Asia in the era of globalization
No. 119, September 1996	Leena ALANEN	The impact of environmental cost internalization on sectoral competitiveness: A new conceptual framework
No. 120, October 1996	Sinan AL-SHABIBI	Structural adjustment for the transition to disarmament: An assessment of the role of the market
No. 121, October 1996	J.F. OUTREVILLE	Reinsurance in developing countries: Market structure and comparative advantage
No. 122, December 1996	Jörg MAYER	Implications of new trade and endogenous growth theories for diversification policies of commodity-dependent countries
No. 123, December 1996	L. RUTTEN & L. SANTANA-BOADO	Collateralized commodity financing with special reference to the use of warehouse receipts

No. 124, March 1997	Jörg MAYER	Is having a rich natural-resource endowment detrimental to export diversification?
No. 125, April 1997	Brigitte BOCOUM	The new mining legislation of Côte d'Ivoire: Some comparative features
No. 126, April 1997	Jussi LANKOSKI	Environmental effects of agricultural trade liberalization and domestic agricultural policy reforms
No. 127, May 1997	Raju Jan SINGH	Banks, growth and geography
No. 128, September 1997	Enrique COSIO-PASCAL	Debt sustainability and social and human development: The net transfer approach and a comment on the so-called "net" present value calculation for debt relief
No. 129, September 1997	Andrew J. CORNFORD	Selected features of financial sectors in Asia and their implications for services trade
No. 130, March 1998	Matti VAINIO	The effect of unclear property rights on environmental degradation and increase in poverty
No. 131, Feb./March 1998	Robert ROWTHORN & Richard KOZUL-WRIGHT	Globalization and economic convergence: An assessment
No. 132, March 1998	Martin BROWNBRIDGE	The causes of financial distress in local banks in Africa and implications for prudential policy
No. 133, March 1998	Rubens LOPES BRAGA	Expanding developing countries' exports in a global economy: The need to emulate the strategies used by transnational corporations for international business development
No. 134, April 1998	A.V. GANESAN	Strategic options available to developing countries with regard to a Multilateral Agreement on Investment
No. 135, May 1998	Jene K. KWON	The East Asian model: An explanation of rapid economic growth in the Republic of Korea and Taiwan Province of China
No. 136, June 1998	JOMO K.S. & M. ROCK	Economic diversification and primary commodity processing in the second-tier South-East Asian newly industrializing countries
No. 137, June 1998	Rajah RASIAH	The export manufacturing experience of Indonesia, Malaysia and Thailand: Lessons for Africa
No. 138, October 1998	Z. KOZUL-WRIGHT & Lloyds STANBURY	Becoming a globally competitive player: The case of the music industry in Jamaica
No. 139, December 1998	Mehdi SHAFAEDDIN	How did developed countries industrialize? The history of trade and industrial policy: The cases of Great Britain and the USA
No. 140, February 1999	M. BRANCHI, A. GABRIELE & V. SPIEZIA	Traditional agricultural exports, external dependency and domestic prices policies: African coffee exports in a comparative perspective

****

Copies of the studies on *African Development in a Comparative Perspective; Proceedings of the International Conference on East Asian Development: Lessons for a New Global Environment; UNCTAD Discussion Papers* and *Reprint Series* may be obtained from the Editorial Assistant, Macroeconomic and Development Policies, GDS, UNCTAD, Palais des Nations, CH-1211 Geneva 10, Switzerland (telephone: +41-22-907.5733; fax +41-22-907.0274; e-mail: nicole.winch@unctad.org).